PSYCHOLOGY

&

MEDICAL CARE

3rd edition

Gerry Kent PhD

Senior Lecturer in Medical Psychology
Department of Psychiatry
The University of Sheffield, UK

Mary Dalgleish PhD

Honorary Lecturer
Department of Psychiatry
The University of Sheffield, UK

W. B. SAUNDERS COMPANY LTD

London Philadelphia Toronto Sydney Tokyo

W. B. Saunders Company Ltd	24–28 Oval Road London NW1 7DX, UK

The Curtis Center
Independence Square West
Philadelphia, PA 19106–3399, USA

Harcourt Brace
& Company
55 Horner Avenue
Toronto, Ontario M8Z 4X6, Canada

Harcourt Brace & Company, Australia
30–52 Smidmore Street
Marrickville, NSW 2204, Australia

Harcourt Brace, Japan
Ichibancho Central Building,
22–1 Ichibancho
Chiyoda-ku, Tokyo, 102, Japan

A catalogue record for this book is available from the British Library

ISBN 0-7020-2065-6

First edition published 1983 by Van Nostrand Reinhold (UK) Co Ltd
Second edition published 1986 by Baillière Tindall
Reprinted 1993

Phototypeset by Selwood Systems, Midsomer Norton
Printed and bound in Great Britain by Butler & Tanner Ltd, Frome and London

PSYCHOLOGY

&

MEDICAL CARE

Dedication

To Michael and Anna

Contents

Preface

This book provides a basic grounding in psychology, drawing out its relevance to medicine. Medical examples are used to illustrate psychological principles and particular attention is given to such aspects of medical care as the doctor-patient interview and compliance with medical advice. We have presented research critically; for example, discussing how a result might be interpreted in more than one way. We hope the book will provide the reader with some of the skills required to appraise research work in the future. Our view is that the ability to evaluate "facts" is as important as the "facts" themselves.

Ideally, the book would be most usefully read from beinning to end as concepts and methods are introduced and developed as the text progresses. To this end, the book is divided into three sections: psychological processes, human development, and doctor-patient communication, the first laying foundations for the second, and both of these adding to an understanding of the third. We have been selective in the choice of topics, covering those areas which seem, to us, most relevant to the psychological aspects of medical care. We have attempted to include sufficient source references to enable the reader to pursue aspects of particular interest, either simply for further detail or for research purposes. Suggested readings are given at the end of each chapter to enable more detailed study of particular areas.

GK MD

Part I

Psychological Processes

1
Making Sense of the Environment

SUMMARY

In order to reduce uncertainty, people actively interpret their environment on the basis of context, past experience, and expectation. This process is illustrated by reactions to a novel and threatening situation – hospitalization.

Have you ever been surprised by the different reactions people have to the same experiences? Your view of a particular film or book may be quite different to someone else's, yet the information presented to you was identical. This difference arises because the information is not simply received passively by your peripheral sensory system. Rather, it is actively *processed* by your central nervous system. Even though ways of collecting and recording data about the world have become increasingly sophisticated, the analysis of this information is open to variations between people because of what they consider important, how they interpret the information, and how they choose to act upon it.

The development of chest X-rays for the detection of lesions associated with active pulmonary tuberculosis provides a medical example of these processes. In the 1940s the development of the radiograph was hailed as one of the most important medical advances of the half-century. However, the enthusiasm was soon tempered by the realization that physicians differed in their interpretations of the information collected. One study examined these differences in a systematic fashion. Initially, several competent radiologists viewed over a thousand films: there was much disagreement between them, with one doctor interpreting the films as showing 56 positive results, while another found 100. The second doctor's cases did not include all of those found by the first. In all, there was disagreement about positive films one time in three. The information was the same but the interpretations differed. When the same films were shown to the same radiologist on two occasions, he found 59 positives on the first run through, but 78 on the second.[1] Thus the way that these experienced doctors processed the information on the films was not straightforward or altogether consistent.

The study of the ways in which people make sense of data is an important topic within psychology. One approach to the ways we process information is in terms of three interdependent phases.[2] This chapter includes a brief description of the first, or *sensory*, phase, using the visual system as an example. The second *interpretive* phase is then discussed. Interpretation is the way in which people organize incoming information in the light of past experience and the context in which events occur. Some aspects of the third phase, *memory*, are covered here, others in Chapter 2.

Sensing the environment

The sensory phase has been studied in several ways. One approach has involved the tracing of neural connections between the sensory receptors (visual, auditory, etc.) and the brain. Here, the concern has been with the ways that the anatomy, physiology and biochemistry of receptors (such as the rods and cones in the eye) affect how the environment is encoded and how the messages are passed along pathways to the cortex.

The visual system

Related to this approach is an interest in patterns of neural firing. Some of this work has involved the recording of single cells in the cortex, exploring the ways in which aspects of the environment are coded neurologically. Perhaps the best-known workers in this field are Hubel and Wiesel, who studied recordings from microelectrodes inserted into the visual cortex of cats. They found that some neurons fired only when a vertical slit of light was presented in the cats' visual fields, while other neurons fired when the line of light was horizontal, and yet others when the line moved.[3] The patterns of firing were found in specific neurons, suggesting that each had a defined and limited function.

Various techniques have been used to investigate how neural pathways develop, generally involving the study of animals reared in controlled or restricted environments. For example, it is possible to rear animals in the dark, examine neurological development and then relate this to behaviour. In such studies, irreversible damage to the visual pathways, such as atrophy of the retinal ganglion cells, has been discovered. When cats were shown only vertical stripes from birth, they were apparently blind to horizontal stripes: both behavioural and electrophysiological measures of these animals indicated little response to horizontal lines. Using Hubel and Wiesel's technique of single-cell recording, no neurons could be found that fired to lines oriented at right-angles to the cats' early visual environment. Conversely, cats which saw only horizontal stripes from birth showed no response to vertical ones. It seems from work of this kind that although the pathways are "hard wired" from birth, exposure to external stimulation is necessary if they are to develop fully.

These approaches to the study of sensation cannot be considered in isolation from higher level processes such as interpretation and memory. An example of their interdependence can be easily arranged by putting this book down and listening to the sounds being produced around you. The first notable feature will probably be the large number of sounds which you probably did not hear when you read the above paragraph. You were attending to the reading and ignoring this irrelevant noise. A similar phenomenon can be experienced at a party: in spite of the music and loud voices, it is possible to attend to one conversation out of many. Your attention may be changed if someone calls your name, a particularly meaningful stimulus.

A second notable feature of the noises around you is that you will find yourself labelling or interpreting each one. As you listen to each sound, you make sense of it by explaining its source. A series of low-frequency sounds outside the room is translated into someone's footsteps; a high-frequency sound outside, a car's brakes. It is difficult to hear the sound alone without making some kind of interpretation about it. The sounds are processed to become integrated into a meaningful environment. It is this feature that characterizes the second phase of information processing, in which the data provided by the sensory systems are given meaning.

Interpreting the environment

It is often difficult to appreciate the fundamental importance of interpretation. Most of the objects we see are unambiguously one thing or another, and we have no apparent difficulty in making sense of them. However, the ease with which interpretations are made is an indication of the familiarity of most objects we encounter in our daily lives rather than evidence for a simple and direct link between sensation and understanding.

This process of fitting together apparently unconnected pieces of information to make a meaningful picture is constantly being performed in daily life. This occurs in many situations. For example, we are often concerned about how other people view us. By piecing together the reactions of others we can arrive at an interpretation of what we are like and how we appear. The process of diagnosis is another example. Initially, a series of seemingly unconnected complaints may be presented by a patient. These symptoms are explored, additional information is gathered, and past experience consulted. Some kind of overall link which connects the previously unrelated symptoms together is sought. These links are hypotheses which are tested through further questioning and physical examination. In a difficult case – where the link is difficult to find – others' views of the condition might be sought in order to make the interpretation. Over time, a diagnosis may be changed: one study indicated that about half the diagnoses for patients admitted with abdominal pain were changed during their stay in hospital. Although controversial, there is increasing interest in computer-assisted diagnosis, with some research indicating that computers are more accurate than senior clinicians for some conditions.

The aim of the following sections is to consider some of the processes involved in making such interpretations. Context, past experience and selective attention are used during the interpretive process.

Context

Context provides a pattern into which ambiguous stimuli can be fitted. It does this in part by arousing expectations about what is to follow. When performing dissection, for instance, the identification of particular structures is aided when you know the surrounding tissues. The process is similar in Figure 1.1. Most people read the top line as A, B, C, D, E, F and the bottom line as 10, 11, 12, 13, 14, yet B and the 13 are

A,B,C,D,E,F
10,11,12,13,14

Figure 1.1 The effect of context on recognition. The same symbol is identified as "B" or "13" depending on its context.

Figure 1.2 The perceived volumes of the cylinders vary according to the lines of perspective. (Reproduced from Lindsay, P. H. and Norman, D. A. (1972) *Human Information Processing*, with permission of Academic Press, Inc.)

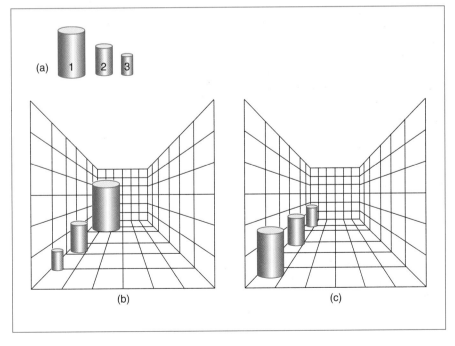

identical. The context in which the symbol is embedded determines how it is "seen".

Psychologists often use illusions to explore the importance of context. Illusions are objects or pictures that encourage the viewer to perceive something which is really non-existent. Representational paintings are illusions, in that the artist attempts to portray a three-dimensional space on a two-dimensional plane. The illusion of depth is achieved in several ways, but primarily through the use of perspective (parallel lines that seem to come together and meet at the horizon), size constancy (although the retinal image of an object varies according to its distance, it is not interpreted as changing in size) and interposition (near objects overlap far objects). The ways in which perspective and size interact are shown in Figure 1.2. Figure 1.2a indicates the relative size of three cylinders. But the same two-dimensional drawings take on different meanings when context is added as in Figures 1.2b and 1.2c.

The social context

In social situations, we interpret others' behaviour within a cultural context. One way in which it plays a role in the perception of other people has been termed the "halo effect" – the tendency to generalize from one attribute to a number of others. For example, in our society physical attractiveness is considered important and provides a context into which we fit additional information. Dion[4] asked people (or *participants* as the volunteers in psychology experiments are usually called) to judge the misbehaviour of young children. All participants were given a description of a child who had behaved in a rather unacceptable fashion, by either being aggressive towards another child or acting cruelly towards an animal. In order to test the importance of physical appearance, Dion attached a photograph to the description: some participants saw a photo depicting a physically attractive child, others viewed a child who was less attractive. The experimental question was whether the child's appearance would affect the participants' interpretations of her behaviour. This was the case: the participants judged the attractive children less harshly than the unattractive children, with more lenient punishments recommended for the same behaviour. It seemed that physical

attractiveness modified perceptions of why the children misbehaved.

Several other assumptions are made about attractive people, including the expectations that they will obtain more prestigious occupations and have happier marriages. There is also evidence that this "beautiful is good" stereotype affects the first impressions of health professionals. In one study, hospital staff were asked to indicate their impressions of patients shown in a series of photos. In some cases the photos depicted a physically attractive man or woman, in other cases the individual shown was unattractive. On 12 of the 15 scales used, the staff indicated more positive impressions of the attractive people than the unattractive ones. For example, they were taken to be more responsible, more motivated and more likely to improve. There were no differences between the professionals, doctors being just as likely to make these assumptions as were the paramedical staff.[5]

Generalizations about people on the basis of who they associate with is another example of the halo effect. Participants were shown a silent film of a man and a woman, who were said to be emotionally involved with each other. In some films, she was made-up to look attractive, in others to look unattractive. The participants' task was to rate the boyfriend on a checklist of characteristics. On virtually every scale, the woman's appearance had an effect: the man was rated as more friendly, intelligent, energetic and physically attractive when the woman was made-up to appear attractive. The woman's perceived intelligence was also altered by saying that she was either a waitress or a medical student. This condition had much less effect on the ratings, although the man was said to be more intelligent, self-confident and talented when she was said to be a medical student.[6] It seemed that the favourable characteristics of one person were attributed to both members of the couple.

The medical context

The medical interview involves the transmission of information between patient and doctor. Both parties seek to inform the other of their ideas, concerns and plans. When conducting an interview, the patient's social class appears to be an important contextual influence in how much information doctors believe their patients want. Pendleton and Bochner[7] videotaped consultations between doctors and their patients and noted that fewer explanations were volunteered for the patients of lower social class than for those of higher social class. This does not seem to be due to the former wanting less information about their difficulties, since they express a desire to know more, not less, than higher social class patients. Despite this, they obtain less of the information they want.[8]

There are other instances where the use of context can have a detrimental effect on patients. Maguire and Granville-Grossman[9] found that 33 per cent of patients suffered from a physical illness in a sample of 200 admissions to a psychiatric unit, yet it had been diagnosed in only half these patients. Conversely, 23 per cent of a sample of in-patients in medical wards were found to have psychiatric disorders, but few cases were recognized by the medical staff.[10] It seems as though each unit provided expectations about patients that made diagnosis of particular complaints less likely.

Another study of psychiatric units illustrates this point in a slightly different way. Rosenhan[11] reported a study in which eight experimenters had themselves committed to various psychiatric hospitals, claiming that they were hearing voices (a symptom often associated with schizophrenia). After admission, these "pseudo-patients" acted in their usual way and the research question was how long it would take before the staff (who were unaware of the study) realized that there was nothing abnormal about these patients and discharged them. In fact, staff recognized none of the pseudo-patients (although some patients did) and some experimenters had difficulty in obtaining their release. Part of the difficulty here seemed to be that although people in psychiatric hospitals are expected to be unusual in some way, they often act normally, making it difficult for the staff to distinguish between the real and the feigning patients. Given this ambiguity, the safe course of action in this context was to assume that the experimenters were suffering from schizophrenia and should not be discharged.

In these studies, the context of a psychiatric unit or a medical ward appears to have led the staff to expect certain conditions but not others, making some interpretations more plausible than others. Context in everyday situations is similarly based on past experience (either directly or through reports by others) and can be modified by future experiences. This second aspect of the interpretive process is considered in the next section.

Experience

Much of the research on the importance of experience has been concerned with visual phenomena. One line of evidence is cross-cultural: people with very different environments from ours perceive the world in quite different ways. One investigator[12] lived with the Bambuti pygmies, forest dwellers whose vistas extend to 30 metres at most. Once, he took a tribesman on to a broad plain where there was a herd of buffalo some miles away. Because the buffalo looked small, the pygmy thought that they were some kind of insect. He became increasingly puzzled and concerned as they drove closer and the buffalo "grew". The pygmy had little experience with large distances and therefore did not, in this situation, use *size constancy* – the tendency for the perceptual system to compensate for changes in retinal size with viewing distance.

Similar observations have been made with adults in Western culture who, having been blind since infancy, have had their sight restored.

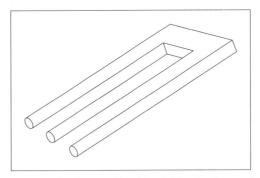

Figure 1.3 An "impossible object". The depth cues in this picture are conflicting, making it difficult to interpret in an integrated way. People unfamiliar with graphic representation have little difficulty in reproducing this figure from memory. (Reproduced from Kimble, G., Garmezy, M. and Kigler, E. (1974) *General Psychology*, 4th edn, with permission of John Wiley & Sons, Inc.)

Figure 1.4 The drawing in (a) can be interpreted as a young woman or an old woman, but seeing (b) first predisposes the observer to see the old woman, whereas seeing (c) first encourages the perception of the young woman.

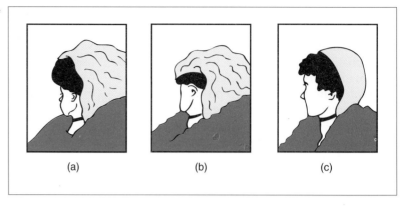

(a)   (b)   (c)

Gregory[13] describes how one such patient thought that he would be able to lower himself to the ground from his window, which was in fact about 10 metres above the ground. Because he had no past experience with depth cues, he was unable to see that the ground was far below.

Conversely, past experience can serve to mislead an observer about objects. Several "impossible objects" have been designed that confuse the viewer and make an integrated interpretation difficult, such as the "devil's tuning fork" (Figure 1.3).

A classic example of the role of experience in perception is the young/old woman demonstration.[14] Figure 1.4a can be seen as a young attractive woman or as an old unattractive one, depending on how her features are interpreted. Looking at Figures 1.4b and 1.4c may make these two possibilities clearer. A simple experiment would first involve showing Figure 1.4b to one group of people and Figure 1.4c to another. Figure 1.4a would then be shown to everyone. Those who saw Figure 1.4b would tend to see the composite drawing as an old woman, while those who saw Figure 1.4c would tend to see the composite as a young woman.

Mental sets

A particular example of how past experience can affect perception is called mental set – the tendency to use a solution which has worked well in the past on further problems, even where this solution is not the best one. The jar problem[13] is a good example of this tendency. Table 1.1 presents six problems, the task being to use jars A, B and C to obtain the amount of water indicated in the right-hand column. After a little thought, a way of obtaining these amounts becomes apparent. Before reading further, it is instructive to perform all the tasks.

All of these problems can be solved in the same way (B − A − 2C), but looking at problem 6 again, it is possible to see how a routine has built up which led to a failure to use the simplest solution (A − C).

Similarly, it seems possible that medical training can induce a kind of mental set in doctors, leading them to solve diagnostic problems and interpret what patients say in certain ways. Since medical training is primarily concerned with physical diseases, doctors may be much more aware of physical aetiologies and treatments than social or psychological ones. One of the first decisions a physician generally makes is to diagnose a complaint as either physically or psychiatrically based, and most doctors tend to exclude the possibility of physical disorders before considering social or psychological issues.

Table 1.1 The jar problem. Use the jars to obtain the amount of water indicated in the right-hand column. (Reproduced from Luchins (1942) *Psychological Monographs*, with permission from the American Psychological Association)

Problem	Jar capacities			Amount to
	A	*B*	*C*	*be obtained*
1	21	127	3	100
2	14	163	25	99
3	18	43	10	5
4	9	42	6	21
5	20	59	4	31
6	23	49	3	20

Maguire and Rutter[16] found that medical students in their final year obtained less social and psychological information while taking case histories than first-year students. It seemed that the senior students asked more questions about and attended more closely to symptoms of physical distress than those of psychological distress.

It also seems that past experience with a particular patient can also lead to a mental set. Stimson[17] outlines the experience of one woman who had a history of respiratory problems which frequently required prescribed antibiotics. It seemed to her that the doctor was too willing to diagnose all her problems as connected with the respiratory condition:

66 No matter what I have got wrong with me, if I go over to the doctor with a terrific headache that I'm getting – 'Oh, it's all to do with your chest' – anything, no matter, if I'm worried about something now, and I want to go to the doctor's, see, perhaps I'm getting these headaches or something and I'm getting a bit concerned about them now, no matter what, I can guarantee when I come out of that doctor's, it's to do with my chest. No matter what I get, you're missing a period and he says – 'It's to do with your chest'. (Ref. 17, p. 102) 99

Apparently, the physician had solved her problem in one way in the past and this prevented him from entertaining alternative possibilities. The idea that once people come to view a problem in a certain way they often attend to information selectively is the next step in the process of making interpretations.

Selective attention

In a sense, people can be regarded as scientists who have developed their own theories which they use to interpret their environment. Since each person has a unique set of past experiences, each individual holds slightly different theories. These theories make it possible to organize the vast amount of data which impinge on our senses. However, these theories also encourage us to attend to information selectively (looking for data which will confirm our hypotheses) and to disregard other kinds of information which appear to be irrelevant. Thus, our perceptions become biased in certain directions.

As an example of this, Abercrombie[18] describes how a child with a persistent cough had a throat X-ray. The radiologist reported that there was nothing in the radiograph to show why the child was coughing. The cough persisted, however, and a second X-ray was taken. This time the shadow of a button was seen in the throat, the button was removed and the child stopped coughing. When the first radiograph was re-examined, the shadow of the button was seen there, too, but the radiologist had explained it away to himself, supposing that the child had been wearing a vest when X-rayed. The information was there, but not processed in the most useful way.

In a further test of his idea that diagnosis of mental illness is influenced by what staff expect to see, Rosenhan[11] led the staff of a teaching hospital to believe that within the next three months one or more pseudo-patients would attempt to have themselves admitted to the psychiatric unit. Of the 193 patients admitted during this time, 41 were alleged to be pseudo-patients by at least one member of staff, 19 by a psychiatrist and one other staff member. In fact, there were no pseudo-patients: the faulty theory led to incorrect expectations and thus to misperceptions.

Thus, once an initial interpretation has been made on the basis of context and past experience, there is a strong tendency to follow up on this impression with further questioning while neglecting other information. This process has been studied in diagnostic interviews by looking at the ways in which clinicians conduct their consultations. Barrows and Bennett[19] coached people to simulate neurological disorders and neurologists were then asked to reach a diagnosis through questioning and examination. Findings elicited by the neurologists were often totally absent from their reports and apparently forgotten unless they were relevant to one of their hypotheses. Once a possible diagnosis had emerged, the doctors asked questions which were aimed at acquiring specific items of information.

Selective attention can be obvious, as in this general practice consultation:

> *Patient:* Am I going to be able to go back to work?
>
> *Doctor:* Let's not worry about that at the moment, let's consider the treatment. (Ref. 20, p. 60)

or less clear, as in this example:

> *Doctor:* Good morning. Sit down. What can I do for you today?
>
> *Patient:* Well, I think I've got the 'flu, doctor.
>
> *Doctor:* Well, there's not much of it about now.
>
> *Patient:* Well, I've got this cold.
>
> *Doctor:* Yes, I can see that. Shivering a bit, are you?
>
> *Patient:* Yes.
>
> *Doctor:* Mmm. Well, there's not a lot to worry about is there? Now you take this to the chemist and you'll be all right in 3 or 4 days. (Ref. 20, p. 102)

In this case, the patient was the last of a crowded morning surgery. He had appeared just before the doctor was about to leave on his morning calls and nine of his previous patients had also suffered from "common colds". This led him to diagnose a cold and not to give either a physical examination or to ask further questions. Unfortunately, this patient was subsequently diagnosed as having pleurisy, but this possibility was not attended to because of the context of the morning's experience.

Self-fulfilling prophecy

Fortunately, many perceptual biases are remedied by further experience. The child with a button in his throat and the patient with pleurisy were subsequently correctly diagnosed. When patients fail to respond to medication prescribed for what was originally diagnosed as organic illnesses, doctors begin to consider social and psychological problems. While an incorrect diagnosis is of course to be lamented, it is easier to understand how it could occur when the complexities of interpreting a patient's symptoms are appreciated.

Other perceptual biases are not so easily corrected, particularly in social situations. An observer may selectively attend only to those features of a situation or of other people that are consistent with expectations and ignore those that are inconsistent. The perception might affect behaviour and perhaps bring about what the person originally expected. Someone who believes that everyone is unfriendly and hurtful is likely to be suspicious himself, selectively attending to instances of rejection. This perception of the world will make him difficult to live with, perhaps resulting in the very behaviour he expects – rejection. This kind of circularity in social situations has been termed the self-fulfilling prophecy.

Some of the more important studies in this area have been conducted in classrooms. Educational theorists have suggested that some pupils do not do well at school because they have a history of failure, a background that teachers use in deciding how intelligent they are and how worthwhile it is to pay careful attention to their work. Meichenbaum et al.[21] studied a group of young women who had been sent by the courts to a training centre. They administered a series of tests that purported to predict intellectual "blooming", and the teachers were then told that certain girls, but not others, could be expected to show remarkable gains in intellectual competence in the coming months. In fact, the tests could not provide such a prediction, so that the only differences between the two groups of girls were in the expectations of the teachers.

Soon the teachers began to note and comment upon relatively insignificant instances that confirmed their expectations. When Meichenbaum checked the school records of exam results several months later, they found that those who were "predicted" to do better did so on objective tests in mathematics and science (but not in literature and history). These girls were also more likely to show "appropriate" behaviour in the classroom (e.g. paying attention to lessons rather than looking distracted or whispering together).

Although some researchers have failed to replicate such findings, many other studies have supported the notion of expectancy effects and the self-fulfilling prophecy. It appears that the person with the expectations changes his or her behaviour to conform with predictions. Teachers with favourable expectations gave more information to supposedly bright students, which may explain why they actually learned more. Similarly, more statements were requested of "gifted" pupils and they were praised more frequently by their teachers. Teachers who had been led to believe that some of their students were very bright leaned forward more when they were addressing them, looked them in the eye, and nodded and smiled more frequently.

At this point, perception becomes more than simply interpreting reality, it becomes part of the *construction* of social reality.

An interesting study on this aspect of the self-fulfilling prophecy is provided by Jahoda.[22] The Ashanti of West Africa believe that infants born on different days of the week have different personalities. Those born on Mondays are supposed to be quiet and even-tempered, those born on Wednesdays aggressive and quarrelsome. Jahoda consulted the police records for the district, trouble with the authorities being his dependent measure of aggression. He found that the Ashanti who had been born on Mondays had a low rate of criminal offences, while those born on Wednesdays had a high rate. It seems possible that the parents reacted to their children in ways consistent with their expectations, and that these expectations were incorporated into the children's personalities, thus fulfilling the prophecy. There has been much discussion of the possibility that many of the differences in behaviour shown by males and females and the way we view ourselves more generally is due to such expectations, a topic considered in Chapter 7.

The self-fulfilling prophecy can play an important role in the medical setting as well. Elderly people are often considered to be in need of much assistance and may be placed in a nursing home at the first signs of mental or physical deterioration. However, there is evidence (discussed in Chapter 8) that deterioration may accelerate if they are discouraged from taking care of themselves by staff who are too keen to help. Placebo effects (discussed in Chapter 10) are based partly on patients' perceptions of the efficacy of treatment and several studies have shown that physicians who are enthusiastic about a particular course of treatment achieve

better results than those who are sceptical. Beecher[23] traced the literature on a particular surgical procedure that was eventually discarded as a result of a properly controlled experiment. Beecher showed that surgeons who were sceptical about the operation and who told their patients they did not expect any change in their condition had low success rates, but that surgeons who were enthusiastic seemed to achieve good results.

In the next section of this chapter the situation of people who enter hospital for treatment or observation is considered. Hospitalization is an unfamiliar event to most people, making it possible to conduct research on the process of interpretation. Principles learned in this setting may apply to other situations. There are also practical implications of research in this area. If it can be shown how patients can be made more comfortable in hospital through helping them to make sense of their environment, this could result in better care and earlier recovery.

Uncertainty and medical care

The previous section indicated that people have a strong tendency to make interpretations about their environment. An explanation for this tendency is that interpretations simplify the complexity of incoming information, thereby leaving cognitive capacity to deal with unexpected or unfamiliar events. Interpretations provide a shorthand, a way of "chunking" information to make it easier to assimilate or remember.

When an interpretation cannot be made easily, people often search for possibilities that would reduce the uncertainty. The experience of having symptoms of illness is a good example of this tendency. Symptoms are often ambiguous and carry implications of threat to health and lifestyle, making them a focus for hypothesis-testing for the patient, family and physician. The threat implied by symptoms cannot be realistically appraised until their cause and potential consequences have been determined. Ambiguity is high because symptoms are often novel, difficult to localize, and of varying severity and this ambiguity can itself be distressing. Evidence suggests that the difficulty in interpreting symptoms is an important cause of delay in seeking help in the critical minutes and hours following myocardial infarction. Thus, the factors involved in the interpretation of external events (past experience, selective attention and context) apply equally well to the perception of internal physiological events.[24]

Anxiety

There are many real-life examples of uncertainty in medical care. Seriously ill patients are often faced with the possibility of disfigurement, loss of social and economic roles and may have difficult choices about treatment. Advances in medical technology hold out the hope for improvement in the quality of life or even a cure, but this can be at the risk of more serious impairments or even death.[25] This type of uncertainty is inherent in most illness and treatment, and is likely to persist even when patients are informed about the risks of treatments or probabilities of recovery. Some of these longer term threats to well-being are discussed in Chapter 9.

However, there is another type of uncertainty to do with receiving medical care and how hospitals work which can be reduced, such as the shorter term threat and uncertainty experienced by patients on admission to hospital. In research studies, anxiety is often measured by the State–Trait Anxiety Inventory, a scale which consists of 40 statements. Twenty of these are designed to measure *trait* anxiety, a personality disposition referring to how people generally feel in a wide variety of situations. An item on this scale is "I lack self-confidence", and a person chooses one of the four alternatives ("almost never", "sometimes", "often" or "almost always") which best describes their feelings. The other 20 statements are designed to measure *state* anxiety, referring to how the individual feels at that moment (e.g. to the item "I feel calm" the patient could choose from "not at all", "somewhat", "moderately so" and "very much"). Typically, replies on the state anxiety scale rise steeply before surgery and fall again afterwards, while trait anxiety scores remain fairly constant throughout.[26]

That patients do feel anxious is not surprising, given the disruption to their lifestyle represented by a stay in hospital. Emotional support from family members is affected, there is a reduction in independence and a lack of privacy. Most germane to the present discussion, patients are troubled by the difficulty of interpreting what is happening to them. Cartwright[27] asked patients to outline their complaints about the hospital they stayed in. The most frequently expressed complaint was: "They didn't tell me what I wanted to know". Another survey found that patients' anxieties centred on the operation (31 per cent) and "not knowing what to expect" (34 per cent).

Preparing the patient (reducing uncertainty)

If these aspects of hospitalization are so important, then helping patients to interpret this unfamiliar environment and to predict what is going to happen to them should make their stay more satisfying and less stressful. They might be able to cope with the threat more easily and perhaps even recover sooner. There is now a large body of research on this topic.

Correlational studies

Some of the evidence is based on correlational research, which is a way of measuring the strength of an association between two variables. For example, Wriglesworth and Williams[28] measured patients' satisfaction with the amount of information they had been given and the degree of their confidence in the medical staff. They found a significant positive correlation, indicating that as satisfaction with information increased, so did confidence in staff.

The problem with correlational studies is in interpretation of the results. It is tempting to conclude from this study that information given to patients was responsible for their confidence. However, it is equally possible that cause and effect work the other way round, that staff members are more likely to give information if the patient has confidence in them. Alternatively, it may be that confidence and information are related to each other only indirectly, through a third variable, such as the patients' personalities. Perhaps some patients would report that they were satisfied with their treatment no matter what it was like, and would therefore say that they were satisfied with both the information they were given and the competence of the staff. Other patients might complain regardless of the quality of their care, and would report that they were dissatisfied with both staff and information.

Fortunately, the area of preparing patients for hospitalization and surgery is open to experimental research. Since preparation is not always given or is given in a rather haphazard fashion, it would not be unethical to give some patients more psychological care than is routinely provided.

The work of worrying

Much of the impetus for research in this area was given by Janis,[29] who identified three groups of patients about to undergo surgery: one group showed high anxiety about the impending operation, feeling very vulnerable, sometimes being unable to sleep and sometimes trying to postpone the operation; a second showed moderate fear, asking for information about the operation and worrying about specific features of the surgical procedure such as anaesthesia; the third showed little fear, sleeping well and tending to deny that they felt worried. These latter patients seemed to feel almost completely invulnerable.

After the operation, the first group (high fear) was found to be the most anxiety-ridden and most concerned with their future. The third group (low fear) was more likely than other groups to show anger and resentment towards the staff and often complained about the treatment. For these two groups the stay in hospital was distinctly unhappy. However, the second (moderately fearful) group was less likely than the other two to display emotional disturbance and showed high morale and co-operation with the medical staff. It seemed that a moderate amount of fear about the realistic threat of the operation was associated with good recovery. These patients could cope with the pain and distress of the after-effects of the operation most adequately.

The reasons why the patients in the moderately fearful group were able to cope with the oper-

ation more successfully were not altogether clear, but Janis suggested that it was because they asked for information about their treatment and were thus able to prepare for its consequences. He came to believe that it is important for people to worry about future events so that they can prepare themselves mentally. This appears to be in direct opposition to the view that patients should not be "worried" by information lest they become upset by it. A case study is illustrative:

◆ Let us consider the reactions of a 21-year-old woman who had earlier undergone an appendectomy. At that time she had been given realistic information by her physician. Before the operation she had been moderately worried and occasionally asked the nurses for something to calm her nerves, but she showed excellent emotional adjustment throughout her convalescence. About two years later she came to the same hospital for another abdominal operation, the removal of her gall bladder. In the pre-operative interview with the investigator she reported that her physician had assured her that "there's really nothing to it; it's a less serious operation than the previous one". This time she remained wholly unconcerned about the operation beforehand, apparently anticipating very little or no suffering. Afterwards, experiencing the usual pains and deprivations following a gall bladder operation, she became markedly upset, negativistic, and resentful towards the nursing staff.

Chronic personality predispositions do not seem to account fully for this patient's reactions, since she was capable of showing an entirely different pattern of emotional response, as she had on a previous occasion. The patient's adjustment to the fear-producing situation appeared to be influenced mainly by the insufficient and misleading preparatory communications she was given before the second operation. Since nothing distressing was supposed to happen, she assumed that the hospital staff must be to blame for her post-operative suffering. (Ref. 29, p. 93) ◆

Experimental studies

If the information received by patients before surgery helped them in coping with post-operative pain and anxieties, then an experiment could be performed to test this hypothesis. One group of patients would be given only basic routine information – the time and duration of the operation and that they would awaken in the recovery room. These patients would form the control group. A second group of patients – the experimental group – would be given much more information about the operation. Such experiments have actually been performed many times. For example, Egbert *et al.*[30] arranged for an experimental group to be given the routine amount of information and also some additional preparation, including:

1 a description of the post-operative pain, including where it would be localized, how

much could be expected and how long it would continue;

2 reassurance that post-operative pain was normal and could be expected;

3 advice on how to relax abdominal muscles and how to move without tensing them (all patients had abdominal operations); and

4 assurance that they would be given pain-killing medication should they require it.

The results indicated that the experimental group required only half as much sedation during the first 5 post-operative days (see Figure 1.5) and had an average of 2.7 fewer days of hospitalization. One patient from the control group complained, "Why didn't you tell me it was going to be like this?".

Since this pioneering work, many researchers have explored the importance of preparatory information. That there are so many studies in this area can itself pose problems, especially when trying to integrate the findings, as described in Box 1.1.

Since Janis's early work, the issues have become more complex. Not everyone seems to benefit from this information, so that psychologists have attempted to develop ways of identifying patients who do not benefit or who are made more anxious. A distinction has been made between those patients who prefer to seek out information about their care and those who prefer to avoid it. There are indications that those who avoid gathering information about the operation can be distressed if it is presented without their request and show somewhat worse adjustment thereafter.[32,33]

Another issue involves the relationship between pre-operative anxiety and post-operative recovery. While Janis contended that moderate anxiety is the preferred state (both high and low anxiety being less desirable), many others have provided evidence that the relationship is more simply linear, with higher anxiety associated with poorer outcome, lower anxiety with better outcome. Many studies have indicated that providing emotional support and help in developing coping strategies are important.[34] As discussed in Chapter 9, the perception of control over events, and not just being able to predict or understand them, may be crucial.[35] Research has also been conducted on timing. Johnson[36]

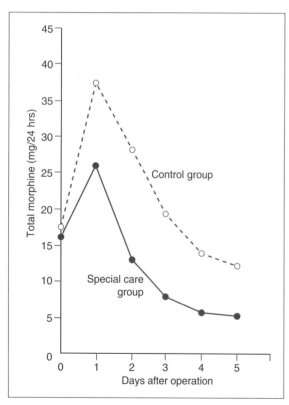

Figure 1.5 Post-operative narcotic treatment of patients given routine and extra preparation for surgery. (Adapted from Egbert, L., Battit, G., Welch, C. and Bartlett, M. *N Engl J Med*, 1964, **270**: 825–827. Copyright 1964. Massachusetts Medical Society. All rights reserved).

BOX 1.1

Reviewing the literature

As studies on a topic accumulate, various researchers are likely to arrive at different conclusions. It is rare that there is one, seminal study which can be used to arrive at a definite conclusion. Different researchers often use different interventions and use different outcome measures. They might also use different populations: for example, a method which might be effective with patients about to undergo dialysis might not be effective with patients who have more minor diseases. These differences can make it difficult for researchers and clinicians to make sense of research results when reviewing the literature.

One way of integrating findings is to use a "voting" procedure. If out of a total of 15 studies on an intervention, 12 indicate that it is effective while 3 do not, one might conclude that there is reasonable evidence in support of the intervention. But what if 8 studies show an effect while 7 are more equivocal? On the face of it, this might be considered weak evidence in support, but if the 8 studies in favour are well designed and give very strong effects while the 7 against are less well designed,

then the conclusions might be different. Such problems of interpretation occur not only in psychology but in many clinical areas.

One method for dealing with such difficulties is to use a *meta-analysis*. This approach to reviewing the literature first involves selecting well-designed studies which have adequate control or comparison groups and which have used similar interventions and outcome measures. Then, the size of the effect is taken into account. A study which shows a very strong effect is more heavily weighted, statistically, than a study which shows a weak effect. This method has been used several times in the area of preparation for surgery, and indicates that interventions are indeed useful. For example, Mumford *et al.*[31] examined 13 studies that used length of stay in hospital as the dependent measure and found that hospital stays for patients receiving psychological assistance averaged about 2 days less than control patients, representing a substantial saving in both financial cost and psychological distress.

---

concluded that anxiety about operations begins well before entering the hospital, indicating that preparation and support could profitably be given before admission.

There is general agreement, however, that for patients who request information it should be specific rather than vague and aimed at the individual patient's concerns and anxieties rather than simply giving the same information to all patients. The opportunity to ask questions results in a greater reduction of anxiety than simply giving the patient a booklet to read.

In general, there has been support for Janis's original recommendations that it is important

1 to give realistic information, so that patients are able to prepare themselves and to correct unrealistic fears;
2 to provide reassurance that others (particularly the medical staff) can be relied on to give

assistance – reassurance counteracts fears of helplessness; and
3 to encourage plans for coping with future difficulties, such as the pain and social consequences of treatment.

To this list should be added a fourth recommendation, that it is important

4 to provide the patient with an opportunity to review the information given.

Written information

Memory does not function well when people are anxious, so that patients may not remember what is said if they are told only once, even if they have a strong wish to understand their treatment. The fourth recommendation can be accomplished by giving the patient a chance to go over the information again with a doctor or nurse, a tape recording of the consultation or a written description to keep. Wilson-Barnett[37] explored the effectiveness of an explanatory leaflet for patients who were to have a barium enema. None of the patients had experienced this before, so that they were all unfamiliar with the procedure and the sensations it produces. The experimental group received a written and verbal explanation of the investigation, an explanation based on both observation and previous patients' comments. The verbal explanation took about 5 minutes, the written information was given to the patients to keep, and any questions were answered. The control group was visited for the same amount of time and asked how they were getting on in hospital.

Giving the control group an equal amount of attention makes this a particularly convincing study. One criticism of research in this area is that many experimenters have neglected to talk with their control group patients, so it is possible that patients in the experimental group find their stay in hospital less stressful simply because someone took the time to talk with them and was interested in their worries, rather than because they gained more information. Such criticism does not

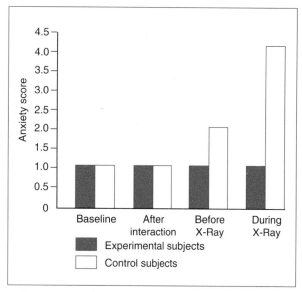

Figure 1.6 Average anxiety scores of patients having a barium enema. The experimental subjects had the procedure explained to them, but the control subjects did not. The control subjects' anxiety began to rise just before the X-ray and continued to rise during it; this was not the case for the experimental subjects. (Reproduced from Wilson-Barnett, J. (1978) *Journal of Advanced Nursing* **3**: 37–40, with permission.)

apply to this experiment because Wilson-Barnett arranged for all patients to have a chat. She also took her measures "blind", so that the investigator who measured anxiety did not know which condition a particular patient was in. Researchers may often find the results they expect and hope to find, not because they "cook" the data but rather because they are more likely to perceive what they expect to perceive.

Measures of the patients' anxieties were taken on several occasions, as shown in Figure 1.6. Before the interaction between nurse and patient, there was no difference in anxiety between the experimental and control group subjects (baseline). Since there was also no difference between the groups after the preparatory information was given, it seems that this knowledge did not adversely affect the patients in the experimental group. But 30 minutes before the X-ray, differences between the groups appeared and were stronger during the X-ray. Although anxiety in the control group patients increased, the experimental subjects showed no such increase. This study indicated that giving well-constructed and designed written information was helpful. Chapter 12 gives some suggestions on how to write such leaflets.

Informed consent

Even if providing information to patients had little effect on their distress and anxiety, there is another important reason for ensuring that patients understand their treatment. This is for the purposes of informed consent. Within biomedical ethics, there is a consensus that people have the right to self-determination: the right to decide what is going to happen to them. This applies equally to medical care as it does to medical research, to minor procedures such as physical examinations as well as to more major invasive procedures such as operations. It is important that patients authorize medical interventions before they occur.

There are five elements which need to be met before consent can be considered "informed", "real" or "valid", as described in Box 1.2. It is clear that these elements are psychological in nature, and concern the communication patterns between doctors and patients. The previous sections in this chapter have covered some of the

BOX 1.2

Informed or real consent

This is designed to protect the right to self-determination, by ensuring that people receive treatment voluntarily and know what they are getting into. It is not enough to explain something – it is the person's understanding and free choice that are important.

There are five elements needed for consent:

1 *Information* Disclosure of those facts which people usually consider material to making their decision to accept treatment, information a doctor considers to be material, and the purpose of seeking consent. People are often provided with an information sheet to keep.

2 *Understanding* The key here is the individual's perspective and his or her participation in the exchange of information. Ordinarily we have only limited insight into the values, hopes, fears and informational needs of other people, so that it is often difficult to assess the level of understanding.

3 *Voluntariness* An absence of control over action, which can be explicit or implicit. In some countries, for example, prison residents cannot be employed in any research projects because of their position within the institution. When students are invited to take part in experiments, care must be taken to ensure that there is no subtle coercion.

4 *Competence* A pre-condition for consent. A person may be incompetent due to immaturity, an illness, or a lack of ability in a particular area.

5 *Consent to intervention* Patients are sometimes asked for written, rather than just verbal, consent. They may require time to consider their decision.

---

issues to do with information-giving and understanding. In Chapter 2 we consider some of the issues to do with cognitive capacity or competence.

Suggested reading

There are a large number of books which elaborate on the principles of perception outlined in this chapter. Lindsay, P.H. and Norman, D. (1977) *Human Information Processing*, 2nd edn, London: Academic Press, provides a good introduction, as does Coren, S., Porac, C. and Ward, L. (1978) *Sensation and Perception*, London: Academic Press. A review of research on preparing patients for surgery is given in Contrada, R., Leventhal, E. and Anderson, J. (1994) Psychological preparation for surgery: marshaling individual and social resources to optimize self-regulation. In: Maes, S., Leventhal, H. and Johnson, M. (eds) *International Review of Health Psychology*, vol. 3, Chichester: Wiley.

References

1. Yersushalmy, J. (1969) The statistical assessment of the variability in observer perception and description of roentgenographic pulmonary shadows. *Radiology Clinics of North America* 7: 381–392.
2. Lindsay, P.H. and Norman, D. (1977) *Human Information Processing*, 2nd edn. London: Academic Press.
3. Hubel, D.H. and Wiesel, T.N. (1965) Receptive fields and functional architecture in two non-striate visual areas (18 and 19) of the cat. *Journal of Neurophysiology* **28**: 229–287.
4. Dion, K.K. (1972) Physical attractiveness and evaluations of children's transgressions. *Journal of Personality and Social Psychology* **24**: 207–213.
5. Nordholm, L.A. (1980) Beautiful patients are good patients: evidence for the physical attractiveness stereotype in first impressions of patients. *Social Science and Medicine* **14A**: 81–83.
6. Meiners, M.L. and Sheposh, J. (1977) Beauty or brains: which image for your mate? *Personality and Social Psychology Bulletin* **3**: 262–265.
7. Pendleton, D.A. and Bochner, S. (1980) The communication of medical information in general practice consultations as a function of patients' social class. *Social Science and Medicine* **14A**: 669–673.
8. Shapiro, M.C., Najman, J., Chang, A., Keeping, J., Morrison, J. and Western, J. (1983) Information

control and the exercise of power in the obstetrical encounter. *Social Science and Medicine* **17**: 139-146.

9. Maguire, G.P. and Granville-Grossman, K. (1968) Physical illness in psychiatric patients. *British Journal of Psychiatry* **114**: 1365-1369.

10. Maguire, G.P., Julier, D., Hawton, K. and Bancroft, J. (1974) Psychiatric morbidity and referral on two general medical wards. *British Medical Journal* **1**: 268-270.

11. Rosenhan, D.L. (1973) On being sane in insane places. *Science* **179**: 250-258.

12. Turnbull, C. (1961) Some observations regarding the experience and behaviour of the Bambuti pygmies. *American Journal of Psychology* **74**: 304-308.

13. Gregory, R.L. (1966) *Eye and Brain*. New York: McGraw-Hill.

14. Leeper, R.A. (1935) A study of a neglected portion of the field of learning. *Journal of Genetic Psychology* **46**: 42-45.

15. Luchins, A.S. (1942) Mechanization in problem-solving. The effect of *Einstellung. Psychological Monographs* **54**.

16. Maguire, G.P. and Rutter, D.R. (1976) History taking for medical students: 1. Deficiencies in performance. *Lancet* **2**: 556-558.

17. Stimson, G.V. (1974) Obeying doctors' orders: a view from the other side. *Social Science and Medicine* **8**: 97-104.

18. Abercrombie, M. (1969) *The Anatomy of Judgement*. Harmondsworth, Middlesex: Penguin.

19. Barrows, H.S. and Bennett, K. (1972) The diagnostic (problem-solving) skill of the neurologist. *Archives of Neurology* **26**: 273-277.

20. Byrne, P.S. and Long, B. (1976) *Doctors Talking to Patients*. London: HMSO.

21. Meichenbaum, D.H., Bowers, K.S. and Ross, R. (1969) A behavioural analysis of teacher expectancy effects. *Journal of Personality and Social Psychology* **13**: 306-316.

22. Jahoda, G. (1954) A note on Ashanti names and their relation to personality. *British Journal of Psychology* **45**: 192-195.

23. Beecher, K.K. (1961) Surgery as placebo: a quantitative study of bias. *Journal of the American Medical Association* **176**: 1102-1107.

24. Skelton, J.A. and Pennebaker, J. (1982) The psychology of physical symptoms and sensations. In: Sanders, G.S. and Suls, J. (eds) *The Social Psychology of Health and Illness*. London: Lawrence Erlbaum.

25. Tymstra, T. (1989). The imperative character of medical technology and the meaning of anticipated decision regret. *International Journal of Technology Assessment in Health Care* **5**: 207-213.

26. Speilberger, C.D., Auerbach, S., Wadsworth, A., Dunn, T. and Taulbee, E. (1973) Emotional reactions to surgery. *Journal of Consulting and Clinical Psychology* **40**: 33-38.

27. Cartwright, A. (1964) *Human Relations and Hospital Care*. London: Routledge and Kegan Paul.

28. Wriglesworth, J.M. and Williams, J. (1975) The construction of an objective test to measure patient satisfaction. *International Journal of Nursing Studies* **12**: 123-132.

29. Janis, I.L. (1971) *Stress and Frustration*. New York: Harcourt Brace Jovanovich.

30. Egbert, L., Battit, G., Welch, C. and Bartlett, M. (1964) Reduction of postoperative pain by encouragement and instruction of patients. *New England Journal of Medicine* **270**: 825-827.

31. Mumford, E., Schlesinger, H. and Glass, G. (1982) The effects of psychological intervention on recovery from surgery and heart attacks: an analysis of the literature. *American Journal of Public Health* **72**: 141-151.

32. Auerbach, S.M. and Kilman, P. (1977) Crisis intervention: a review of outcome research. *Psychological Bulletin* **84**: 1189-1217.

33. Miller, S.M. (1987) Monitoring and blunting: validation of a questionnaire to assess style of information seeking under threat. *Journal of Personality and Social Psychology* **52**: 345-353.

34. Contrada, R., Leventhal, E. and Anderson, J. (1994) Psychological preparation for surgery: marshaling individual and social resources to optimize self-regulation. In: Maes, S., Leventhal, H. and Johnson, M. (eds) *International Review of Health Psychology*, vol. 3. Chichester: Wiley.

35. Miller, S., Combs, C. and Stoddard, E. (1989) Information, coping and control in patients undergoing surgery and stressful medical procedures. In: Steptoe, A. and Appels, A. (eds) *Stress, Personal Control and Health*. Chichester: Wiley.

36. Johnson, M. (1980) Anxiety in surgical patients. *Psychological Medicine* **10**:145-152.

37. Wilson-Barnett, J. (1978) Patients' emotional responses to barium X-rays. *Journal of Advanced Nursing* **3**: 37-40.

2

Cognitive Abilities

SUMMARY

This chapter outlines two key cognitive processes: memory and intelligence. Memory is considered in three stages: encoding, storage and retrieval. *Encoding* or learning information is aided by preparation, repetition and rehearsal. Three kinds of *memory store* are identified: a sensory store based on auditory or visual after image; a short-term store; and a long-term store that material enters if rehearsed. Information in long-term store may be changed in order to be consistent with existing themes and expectations. *Retrieval* involves both recall (which depends on emotional state and context) and recognition (as in multiple-choice questions). The principles of memory research have been applied to improving patients' memory processes.

Intelligence can be measured by IQ (Intelligence Quotient) tests. Intelligence depends on both hereditary and environmental factors such as pre-natal influences and parental attitudes. Because children's understanding differs from that of adults in some fundamental ways, there are several implications for the medical care of children and for obtaining their consent to medical treatment.

This chapter considers some aspects of ability and behaviour which are closely related to neuropsychology. *Neuropsychology* is the study of the ways that the brain and its structures control behaviour and cognitive processes. The effects of brain damage due to injury or disease have helped in the development of neuropsychology. By correlating anatomical damage to changes in behaviour, it has been possible to chart the functions and locations of many neurological structures. Such research has added to our understanding of the difficulties which patients face when they experience a stroke or have a head injury: not only can this aid in diagnosis but it can also point to possible interventions.

First, a brief overview of brain functions is provided, especially as it relates to damage to the central nervous system. Second, there is an examination of memory processes. This section is relevant not only to helping patients with memory losses but also for students learning new information, as in studying for examinations. Third, there is a discussion of intelligence as it is studied by psychologists. This section includes information on IQ testing and the development of cognitive abilities.

Brain functions

Compared to other animals, humans have the highest brain to body weight ratio, with about 20 per cent of the blood from the heart flowing to the brain, attesting to its importance for humans.

Unconsciousness results if the flow is interrupted for as little as 6 seconds and a brain starved of oxygen for only a few minutes is likely to be damaged irreversibly. Neuroanatomy is a complex area, but for a psychologist the interest lies in how the structures of the brain are related to behaviour, emotions and cognitive abilities.

Localization of function

One of the oldest controversies in neuropsychology has concerned the degree of localization of function within the brain. There is ample evidence that lesions in different parts of the brain have different effects. Two good examples are Broca's and Wernick's areas. In the nineteenth century Paul Broca was able to show, by reviewing the evidence on brain injuries, that a small area in the left cerebral hemisphere was closely associated with the production of speech, but not its understanding. *Broca's aphasia* is the term given to slurred and laboured speech after damage to this area. Soon afterwards, Carl Wernick argued that damage to a nearby area was responsible for *Wernick's aphasia,* in which speech is rapid and articulate, but has little or no meaning. Damage to the pathway between these two areas results in a disruption between speaking and understanding.

Language disorders generally result from damage to the left hemisphere, indicating that speech centres are located on the left. This is almost always the case for right-handed people, but left-handed people often have their speech centres within the right hemisphere or have a mixed localization.

The right or non-dominant hemisphere has a number of important functions, particularly those associated with the perception and memory of complex visual and spatial stimuli. People who have suffered damage to some parts of the right hemisphere have difficulty in remembering familiar faces, for example.

When the connection between the right and left hemispheres – the corpus callosum – is severed, people can suffer a number of odd and surprising deficits. A person may be able to give an accurate report about the size of an object if it is presented in their left hand, but not if it is presented to their right hand.[1]

On the other hand, there is certainly no one-to-one relationship between individual functions and particular parts of the brain, so that a simple mapping of areas is an oversimplification. If damage occurs gradually or before or shortly after birth, other parts of the brain may develop to compensate, so that a child brain-damaged at birth may go on to develop virtually normally. In fact, there is even some question about the need for all the structures which are normally present. Lewis[2] describes a young man who was born hydrocephalic yet was able to accomplish much intellectually:

◆ There's a young student at this university who has an IQ of 126, has gained a first-class honours degree in mathematics, and is socially completely normal. And yet the boy has virtually no brain ... Instead of the normal 4.5 centimeter thickness of brain tissue between the ventricles and the cortical surface, there was just a thin layer of mantle measuring a millimeter or so. His cranium is filled mainly with cerebrospinal fluid. ◆

Such observations indicate that the relationship between anatomy and behaviour is very complex, a complexity which is supported by psychological research on memory and on intelligence.

Memory

In Chapter 1 an information-processing model of perception was outlined. According to this model, there are three stages involved in perception – sensation, interpretation and memory. The aim of this section is to consider some aspects of memory, particularly as they apply to learning information, as in studying for examinations, and to clinical practice, as in giving information to patients.

The hippocampus and the Papez circuit generally (hippocampus – fornix – mammillary bodies – thalamus – ungulate cortex – hippocampus) have been implicated by several studies exploring the effect of brain lesions on memory. It seems that bilateral damage to any part of this circuit will disrupt memory processes. Some of the more striking case studies are those reported by Milner.[3] In an attempt to relieve patients of severe epilepsy, and when more conservative treatments had little effect, the mesial parts of both temporal lobes were removed, thus destroying two-thirds of the hippocampus bilaterally. Unfortunately, the operation led to severe memory impairment in several patients. For example:

◆ [T]en months after the operation the family moved to a new house which was situated only a few blocks away from their old one, on the same street. When examined nearly a year later, H.M. had not yet learned the new address, nor could he be trusted to find his way home alone, because he would go to the old house. Six years ago the family moved again, and H.M. is still unsure of his present address, although he does seem to know that he has moved. Moreover, his mother states that he is unable to learn where objects constantly in use are kept; for example, although he mows the lawn regularly, and quite expertly, she still has to tell him where to find the lawnmower, even when he has been using it only the day before. His mother also observes that he will do the same jigsaw puzzles day after day without showing any practice effect, and read the same magazines over and over again without ever finding their contents familiar. The same forgetfulness applies to people he has met since the operation, even to those neighbours who have been visiting the house regularly for the past six years. He has not learned their names and he does not recognize any of them if he meets them in the street. Conversely, he cannot now be left alone in the house, because he has been known to invite total strangers in to await his mother's return, thinking that they must be friends of the family whom he has failed to recognize. (Ref. 3, pp. 113-114) ◆

It is hard to imagine what it must be like to be H.M. In many respects, we *are* our memories – how we see ourselves, how we choose our careers and how we conduct our relationships with other people are all based on our memories of past experiences.

While it is clear that memory is vital to our everyday functioning, it is tempting to consider it as a rather straightforward process: information is learned and either remembered or forgotten. We also tend to think of memory in terms of facts, but it seems that memories are organized in terms of *meanings*, rather than discrete pieces of information. Sometimes information cannot be recalled when every effort is made (say, during an examination), only for it to pop up later (during the walk home afterwards). Some kinds of information are very difficult to learn, whereas other kinds can be recalled without any intention to remember. Further, over time the information stored in memory can change. Memory consists of a complex array of systems and subsystems which can interact in surprising ways.

It has proved useful to distinguish between two different types of memories:

● *Episodic* memories concern the types of autobiographical experiences we have on an everyday basis, such as what we had for breakfast or the content of a conversation. These are temporally coded memories of particular times and places.
● *Semantic* memories are more conceptual. Although they contain factual information (the type needed to pass an anatomy examination), they also involve more generic information, such as how to order a meal in a restaurant or how to use public transportation to see a friend.

Sometimes, one type of memory but not the other is affected by how we feel (our mood) and by our past experiences. In trying to understand a very complex process, it is useful to consider memory in three stages: learning information (encoding), storing it and retrieving it.

Encoding information

The way in which information is learned or encoded has an important influence on how easy it is to recall. One of the most important figures in the study of memory was Hermann Ebbinghaus who, in the nineteenth century, studied his own memory processes by learning long lists of what are called "nonsense syllables", such as KYH or ZIW. He found that syllables in the middle of these long lists were recalled less easily than those at the beginning (the primacy effect) and those at the end (the recency effect). He also found that most forgetting occurred within the first few hours and that it was reduced if the list was "over-learned" (i.e. instead of stopping his reviews of the lists when the syllables were accurately recited for the first time, he would recite them once or twice more). Material that was repeated soon after it was first encountered was also more likely to be recalled later. The timing of such rehearsals is very important: although an immediate rehearsal is helpful, subsequent repetitions should be spaced over time for maximum learning, rather than being massed into a short time-interval.

Recall can also be enhanced by some preparation for learning by first skimming over the material. This gives an overall idea of the content so that expectations about the information can be raised and the material more easily organized. For the reader of this book, some of the organizational work has already been done: at the beginning of each chapter there is a short description of aims and a list of contents. There is much evidence that skimming is effective. In one study participants were given a short tutorial, being shown how to skim over the headings and summaries of the passages they were to learn before they settled down to read. When given a new passage to learn, this group read 24 per cent faster than those not encouraged to skim first, and there was no loss in accuracy.

Baddeley[4] terms this direction of attention towards particular aspects of the environment our *working memory*. As you read these words, part of the working memory – called the executive – allocates attention towards the words on the page. The executive is involved in all attentionally demanding tasks such as problem-solving, reading and writing, and resists distraction to other tasks.

Storing information

Memory seems to have three kinds of store. The first type – sensory store – may last less than a second and seems to be based on an auditory or visual after-image. If this information is not attended to, it fades and seems to be permanently lost. If attention is paid to the information via the working memory, it enters the second type of storage – short-term storage (STS). As this sentence is read, the previous one will be in STS and will be available for only about 18 seconds if it is not rehearsed or reviewed.

The capacity of STS is very limited, often considered to be able to hold only about seven items of information. However, it is the meaning of this information which is significant, not simply the number of items. For example, it would be difficult to remember the following series of digits:

1066177619391812

However, they would be relatively easy to recall if you noticed that the sequence is made up of the dates of the Battle of Hastings, the American Declaration of Independence, the outbreak of the Second World War and the Battle of Waterloo. In this case, there are only four bits of information to recall, a comparatively simple task.

This is because you are relying on information already held in the long-term store (LTS). It holds past experiences which have been integrated from the STS. Rehearsal over spaced time intervals and skimming facilitate this process. Whatever biochemical or anatomical changes are involved in transfer to the LTS,[5] forgetting from this store seems to be very slow and its capacity is very large.

The reconstruction of memories

An important feature of the LTS is its active nature. It is not simply a warehouse full of past experiences, holding memories that correspond exactly to what was learned or experienced. Rather, memories can change or be reconstructed. After a period of time, material recalled from the LTS may not necessarily correspond to that which was originally learned but may be distorted to fit into themes or ideas. It is as if the gaps in memory are filled with pieces of general information about the world. Inferences are made and integrated into memory.

This is because our memories are organized into *schemata*, or mental representations about the world. Schemata are basic assumptions about how the world is organized. New information is processed to be consistent with already-existing premises which have been built up over time. An illustration of how they operate is provided by a study on anxiety. One of the more puzzling features of some kinds of anxiety is that people remain anxious about a situation despite repeated experiences when nothing aversive occurs. Although theories of anxiety reduction predict that anxiety will reduce with experience, it can be slow to decline in real-life settings. Dental anxiety is a good example: anxious patients typically expect considerable pain when they visit the dentist, but they find this rarely occurs. Why, then, do they continue to expect discomfort on their next visit? It seems to be due in part to the reconstruction of memory.

In one study,[6] patients who were attending a dentist were asked to fill out a questionnaire designed to measure their degree of dental anxiety and the amount of pain they expected. After the appointment, they were asked about the amount of pain actually experienced. When the patients were contacted 3 months later and asked to recall the amount of pain they had felt at the appointment, the anxious patients recalled much more pain than they had originally reported, whereas the less anxious patients were more accurate in their recall. It seemed that the memories of the anxious patients had changed in order to become consistent with what they had expected their appointment to be like, rather than reflecting actual experience. In this case, the episodic memory (what actually happened) was altered to be consistent with the semantic memory (what they expected dental appointments to be like).

These distortions of memory are due to a tendency that we all share to fit what we experience into what we believe. This process, called "effort after meaning", is important in much psychological research and medical practice. Whenever a person in a psychological study or a patient under the care of a doctor is asked for retrospective data, there is the possibility that the memories will be matched not simply to events but also to previous and subsequent experiences. People may be more likely to remember and embellish an event if it is followed by a change in health, for example (see Chapter 9 on stress), or to forget a doctor's advice if it does not fit into a pre-existing pattern of memories and expectations (see Chapter 12).

Retrieving memories

Not all information stored in LTS can be recalled. Ebbinghaus distinguished two types of retrieval – recall and recognition. You may have experienced the "tip of the tongue" phenomenon, the certainty that you know a piece of information, but cannot recall it: someone's name, perhaps, or an important fact on an examination. Once the name or fact is given, however, it can be immediately recognized.

There are many factors which affect retrieval. One involves the circumstances in which the information was originally learned, called *state-dependent* retrieval. It seems that we are able to retrieve information more readily if we do so in circumstances similar to those in which it was learned. Thus it is easier to recall factual information in an examination hall if the material was originally learned in a similar setting, such as a library.

Another factor is termed *mood-dependent* recall. We tend to recall memories which are consistent or congruent with our current mood. When we are feeling happy, we tend to remember pleasant episodes in our lives, but when we feel sad or depressed we tend to recall unpleasant experiences. It has been possible to explore this phenomenon experimentally through mood-induction techniques. In these studies, people are asked to read sad (or happy) stories, or to listen to sad (or uplifting) music. These induction techniques are very effective and do result in changes of emotion.

Many studies have shown that our current emotion will affect recall of episodes. Bower[7] examined this process by first inducing a happy or sad mood in his subjects and then asking them to recall childhood incidents. Some of his results are shown in Figure 2.1. When a happy mood was induced, they were much more likely to recall pleasant experiences, but when they were in a sad mood more unpleasant experiences were recalled.

This line of research is clinically important for two reasons. One is that people tend to recall episodes in their life which are congruent with their current experiences. A person who has been recently bereaved, for example, is more likely to recall earlier sad experiences. It is also

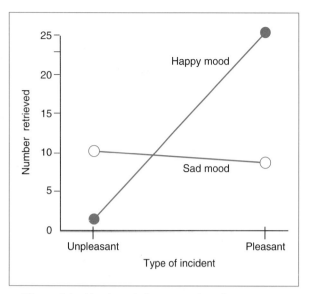

Figure 2.1   Number of pleasant and unpleasant childhood incidents recalled when the recaller was in a happy or a sad mood. (Reproduced from Bower, G. (1981) *American Psychologist* **36**: 129–148. Copyright © 1981 by the American Psychological Association. Reprinted with permission.)

possible that mood is self-perpetuating. When we feel sad, we are more likely to stay sad in a circular fashion. This is one explanation for the persistence of clinical depression: when depressed, people are more likely to recall negative experiences, perhaps when they had failed rather than succeeded on tasks, which serves to exacerbate their lowered mood.[8]

This distinction between types of retrieval also has implications for studying, since the type of examination should influence how the material is studied. Multiple-choice questions rely mainly on recognition, while essay-type examinations require accurate recall. In one experiment, students were given a passage to read and then examined on it. One group of students was told that they would receive short-answer, open questions, whereas the other group expected multiple-choice questions. However, half of each group was given the kind of test they did *not* expect, so that their preparation may have been inappropriate. As predicted, those who received the expected type of test did better than those who received the unexpected one.[9] Preparation and retrieval can be aided by checking the type of questions used in past examinations in a subject.

Practical applications

These types of research on memory have many practical implications. In Appendix 1, there is further discussion of study aids, but here we consider how memory research might help medical staff to impart information to patients and how it aids the diagnosis of people with certain kinds of brain damage.

Imparting information to patients

Simply because a patient has been told something, it cannot be assumed that the information will be retained or recalled. This could be because they are given material which is unfamiliar and difficult to link with already existing ideas and beliefs, or because they are anxious and find it difficult to attend to everything a doctor says. It seems to be the case that people in a shocked state retain little of what is said to them. This could apply equally to informing someone of a terminal prognosis as to telling parents that their child is handicapped. As one mother recalled,[10] when asked what she was told during the consultation when she first heard her child had Down's syndrome: "I can't really remember; I think we were too shocked at the time that anything else he said just went into one ear and out the other" (p. 26). This implies that it is important for doctors to make themselves available on subsequent occasions and to be prepared to repeat information that has already been given.

In Chapters 11 and 12 some ways in which doctors can present advice to patients to make it more likely to be retained are described. These include being aware of the primacy effect (material given early in the consultation is more likely to be remembered), stressing the crucial aspects, and not giving patients too much to remember. There has also been interest in using tape recordings of consultations, as illustrated by studies in which patients were given audio tapes to take home and replay whenever they wished. In one study they were given a tape recording of the final discharge interview. At this time the history was reviewed, a final physical examination was given, the laboratory findings were outlined and the treatment discussed. When asked about the usefulness of the tape recording later, the patients reported that they had listened to it three and a half times on average, indicating that most were unable to assimilate all the information on first or even second hearing.[11]

In another study,[12] patients who were suffering from cancer were randomly assigned to one of two conditions: either being given a tape recording of their consultation, or not. One week later they were asked to return to the clinic, when they were asked to recall information about the consultation and to complete questionnaires designed to measure their levels of anxiety and depressed mood. Not only could the patients given the tape recall more information (they had listened to it an average of four times), but they were less anxious and only one reported being "mildly upset" by it. This approach is inexpensive, easy to introduce and highly appreciated by patients.

Memory impairment

Techniques developed from memory research have also proved useful with patients suffering from memory impairments. They can assist in diagnosis, they can be used to monitor changes in a patient's condition, and they can give patients some insight into their difficulties and suggest ways in which these might be overcome.[13,14]

Brain injury can lead to amnesia. *Anterograde amnesia* is an inability to retain new experiences, as occurs following brain injury or during recovery from a general anaesthetic. *Retrograde amnesia* refers to the difficulty in remembering events before the injury: concussed patients are often unable to recall the incident causing the concussion or the events just preceding it. The degree of such post-traumatic amnesia is often used as an index of the severity of a closed head injury. Patients usually recover their ability to remember new experiences but rarely completely fill the retrograde gap.

Memory difficulties in general are considered to be early warning signs of organic disorders, with problems occurring at the learning, storage or retrieval stages. In Korsakoff's amnesia syndrome, due to chronic alcoholism, there is an almost complete inability to learn new material and much difficulty in recalling past events. Dementia is the term given to a profound and progressive deterioration of all intellectual faculties.

The exact nature of such deficits, however, can be very subtle. Sometimes it is not clear whether the difficulty is in encoding, storage or retrieval. For example, Baddeley[4] describes a study with Korsakoff patients. They were asked to solve the same jigsaw puzzle on a number of occasions. Since there were severe short-term memory difficulties, they could not recall having encountered the puzzle before. However, they were able to become more fluent in solving the puzzle, indicating that the skill had improved, even if they could not recall their earlier experience consciously.

While deficits in memory can indicate organic damage, there are other possible explanations for any deterioration. Anyone who is severely emotionally disturbed may be troubled by forgetfulness. Memory can also decline due to social and environmental factors, as in the case of some elderly people who are resident in nursing homes where there is little stimulation and few opportunities to practise memory skills. Langer *et al.*[15] argued that many cognitive abilities can diminish with disuse. They reasoned that if nursing home residents could be encouraged to practise such skills then any deterioration could be stopped or even reversed, an argument discussed further in the next chapter.

Intelligence

Most people, at some time in their lives, undergo tests of ability. Tests may be overt, such as an examination designed to give an indication of how well a student has learned a subject, or they may be less obvious, such as a consultant unobtrusively assessing the ability of a student. These kinds of test are very specific: the interest is only in one aspect of a person's life, often at a particular time. Psychologists have attempted to gain a more general measure of ability through the development of IQ (Intelligence Quotient) tests. These are used by many educational and clinical psychologists in their assessments of, say, a child who is not doing well in school or an adult whose capacities may have been damaged by a stroke or an accident.

Different types of psychologists

Psychologists come in many shapes and forms. All will have completed an undergraduate degree in psychology, covering the areas of perception, memory, intelligence and human development. After this initial training, psychologists go on to specialize in various areas.

Some are academically based, with their main concerns in research and teaching. They will have completed a PhD in a particular topic and gained a post in a university or other higher-level academic institution. Most of the research reported in this book has been conducted by academic psychologists who have a particular interest in health psychology. *Clinical psychologists* will have undertaken additional training in helping people with emotional difficulties such as anxiety or depression, intellectual difficulties, and rehabilitation of people who have suffered strokes and other injuries. Some of the issues they encounter are discussed here, others in Chapters 3 and 4. *Educational psychologists* work with schools, where they attempt to help teachers and children to deal with behavioural and emotional issues. *Occupational psychologists* tend to work in organizations, such as private companies, examining how relationships between workers and management affects the efficiency of the company and well-being of the workforce.

Psychiatrists are medically trained. After completing their basic training, they specialize in mental health. Although they may often use the same interventions as clinical psychologists, such as behavioural therapies and psychotherapy, they have wider powers to prescribe medications.

In such cases, IQ tests may aid diagnosis. The child whose school grades are low might have difficulties in learning or, alternatively, have emotional or interpersonal problems. If a high score were achieved on an IQ test, this could effectively rule out intellectual impairments. Since IQ tests measure various abilities, the particular difficulties experienced by a patient can sometimes be pinpointed and rehabilitation programmes devised.

Although there is a wide variety of suggested definitions of "intelligence", as measured by IQ tests it refers to an ability to solve problems and to think in the abstract. Measurements of this ability run into numerous problems. For instance, can intelligence be regarded as one global ability or does it refer to several independent abilities such as competence in solving problems, memory or word fluency? Can it be measured without taking into account a person's motivation to succeed at the task? Is it possible to devise tests which measure aptitude rather than prior learning? Once a measurement has been made, does it show that a person has inherited their intellectual ability or does it depend on past experiences? What, if anything, does current performance indicate about a person's future capabilities? In this section of the chapter we look at how people have studied intelligence, with particular attention to the development and use of IQ tests.

Measurement of IQ

Several ways of measuring intelligence have been explored. As far back as 1884, Sir Francis Galton tried, unsuccessfully, to relate head size and reaction times to intellectual performance. More recently, attempts have been made to relate the speed of brain functioning and myelination,[16] but the most successful approach to intellectual measurement has been the IQ test.

IQ tests

The forerunner of current individual IQ tests was a scale developed by Alfred Binet at the beginning of this century. By giving a large sample of children various problems to solve, he identified items which could be done by, on average, half the children of each age. For example, he found that half the 8-year-olds could count backwards from 20 to zero, and half the 10-year-olds could name the months of the year. His test consisted of a set of these age-graded items. When the test was administered to a particular child, he or she would initially be presented with the items for an age lower than his or her *chronological* age and then given successively harder items until several in a row were failed. This procedure established the child's *mental* age.

The original Binet test has been revised many times but remains in common use as the Stanford–Binet test, along with a similar test developed by David Wechsler (the Wechsler Intelligence Scale for Children, or WISC). In the current version of the Stanford–Binet, an 8-year-old child would be asked to define certain words (e.g. a straw, an orange, an envelope, a puddle), to point out absurdities in statements (e.g. "An old man complained that he could no longer walk around the park as he used to; he said that now he could only go half-way round and then back again"), to say how two things were alike and how they differed (e.g. sea and river) and to indicate comprehension of situations by answering questions appropriately ("What's the thing for you to do when you are on your way to school and think you are going to be late?").[17]

The Stanford–Binet and the WISC are for children aged 2-16 years, but there are also various tests for children below the age of 2 years. A 6-month-old infant would be expected to pick a cube off a table; to lift a cup from a table; to finger his or her reflection in a mirror; to reach out for objects with one hand and to stretch persistently towards an object which was just out of reach. There are also tests designed for people over the age of 16, such as the Wechsler Adult Intelligence Scale or WAIS. Like the WISC it samples a variety of cognitive abilities, mainly of the verbal (e.g. general knowledge, vocabulary and comprehension) and performance (e.g. block design and picture arrangement) types. Most recently, there has been a concern that they assess too few abilities. Although these IQ tests sample performance in a variety of areas, they do not include many important competencies. The British Ability Scales have 24 tests, which can be selected according to the individual's needs.

Calculating IQ

For children, the intelligence quotient or IQ is derived from the formula mental age (MA)/chronological age (CA) × 100. In the case of an 8-year-old child who passed only the items expected of an average 6-year-old, the IQ would be $6/8 \times 100 = 75$, whereas the IQ of the child whose answers indicated the ability of a 10-year-old would be $10/8 \times 100 = 125$. An "average" child, with a mental age equivalent to the chronological age, would have an IQ of 100.

Beyond the age of 16-18 years, chronological age is no longer used to calculate IQ. It is not easy, for example, to find items that can be done by a 23-year-old but not by a 22-year-old. An IQ can still be calculated for an adult, however, by comparing his or her performance with that of a large group of people of similar age. It is not the absolute score which is important, but how the score compares with the results given by other, similar, people. Only if people come from similar cultural backgrounds can the comparison be made. When an IQ test has been given to a large group of people it is said to be "standardized" for that population and their results are called "norms".

IQ tests are designed so that the average is 100. IQ is considered to be normally distributed in the population, allowing for a curve to be constructed which indicates the number of individuals likely to obtain a particular score. In fact, standard IQ tests are devised so that almost everybody lies within a range of 90 IQ points, from 55 to 145.

Reliability and validity

The results of IQ tests can only be taken seriously if they can be shown to be *reliable* (the same result is obtained by different testers or on different occasions) and *valid* (the tests are measuring problem-solving abilities and abstract thinking rather than something else, say, prior training in how to do the test).

Reliability can be measured in various ways: by seeing if people achieve a similar score on subsequent administrations of the test (called test–retest reliability); by preparing alternative or parallel forms of the test and seeing whether people score similarly on both; or by comparing scores on one half of the test with scores on the other half (split-half reliability).

One way in which reliability is maintained is by standardizing the way the tests are given, so that each testing is seen as a well-controlled experiment. Manuals describe precisely how the tests must be administered and the trained psychologist must follow this agreed procedure, down to the exact words. Great emphasis is placed on these standard procedures because scores are open to social influences. An examiner who encourages the client to try harder, or who is warm and reassuring, may obtain different results from an examiner who does not show these qualities. This point is illustrated by a study in which children were tested using the Stanford–Binet by graduate students in psychology. The students were asked to test two children each, being led to believe that one was capable of high academic achievement whereas the other had shown only poor academic ability. In fact, there was no such systematic sorting of children, yet the examiners' results corresponded to their expectations. Those children said to be more able attained significantly higher scores than those said to be less able.[18] At least in part, measuring IQ is a social process.

As far as validity is concerned, IQ tests do correlate with academic achievement, the original purpose behind Binet's scale. The Stanford–Binet and Weschler tests correlate between 0.40 and 0.60 with school grades. IQ test results also correlate with occupational achievement and the average IQ of people in different jobs (such as lawyer or butcher) has been found to correlate with independent rankings of how intelligent such workers would be considered to be.

Within more restricted ranges, however, IQ correlates less well with achievement. Doctors in the top and bottom thirds of their graduating class displayed only very slight differences in the quality of practice thereafter and even these decreased after the first few years.[19] This was because the IQ test was not designed to discriminate between people of similar high (or low) ability but rather to distinguish between the high and low scorers. Since almost everyone who goes to university will have a high IQ, this lack of correspondence is not surprising.

Attempts have been made to develop "culture-fair" tests which do not rely on linguistic ability. However, it is clear that cultural influences extend beyond language: the motivation to succeed at the task may be quite different, for instance. Intelligence is highly prized in Western societies, while there is not even an equivalent concept in some other cultures. It now seems apparent that, although some tests may be less culture-biased than others, no test is completely culture-fair. This means it is impossible on the basis of IQ tests to say people from one culture are more intelligent than people from another. This has been well demonstrated by a study investigating groups of children in various parts of the world. Each group showed definite variations in the pattern of abilities. Children in less developed countries sometimes surpassed Western standards on some tasks but scored very low on others.[20] Such studies illustrate that the global concept of intelligence provides only a crude measure.

Factors affecting IQ

An individual's score on an IQ test is generally considered to be a function of both heredity and environment. The environment is important since genes provide only a potential for growth. They do not determine its course independent of the environment. The importance of genetics in height, for example, is clear, but the general population in Western countries has been becoming appreciably taller over the last generations. This seems to be due to better diet and living conditions. Specific gene mutations that affect IQ highlight the complexity of the interrelationship between nature and nurture. Children born with phenylketonuria (PKU) used to suffer brain damage due to the build up of phenylalanine in toxic quantities in the bloodstream. Now, however, every infant is routinely tested a few days after birth (the Guthrie test) and in the rare cases that the condition is detected, amelioration is possible by the provision of a special diet. By providing the right environment, the potentially damaging effects of the individual's genetic make-up are averted.

There is considerable disagreement about the relative importance of genetic and environmental influences in the development of intelligence. Some hold that heredity is primarily responsible for scores in IQ tests, others argue that environment is the critical factor. This debate, which is found among geneticists as well as psychologists, has been fiercely argued by both sides, with accusations of fraudulent reporting of data (see Box 2.2). It is not possible adequately to summarize the debate here except to make some general points.

BOX 2.2

Fraud and misconduct in research

There are two main types of fraud in scientific research: using others' ideas without acknowledging their previous efforts (plagiarism) and making up or altering data. These forms of fraud are very important for several reasons. One reason is that the scientific enterprise depends on honesty. If a scientist's results are fraudulent they can mislead others into making incorrect assumptions. A second reason is that educational and public health policies are often based on scientific findings. If educational policies are based on erroneous ideas or resources are allocated to what is in fact an ineffective intervention, harm may result.

Fraudulent researchers can have any one of a number of motives. While it is true to say that most researchers have an overriding interest in the truth, they also have many other obligations. They have obligations to themselves and their careers and to their institutions: because allocation of grants and status fall to those who publish in prestigious journals, and because interesting results are much more likely to achieve publication, there is always the temptation to alter or invent data.[21]

The problem in disentangling the effects of genes and environment is that people who are related to one another genetically are usually related to one another socially as well. If they live in the same household, they will have many shared experiences, so that any correlation between their IQs could just as easily be attributed to similarities in environment as to similarities in genetic endowment. Children who are given "good" genes by their parents are also likely to live in an enriched environment, with plentiful books, lots of conversation and encouragement to do well at school. Any genetic potential is more likely to be fulfilled in such conditions.

Studies attempting to disentangle genetic and environmental effects run into many problems.

For example, many studies have compared the IQs of monozygotic twins reared together with those reared apart. The similar correlations found have supported the genetic position. However, even for those twins reared apart the environments may be very similar. In one study, many of the separated twins were raised in related branches of the same family, such as by the biological mother's sister. Furthermore, testing has not always been conducted "blind". There is the possibility that the examiners expected to find similar IQs amongst the twins and unconsciously biased their examination.

The debate between the two camps is likely to continue for some time yet.[22] As in other areas of psychology, it is those studies which have important social implications that are most critically examined, each side looking for flaws in the other's research. Rather than attempt to determine the relative influence of genetic versus environmental factors, it seems more helpful to explore the ways in which each influences intellectual growth. Some of the environmental influences are outlined below.

Environment

The effect of a wide range of environmental circumstances on intellectual ability (again, as measured by IQ tests) have been studied, including the pre-natal environment, family, social class and education.

Influences on the foetus in the womb can affect the IQ of the child, depending on their timing. An organ system is most sensitive when it is developing most rapidly. Although in the majority of cases of mental handicap no physical cause can be discovered, if the mother catches rubella (German measles) in the first 3 months of pregnancy, for instance, the infant's hearing may be impaired and heart defects or other physical abnormalities caused. The number of brain cells in the child is reduced if the mother's diet is inadequate (too little protein or too few calories) particularly in the final 3 months of pregnancy, and maternal alcoholism has been shown to lead to mental handicap in the child. Certain drugs taken by the mother or smoking during pregnancy can also affect the child.

Numerous studies have shown clear relationships between parental social class and both the

IQ and scholastic achievement of their children. Part of this social-class influence may be related to differences in the quality and quantity of language used in the home. Many studies have found marked social-class differences in the language used by parents to their children which put working-class children at a disadvantage on traditional IQ tests (and, indeed, in educational settings generally) compared to middle-class children. It is not the amount of stimulation, but rather the quality, meaningfulness and range of experiences available to the child that are important.[23]

Parental attitudes to learning and education and the literacy of the home may also be part of the social-class related influences, as, indirectly, are poor material circumstances such as poverty, overcrowding and lack of basic household facilities. There is a high correlation between large family size and low attainment, larger families also tending to be those with less financial and material resources. The different forms of social disadvantage all tend to affect the same group of families. Verbal skills are particularly affected. McCall et al.[24] compared children whose IQ scores increased over time with those whose IQ scores decreased, and found the former had parents who placed more emphasis on intellectual tasks and achievements.

Education has been shown to affect IQ, but to account for much less of the variance than features of family and home. There have been various attempts to help children from disadvantaged homes by means of compensatory education, generally at pre-school level. In one attempt to raise intellectual ability,[25] 40 children were selected at birth whose mothers had an IQ of 80 or below. Twenty of the children served as a comparison group, being given no special attention. The other children were given extensive educational advantages – attending a centre for 7 hours a day, 5 days a week. The programme included assistance in language, thinking and sensorimotor skills. Their mothers were also included, being given vocational and child-care training. Both groups of children were periodically tested and after the age of 14 months differences between the groups became apparent. At about 5 years of age the experimental group children averaged 120 IQ points while the control

group children had an average IQ of about 95. It seems that attempts at compensatory education that involve the family and which continue into the school years seem most likely to succeed.

Thus, intelligence is affected by both genetic endowment and experience. Those psychologists who emphasize the genetic component cite the studies on twins, where there are high correlations between monozygotic twins reared apart in separate families. On the other hand, there are clear environmental influences as well, since experiences (including pre-natal experiences) have effects on IQ.

Development of intelligence

The intelligence tests so far described are empirical, simply identifying tasks that an average child of a particular age can do. The researchers who devised the early tests were not primarily concerned with explaining how such skills develop. Some child psychologists have argued that there is a sequence of stages through which every child progresses. Although the order of these stages is common to all, some children may pass through them more quickly than others. Progression through such stages might be due primarily to maturation (growth processes that are governed by automatic, genetically determined signals) or perhaps learning should be given more emphasis. Both processes are involved to some extent: for example, maturation is clearly important in the infant's ability to reach or to walk, but there is evidence that both skills can be hastened by experience.[26,27]

Gesell

A major proponent of the maturational approach is Arnold Gesell, who made many detailed observations of infants' and pre-school children's abilities. By examining large groups of children, Gesell charted the normal (or average) course of development. An individual child's abilities could then be compared with these norms. The tests devised from this work are easy to administer, score and interpret, being concerned with the average age at which such skills as smiling, sitting without support or standing emerge.[28] Such normative studies of development form the basis of routine paediatric assessments. By checking all children in this way as a matter of course, developmental lags can be monitored, allowing the early detection of sensory handicaps or intellectual impairments and early intervention to deal with these. Gesell believed behaviour unfolded in a sequence of stages, determined by inherent maturational mechanisms. Although this work shows the average ages at which skills emerge, it is important to realize that there is a large normal range of ages at which skills develop. The average age of walking is 14 months, for example, but many children do not accomplish this until some months later.

Piaget

A more active view of the developmental process was taken by Jean Piaget. Rather than simply accumulating experiences or maturing physically, he argued, the child comes to understand the world through actively working with, modifying and organizing these experiences. Like Gesell, Piaget believed that each child goes through a series of distinct stages: some may progress further than others, but the order remains invariant. Each stage builds on the previous one and, once new concepts are mastered, allows the child to explore new aspects of the environment.

Piaget suggested that the child under the age of seven is in many ways extremely limited in his or her ability to think or reason. The pre-school child, for example, is not supposed to know what an object would look like from the other side, being unable to consider any viewpoint other than his or her own (called egocentrism); the child is supposed to think that if you pour water from one jar into another of a different shape, you change the quantity of water (conservation of volume). These and other limitations were brought to light in a series of careful – and much replicated – observations of children in defined situations.

However, some aspects of Piaget's theory have been called into question. It seems that children can reason in many of these ways if the situation is made more relevant to their own experiences and if ambiguities in language are removed. More recent research has indicated that children's responses may be due more to a failure of communication between the adult and the child than a lack of ability.[29]

Despite such problems with aspects of Piaget's work, his theories remain influential and have made psychologists more aware of the ways that children come to understand their world. Piaget's theory holds that children are motivated to explore their world. Curiosity may be as important a motivator of behaviour as the biological pressures of hunger and thirst. Hospitalization may have disturbing effects on the child if these cognitive requirements are not met. The opportunity to explore and experiment with their world may be restricted in hospitals due to staff shortages, or lack of toys and space. Particularly when chronic illnesses requiring lengthy stays in hospital are involved, a chance to play may be crucial for well-being.[30]

Like adults, children respond to instructions in ways consistent with their expectations and interpretations of a situation. A child is unlikely to have clear and realistic expectations about medical settings which may be novel and anxiety-provoking. Adults involved with children need to be sensitive to the ways in which they use and interpret language. Their understanding of concepts such as health and illness may be very different from an adult's view.[31] The concept of cause and effect is a very complex one in medicine, and it may not be until the age of nine or ten that a child can understand these ideas. Similarly, children's views about death are often different from adults'. Below the age of about five, death may be confused with "going away" for a short time or with sleep. It might be seen as a form of punishment. Later, death becomes more final and inevitable, but it is not until adolescence that most children can view it in a philosophical way.[32]

Consent to treatment

There are also implications for asking children to give their consent for medical interventions. Until recently, most health professionals have assumed that children, especially young children, are incapable of understanding enough about treatment for their views to be recognized and taken into account. Parental decision-making – decision by proxy – has been taken as sufficient.

This view is now less prevalent and in some countries the child's right to have his or her voice heard has legal force.[33]

When children are interviewed they can show remarkable insight into their difficulties and choices, as illustrated by the following section of an interview with a 10-year-old who had congenital scoliosis. The interview suggests that children have many of the same needs for understanding and information that apply to adults. When asked whether anything unexpected had happened, the child described being in the anaesthetic room:

> *Child:* I had pads on my arms to measure the pulse and other things, and one on my toe. I worked out that it measures the oxygen in my blood. I saw the instructions on the wall. They asked mum to come in at 9:30 one evening. I was having trouble breathing. I had an oxygen mask and I was on 72% oxygen.
>
> *Interviewer:* Do you wish anything had been explained that wasn't?
>
> *Child:* All the tubes, what they were for. They told me there would be tubes, but I had to listen hard to find out what they were. They took a graft off my hip to strengthen my spine. I didn't hear about that until afterwards, and I would prefer to know beforehand. (Ref. 34, p.131)

Although children are often more competent than we give them credit for, they may have difficulties in other situations. Schwartz[36] examined the effects of hospitalization of a purely research nature on children from 4 to 18 years of age. The researchers gave each child and the parents careful preparation before the research work began, explaining its purposes, duration and possible benefits. Later, however, despite having been told that the purpose of the hospitalization was research, there was no indication that any of the children under the age of 11 understood why they were in hospital. This abstract idea was either beyond their capacity to understand or was not explained in a way that made sense to the children, so their consent to participate could not have been "informed".

BOX 2.3

Proxy decision-making

Decision-making by proxy means that one person makes a choice for someone else who is not competent to make the decision themselves. There are two types. One involves "best interests", meaning that a choice is made on behalf of someone who has never been competent. This could be applied to very young children, where they might refuse treatment which is manifestly in their best interests.

The other type of proxy decision-making is termed "substituted judgment". This occurs when someone has been competent previously, but is not competent at the time when a decision has to be made. A person might be unconscious, for example, or has become demented. In substituted judgment, a decision is made on the basis of what the person "would have wanted". A person might have indicated previously that they would not wish to be resuscitated after a traumatic injury to the brain, for example, or would not wish to be kept on a life-support machine.

One problem with proxy decision-making is that the decision-maker might not have an accurate view of what is in the patient's best interests or what the patient would have wished. In several studies, psychologists have asked patients about their views and feelings and then asked their carers about what they believed these views would be. Often, there is a considerable discrepancy between these. For example, Johnson[35] asked patients and nursing staff to describe the patients' worries. Despite having had considerable contact with the patients, the nurses were not especially accurate. In fact, other patients on the ward were considerably more accurate. Thus it is not clear whether doctors and nurses can, in fact, make the types of decisions which patients would prefer.

Use of intellectual assessments

Although, as discussed above, IQ scores obtained from infants have low correlations with later scores, scales based on the work of Gesell are widely used, especially by paediatricians and health visitors to diagnose sensory and mental handicaps in infants during the first years of life. Although the earlier the diagnosis is made the better, since the environment can then be structured to optimize development, it is important to ensure that re-assessments occur: 21 per cent of one sample who were originally diagnosed as handicapped were not, at future testings, intellectually handicapped on any criterion despite their earlier scores.[37]

In educational settings, standard IQ tests such as the WISC have proved useful in assessing individual children who have problems at school. They provide a way of seeing whether a child's difficulties are due to below average intelligence, for which a remedial programme might be suggested, or whether there are sensory difficulties, such as impaired vision or hearing; or whether there are specific perceptual difficulties, such as dyslexia, that would affect a child's ability to read but not affect his or her score on an individually administered IQ test. The different subscales of the WISC allow a comparison between verbal and performance measures (the latter comprising manipulation or arrangement of blocks, beads, etc.) that can pinpoint more specific problems.

In psychiatric settings, individual IQ tests of adults can provide helpful information. Stress at work, for instance, could arise from lack of capacity to cope with a too-demanding job or could result from a person's over-capacity in an undemanding job. Some clinical conditions cause deterioration of intellectual performance, leading to dementia. In the early stages, such conditions can resemble other psychiatric disorders. In conjunction with psychiatric evidence, IQ tests may enable elderly people with intellectual difficulties associated with functional disorders to be distinguished from those related to more severe degenerative senile processes.[38] The course of any deterioration can be charted by testing over time. It is very important to take account of the state of the patient during the testing and the nature of the referral may provide clues; for instance, someone showing signs of depression may be particularly handicapped on timed items.

Intellectual impairments

The use of intellectual assessments in paediatric and educational settings can identify people with intellectual impairments. Care policies have changed in recent years. It is now recognized that long-stay hospitals, into which they were often admitted as a matter of course, provide an unsuitable environment (see Chapter 5). Although IQ tests can be helpful in identifying impairments (traditionally defined as IQs less than 70), they do not provide information on appropriate care. Despite low intellectual capacity, many people can, with time, learn to cope effectively with familiar situations. Their adaptive behaviour, or ability to cope independently, is what is important, and there are tests available which attempt to measure this.[39,40]

Stage approaches to intellectual development may also be helpful in assessing and treating intellectually impaired people. Early stimulation of handicapped children by parents has been found to produce significant gains compared with controls.[41] Self-help guides for parents have been produced, based on Gesell's work. As well as enabling parents to chart their child's progress, they indicate the next likely step in development, allowing parents to provide opportunities for the child to practise the necessary skills.

Dementia

Dementia refers to a progressive and profound loss of all intellectual abilities. It is most commonly found in elderly people, and is known as senile dementia, but can also be present in AIDS, Huntington's disease, Parkinson's and multiple sclerosis. About 1 person in 100 between 65 and 75 years of age and 10 in 100 over the age of 75 become demented.

Three stages can be identified. In the early stage, memory deficits occur, especially the loss of short-term memory, and these are most commonly noted by family and friends. There may also be mood and behavioural changes, such as irritability, depression and perhaps disinhibitions. In the middle stage, psychological abilities have deteriorated further, so that the individual may not be able to recall their date of birth, or the names of important people in their lives. In the final stage, people may not even be able to remember their own name. Histologically, dementia is associated with a large number of plaques and tangles in the brain, but diagnosis in the early stages can be problematic, since there are other diseases, such as severe depression and acute confusional state resulting from metabolic disorders, which can mimic dementia.

From a psychological point of view, there are several issues. One is diagnosis. This is important because if the confusion is due to other factors, such as metabolic failure or depression, immediate remedial steps can be taken. A second issue is the development of interventions which can be used to help both the patient and the caregiver, such as ways of gaining the patient's attention and making tasks more easy to complete. The third issue concerns the caregiver's well-being. As discussed in Chapters 8 and 9, caring for a person who is dementing can be a draining and exhausting experience.

Suggested reading

For an excellent and personalized review of research into the biochemistry of memory, see Rose, S. (1993) *The Making of Memory. From Molecules to Mind*, London: Bantam Books. Cohen, G., Kiss, G. and LeVoi, M. (1993) *Memory. Current Issues*, Buckingham: Open University Press, provides a good review of current views of memory processes.

References

1. Nebes, R. (1974) Hemispheric specialization in commissurotomized man. *Psychological Bulletin* **81**: 1-14.
2. Lewis, R. (1980) Is your brain really necessary? *Science* **210**: 1232-1234.
3. Milner, B. (1966) Amnesia following operation on the temporal lobes. In: Whitty, C. and Zangwill, O. (eds) *Amnesia*. London: Butterworth.
4. Baddeley, A. (1990) *Human Memory. Theory and Practice*. London: Lawrence Erlbaum.
5. Rose, S. (1993) *The Making of Memory. From Molecules to Mind*. London: Bantam Books.
6. Kent, G. (1985) Memory of dental pain. *Pain* **21**: 187-194.
7. Bower, G. (1981) Mood and memory. *American Psychologist* **36**: 129-148.
8. Teasdale, J. and Spencer, P. (1984) Induced mood and estimates of past success. *British Journal of Clinical Psychology* **23**: 149-150.
9. d'Ydewalle, G. and Rosselle, H. (1978) Text expectations in text learning. In: Gruneberg, M.M., Morris, P.E. and Sykes, R.N. (eds) *Practical Aspects of Memory*. London: Academic Press.
10. Hannam, C. (1975) *Parents and Mentally Handicapped Children*. Harmondsworth, Middlesex: Penguin Books.
11. Butt, H.R. (1977) A method for better physician-patient communication. *Annals of Internal Medicine* **86**: 478-480.
12. North, N., Cornbleet, M., Knowles, G. and Leonard, R. (1992) Information giving in oncology: a preliminary study of tape-recorder use. *British Journal of Clinical Psychology* **31**: 357-359.
13. Grafman, J. and Mathews, C.G. (1978) Assessment and remediation of memory deficits in brain-injured patients. In: Gruneberg, M.M., Morris, P.E. and Sykes, R.N. (eds) *Practical Aspects of Memory*. London: Academic Press.
14. Wilson, B. and Moffat, N. (eds) (1992) *Clinical Management of Memory Problems*. San Diego: Singular Publishing.
15. Langer, E.J., Rodin, J., Beck, P., Weinman, C. and Spitzer, L. (1979) Environmental determinants of memory improvement in late adulthood. *Journal of Personality and Social Psychology* **37**: 2003-2013.
16. Miller, E. (1994) Intelligence and brain myelination. *Personality and Individual Differences* **17**: 803-832.
17. Terman, L.M. and Merrill, M.A. (1961) *Stanford-Binet Intelligence Scale: Manual for the Third Revision*. London: Harrap.
18. Hersch, J.B. (1971) Effects of referral information on testers. *Journal of Consulting and Clinical Psychology* **37**: 116-122.
19. Vernon, P.E. (1969) *Intelligence and Cultural Environment*. London: Methuen.
20. Becker, H.S., Geer, B. and Miller, S.J. (1972) Medical education. In: Freeman, H.E., Levine, S. and Reeder, L.G. (eds) *Handbook of Medical Sociology*, 2nd edn. Englewood Cliffs, New Jersey: Prentice-Hall.
21. Lock, S. and Wells, F. (eds) (1993) *Fraud and Misconduct in Medical Research*. London: British Medical Association.
22. Eysenck, H.J. and Kamin, L. (1981) *Intelligence: The Battle for the Mind*. London: Pan Books.
23. Douglas, J.W.B. (1967) *The Home and the School*. St Albans: Panther.

24. McCall, R.B., Appelbaum, M. and Hogarty, P. (1973) Developmental changes in mental performance. *Monographs of the Society for Research in Child Development* **38**: 150 pp.

25. Garber, H. and Heber, F. (1977) The Milwaukee project. In: Mittler, P. (ed.) *Research to Practice in Mental Retardation*. Baltimore: University Park Press.

26. White, B.L., Castle, P. and Held, R. (1964) Observations on the development of visually-guided reaching. *Child Development* **35**: 349-364.

27. Zelazo, P.R., Zelazo, N. and Kolb, S. (1972) "Walking" in the newborn. *Science* **176**: 314-315.

28. Frankenburg, W.K. and Dodds, J.B. (1967) The Denver developmental screening test. *Journal of Pediatrics* **71**: 181-191.

29. Donaldson, M. (1978) *Children's Minds*. Glasgow: Fontana.

30. Crocker, E. (1978) Play programmes in pediatric settings. In: Gellert, E. (ed.) *Psychosocial Aspects of Pediatric Care*. London: Grune and Stratton.

31. Eiser, C. (1984) Communicating with sick and hospitalised children. *Journal of Child Psychology and Psychiatry* **25**: 181-189.

32. Blos, P. (1978) Children think about illness: their concepts and beliefs. In: Gellert, E. (ed.) *Psychosocial Aspects of Pediatric Care*. London: Grune and Stratton.

33. Herbert, M. (1993) *Working with Children and the Children Act*. Leicester: British Psychological Society.

34. Alderson, P. (1993) *Children's Consent to Surgery*. Buckingham: Open University Press.

35. Johnson, M. (1982) Recognition of patients' worries by nurses and other patients. *British Journal of Clinical Psychology* **21**: 255-261.

36. Schwartz, A.H. (1972) Children's concepts of research hospitalisation. *New England Journal of Medicine* **287**: 589-592.

37. Illingworth, R.S. (1971) The predictive value of developmental assessment in infancy. *Developmental Medicine and Child Neurology* **13**: 721-725.

38. Savage, R.D., Britton, P., Bolton, N. and Hall, E. (1973) *Intellectual Functioning in the Aged*. London: Methuen.

39. Gunzburg, H.C. (1969) *The P-A-C Manual*. London: National Association on Mental Deficiency.

40. Nihira, K., Foster, R., Shellhaas, M. and Leland, H. (1974) *AAMD Adaptive Behaviour Scale for Children*. American Association on Mental Deficiency.

41. Gath, A. (1979) Parents as therapists of mentally handicapped children. *Journal of Child Psychology and Psychiatry* **20**: 161-165.

3

Under-standing Behaviour

SUMMARY

This chapter considers the theories held by psychologists who have attempted to understand behaviour by relying mainly on environmental, observable determinants.

In *respondent* or *classical* conditioning, associations between unconditioned and conditioned stimuli are viewed as the fundamental building blocks of behaviour. Treatments based on this model include aversion therapy, flooding, and systematic desensitization. Individuals learn actively as well, by relating actions to consequences. This is recognized in *instrumental* or *operant* learning theories, where actions which are reinforced or rewarded are repeated, while those which are not become less frequent. *Observational* learning is a way of accounting for the learning which results from viewing the actions of others. This approach has helped individuals cope with stressful situations and develop social skills.

Although these theories are able to predict behaviour much of the time, they do not consider beliefs. Learning occurs when there are no apparent rewards. These considerations have led to methods of helping patients which take *cognitive factors* into account, such as structured self-instruction and self-control techniques.

In Chapter 1, the idea that human beings have a need to understand their environment was discussed. In explaining events, people use the context, their own past experience and selective attention in order to come to an interpretation of what they experience. Psychologists are no different in this respect, except they collect data very systematically (the *methods* used in experimental and observational studies) and are careful not to make interpretations (their *theories* about the causes of events) which are unsupported by these data.

Historically, there has been a major dispute between psychologists about the most useful way to achieve this aim of understanding behaviour. There was an important debate in psychology at the turn of the twentieth century which had a profound effect on the way that the subject developed. Some psychologists thought that the *inner life* of people was the proper area of psychological study. They argued that if psychology was to develop a way of understanding behaviour then it would be necessary to understand how people thought and felt about their world and themselves. After all, they argued, behaviour is an outward manifestation of attitudes and beliefs. Some of these views developed into theories about personality and personality development. The interest in this approach has been in how one person with particular personality characteristics can differ in behaviour from someone else with other traits. This view, held by such clinicians as Freud, is discussed in the next chapter.

Other psychologists hotly disputed this approach, arguing that these inner states could never be scientifically validated or measured. It was impossible, they claimed, to know if one person has the same image of an event as another person, or to prove that such images exist at all. The only way anything could be discovered about people was from their observable behaviour; everything else is inferred. It was behaviour which was important, not the subjective feelings of an individual. Taking classical physics as their model, these psychologists wanted to find mathematical equations that could predict how someone would behave in a given situation. This approach came to be known as *behaviourism*.

Behaviourism

The current chapter concentrates on the theories developed by these psychologists, who concentrated on the environmental determinants of behaviour. According to this approach, differences between people occur not because they have different personalities but because they have different learning histories. In chronological order, the respondent (or classical) model, the instrumental (or operant) model and the observational model have been suggested as ways of explaining how the environment influences behaviour. Most recently, these theories have been expanded to include cognitions.

Applications from these theories are termed behaviour therapy or behaviour modification to distinguish them from psychotherapies that involve techniques based on the personality theories of the next chapter (but note that some writers use the term psychotherapy to include behavioural treatments). These behaviour therapies are relevant because they may be used by clinical psychologists who form part of the paramedical services increasingly associated with general practitioners and hospitals.

Applications of behavioural therapies

Behaviour therapies are of particular use in the treatment of anxiety. There are several categories of anxiety disorders, including panic attacks (periods of intense fear or discomfort where the symptoms can include shortness of breath, dizziness and palpitations), specific phobias (fear and avoidance of specific objects or situations), social phobia (where there is a great fear of social scrutiny) and obsessive–compulsive disorders (where a person continually ruminates over anticipated calamities or feels compelled to keep checking against possible dangers). Generalized Anxiety Disorder is a more diffuse difficulty, manifest in excessive anxiety and worry about life circumstances.

Behaviour therapists consider these problems to be *learned* difficulties. That is, they are considered to be a result of previous experiences of various kinds. Because they have been learned, they ought to be amenable to changes through further experience. However, there could be a biological substrate. Gray[1] has explored the neuroanatomy of anxiety, and has suggested that anxiety is a result of activity in the septo-hippocampal system of the brain. The hippocampus is said to act as a comparator, matching expected with actual events. If there is some kind of mismatch between these, the organism reacts with increased arousal, attention and inhibition of behaviour. The kinds of therapeutic interventions used by psychologists could operate by altering this neurological pattern in some way.[2]

Clinical psychologists have much to offer to the medical profession in helping patients with anxiety difficulties, often being able to help doctors who either do not have the time or the expertise to apply the therapies outlined in this chapter. For instance, Koch[3] describes how he used these approaches with 30 patients who had been referred by a general practitioner. All the patients (who suffered from a variety of problems including psychosomatic disorders, anxiety, smoking, drinking and eating disorders) were seen at the surgery. In the year before referral, these patients made an average of 9.27 consultations (as opposed to the practice's average of 3.31), but in the year after treatment this dropped to 5.46 and the repeat prescription rate for psychotropic drugs also dropped significantly. Although some of this improvement could have been due to spontaneous recovery, it seemed as though contact with clinical psychology services considerably reduced the demand made by these patients for general practitioner time.

Using animals in basic research

Some of the studies mentioned in this chapter are based on experiments with non-human animals, such as rats and pigeons, in artificial laboratory situations, such as learning to press a lever in order to gain a drink or a pellet of food. You may feel that this work provides a poor basis for forming conclusions about how humans learn, with their much greater abilities. Simply because rats seem to learn in a certain way does not necessarily mean that humans do the same. What similarities could there be between a rat pressing a lever for food and a student preparing for an exam?

There are several answers to such a criticism. First, the use of lower animals in experiments means that some of the ethical problems involved in experimenting with humans can be overcome to some extent. Just as society considers it more acceptable to test drugs first on other species before trying them out on humans, so too is it more accepting towards keeping rats hungry or thirsty or giving them electric shocks. It seems likely that many of the methods which can be used to alleviate human distress described in this chapter would not have been discovered if only humans had been used. (Of course, many people in our society argue that animals should not be used for any kind of experimentation; see Chapter 9.)

A second reply to this criticism is empirical:

many of the principles and theories developed through work with other species *do* seem to apply to humans as well. In keeping with the Darwinian insight that the differences between species is only a matter of degree, there are also many similarities between us and other animals. The argument is that, in principle, there is little difference between lever-pressing and studying, since they result in consequences that aid the organism. In the first case it is food to relieve hunger, whereas in the second a pass mark provides a qualification that, in turn, might lead to a job. For psychologists, the term "learning" is used in a wide sense, applying to many kinds of adaptive changes.

Respondent conditioning

Pavlov's experiments

The origins of the respondent or classical conditioning approach lie with Ivan Pavlov (1849–1936), a Russian physiologist who studied the digestive system of dogs. He was interested in the notion of a "reflex", which was an unlearned and predictable response to environmental events, such as withdrawal from a painful stimulus and eye-blinking in response to a puff of wind. All reflexes were thought to have adjustment or protective purposes. Reflexes also occurred when food was tasted, including the production of saliva and the secretion of stomach juices.

Pavlov's great contribution was that he noticed that his dogs would begin salivating not only at the taste of food but also at the sight of food and even at the sight of the handler who regularly fed them. It seemed as though a connection or association had been made between the sight of food and salivation. He called salivation in this latter instance a *conditioned reflex*, because its occurrence was conditional upon a prior association between seeing the food and tasting it.

Pavlov hypothesized that many such associations could be learned, and performed several experiments to test the limits of this prediction. Typically, a stimulus that the animal was likely to notice but that had no prior association with salivation was presented – a light, for example (called the conditioned stimulus). This stimulus

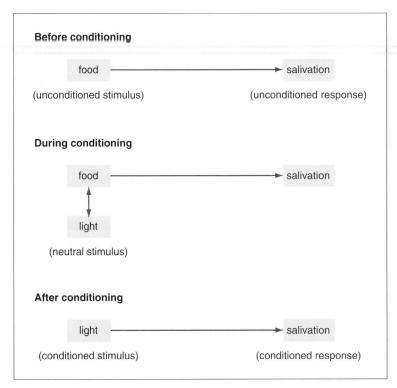

Before conditioning

food ———————————————→ salivation

(unconditioned stimulus)   (unconditioned response)

During conditioning

food ———————————————→ salivation

↕

light

(neutral stimulus)

After conditioning

light ———————————————→ salivation

(conditioned stimulus)   (conditioned response)

Figure 3.1 The classical conditioning paradigm. Before conditioning, food elicits salivation. During conditioning a neutral stimulus such as a light is presented at about the same time as the food, so that they are paired together. After conditioning, the light alone will elicit salivation.

was then followed closely in time by food, which normally elicited salivation (the unconditioned stimulus). Several pairings, or *acquisition trials*, were conducted in this way. The process is shown diagrammatically in Figure 3.1. Then, in order to test for the presence of an association, the light was turned on but no food presented: if salivation occurred, a conditioned reflex (or conditioned response as it is usually called) has been formed.

Pavlov showed that many previously neutral stimuli could come to elicit salivation, even though the response may be somewhat weaker (fewer drops of saliva) compared to the original unconditioned stimulus (the food). The more pairings made, the more similar did the conditioned reflex become to the unconditioned one (i.e. the quantity of saliva increased). If only the light were shown on several occasions, the response became progressively weaker and gradually fewer and fewer drops of saliva were elicited. This is known as *extinction*. Pavlov came to view the learning of associations between unconditioned and conditioned stimuli as the fundamental building block of all behaviour, contending that all learning could be reduced to

associations between unlearned reflexes and previously neutral stimuli. Owing to many experiments conducted by Pavlov and others, the respondent (or classical) conditioning model gained many adherents.

Although Pavlov's results were important in their own right, perhaps his greatest influence was in providing a method of studying *behaviour*, as distinct from inner thoughts, images and imagination. While Darwin provided a way of understanding how species adapted to their environment over many generations, Pavlov seemed to provide a way of understanding how an individual learns about and adapts to its environment during a lifetime.

Although conditioned responses could not always be shown in humans,[4] it was argued that many types of behaviour could be the result of this type of associative learning. Respondent conditioning has often been used to explain the development of fear and anxiety, for example, where an association between an event (such as a visit to the dentist) has been formed with an aversive event (such as a painful experience). Thereafter, a visit to the dentist might result in a conditioned fear response.

Preparedness

It appears that some conditioned associations are more readily learned than others. For example, relatively few people are very anxious about travelling at high speeds on the roads, although this is objectively very dangerous. And phobias (see Box 3.1) about electrical equipment are uncommon, although electric shocks can be lethal. Conversely, many people are extremely anxious about being enclosed in small spaces, public speaking, spiders, and domestic pets such as cats and dogs, but there is little objective danger present. Such observations have led some psychologists to propose that humans have innate propensities to become anxious about some situations more easily than others.

Known as *preparedness*, the argument is that in our evolutionary past some objects and situations did, in fact, threaten our physical well-being. Small animals which scuttle in unpredictable ways might have been the carriers of infectious diseases – leading to specific phobias about small animals – and, being social creatures dependent on acceptance by other people, humans might easily learn to be very anxious about being scrutinized by others – leading to social phobias.

In this way it is easy to understand why some people are phobic about injections, or why the sight of blood can be so distressing. It may, for example, have been adaptive for a child to avoid being pierced in the arm by an unknown adult. Although there might not be an objective threat in the present, evolution may have favoured "anxious genes".[5]

Phobias

A phobia is a persistent and excessive fear of an object or situation that is objectively not dangerous. The fear leads people to avoid such situations, even though they may recognize, rationally, that such avoidance is not necessary. Five characteristics of specific phobias are that:

1 there is a persistent fear of a circumscribed situation or object;
2 exposure to the stimulus almost invariably provokes an immediate anxiety response;
3 the object or situation is avoided or endured with intense anxiety;
4 the fear or avoidant behaviour significantly interferes with the individual's normal social routines or activities; and
5 the individual recognizes that the fear is excessive or unreasonable.

There are many types of phobias, such as specific phobias (where the feared object is circumscribed, such as fears of spiders, heights or cats), social phobias (where there is a great fear of negative social evaluation) and agoraphobia (fear of being away from home in such areas as crowded spaces). Phobias are very common in the general population, especially in children, yet people are often ashamed of their reactions.

The essential characteristic of phobias is avoidance and the need to flee from the situation or object, but there can be heightened physiological arousal and distressing thoughts (such as "I am going to make a fool of myself"). Phobias can also be extremely debilitating, since people may feel unable to take part in all the activities they wish to and may restrict their lifestyles in order to avoid the feared situation. The treatment of choice for phobias is graded exposure, in which the person gradually approaches the feared object or situation while being given support to cope with the rising anxiety.

Anticipatory nausea

Chemotherapy is the treatment of choice for hundreds of thousands of patients suffering from cancer. Unfortunately, it has a number of unpleasant side-effects including hair loss, tiredness, nausea and vomiting. These latter two side-effects are very common, with perhaps two-thirds of patients experiencing them frequently during and after treatment. Not only can nausea and vomiting be uncomfortable and embarrassing, but they can also lead to avoidance of the hospital and a decision not to continue treatment.[6] Anticipatory nausea refers to the nausea which can occur – in about 10–15 per cent of patients – *before* a chemotherapy session begins. Psychologists have described a number of instances in which the sight of the hospital, tastes associated with the drugs and the smell and sounds associated with the clinic have led to nausea.

Such symptoms are psychologically rather than pharmacologically induced and are usually explained in terms of respondent conditioning. According to this explanation, the drugs act as an unconditioned stimulus for the nausea and vomiting. Stimuli which were originally neutral but which are present at the time of the drug administration (such as sight of the hospital) then become associated with the drugs and lead to the conditioned nausea.[7,8]

Before attempting to help patients with such difficulties, psychologists would conduct a careful assessment of the problem. In keeping with a behaviourist approach, they would be interested in taking precise measures of the extent of the nausea and vomiting. A good example of such a measurement tool in this area has been developed by Morrow,[9] and has been used in several intervention studies. Morrow used a questionnaire to measure the frequency, severity and duration of the symptoms by asking such questions as:

◆ I have experienced vomiting:
   1. before every treatment
   2. before many of my treatments
   3. before about half my treatments
   4. rarely before a treatment
   5. never before a treatment
   I would describe the vomiting before my treatment as:
   1. very mild
   2. mild
   3. moderate
   4. severe
   5. very severe
   6. intolerable ◆

This assessment questionnaire is typical of many used by psychologists to gather baseline data before attempting an intervention. This is needed so that the efficacy of treatment can be gauged and any alterations in the treatment package made.

Treatments based on respondent conditioning

The respondent approach to psychological difficulties considers it unnecessary to examine a patient's personality or to discover any unconscious conflicts that might have led him or her into difficulty. Instead, principles discovered and validated in the laboratory such as the pairing of conditioned and unconditioned stimuli and extinction would be employed. Several methods have been developed within this orientation, including aversion therapy, flooding and systematic desensitization.

Aversion therapy

Aversion therapy is a particular approach which is favoured by very few clinical psychologists and is rarely used in practice. It is designed to reduce the frequency of behaviour that is considered undesirable. The idea is to pair the undesired behaviour with a noxious stimulus, thus making the behaviour unpleasant and likely to be avoided, just as chemotherapy patients who experience nausea might wish to avoid the hospital. Any aversive stimulus could be paired with any undesired behaviour in theory, but in practice there are cultural and methodological constraints. A particular behaviour may become more or less acceptable depending on current social values and knowledge. In the 1960s and early 1970s homosexuality was considered undesirable and there are many papers in the literature from this time exploring the effect of aversion therapy on homosexuals. But as this sexual orientation has become more accepted fewer reports have been published. Conversely, smoking has only been viewed as undesirable in recent years, reflected by an increase in the number of studies attempting to modify this behaviour.

The ethics of aversion therapy have played an important role in the reluctance of many psychologists to use this technique. It is not always clear why someone seeks therapy for a problem. Many of the people who seek assistance for socially unacceptable difficulties only do so after they have been detained by law or have been isolated by family and society. It is important to question whether it is reasonable to subject patients to aversive stimuli for the sake of society rather than the individual. As discussed in Box 3.2 there is a tension between the ethical principles of "doing good for others" and "doing no harm" in the use of aversion therapy. Given the cultural relativity of many behaviours, psychologists are often unwilling to pursue this kind of treatment.

Flooding

This is another technique which uses the classical conditioning model. The approach is based on the possibility that once fears and phobias are learned they are not extinguished because patients avoid the fear-provoking situation. By never placing themselves in the situation again there is no opportunity for extinction to occur. For example, a person who is afraid of the dark will avoid dark places and thus the strength of the response will not diminish.

Therapists who use flooding encourage patients to confront the situation repeatedly until they discover that dark places (or spiders or snakes) are not really all that frightening. For example, Sreenivasan et al.[10] report the effects of flooding on a young girl who had been extremely fearful of dogs for about 5 years. The fear did not lessen in response to other kinds of therapy and flooding seemed justified in this case. A passive and friendly dog was chosen and taken off the leash while the girl was in the room:

◆ For the first session, Colleen was apprehensive for several hours before. On arrival in the treatment room she was anxiously scanning the area for the dog. When the dog was led in she froze, visibly paled and her pupils were dilated. Staff talked reassuringly to Colleen, but when the dog was freed she jumped on a chair. She cried and pleaded that the dog should be placed on its leash. Gradually she relaxed slightly but stayed on the chair, becoming anxious and

---

> ### BOX 3.2
>
> #### Do no harm
>
> One of the basic ethical principles in the health professions is to do no harm to patients. Enshrined in the Hippocratic Oath, doctors and others in the caring professions have an obligation not to inflict harm on their patients or expose them to unnecessary risks. This is known as the principle of *non-maleficence*.
>
> While this principle is clear, its application may be complicated. For example, treating a patient with cancer with chemotherapy is harmful in one respect, because the drugs can have many painful and impairing side-effects. We feel that the use of such drugs is ethical because although the short-term side-effects are negative the longer term prospects can be improved. In other words, there is a balance between the principle of non-maleficence and the principle of doing good – known as *beneficence*.
>
> Sometimes it is difficult to achieve a satisfactory balance between these principles. While it may be ethical to persuade a person to undergo painful treatment if it is in their longer term interests, at what point do the possible returns fail to outweigh the short-term consequences of treatment? For example, at what point is it unethical to continue treatment for a cancer patient? Perhaps it will be difficult to tell when the likelihood of success is so low that the balance in favour of treatment changes to a balance against.
>
> Similarly, psychologists must balance the possible benefits of aversion therapy or flooding with distress. Would it be ethical to use aversion therapy for the treatment of obesity, for example? A person may volunteer for aversion therapy to reduce homosexual leanings, but any stigma still attached to being gay or lesbian is a cultural issue. Would the ethical dilemma be any different for smoking, or for severe drug abuse?

entreating if the dog moved towards the chair. Two of the staff played table tennis and tried unsuccessfully to persuade

Colleen to join them. In the second session she was equally anxious but would get down from the chair or table she stood on for a few seconds but was never at ease. Prior to the third session Colleen appeared excited, although she expressed fear and dislike of the sessions. She managed to take part in the table tennis game for brief periods, sitting on the table if the dog ambled towards the table. In the fourth session she could pat the dog if it was not facing her. In the sixth session she tolerated the dog in her lap, and then took the dog for a walk holding the leash to the amazement of her parents who happened to arrive. After this, she was able to take the family pet for a walk and then to go for a drive with the puppy in the car. (Ref. 10, pp. 257-258) ◆

After only six sessions of about an hour each her fears appeared to subside, as measured by the therapist and subjectively validated by the girl herself. Further, she was no longer troubled by thoughts about dogs attacking her and was now doing well in school. Although flooding was effective in this case, there are clearly ethical issues here as well. Systematic desensitization (discussed next) is generally preferred because it is less stressful for the patient.

Systematic desensitization

Whereas flooding involves long periods of intense experience with the feared object, systematic desensitization (or SD) involves a gradual approach to the feared object. Developed by Wolpe,[11] it may best be described by outlining a case study of a patient who had a phobia about visiting the dentist.[12] This 32–year-old man had been taken to the dentist at the age of 5 or 6 but tried to flee from the office. At 8 years of age, he refused to have any dental work done and at 18 he had one filling and then refused to return. Later, after a toothache lasting 3 weeks, he finally went to a dentist who placed him under a general anaesthetic. Several teeth were removed and several restorations completed at this time. Over the next 12 years or so he suffered repeated toothaches but had not seen a dentist.

During systematic desensitization, the patient was seen by a therapist for nine sessions of one hour each. At the first session his history was taken and the therapist began to give relaxation training. The idea behind this training is that anxiety is associated with physiological arousal – high heart rate, muscular tension and sweating. If a patient could be taught to relax, these signs of arousal could be reduced and anxiety alleviated. The most common method for teaching relaxation is called progressive muscle relaxation. The patient is asked to sit in a comfortable reclining chair. The therapist then asks the patient first to tense and then relax the major muscle groups in the body. This often starts with the toes, progressing through the ankles, calves, thighs, and so on. Slow and controlled breathing with the eyes shut is finally achieved. The exercise takes 15-25 minutes to complete and for most people it results in a general feeling of calm and relaxation, a feeling very different from that engendered by anxiety. The patient would be asked to remain in this state for a further 10 minutes or so.

After several training sessions people can generally relax themselves fairly quickly without the therapist's instructions. In the second session, further relaxation training was given to this patient and he was asked to list his fears about the restoration of his teeth. These fears were ordered in a hierarchy, as shown in Table 3.1. The least anxiety-provoking situation was thinking about going to the dentist, while the worst was receiving two injections, one on each side. In the third session relaxation training was completed.

The next six sessions were devoted to pairing the relaxation with the items in the hierarchy. In systematic desensitization this is done by asking the patient first to relax as fully as possible. He is then requested to visualize the situations which he finds frightening, starting with the least frightening one. Whenever he begins to feel anxious, the therapist instructs him to stop thinking about the situation and concentrate again on the relaxation. By pairing relaxation with the image, the situation begins to lose its anxiety-provoking properties. When the patient can visualize the least frightening situation without feeling anxious, he moves on to the next step of the

Table 3.1 Hierarchy of patient's fears from least (1) to most (13) feared situations (Reproduced from Gale, E. N. and Ayer, W. A. (1969) *Journal of the American Dental Association* **78**: 1306. Reprinted by permission.)

1	Thinking about going to the dentist
2	Getting in your car to go to the dentist
3	Calling for an appointment with the dentist
4	Sitting in the waiting room of the dentist's office
5	Having the nurse tell you it's your turn
6	Getting in the dentist's chair
7	Seeing the dentist lay out his instruments, one of which is a probe
8	Having a probe held in front of you while you look at it
9	Having a probe placed on the side of a tooth
10	Having a probe placed in a cavity
11	Getting an injection in your gums on one side
12	Having your teeth drilled and worrying that the anaesthetic will wear off
13	Getting two injections, one on each side.

hierarchy. This is repeated until he can think of the most frightening situation without anxiety. SD was very successful with this particular patient. Just before the ninth session, he made and kept an appointment with a dentist. Afterwards, all dental treatment was completed and he found the experience "relaxing".

Instrumental conditioning

Pavlov argued that learning comes about because events happen to occur at about the same time and these become associated within the organism. But this point of view neglects the fact that animals often actively explore their environment and appear to make attempts to influence events. They are active operators as well as passive recipients and rarely wait for a stimulus to occur. It was the recognition of the importance of this aspect of behaviour that led psychologists in the 1930s to explore another area of learning.

This approach has come to be known as instrumental or operant learning. According to this viewpoint, it is the *consequences* of behaviour that determine what a person will do. When behaviour is followed by pleasant consequences

it is likely to be repeated, but when the consequences are negative its frequency will decrease. This simple but important idea is known as the *Law of Effect*. While patterns of behaviour might be random in the first instance, as experience with the consequences increases certain behaviour will be repeated while other behaviours will become less frequent. The basic idea is illustrated in Figure 3.2, but according to operant theorists the principle holds in many much more complex situations as well.

The rat running up the T-maze is equally likely to turn right or left from the starting box. But when it happens to turn right, it finds food, and if it is hungry this is a gratifying result. In time, it will learn that a right turn results in food and will turn that way more often. The speed of learning would be affected by the intensity of the rat's hunger (which could be manipulated by denying it access to food for a specified time) and by the amount of food it would find.

Reinforcement

The food in this example is called a *reinforcer*, a concept that plays an important part in understanding operant behaviour. According to

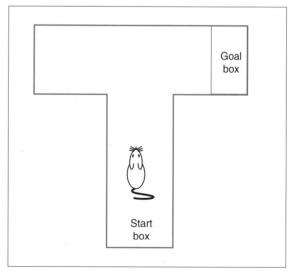

Figure 3.2 A T-maze. The first time the rat runs up the maze it is equally likely to turn right or left. However, if it happens to turn right it finds food. In time, it will learn that turning right results in food and it will turn that way more often.

behaviourist B.F. Skinner, a reinforcer could be any experience (food, water, praise) which increases the probability of a certain response. If you have attempted to train a dog by giving it biscuits you will have employed this principle. By giving a biscuit when a stick is retrieved, for example, the dog is more likely to fetch it again. Similarly, if you have been rewarded in any way for behaviour in the past (e.g. doing well in an examination after studying hard) operant conditioning could be said to have occurred. Getting a good grade may have influenced you to study hard for the next exam. Skinner has written extensively about the ways that the principle of reinforcement can be applied to humans, notably in his novel about the utopia *Walden Two*.[13]

Reinforcers can be positive or negative. In the case of a positive reinforcer, *presentation* increases the probability of a response, whereas the *removal* of a negative reinforcer increases the chance that a response will occur. A hungry rat will learn to press a bar in order to obtain food through positive reinforcement if, when the bar is pressed, food arrives. The rat will also learn to press the bar through negative reinforcement, if an aversive stimulus like an electric shock is terminated by bar-pressing. An everyday example of this is a mother picking up a crying infant. If the baby stops crying when picked up, the probability of the mother repeating the same behaviour increases since the cessation of the baby's crying is reinforcing.

Punishment is not the same as negative reinforcement. Technically, punishment is an event that *reduces* the probability of behaviour. This can occur when a positive event is with-drawn (e.g. a parent might refuse to allow a child to watch a favourite TV programme when he has been badly behaved) or when an aversive stimulus is presented (e.g. a parent might reprimand a child). The different contingencies are shown in Figure 3.3.

Reinforcers can also be primary or secondary. Primary reinforcers are those which satisfy basic biological needs, such as hunger or thirst. Secondary reinforcers are events that have become rewarding through their association with primaries. Money is an obvious example of the latter: cash will increase the probability of behaviour not because it is innately reinforcing, but because people have learned that they can satisfy their needs with it. It then takes on reinforcing characteristics of its own.

Treatments based on instrumental conditioning

Operant learning procedures thus gave psychologists another way of predicting and changing behaviour. The theory suggested that, by discovering the reinforcement contingencies involved in maladaptive behaviour, it would be possible to change these and substitute more appropriate reinforcement patterns. For example, some children become disruptive, disturbing classes at school and being difficult to control at home. Although many children do this occasionally, constant disruption is a problem for teachers and parents and, in the long run, for the children themselves. Some children become very isolated, refusing to take part in social play and preferring to stay on their own. Again, although

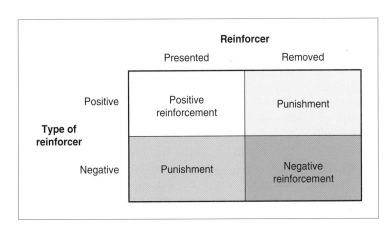

Figure 3.3 Ways in which positive or negative reinforcers can be presented or removed in order to change behaviour.

such behaviour is sometimes desirable, prolonged isolation from others may be considered
maladaptive.

Harris *et al.*[14] describe how they used operant
methods to help a child in such an isolated position. They first observed the child's behaviour
and the behaviour of others around him. The aim
was to discover the frequency of the problem
behaviour and its function: the context in which
it occurred and the reactions it evoked from
others. Whenever this particular child sat alone,
teachers talked to him and showed concern. But
whenever he joined the other children his
contact with the teachers lessened. Effectively,
the teachers were reinforcing the isolation by
providing attention when he was alone and pun-
ishing the child's social behaviour by with-
drawing the attention when he was in the larger
group. In operant terms, the isolation served the
function of eliciting attention from staff.

When this was pointed out by the psychologists, the teachers stopped reinforcing
seclusion (by ignoring the child when he was
alone) and began to reward social behaviour (by
giving attention during the times when he was
with other children). As a result, the child's tendency to play alone lessened and he began to play
with the other children more often.

This study illustrates several important features
of operant behaviour therapy. First, there is the
functional analysis of the behaviour to be modified, depending upon careful observation and
description. Behaviour must be described in very
specific terms and small steps towards the
desired (or target) behaviours rewarded. Second,
the reinforcers are chosen to suit each individual,
since what might be reinforcing for one person
might be aversive to another. If a person is particularly fond of a food, that food may be a suitable
reinforcer: if he or she chooses to sit on a particular chair whenever possible, an opportunity
to do so is a reinforcer. Parents use this regularly.
Since children often play when they have the
opportunity, playing can be used as a reward, as
in "if you finish your dinner you can go out with
your friends".

Once the targets and the reinforcers appropriate to the individual case are chosen, the treatment procedures can be started. Generally,
positive aspects of behaviour are emphasized by
the introduction of the reinforcers at the appropriate times. Decreasing the probability of undesirable behaviour is a secondary consideration.
Coercive procedures (e.g. threats) and punishment are rarely used. Undesirable behaviour,
such as the isolation of the child in the case study
above, is left to extinguish when it is no longer
reinforced.

However, there are some examples in the literature which suggest that punishment can be effective as a last resort. Lang and Melamed[15] describe
a case in which a 9-month-old child, weighing
only 5.4 kg, was vomiting persistently. When
other physical and psychological treatments
were unable to discover the cause or alleviate
the problem, aversion therapy was used. In an
attempt to save the child's life, an electric shock
was administered to the infant's leg when he was
about to vomit. This treatment had quick and
dramatic effects: the vomiting ceased almost
immediately and the child began to gain weight.

Incentives for memory improvement

As mentioned in Chapter 2, psychologists have
argued that some cognitive skills can be lost or
deteriorate if people have little incentive to practise their cognitive abilities. A lack of incentive
could occur, for example, in nursing homes
where elderly people may find that they no longer
encounter many of the cognitively demanding
tasks that they used to master, since their cognitive as well as physical needs are met for them.
Langer *et al.* reasoned that if residents could
be encouraged to practise such skills then any
deterioration could be stopped or even reversed.

In order to test this hypothesis, Langer *et al.*[16]
used the notion of reinforcement to motivate
some residents to attend to and try to remember
their experiences. If the patients could, for
example, discover and remember the names of
some of their nurses and recall the nature of some
of the activities in the home, they would be given
tokens which could be redeemed for gifts or
attendance at social events. Thus, these tokens
served as motivators for practising memory skills.
To serve as a comparison group, other residents
were also given the tokens, but these were
described simply as presents.

Later, Langer *et al.* tested the memory abilities
of patients in the two groups. Not only could

those in the first group recall more information about their activities but they could also remember new material more accurately. Furthermore, these patients showed an improvement in their general alertness while others showed a decline. Thus, this study suggests that the memory loss shown by some elderly patients is, at least in part, due to their unchallenging environment rather than to organic deterioration. This point is taken up again in Chapter 8 when old age is discussed in more detail.

Shaping

When attempting to make complex changes in behaviour, a procedure called *shaping* is used. Horner and Keilitz[17] describe how they used shaping to teach people with severe intellectual impairments how to brush their teeth. Tooth-brushing involves a complex series of behaviours which can be a formidable task for them, although it is relatively easy for most people. Horner and Keilitz first videotaped a person skilled at brushing his teeth. This allowed them to analyse the task closely and from this tape they identified several small steps including:

1 Pick up and hold the toothbrush
2 Wet the toothbrush
3 Remove the cap of the toothpaste
4 Apply the toothpaste to brush
5 Replace the cap on the toothpaste.

Steps 6–15 involved brushing parts of the mouth, rinsing the toothbrush and putting the equipment away. The teaching of each of these steps was accomplished by giving rewards. When the patient picked up and held the toothbrush, for example, he or she was praised or given tokens which could be later exchanged for sugarless gum, and was therefore more likely to repeat this action again. When this learning was accomplished, the next step was taught: rewards were given only when the toothbrush was wetted. These two pieces of behaviour were then *chained* together so that the reward was given only when the patient both picked up the toothbrush and wetted it. Then the next step was taught. This procedure was followed until the whole series of actions could be accomplished. Brushing one's teeth might form only a small part of an overall programme of self-care which might also include such skills as dressing, eating with utensils, and so forth.

Enuresis

A third example of the use of operant methods in patient care is the "bell and pad" method for children who suffer from nocturnal enuresis. This problem is defined as bedwetting of at least twice per month in a child 5 years of age or older. While it is very common in younger children, by the age of 7 it is of concern. About 7 per cent of 8-year-olds and as many as 3 per cent of young adults wet their beds. As children become older the social and emotional consequences can become severe. Organic difficulties are found in about 10 per cent of enuretic children, so that most are functionally enuretic. When children have learnt to be dry but later become enuretic, stressful life events may play a role.

Approximately 40 per cent of enuretic children are taken to their doctors, and most of these are treated pharmacologically. However, the psychological bell and pad method is very effective, simple and without side-effects. Every time the bed becomes wet, a pad placed under the sheets triggers an alarm which awakens the child. In instrumental learning terms, the bell and the awakening are negative consequences to be avoided, so that the child begins to learn when the bladder is full and needs emptying. It is very effective, with about two-thirds of children soon learning to be dry throughout the night.[18]

Observational learning

A type of learning which neither the classical nor the operant approach explains adequately is the fact that we often change what we do after observing the behaviour of other people. For instance, much of the learning involved in becoming a member of a profession involves observation. Watching a consultant during his or her rounds provides much information for a medical student about behaviour with patients. We might see a doctor behave in a certain fashion, for example, and resolve to act in that way ourselves. Two processes can be used to explain such changes.

One is *imitation*, in which one person makes an observation and then repeats the behaviour as closely as possible. Imitation is not limited to humans. There are several reports of dolphins and chimpanzees also learning in this way. For example, chimps raised in psychologists' homes have been seen to sit at typewriters striking the keys and to apply lipstick in front of a mirror without prior tutoring.[19] Particularly charming are the descriptions of dolphins kept in zoos, who often imitate their handlers' behaviour. For example, just as divers use scrapers to remove algal growth from their tanks, dolphins have been known to grasp loose tiles in their mouths and to scrape the viewports of the tanks. They have also been seen to release air bubbles, just like the divers. There are many examples of such learning in humans. It may be the case that imitation is in itself pleasurable and so external rewards or punishments are not necessary for learning.

During the 1960s, Albert Bandura put forward another explanation for observational learning. He argued that the observer expects to be treated in a similar way to the person watched, so there is *vicarious reinforcement*. If the observed person is reinforced for their behaviour, we expect to be rewarded if we behave similarly. If that person is punished in some way, we would expect the same to happen to us, and so we would avoid behaving in that way. For example, if the behaviour of a senior doctor appears to put patients at ease and help them to discuss their difficulties, a junior doctor might try out the same approach. But if patients react badly, then the junior doctor would probably choose not to use that approach him or herself. Thus, the central idea here is that we expect to receive the same consequences as others have received for the same behaviour. The person we observe acts as a *model* for our own behaviour.

Bandura's approach is called social learning theory, and has been tested in many situations. For example, children in one study viewed a film of another child who was acting aggressively. The child was seen to punch and throw toys about a room. Sometimes the aggressive behaviour was rewarded and sometimes it was punished. When placed in a similar situation themselves, the children acted as if vicarious reinforcement were taking place: those who saw aggression rewarded tended to be aggressive whereas those who saw it punished showed no aggression.[20]

Treatments based on observational learning

The emphasis in this kind of social learning is on the importance of models, their behaviour and the consequences of their behaviour. Extensive research has been conducted in various situations on the characteristics of models which are effective in encouraging imitation (high prestige and similarity to the observer are important), on how the modelling should be accomplished (e.g. phobic patients benefit more from watching initially fearful models gradually overcoming their fear than initially confident models) and on how this type of learning could be used clinically. The latter has resulted in two important techniques: the use of models in helping patients cope with anxieties (such as phobias and hospitalization) and social skills training.

Coping with anxieties

The idea behind the use of observational learning in treating anxieties and phobias is that behaviour which the observer has previously regarded as hazardous in some way is repeatedly shown, under various circumstances, to be safe. Through vicarious reinforcement, the observer is encouraged to perform the actions that he had previously avoided. Someone with a phobia about snakes, for example, is more likely to approach them after seeing a model handle one without negative consequences. A variation of this method is participant modelling, which involves the therapist first modelling the desired behaviour and then the patient repeating the performance, at his or her own pace, until imitation is achieved.

More relevant here perhaps is one study that has used the modelling technique to help patients cope with their fears about admission to hospital and surgery.[21] In one such study, films were shown to children (between 4 and 12 years of age), who were about to enter hospital for surgery (e.g. tonsillectomy). None of the children had been in hospital previously and two groups of children were matched for sex, age, race and type of operation. One group saw a film of a child who attended hospital for minor surgery. The model in the film was initially hesitant and showed some anxiety during the admission procedure. Later the model talked with the surgeon and anaesthetist about what to expect. After waking in the recovery room, he regained his composure as he prepared to go home. He talked about his feelings about his stay, as did other children in the hospital playroom. These uncomfortable aspects of the operation were balanced by a rewarding atmosphere, with medical staff and the mother on hand to give comfort and support. The model was given a present after the operation and was shown leaving the same way as he arrived, which included carrying his toy dog, Ruffy. The children in the control group were also shown a film, but it was not related to hospitals. This film, about a fishing trip, controlled for length of time, interest value and a peer model coping with a new experience.

Children who observed the film of a model going through the hospital procedure and arriving safely home again showed better adjustment both just before the operation and after it. Figure 3.4 illustrates the results for observers' ratings of anxiety. It shows that there was little difference between the groups before the children saw the film, and there was little change immediately afterwards. However, just before the operation the children who had seen the hospital film were less anxious than the control group children, and this difference was maintained at the follow-up visit 4 weeks later.

Results such as these indicate that modelling is a powerful procedure in helping patients to overcome their anxieties about medical care, but it is important not to over-generalize. There is evidence, for example, that the distress of children who have intellectual impairments may increase after viewing such films.[22] Furthermore, showing the films to children who are attending for day surgery – before they have had an opportunity to integrate the information – may also increase distress.[23]

Social skills training

Social skills training (SST) has been used with considerable success with people whose relationships with others are considered to be inadequate in some way. As in the behaviour therapies previously mentioned, this type of learning is not primarily concerned with bringing about changes in inner personality states but in learning useful behavioural skills. This could apply equally to a manager who alienates employees as to a person who complains of an inability to get along with other people.

Several methods are used. *Role playing* involves the person acting in situations which approximate to the real ones. An excessively shy person, for example, might role play someone

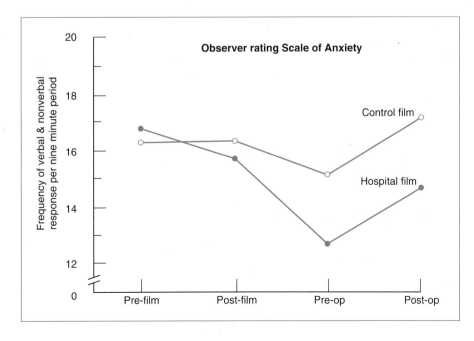

Figure 3.4 Changes in anxiety levels shown by children shown either a film of a peer attending hospital or a film of a peer having a non-medical experience. (Reproduced from Melamed, B. G. and Siegel, L. J. (1975) *Journal of Consulting and Clinical Psychology* **43**: 511–521. Copyright © 1975 by the American Psychological Association. Reprinted with permission.)

who engages another in conversation. By practising the skill in a relatively non-threatening situation, some of the anxieties can be allayed. *Role reversal* is similar in that an artificial role play is used, but in this case the person takes the role of the other individual with whom he or she has difficulty. In many medical schools, students are asked to role play patients, to help them appreciate patients' reactions to medical care. Another technique is *modelling*, in which actors or therapists demonstrate effective ways of behaving. Watching a peer handle a difficult situation seems particularly effective.

The *instructional* component of SST entails giving information about non-verbal communication. For instance, eye gaze is very important in conversation, indicating interest and attention. Someone who does not look at his or her conversational partner may seem disinterested and unfriendly, making it difficult to achieve satisfactory social relationships. The instructor might suggest to the patient, "When you're listening to people, show that you're interested by looking at them more often".

Finally, there is the *feedback* component. Social skills can be likened to other kinds of skill, such as riding a bicycle. In order to learn to ride a bike, it is necessary to acquire knowledge of results – the effect of a shift of weight on balance, for example. Similarly, videotapes provide an opportunity for patients to see and hear themselves less subjectively, and when they cannot see where they have gone "wrong" the instructor can point out the difficulty. The uses of this training are various, including marriage guidance and the rehabilitation of adolescent offenders and psychiatric patients.[24] A method which uses social skills training in helping students and medical staff learn to interview patients is discussed in Chapter 11.

Cognitive–behavioural learning

In the kinds of learning previously discussed little or no emphasis is placed on the inner workings of the mind. In many respects, this is quite satisfactory, since these approaches are able to account for behaviour much of the time (at least in restricted environments). This is a valid criterion for any theory.

In other respects, the strict behavioural approach is not as satisfactory. Cognitive factors appear to play a role in some learning, such as in the case of latent learning. In the classic experiments, some rats were allowed several days to wander around a complicated maze, but they were given no reinforcements. Another group of rats was regularly rewarded if they found their way through the maze to a goal box which contained some food. According to a strict behavioural approach, the first group of rats should have learned nothing about the path to the goal box, since they were not given any positive consequences for any learning.

However, this was not the case. As soon as the first group of rats were given food in the goal box they were able to find their way through the maze as quickly as the always-rewarded rats, indicating that learning had taken place without reinforcement.[25] This finding suggests that inner maps or cognitive structures are learned through experience, but that this learning becomes apparent only if some incentive is given for performance.

One explanation for these findings has been given by Bandura.[26] He suggests that the critical factor in learning is not simply that events occur together in time, but that people become able to predict them and summon up appropriate actions. Thus, the conditioned stimuli (the light) in Pavlov's experiments provides a predictive signal for the presentation of food. Extinction occurs when the animal discovers that the signal is no longer predictive. Similarly, it may be that operant methods are useful in changing behaviour because the person learns that the consequences of his behaviour depend on his actions in a predictable way: if he performs X in all probability Y will occur.

The important point here is that cognitions about the environment have an important effect on behaviour. The cognitive–behavioural approach argues that the way we interpret our world has an important effect on how we behave. Although this may seem obvious to many readers, it was not until the 1970s and 1980s that this became widely accepted within experimental psychology.

The internal dialogue

In a new or stressful situation, people often talk to themselves, reflecting on how they feel and act. Before going into an examination, for example, you might be thinking: "I wonder what the exam will be like" and "Remember to read each question carefully". If feeling confident, you might be saying: "I know all about this subject so calm down and relax"; but if lacking in confidence, something like: "I'm going to make a mess of this" or "I don't know enough to pass" might be going through your mind.

Clinically, this self-talk – the internal dialogue – has many implications. The interests of clinical psychologists have shifted away from a sole concern with the environmental consequences in which behaviour occurs (although this is still important), towards an understanding of how our interpretations of the environment affect our behaviour. Within cognitive models of emotional disorders, two different levels of disturbed thinking have been postulated. One is called *automatic negative thoughts*, which are thoughts or images that occur quickly and automatically. For example, a person who is anxious about public speaking might automatically think that "everyone will be bored by what I have to say" or "everyone will think that I'm useless at my job". A student who has lost confidence in his or her ability to do well might be thinking "I am going to fail this exam".

The second level of disturbed thinking is called *dysfunctional rules and assumptions*, which are general beliefs which a person holds about the world and themselves. Such beliefs could include "unless I'm liked by everyone I'm worthless" or "I must do everything perfectly well or else I'm a failure". Such assumptions lead people to interpret many situations as threatening. For example, someone who makes the assumption that other people find him or her boring might interpret a long silence in a conversation as confirmation of this assumption,[27] and someone who believes they have to do extremely well in an examination may feel very threatened if they cannot answer one question on the paper.

Smoking

There are many reasons why people begin to smoke (having friends who smoke, the need for peer approval, curiosity and perhaps advertising). Once the pattern has been established, the instrumental approach to behaviour provides a useful way of understanding why people continue, despite so much evidence that it is harmful to health. Although most smokers recognize and accept its dangers, the benefits of stopping are felt in the longer term, while the costs of stopping are experienced in the short term. When smokers switch to low tar and nicotine cigarettes, they often draw harder and smoke more frequently, thus maintaining their dosage of the drug. These types of behaviour are exactly what the instrumental approach would predict.

However a cognitive–behavioural approach is useful for understanding the processes involved when smokers attempt to quit. Shiffman[28] was interested in identifying how people cope with the temptation to smoke when they are trying to give it up. In his study, callers to a telephone hotline designed to help ex-smokers maintain their abstinence were asked to indicate what they said or did when they were tempted to smoke.

The callers reported that they used a wide range of behavioural strategies, including relaxation, distraction (e.g. "keeping busy"), delaying tactics and leaving the tempting situation, and many cognitive methods, such as thinking about the positive health consequences of not smoking and the negative consequences of relapsing, and thinking about other interests. Interestingly, callers who used punitive self-statements (e.g. "you weakling") and willpower were more likely to have relapsed. It was not the number of coping strategies which was important but the combination of behavioural and cognitive strategies which was most effective. Another study[29] indicated that those who strongly believed in the addictive properties of nicotine and had little confidence in their ability to resist were least likely to be able to quit.

Panic attacks

A good example of how this interest in thoughts and personal interpretations can be used to understand behaviour is given by the research on panic attacks. Panic attacks involve the experience of intense somatic symptoms, such as muscle tension, twitching and shaking, breathlessness, palpitations and sweating. Although we all feel anxious on occasions, panic attacks are extremely frightening, especially since they occur very quickly and apparently uncontrollably. For some people they occur "out of the blue", while others can predict the situations in which they are likely to happen. Clark[30] has developed a cognitive–behavioural model of this difficulty, in which he has asked patients to describe what they say to themselves just before the onset of their attacks. Sometimes it is difficult to elicit these self-statements, but usually patients are able to say that they interpret any anxiety symptoms as indications that they are seriously ill and perhaps likely to die.

To make this clearer, Clark's model is shown in Figure 3.5. In it, Clark argues that panic attacks usually occur in situations where the patient feels under some kind of threat. The threat can be external, such as having to speak in front of a group of people, or it might be internal, as when the patient *thinks* about having to speak. For example, if a person begins to imagine how people will react to a speech while he or she is preparing it, they might find themselves becoming apprehensive.

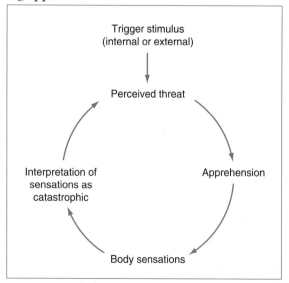

Figure 3.5 The suggested sequence of events in a panic attack. (Reproduced from Clark, D. M. (1986) A cognitive approach to panic. *Behaviour Research and Therapy* **24**: 461–470, with kind permission from Elsevier Science Ltd, The Boulevard, Langford Lane, Kidlington, OX5 1GB, UK.)

An increase in anxiety after having such thoughts is very common (you might have found something similar, as you have thought about how much preparation you have to do before an important examination), but Clark contends that there are two additional processes which occur in panic attacks. First, the person begins to attend more and more to their bodily sensations. Furthermore, these sensations are interpreted in a catastrophic way, being taken as indications that they are about to die or suffer a heart attack. These interpretations serve to complete a vicious circle where the threat escalates. Such interpretations may occur due to the experience of the death of a significant person, which sensitizes the person to their own health status. Interviews with patients support the idea that many people with panic attacks have recently experienced the loss of an important person in their lives though illness, often through a heart attack.

Treatments based on cognitive–behavioural learning

Thus, a cognitive–behavioural approach to clinical difficulties involves an analysis of the situation, the patient's interpretation of the situation and the effects of this interpretation on subsequent behaviour. In this section, cognitive–behavioural interventions designed to help people with three different problems are outlined.

Situational anxieties

The self-statements used by patients in clinical settings are also associated with their levels of anxiety. Kendall *et al.*[31] examined the self-statements of patients who were undergoing cardiac catheterization, asking them to indicate the kinds of thoughts they experienced during the procedure. Some of the thoughts were positive (e.g. how little pain the procedure caused and how easy it was to go through it) but many more were negative (e.g. thinking about the possibility of the catheter breaking off). When the attending physicians' and technicians' ratings of adjustment made during the procedure were compared with the patients' self-statements, there were significant relationships between them, with poor adjustment being correlated with the frequency of negative self-statements.

Cognitive theorists argue that such self-statements are not simply the result of any anxiety felt by a patient during cardiac catheterization, but actually contribute to the anxiety. The implication is that if these self-statements can be modified, the anxiety level will be changed. Kendall *et al.* tested this possibility by giving some catheterization patients a short introduction to the idea that what people say to themselves can affect their level of anxiety. The patients' specific fears were addressed. If, for example, a particular patient was to say that he was anxious about all the machinery at the hospital, a new self-statement such as "science has come such a long way to be able to have and to use all of this expensive equipment, and the doctors are very skilled in their use" would be encouraged. Other patients formed a control group: they were given a chat which was generally supportive of their concerns, but no specific coping skills were discussed. Both the doctors' and technicians' ratings of adjustment and the patients' reports of anxiety experienced during the subsequent procedure indicated that the patients encouraged to use coping self-statements fared better during the catheterization. Thus, positive self-talk modified the level of anxiety.

An application of self-instructional training which may be of personal relevance to you concerns test anxiety. The deleterious effects of high anxiety in the performance of complex tasks are well-documented, and are a problem often encountered by students taking important exams. Part of the difficulty seems to be that highly anxious students tend to be self-deprecating about their performance and ruminate on the performance of others in the examination hall. There seems to be a failure to attend to the relevant aspects of the task, with irrelevant thoughts intruding frequently and a concern with feelings. That is, attention is directed inwardly rather than outwardly to the task at hand.

In an attempt to help with this problem, students were encouraged to become aware of their thoughts and self-statements during exams. They were then asked to imagine themselves taking an exam but instead of ruminating on irrelevant thoughts to instruct themselves positively; for

instance, to say to themselves "This is a difficult exam, I'd better start working at it" rather than "I'm really nervous, I can't handle this". Compared with students who were waiting to take the cognitive modification programme, this procedure had a significant effect on grades and self-reports of improvement.[32]

Self-control

Self-control techniques do not involve "use your willpower" or "pull yourself together" admonitions. Self-control methods are much more detailed and structured than these kinds of advice. There are two main components. First, there is careful observation of the conditions that evoke the undesired behaviour. Someone who wants to stop smoking, for instance, would be encouraged to monitor the occasions when a cigarette is taken. This could be done by keeping a diary of the circumstances in which smoking occurs, the number of cigarettes smoked, and so on. Since people are not particularly accurate at observing their own behaviour, the therapist would provide instructions on how this monitoring could be accomplished.

The second component of self-control involves the idea of self-reward, in which people give themselves rewards contingent on their behaviour. This can be encouraged by either direct instruction or by modelling. In the case of direct instruction, the therapist tells the patient to choose something pleasant whenever a certain standard of behaviour is reached. When the patient has no cigarette with morning coffee he or she could have a piece of cake, for instance. In modelling, the individual observes models rewarding themselves for performing a certain action and is encouraged to do the same. Once people have learned to reward themselves in this way, the behaviour is typically maintained for longer periods of time than when reinforcement is always given by the experimenter or therapist. Self-punishment, by contrast, has relatively little effect on self-control.[33]

This approach is nicely illustrated by some research that explored the self-control shown by students attempting to study. Students were initially asked to examine their own study methods, noting when and where they usually revised. To increase motivation, the students were also requested to make lists of all the reasons why they should study. Two methods were used to increase self-control. The first involved stimulus control: the students were encouraged to use only one or two places for study, places not associated with behaviour incompatible with studying. This method was based on the notion that the environment has an important effect on behaviour.

The second method involved asking the students to reward themselves whenever they studied for a specified length of time. At first, this time was short, about 20 minutes, but this increased as the programme progressed. They chose their own reinforcers, which could have been food, or watching TV. The students were also taught to graph the number of hours they spent studying, so that they could see the results of their efforts. The programme was supplemented by information about the SQ3R, a method outlined in the Appendix. The results were very encouraging. A significant improvement in grades in the university exams was found for these students, compared with those not involved in the programme and those who dropped out after the introduction. While these researchers could not attribute the results to self-reinforcement alone owing to the design of the experiment, others have shown more clearly that self-reinforcement is effective in changing study patterns.

Hypochondriasis

Hypochondriasis refers to a preoccupation with the fear of having a serious illness which cannot be explained by the presence of disease and is resistant to medical reassurance. As is the case with panic attacks, anxiety about one's own health can be very debilitating and is based on misinterpretations about bodily signs. Patients with such difficulties may become very dissatisfied with the investigations carried out by staff as they continually seek reassurance while paying undue attention to their bodily state. Although patients with such difficulties can be maligned or ignored, a clinical psychologist would be interested in helping them to understand how their beliefs and cognitive processes serve to exacerbate and maintain the difficulty.

Salkovskis[34] explains how an important initial step in this intervention is to take the patients'

concerns seriously. Although no organic cause might be found, the pain or discomfort is very real to the patient. This is important since such patients are often very resistant to the idea that their symptoms could be psychologically based, and only a gradual introduction of a psychological explanation is likely to succeed. Another important aspect of treatment is to avoid reassuring the patient that nothing is wrong. He argues that reassurance and extensive medical tests actually make the problem worse since they further focus the patient's attention on his or her health.

Salkovskis provides a case study to illustrate his view. In this instance, a patient became convinced that he was suffering from leukaemia, partly due to a misinterpretation of some information given to him by his dermatologist about a skin rash. He inspected this rash frequently, read textbooks in an effort to discover the cause and could talk of little else to his wife, family and friends. Eventually he was hospitalized for emotional difficulties.

Therapy began by asking the patient to entertain the possibility that he had a difficulty with anxiety, rather than a serious disease, which was maintained by repeated medical consultations and checking of his skin. The notion that he was selectively attending to aspects of his body was also emphasized. Instead of continually thinking about how he felt, Salkovskis encouraged him to engage in ward activities on a regular basis, rather than waiting near the nurses' station hoping to talk to his doctor. Ward staff, his family doctors and his family were instructed to stop giving him reassurances about his health.

Some of the results of this intervention are shown in Figure 3.6. The patient was asked to complete some scales which indicated how strongly he held the belief that he was seriously ill. First, a baseline was taken over 3 days, then there was a period when staff sought to give him reassurances that he was not ill, which had little effect on his beliefs, and then the treatment was instituted. As Figure 3.6 indicates, his belief that he was ill decreased substantially over the treatment sessions.[35]

Thus, the cognitive approach to learning emphasizes the ways that people perceive their environment and themselves. Their thoughts are seen to be crucial, with self-statements about

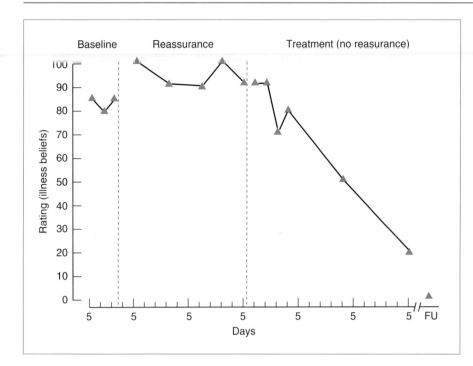

Figure 3.6 Patient's rating of how firmly he held the belief that he was ill with leukaemia during baseline, during a period when he was reassured about his health, and during the cognitive–behavioural treatment sessions. (Reproduced from Salkovskis, P. and Warwick, H. (1986) *Behaviour Research and Therapy* **24**: 599, with kind permission from Elsevier Science Ltd, The Boulevard, Langford Lane, Kidlington, OX5 1GB, UK.)

feelings and about what to do in new situations affecting behaviour. The argument is that if these self-statements can be modified, then behaviour and feelings will also change, an idea that is gaining much support in a variety of situations from encouraging compliance to helping students take exams.

Comparing therapies

There are thousands of studies addressed to the issue of treatment efficacy. The topic is an important one, having many practical implications. If one treatment can be shown to be more effective than another, then therapists would have a responsibility to use the superior treatment for the good of their patients. The type of approach a therapist advocates may not only affect the treatment used but also which signs and symptoms will be observed.[36]

The usual approach is to assign patients, with similar severity and types of difficulties, randomly to one of three groups. Two of the groups would be treated by two different methods (for example, systematic desensitization and

modelling), whereas the patients in the third group would serve as waiting-list controls. Baseline measures would be taken before treatment, and a follow-up conducted some months after treatment is completed.

As well as experiments which have considered differences between treatments, researchers have been interested in ascertaining the most important aspects of any one procedure.[37] Several general principles have emerged:

1 Generally, when compared with waiting-list control groups, these therapies have proved effective in the treatment of a wide variety of emotional difficulties such as phobias and various types of anxiety and behavioural disturbances.

2 There are many experiments and individual case studies in the literature testifying to the efficacy of behaviour therapy. While these cases provide evidence, a therapist is unlikely to seek to publish instances where his or her therapy has not been successful.

3 Treatments that involve the patient in actually engaging in the feared behaviour are more effective than those which rely on imagination. *In vivo* treatments, such as participant-

modelling, produce more change than, say, modelling alone.

4 Studies using cognitive behaviour modification have generally proved superior to the more traditional kinds of behaviour therapies, providing better generalization with less cost in therapists' time.

5 Programmes which use multiple treatments have tended to be more effective than those that use a single method. This may be because many psychological difficulties have several components and each approach is best suited to a different component. Fear of a spider, for example, can involve physiological reactions, subjective perceptions and behavioural actions. Each component might best be altered by a different kind of therapy: a classical approach for the physiological component, a cognitive approach for the subjective one and an operant approach for the behaviour. Perhaps a fear is caused via the classical conditioning model but is maintained through the operant: for example, a person may run out of a room whenever a spider is sighted, thus gaining some relief from the feared stimulus. By combining several methods, each component is treated.

Behavioural therapies versus medication

Researchers have also been interested in comparing psychological and pharmacological approaches.[38] There are several medications which can be used to help people who find themselves anxious in situations, such as the beta-blockers, which control the signs of physiological arousal (rapid heart rate, tremors and blushing) that are associated with anxiety. Turner *et al.*[39] were interested in comparing the effects of beta-blockers with flooding in helping patients who suffered from social phobia.

Patients suffering from social phobia were assigned to one of three groups: flooding, atenolol (beta-blocker), or placebo. The flooding intervention involved asking the patients to place themselves in the types of situation they feared, both in imagination and *in vivo*: for example, participating in group discussions where their

opinions were asked. In the atenolol and placebo interventions, patients were asked to take tablets each morning, but no psychological assistance was given.

In order to assess the effects of the interventions, each patient was asked to give a 10-minute speech in front of three people both before and after treatment. Measures of the patients' actual behaviour (whether they could manage the speech), how they felt during the speech (their subjective level of distress) and physiological arousal (blood pressure and pulse rate) were taken. The results indicated that flooding was superior to the atenolol and placebo interventions. Overall, 89 per cent of the patients given the flooding intervention showed moderate or significant improvement in their ability to give the speeches, but only 47 per cent of the atenolol and 44 per cent of the placebo group patients. Furthermore, at a 6-month follow-up, the flooding patients continued to improve, whereas the atenolol patients remained unchanged or deteriorated. Such studies as this indicate that the psychological interventions have greater and longer term effects than medical approaches. Perhaps this is because when medications are given people attribute their success to the tablets (e.g. "I was able to do this because of the medication") rather than to their own ability.

Suggested reading

Rachman, S. and Wilson, G. (1980) *The Effects of Psychological Therapy*, Oxford: Pergamon, and Hawton, K. *et al.* (1988) *Cognitive Behaviour Therapy for Psychiatric Problems*, Oxford: Oxford Medical Publications, provide reviews of the many ways in which behavioural approaches can be helpful to people with a variety of difficulties.

References

1. Gray, J. (1982) *The Neuropsychology of Anxiety: An Inquiry into the Functions of the Septo-Hippocampal System*. Oxford: Clarendon Press.
2. Kent, G. (1991) Anxiety. In: Dryden, W. and Rentoul, R. (eds) *Adult Clinical Problems*. London: Routledge, pp. 27–55.

3. Koch, H. (1979) Evaluation of behaviour therapy intervention in general practice. *Journal of the Royal College of General Practitioners* **29**: 337–340.

4. Harris, B. (1979) Whatever happened to Little Albert? *American Psychologist* **34**: 151–160.

5. De Silva, P. (1988) Phobias and preparedness: replication and extension. *Behaviour Research and Therapy* **26**: 97–98.

6. Carey, M. and Burish, T. (1988) Etiology and treatment of the psychological side effects associated with cancer chemotherapy: a critical review and discussion. *Psychological Bulletin* **104**: 307–325.

7. Watson, M. and Marvell, C. (1992) Anticipatory nausea and vomiting among cancer patients: a review. *Psychology and Health* **6**: 97–106.

8. Jacobsen, P., Bovberg, D., Schwartz, M., Hudis, C., Gilewski, T. and Norton, L. (1995) Conditioned emotional distress in women receiving chemotherapy for breast cancer. *Journal of Consulting and Clinical Psychology* **63**: 108–114.

9. Morrow, G. (1982) Prevalence and correlates of anticipatory nausea and vomiting in chemotherapy patients. *Journal of the National Cancer Institute* **68**: 585.

10. Sreenivasan, U., Manocha, S.N. and Jain, V.K. (1979) Treatment of severe dog phobia in childhood by flooding: A case report. *Journal of Child Psychology and Psychiatry* **20**: 255–260.

11. Wolpe, J. (1969) *The Practice of Behavior Therapy*. New York: Pergamon.

12. Gale, E.N. and Ayer, W.A. (1969) Treatment of dental phobias. *Journal of the American Dental Association* **78**: 1304–1307.

13. Skinner, B.F. (1976) *Walden Two*. London: Collier Macmillan.

14. Harris, F.R., Wolfe, M.M. and Baer, D.M. (1964) Effects of adult social reinforcement on child behaviour. *Young Children* **20**: 8–17.

15. Lang, P.J. and Melamed, B.G. (1968) Case report: Avoidance conditioning therapy of an infant with chronic ruminative vomiting. *Journal of Abnormal Psychology* **74**: 1–8.

16. Langer, E.J., Rodin, J., Beck, P., Weinman, C. and Spitzer, L. (1979) Environmental determinants of memory improvement in late adulthood. *Journal of Personality and Social Psychology* **37**: 2003–2013.

17. Horner, R.D. and Keilitz, I. (1975) Training mentally retarded adolescents to brush their teeth. *Journal of Applied Behaviour Analysis* **8**: 301–309.

18. Houts, A., Berman, J. and Abramson, H. (1994) Effectiveness of psychological and pharmacological treatments for nocturnal enuresis. *Journal of Consulting and Clinical Psychology* **62**: 737–745.

19. Hayes, K.J. and Hayes, C. (1952) Imitation in a home-raised chimpanzee. *Journal of Comparative Physiological Psychology* **45**: 450–459.

20. Rosekrans, M.A. and Hartup, W.W. (1967) Imitative influences of consistent and inconsistent response consequences to a model on aggressive behaviour in children. *Journal of Personality and Social Psychology* **7**: 429–434.

21. Melamed, B.G. and Siegel, L.J. (1975) Reduction of anxiety in children facing surgery by modelling. *Journal of Consulting and Clinical Psychology* **43**: 511–521.

22. Boj, J. and Davila, J. (1980) A study of behaviour modification for developmentally delayed children. *Journal of Dentistry for Children* **56**: 452–457.

23. Faust, J., Olson, R. and Rodriguez, H. (1991) Same-day surgery preparation: reduction of pediatric patient arousal and distress through participant modelling. *Journal of Consulting and Clinical Psychology* **59**: 475–478.

24. Argyle, M. (ed.) (1981) *Social Skills and Health*. London: Methuen.

25. Tolman, E.C. (1948) Cognitive maps in rats and men. *Psychological Review* **55**: 189–208.

26. Bandura, A. (1977) *Social Learning Theory*. Englewood Cliffs, New Jersey: Prentice-Hall.

27. Clark, D.M. (1986) A cognitive approach to panic. *Behaviour Research and Therapy* **24**: 461–470.

28. Shiffman, S. (1984) Coping with temptations to smoke. *Journal of Consulting and Clinical Psychology* **52**: 261–267.

29. Katz, R. and Singh, N. (1986) Reflections on the ex-smoker: some findings on successful quitters. *Journal of Behavioral Medicine* **9**: 191–202.

30. Clark, D.M. (1988) Anxiety states: panic and generalised anxiety. In: Hawton, K., Salkovskis, P., Kirk, J. and Clark, D. (eds) *Cognitive Behaviour Therapy for Psychiatric Problems*. Oxford: Oxford Medical Publications, pp. 52–96

31. Kendall, P.C., Williams, L., Pechacek, T.F., Graham, L.E., Shisslak, C. and Herzoff, N. (1979) Cognitive-behavioural and patient education interventions in cardiac catheterization procedures. *Journal of Consulting and Clinical Psychology* **47**: 49–58.

32. Meichenbaum, D. (1972) Cognitive modification of test-anxious college students. *Journal of Consulting and Clinical Psychology* **39**: 370–380.

33. Thorensen, C.E. and Mahoney, M.J. (1974) *Behav-*

ioural Self-control. New York: Holt, Rinehart and Winston.

34. Salkovskis, P. (1988) Somatic problems. In: Hawton, K., Salkovskis, P., Kirk, J. and Clark, D. (eds) *Cognitive Behaviour Therapy for Psychiatric Problems*. Oxford: Oxford Medical Publications, pp. 235-276.

35. Salkovskis, P. and Warwick, M. (1986) Morbid preoccupations, health anxiety and reassurance: a cognitive–behavioural approach to hypochondriasis. *Behaviour Research and Therapy* **24**: 597-602.

36. Langer, E.J. and Abelson, R.P. (1974) A patient by any other name. *Journal of Consulting and Clinical Psychology* **42**: 4-9.

37. Kazdin, A.E. and Wilson, G.T. (1978) *Evaluation of Behavior Therapy*. Cambridge, Mass.: Ballinger.

38. Kendall, P. and Lipman, A. (1991) Psychological and pharmacological therapy: methods and modes of comparative outcome research. *Journal of Consulting and Clinical Psychology* **59**: 78-87.

39. Turner, S., Beidel, D. and Jacob, R. (1994) Social phobia: a comparison of behaviour therapy and atenolol. *Journal of Consulting and Clinical Psychology* **62**: 350-358.

4
Personality and Meaning

CONTENTS

SUMMARY

Two major trends in the study of personality are considered in this chapter, based on the descriptive and psychotherapeutic approaches. In the descriptive approach, personality questionnaires have been developed for ease of measurement and statistical analysis. These questionnaires are composed of statements or items which describe people as possessing certain traits, such as introversion–extroversion or neuroticism.

Approaches based on therapeutic work with clients are more concerned with personal meanings. While Freud placed much emphasis on the unconscious, more recently there has been an emphasis on how a therapist can help clients to develop their own orientation to life or to re-evaluate unhelpful interpretations of their experiences.

In the previous chapter, the behaviourist approach to understanding behaviour was outlined. Although the role of cognitions has recently been examined, the emphasis there was on the environmental determinants of behaviour. Psychologists who have been interested in personality variables have taken an almost opposite approach. For them, behaviour is determined by internal characteristics. This way of understanding behaviour holds the view that "personality *is* something and *does* something . . . It is what lies *behind* specific acts and *within* the individual".[1]

This approach to understanding behaviour is intuitively attractive. However, the study of personality has proved to be remarkably complex and difficult. Forer[2] conducted one of the classic studies in psychology. He asked people attending an open-day in a psychology department to complete several questionnaires, which were supposed to be able to provide unique and detailed insights into their personalities. After the results of the questionnaires were analysed, the participants were given a brief description of their personalities, and asked to indicate how accurate the description was, and whether it applied to them much more than to other people. When shown the description, most participants believed that it was remarkably accurate and unique to them. Unknown to them, however, the description was actually the same for everyone, as follows:

" You have a strong need for other people to like you and for them to admire you. At times you are extroverted, affable and sociable, while at other times you are introverted, wary and reserved. You have a great deal of unused energy which you have not turned to your advantage. While you have some personality weaknesses, you are generally able to compensate for them. You prefer a certain amount of change and variety and become dissatisfied when hemmed in by restrictions and limitations. You pride yourself on being an independent thinker and do not accept others' opinions without satisfactory proof. You have a tendency to be critical of yourself. Some of your aspirations tend to be pretty unrealistic. "

This study has a number of implications for understanding personality. The description is so vague and multi-faceted that there will be many characteristics which will correspond with how everyone sees themselves. We all like to think of ourselves as being independent thinkers, dislike feeling hemmed in, and so on. We may like to think that we are unusual in these ways, but in fact we are not. Does this mean that personality is a myth, or is it possible to be more specific than this, so that individual differences can be described accurately and with reference to our own uniqueness?

This chapter considers two approaches which have been used to understand our personalities. One approach is mainly descriptive, where the interest lies mainly in developing questionnaires which can be used to *distinguish* between different people, while the other approach is more therapeutically orientated, the interest lying mainly in being able to *understand* the personal problems experienced by individuals.

Personality tests

This section considers methods of assessing personality whose aim is to predict how different types of people might act in certain situations. Such measures are used in, for example, personnel selection, as well as in research studies (e.g. identifying people who are most susceptible to certain kinds of illness). Although there is a brief description of projective techniques here, most of the research in this area has been conducted using self-report questionnaires and this will form the main discussion.

Projective techniques

Two of the best-known projective tests are the Thematic Apperception Test (TAT) and the Rorschach Inkblot Test. In both instruments the person is presented with vague and ambiguous pictures and asked to describe them. The TAT consists of 20 cards, one of which is actually blank. The examiner asks the person to imagine a story that tells what led up to the event shown, what is presently occurring, and what the outcome might be. There are no right or wrong

descriptions, the assumption being that the way the person makes sense of the pictures is a reflection of personality, aspirations and needs. These are said to be shown through the use of repeated themes. If, for example, an individual often describes the pictures in terms of parent–child relationships, then the relationship with his or her parents might be particularly important.

In the Rorschach test, subjects are shown ten inkblots in reds, greens and blacks and asked to suggest what they might represent. The responses are coded in terms of their number and the parts of the inkblot that are included in the description. The actual content is not considered to be so important unless the description is very unusual.

Projective techniques have not been well-accepted by psychologists for several reasons. One requirement of a measuring instrument is that observations taken at one time are similar to observations taken at another. In addition, it is important to have agreement between different observers when applying the measure in the same circumstances. The *reliability* of projective techniques is not good since the same description of the TAT or Rorschach materials produces differing interpretations from different examiners.

Another important requirement of personality instruments is that they measure what they purport to measure (i.e. underlying personality factors) rather than something else (e.g. what the examiner wants to hear). This is termed *construct validity*. There is evidence that responses on projective techniques are subject to temporary mood changes: if, for example, people are asked not to eat breakfast before describing the pictures on the TAT, they are more likely to give responses concerning food. A further difficulty is that they are not particularly suitable for research purposes. Examiners require long training in order to interpret the responses and even then the materials do not lend themselves easily to numerical assessment. For testing large numbers of people, instruments that can be scored easily and provide data which can be readily analysed using statistical techniques are preferred.

Such difficulties with projective materials have led many psychologists to question their usefulness in assessing personality. While they can be helpful in providing a global view of individuals when precise descriptions are not needed and may be useful in opening conversation between a therapist and a patient when the patient is feeling unsure or hesitant,[3] other forms of personality questionnaire are used much more commonly.

Personality questionnaires

When describing someone, you may well use a series of adjectives – honest, shy and hardworking, for example. Someone else might be described as less honest and shy but more outgoing and independent. Such descriptions illustrate that people have everyday ways of understanding personality which not only include adjectives but also scales as well – one individual might be more or less shy than another. Psychologists have systematized this commonsense approach to studying personality through the use of self-report questionnaires. The aim has been to develop instruments which measure the extent to which a person possesses certain characteristics, or traits, and to compare the results with others.

In this method, people are asked a number of questions about their behaviour, feelings or thoughts, and are given a choice of answers, often a simple "Yes" or "No". The decision about which questions (or items as they are usually called) are included depends on the purpose of the questionnaire. There are three main ways of selecting items: observation, use of criterion groups, and factor analysis.

Observation

First, the items may be suggested through observation. For example, clinicians noted that patients with coronary heart disease often have distinctive personalities, characterized by striving for achievement, competitiveness and impatience. This constellation of traits has become known as the Type A personality, as compared to those who do not have these characteristics (known as Type B personalities). Jenkins et al.[4] constructed a number of items from interviews and observations which seemed to tap this distinction, arriving at the Jenkins Activity Survey. In this questionnaire people are given a number of situations (e.g. waiting to be served in a restaurant or post office) and asked how they typically react in them (e.g. a choice between "accept it calmly", "feel impatient but do not show it", "feel so impatient that someone watching could tell that you are restless" and "refuse to wait, and find ways to avoid such delays").

Criterion groups

Second, items may be selected empirically. Perhaps a researcher aims to distinguish people who belong to different groups, such as those who have or have not been diagnosed as having a particular psychological difficulty. The investigator could ask a large number of questions of the people in each group and then subsequently include those items which a majority of one group answered one way and the other group the other way. These items could then be later used as a diagnostic tool, assuming, of course, that the diagnosis of the original criterion group was a valid and reliable one and that the selection of the original control group was representative of the general population.

This empirical approach was used in the development of the Minnesota Multiphasic Personality Inventory (the MMPI), which is widely used in the United States. The MMPI contains 13 scales, each of which is intended to differentiate between various criteria and control groups. The scales include hypochondriasis, depression and social introversion–extroversion. Like the Jenkins Activity Scale, the MMPI is purely descriptive and there is no explanation given as to why the people in the various groups answer in particular ways or why they came to enter that group in the first place. While some of the items are obvious (e.g. "I am happy most of the time" is an item on the depression scale), others are less so (e.g. "It takes a lot of argument to convince most people of the truth" in the same scale). The inclusion of an item is not dependent on being obviously applicable but only on whether or not it discriminates.

An example of how the MMPI could be used in practice is given by a study on reactions of cancer patients to their diagnosis. The questionnaire was given to 133 newly diagnosed patients who were followed up monthly for the next 6 months. A social worker, who did not know the MMPI results, took several measures of their emotional distress, so that the patients could be divided into those who showed a high degree of emotional distress and those who showed a low degree of distress. The highly distressed group scored higher on several scales of the MMPI, including emphasis on physical complaints, depression, anxiety and withdrawal. About 75 per cent of the patients could be classified as showing high or low distress by the MMPI results gathered 6 months previously, suggesting that the questionnaire might be used to predict patients' reactions to the diagnosis.[5]

Factor analysis

A third approach to the design of personality questionnaires is based on factor analysis. Essentially, this method involves correlating answers on one item with answers on all other items. In some cases people would give similar responses to a group of questions: if they scored high on one they would score high on others. In other cases, the scores on one item would not correlate with scores on others. Each group of items which correlate or cluster together constitute a factor, and this factor is given a label which reflects the kinds of items which were found to cluster together. For example, people might respond to items about their relationship with parents and with friends in similar ways that may be appropriately subsumed under a factor labelled dependency.

Eysenck[6], who developed the Eysenck Personality Inventory (EPI) and the later version the Eysenck Personality Questionnaire (EPQ), suggests that there are three important factors – neuroticism, introversion–extroversion and psychoticism. Someone who scores high on the neuroticism or N scale is said to be emotionally reactive, being easily upset in a variety of situations: a high scorer on the extroversion scale (E) is outgoing, impulsive and sociable. The EPQ consists of 90 items, each of which is answered by a "Yes" or "No". The individual's responses are compared to a large sample of others' answers in order to discover how unusual the responses are, so that this questionnaire, like the others mentioned, does not give an absolute measure of personality but simply a *relative* one. Someone is said to be extroverted, for example, if he or she replies to more of the items in an extroverted way than most other people. Another feature of this questionnaire, again shared by others, is that the personality characteristics are considered to be continuous rather than discrete entities. The assumption is that everyone possesses these traits to some extent.

An example which illustrates the relevance of these ideas is shown by a study with women who were about to undergo elective Caesarian section under regional anaesthesia. Many patients awaiting this type of surgery experience anxiety beforehand, but it can be difficult to identify who they will be early enough to offer assistance. In an attempt to identify women who were likely to experience distress, Thorp *et al.*[7] asked women to complete the Eysenck scale and an anxiety scale the day before surgery. As Eysenck would predict, women who scored highly on the neuroticism scale and low on the extroversion scale also scored highly on the anxiety scale. Thus it might be possible to predict those women who are in most need of emotional help well before they enter hospital, making a pre-operation intervention designed to reduce anxiety more feasible.

One further aspect of personality questionnaires merits attention. It is important that the examiner has some idea of how honestly and carefully the person has answered the items. For several reasons, people may present a picture of themselves which is not an accurate one but, rather, a picture that is socially desirable. Some people may not want to admit, even to themselves, their foibles and embarrassing thoughts, so that questionnaires often include some indication of how honestly the person is reporting his or her personality. Most questionnaires include one or more "Lie" scales, in which questions about common frailties are asked. For example, on the EPQ, questions such as "Have you ever taken advantage of someone?" are included. If the person answers too many of these kinds of items in a socially desirable way, then the validity of the answers on the other scales is called into question.

Biological explanations for personality

There is a common tendency to use traits to explain behaviour but this is logically incorrect. Traits are inferred from behaviour and cannot, therefore, be used to explain it. For example, if someone behaves in an honest way, people may attribute this behaviour to a trait of honesty. If this person returns some money which he had found, his friends may explain this by saying, "Well, he returned the money because he is honest". But this is a circular explanation and tells us little about any underlying mechanisms.

This is a tempting mistake to make, one which Eysenck has avoided. He considers the responses on the EPI and EPQ to be strongly influenced by genetic factors. Vulnerability to psychotic behaviour is considered to be inherited, the predisposition becoming apparent when the person is under stress. High scorers on the neuroticism scale (who are easily upset and lack confidence) are thought to have over-reactive autonomic nervous systems, whereas high scorers on the extroversion scale (who are impulsive and sociable) are said to be cortically inhibited.

The attraction of Eysenck's position is that he has attempted to provide an understanding of why people have certain traits rather than simply describing them. There is some evidence that there are biological differences between Type As and Type Bs as well. At admission to hospital, Kahn *et al.*[8] assessed the personality of patients due to have coronary bypass surgery. During the operation, the Type As were more likely to show rises in systolic and diastolic blood pressure than Type Bs. Since the anaesthetized patients were presumably free from consciously mediated determinants of blood pressure, these results suggest that there are constitutional differences between As and Bs.

Validating personality questionnaires

A good indication of the validity of a personality test would be if it could predict how someone behaves. There are two basic assumptions behind the use of personality questionnaires: (1) that they tap underlying dispositions which are relatively independent of circumstances, and (2) that people act consistently in different situations. If person A is more assertive, aggressive and honest than person B in one situation, then A should be more assertive, aggressive and honest in other situations as well. If a theory is unable to predict how someone will act (i.e. it has little *predictive*

validity), then it could be argued that it should be discarded.

Eysenck's theory has met with some success in these respects. In several objective tests (e.g. under experimentally imposed stress) high scorers on the extroversion and neuroticism scales give different results from low scorers. Reactions to analgesics vary along lines similar to those which Eysenck's theory would predict (see Chapter 10) and high scorers on the neuroticism scale are more likely to have complications and to recover less well after surgery than those who score low.[9]

Other personality questionnaires which have been designed for specific purposes have also been useful. The Jenkins Activity Survey, for example, has been validated in a prospective study. Over 3000 people were monitored in a long-term study of the correlates of coronary heart disease. Some 8 years after the initial tests were given, 257 males in the sample who were initially healthy had some kind of heart complaint. Even when serum lipids, blood pressure, obesity and smoking were taken into account, Type A men had over twice the risk of heart disease than Type B men. Of course, many of the Type As did not report heart disease and many Type Bs did, indicating that other factors besides personality were also significant.[10,11]

Limitations of personality tests

However, the relationship between scores on personality tests and observations of behaviour have often been found to be tenuous, correlations being quite low.[12] A similar lack of correspondence between what people say they would do and what they actually do in practice has been found in research on attitudes. Attitudes are said to be general predispositions to respond towards objects or people in positive or negative ways, but they have been found to be poor predictors of behaviour.[13]

Similarly, there is evidence that how a person behaves in one set of circumstances often provides a poor predictor of behaviour in dissimilar situations. Ellsworth *et al.*[14] asked both the staff of a psychiatric hospital and the patients' family and friends for assessments of patients' behaviour: the way in which they acted in hospital showed little congruence with the ways they acted at home. Patients who showed improvements in hospital were not necessarily those who were improved once they rejoined the community. Such studies have important implications for medical care. Simply because a patient appears hostile in a hospital or a consulting room may not provide clues as to his or her behaviour elsewhere. As mentioned above, there seems to be a strong tendency for people to cite personality variables as causes of behaviour, a tendency that may often be misplaced.[15] For example, physicians often attribute lack of compliance in their patients to an uncooperative personality, but there are few indications that this provides an accurate assessment of the reasons for their behaviour (see Chapter 12).

Some psychologists have argued that personality is simply an illusion and advocated rejection of the concept. Although people do act consistently, perhaps this consistency is not due to personality factors but to recurring patterns in the environment. For example, people tend to appear the same over time because their physical appearance changes only slightly and they have many routines which they repeat daily. For some of these psychologists it is the roles and expectations that people have of others which form the important variables (see Chapter 5).

Other psychologists have argued that it is idiosyncratic meanings which need to be explored. Such an approach stresses the importance of assessing individuals' views and understandings, an emphasis given by psychologists who work in clinical settings.

Clinical approaches to personality

This part of the chapter considers approaches to personality which have developed out of psychotherapy with clients who have a variety of emotional difficulties. The emphasis in these approaches is in understanding the life circumstances and emotions faced by individuals, with the aim of developing general principles that can be applied to everyone. A theme of these approaches is that most psychological difficulties are a matter of degree and that a person who needs to consult a clinical psychologist or psychiatrist is not fundamentally different from anyone else.

Freud

Sigmund Freud is considered to be the father of the *psychodynamic* approach to personality. Although many aspects of his original theory have been modified by later therapists, his contribution to psychiatry and psychology is enormous and it is important to give at least a brief outline of his thinking. His perspective grew out of experiences with the patients he treated in Vienna at the turn of the century, and his theory is much easier to understand in the context of this cultural background.

Trained as a neurologist, Freud was steeped in the medical model. One tenet of medical training is that complaints are symptoms of an underlying cause. They are important only in so far as they point to an underlying pathology of some kind. If this pathology is treated then the symptoms will disappear. Thus, Freud was more interested in discovering what his patients' symptoms indicated than in the symptoms themselves.

The unconscious

Freud was born in 1856, and many contemporary ideas were included in his theory. Although Freud is sometimes credited with discovering the unconscious, the idea seems to have been present in Victorian culture. Stevenson's *Dr Jekyll and Mr Hyde* provides an example: by drinking a potion, a hidden side of the doctor's personality was expressed. Further, this unknown personality was destructive and needed to be controlled. Freud argued that the unconscious formed the greater proportion of everyone's personality, with consciousness being only a small part of our personality, like the tip of an iceberg. The unconscious contained feelings and experiences of which, under ordinary circumstances, the person was unaware but which motivated actions or desires.

Freud's theory was also consistent with an important trend in Western thinking – biological determinism, the idea that what people do and think is set by their biological make-up. William Harvey's contention that the heart was not a "vital" organ (i.e. not the seat of life) but simply a pump, was one example; Charles Darwin's theory of evolution was another. Freud saw no reason to believe that thinking and perceiving were any different from breathing or walking. Both kinds of process were seen to be manifestations of the same underlying biological machine.

Like physical energy, he contended that psychic energy (which he called libidinal energy) was present in finite amounts and could be neither created nor destroyed. Since intake of food resulted in the production of psychic as well as physical energy, this energy must find expression. If for some reason the expression of energy was blocked, then, like a hydraulic system, the energy found expression elsewhere. For example, Freud contended that a person who had a compulsion to wash their hands repeatedly was using up the energy from a blocked impulse. There would be little point in treating the hand-washing alone since the energy would simply find expression elsewhere – *symptom substitution*.

The components of personality

Freud postulated three systems within the personality. The most basic was the *id*. The id was like a reservoir, supplying the energy required for human behaviour. Freud argued that the *ego* developed as a system that was responsible for mediating between the id's demands for pleasure and the demands of external reality. The ego did not have energy of its own but only borrowed it from the id in return for satisfying the id whenever possible. He also postulated the existence of a third system, the *superego*, as a means of incorporating society's values into the individual. The superego developed in two ways, through rewards and through punishment. Punishments given by others, parents in the first instance, resulted in the conscience which inhibited transgression of rules. Rewards resulted in the development of the positive side of the superego, the ego-ideal. This was responsible for endeavours to please parents, friends and self. When the superego was fully developed, parental and societal values were internalized so a person no

longer needed direct control from others but was self-controlled.

These three systems, the id, ego and superego, interacted with and counterbalanced each other in Freud's theory. The ego was a kind of executive, trying to satisfy the often conflicting demands of the id and the superego. Symptoms were said to arise when one or two systems contained an undue share of libidinal energy, so that someone who had too much energy in the conscience may be over-inhibited and fearful lest he or she be punished for allowing the id to express itself.

Many of the patients that Freud originally treated, who would now be classified as "neurotic", seemed to have an undue amount of energy invested in the superego. They showed hysterical symptoms such as paralysis for which no physical cause could be discovered. Freud found that by "working through" patients' emotions and helping them gain insight about themselves, these symptoms would disappear. "Working through" involved an exploration of childhood experiences, particularly those that were emotionally painful. This was considered to be difficult because many of these childhood memories were no longer conscious but could only be rediscovered through the use of analytic techniques.

Defence mechanisms

Freud argued that memories became unconscious because the ego, in its attempts to satisfy the demands of both the id and the superego, used *defence mechanisms*. All of these mechanisms involved distortion of some kind, either of reality or of one's own impulses. For example, *repression* might be an ego-response to a painful memory: the memory might be of being hurt by a parent as a child, but this would be unacceptable to a superego which demanded that parents should always be loved and respected in an unambivalent way. *Denial* was a refusal to accept the existence of a situation which was too painful to tolerate, such as inscribing "Only Sleeping" on a gravestone. *Rationalization* was the attempt to find socially and personally acceptable reasons for behaviour that would otherwise be threatening in some way. If, for instance, you have ever cheated in an exam (behaviour which might be unacceptable to the superego), the rationalization "Well, it's all right to cheat if they make the examinations so ridiculously difficult" might be used. Freud believed that these and the other defence mechanisms had two properties in common. First, they were present in everyone, not only those with psychological difficulties. Second, the individual was not aware that he or she was using them. These mechanisms were usually unconscious but could be brought into consciousness during psychoanalysis.

Thus, Freud understood his patients' difficulties in terms of different kinds of conflict between the id, ego and superego. For some patients, the problem was seen as being due to a damming-up of libidinal energy: failure to discharge the energy adequately left a residue that could result in a state of anxiety. The problem could be quite transitory and deep psychoanalysis not needed. For other patients, however, a detailed analysis of personality development was needed. The growing individual was said to pass through oral, anal, phallic and genital stages, each of which marked a particular kind of libidinal expression. During the oral phase, for example, libidinal energy was expressed through the mouth: this is exemplified by the first months of an infant's life, where sucking is the main activity. Gradually, libidinal energy was transferred to the anal zone, and so on.

When patients consulted Freud, he saw their difficulties as manifestations of incomplete or inadequate transfer of energy from one bodily zone to the next and the kinds of problems they presented as being a result of regression to this earlier phase. This model of psychological growth is analogous to the development of the foetus *in utero*. If an infant is born with some physical handicap, it is possible to specify the time when something went wrong in its development. For example, the limb defects caused by thalidomide were due to prescription of the drug during the critical weeks of limb growth in the foetus. Similarly, Freud attempted to discover what "went wrong" in a patient's psychological development by exploring the relevant phase. Someone who presented with an hysterical complaint (such as paralysis of a limb with no physical cause), for example, was said to have regressed to the phallic phase.

Developments in psychodynamic theory

It would be a mistake to consider psychodynamic theory and therapy as currently practised to be the same as Freud originally outlined. Although many of his concepts are still in common use, their meaning has been modified in the light of further clinical experience. Many of Freud's students broke with him early on, particularly over his emphasis on sex and aggression as motivators of behaviour, and there is now a wide range of psychodynamic theories.

During the 1940s and 1950s there was an increasing emphasis on the interpersonal aspects of personality and personality growth. The infant's first and intense relationship with a mother or mother-figure became all important. The quality of mothering was seen to be crucial, providing the context in which the child first begins to form ideas about the self and the world. If the world (i.e. the mother) were frustrating and inconsistent, then the infant was thought to internalize these experiences and use them as a basis for all later relationships. One result of the increased emphasis on the mother–infant relationship is the concern with attachment and maternal deprivation, a topic raised in Chapter 6.

Some psychiatrists and psychologists have gone so far as to question the validity and usefulness of the idea of personality residing solely within the person, arguing that it is a meaningful concept only when seen in relation to other people. The American psychiatrist H.S. Sullivan contended that "personality is the relatively enduring pattern of recurrent interpersonal situations which characterize a human life" (Ref. 16, pp. 110–111). According to this position, personality has to do with the individual's relationship to his or her world, particularly with other people, and psychological difficulties are mainly disturbances of communication in interpersonal relationships.

An important criticism of Freud's work concerns his view that many of the reports of sexual and physical abuse reported by his patients were fantasies. He argued that, since such reports were unlikely to have validity, they must be the result of unconscious processes and defence mechanisms.

Specifically, he argued that the reports must be indications of unconscious sexual wishes. We now know that sexual abuse is very prevalent (see Chapter 8), and Freud's misinterpretation of his patients' reports must be considered one of his most unhelpful conclusions.[17]

The humanistic approach

An important development to personal therapy was contributed by Carl Rogers.[18] While Freud placed much emphasis on the unconscious, which required the technical assistance of a psychoanalyst to explore, Rogers took a very different view, arguing that interpretations of feelings, thoughts and concerns were not necessary. For Rogers, the correct approach should be *non-directive*. In order for people to change, he believed it is necessary to develop an open and trusting relationship with another person. The aim was not to change the person in ways that the therapist thinks are correct, or to make interpretations about unconscious defence mechanisms, but to allow the patient an opportunity to explore their feelings and to develop in ways that are personally helpful.

Therapeutic principles

For Rogers, the three important principles in therapy were as follows:

1 The therapist should give *unconditional positive regard* or acceptance of the patient's statements, wishes and concerns without condemnation or castigation. Acceptance is regarded as a crucial aspect of this form of psychotherapy because as soon as someone is penalized for their feelings, these feelings cannot be explored satisfactorily.
2 *Empathy* with the client is needed, in order to understand their experiences, beliefs and feelings. When empathy is achieved, the therapist can provide his or her own impressions, thus providing important feedback.
3 The therapy must concentrate on the feelings experienced in the *here and now*, rather than on childhood experiences. This provides an opportunity for the client and therapist to explore the personal meanings of situations.

This does not mean that patients are simply allowed to talk while the therapist listens passively. Psychotherapy often involves a degree of confrontation and challenge. A therapist might challenge his patient with the observation that, while the patient is professing relaxation, he or she is moving or sitting uncomfortably. Or that he or she is talking about the death of a parent intellectually, without depth of feeling. Most psychotherapists would agree that giving advice is inappropriate, since this implies taking responsibility away from the patient. One aim of therapy is to help patients cope with their "problems of living" in ways of their own choosing, and this is impeded if the therapist advises or makes value-judgements.

The therapist's own personality

According to this approach, the development of techniques for helping patients is less important than the personal development of the therapist. As Truax and Mitchell[19] put it:

◆ Basically, the personality of the therapist is more important than techniques . . . [although they] can be quite potent in the hands of a therapist who is inherently helpful, and who offers high levels of empathetic understanding, warmth, genuineness . . . We want to emphasize the therapist-as-person before the therapist-as-expert or therapist-as-technician. We want to emphasize the commonality that psychotherapy has with other aspects of life. We want to emphasize the therapist as a viable human being. (Ref. 19, p. 341) ◆

Thus, psychotherapists in this tradition often place strong emphasis on the need for therapy for themselves as well as their clients. Just like everyone else, psychotherapists have problems in their relationships with others – parents, friends and spouse. They, too, have "problems of living" and these will affect their relationships with patients.

Psychotherapy can involve strong emotional reactions from clients, both positive and negative. It is not uncommon for a client to become very dependent on the therapist during treatment, for example, and the ways such dependency is dealt with may well affect the course of treatment. A therapist who fosters inordinate dependency may make it difficult for the client to progress or to end therapy. Anger is another commonly aroused feeling in therapy: a therapist who finds anger particularly distressing may not be able to help the client explore his or her feelings of hostility.

There seems little doubt that the way therapists approach patients has an effect on the success of an intervention, even when medication is also employed. Whitehorn and Betz[20] examined the importance of the therapist's approach in a psychiatric hospital by comparing seven doctors whose patients showed good improvement with seven doctors whose patients showed least improvement. Several differences were found between the two groups of physicians. The first group tended to see their patients' behaviour in terms of personal meanings, rather than a way of arriving at a descriptive diagnosis. When case histories were taken, the personal relevance of past experiences was considered and discussed. They worked towards goals which were oriented towards the perceptions of the patients, rather than curing symptoms, and they were more likely to build trusting relationships with their patients.

It is sometimes difficult to see how psychotherapy differs from a close friendship and, indeed, there are many similarities (see Box 4.1). Caring, attention and commitment are common to both, but they are different in psychotherapy compared with a friendship. Contact between therapist and patient is usually limited to hourly sessions (often once a week) and there is an inevitable difference in power. A degree of objectivity is important lest the therapist become so involved that he or she is unable to see where the relationship is floundering. The people involved in a friendship also have vested interests in keeping the relationship fairly constant, whereas the essence of psychotherapy is change. While few people in their everyday lives set out to end a relationship, an important aim in psychotherapy is to help the patient eventually cope with his or her difficulties without the assistance of the therapist.

BOX 4.1

Seeking help

Talking things over with friends is undoubtedly helpful, but there are times when people may feel the need to talk with someone who is not so involved in their lives, or when friends cannot seem to help. At such times, it can be useful to contact a counselling service.

There are many reasons why people hesitate to ask for professional assistance. Perhaps feelings of shame or concerns about stigma might dissuade someone from requesting assistance. There may be concerns that the difficulty may be seen as trivial or perhaps there is the uncertainty of not knowing what to expect. Counselling services emphasize the importance of acceptance and respect for each client, and seek to understand the client's concerns from the client's perspective. Problem-solving methods, where appropriate, may also be used.

Counselling services often have a waiting list, sometimes a few weeks long, but they always attempt to make an appointment as soon as possible after first being contacted.

Two quotations from Carl Rogers illustrate the viewpoint:

◆ The relationship which I have found helpful is characterized by a sort of transparency on my part, in which my real feelings are evident . . . I become a companion for my client, accompanying him in the frightening search for himself. (Ref. 18, p. 34)   ◆

◆ [S]o if I sense that I am feeling bored by my contact with this client and this feeling persists, I think I owe it to him and to our relationship to share this feeling with him. The same would hold if my feeling is one of being afraid of this client, or if my attention is so focused on my own problems that I can scarcely listen to him. But as I attempt to share these feelings I also want to be constantly in touch with what is going on in me . . . I also feel a new sensitivity to him now that I have shared this feeling which has been a barrier between us. I am very much more able to hear the surprise or perhaps the hurt in his voice because I have dared be real to him. I have let myself be a person - real, imperfect - in my relationship to him. (Ref. 21, p. 57)   ◆

Cognitive approaches

Psychologists who take a cognitive approach contend that personality is the way the person interprets the world. The assumptions and expectations made about the environment determine behaviour and reactions. Two examples of therapists who take this position are George Kelly and Aaron Beck.

George Kelly

Just as a scientist makes observations, has expectations about what will be found and modifies theories in the light of new results, Kelly suggested that people use the scientific method in their everyday lives. Individual theories about how the world works help the person to make sense of the environment and to make predictions about future events. For example, someone might have the theory that the world is a kind place and that everyone can be trusted. This theory could lead to the prediction that if money is left on a table in a public place, it would still be there when the owner returns. If the money is not there, the person might predict that someone found it and turned it in to a lost property office - a way of fitting the event into the theory. If the money could not be traced, the person may decide the theory is not a good one and change it. Not only do people have theories about the actions of others, they also have theories about themselves. To say "I'm not the sort of person who does that kind of thing" indicates a theory about oneself that will determine to some extent how events are perceived and which behaviour will be shown.

For Kelly, life is said to be like a series of experiments, where predictions are made and tested on an everyday basis. Each person holds theories about how life works, selectively attending to some phenomena and ignoring others. Scientists work first by inductive reasoning, looking for a general rule that explains or accounts for their observations. In the same way, infants initially perceive the world with no theory, but gradually build up a view which can be used to explain why people react to them in the way they do. If adults react negatively towards a child, he or she might conclude: "I am worthless" or "the world is essentially a hurtful place". These conclusions eventually become premises upon which behaviour and interpretations of others' behaviour are based.

Different people place emphasis on different aspects of their world. For one person, generosity may be important, for another, happiness. When asked to describe someone, the first person might be more likely to use a generosity–miserliness dimension, while the second would tend to select happiness–sadness. These descriptions are known as *personal constructs*. In order to make a person's constructs explicit, Kelly devised a technique which involved the individual naming three objects: three cars, for example, or three people. The person is then asked to say how two of the objects are similar to each other but different from the third. Through questioning, the terms in which the world is viewed can be discovered. Rowe[22] provides an illustration, in which a student is asked to name three cars:

◆Let us suppose the student names a Rolls-Royce, a Lamborghini and a Ford. Then the psychologist asks the student to tell him one way in which two of these are the same and the other different. The student could reply in a number of ways. He could say that two are fast and one is slow or two are elegant and one ordinary, or two are expensive and one cheap . . .

Suppose the student replies that two are fast and one slow. Then the psychologist asks, "Which would you prefer, the fast or the slow?"

Suppose the student replies "The fast". Then the psychologist asks, "Why is it important for you to have the fast one?"

"Because", the student might reply, "I like driving fast. I'm really feeling alive when I'm driving fast."

"Why", the psychologist will then ask, "is it important to feel really alive?"

"Because I want to make the most of my life while I'm here to enjoy it," says the student, thereby defining an aspect of his philosophy of life. (p. 14) ◆

The last statement made by the student seems to be an important rule for him and could be expected to influence his approach to many situations.

When applied to patients in therapy, the objects (or *elements* as they are termed) are often people (mother, father, self, for example) and the terms the patient chooses to distinguish between them are taken as important constructs. Additional elements can then be added – usually individuals important in the patient's life – and each categorized in terms of the previously elicited constructs, to provide a grid (a "repertory grid").

Figure 4.1 illustrates how this information can be presented. In this particular case, five elements were elicited – mother, father, sister, self and ideal self (how the patient wishes to be). There were also a number of constructs, including depressed, happy, careful with money. The distance between elements and constructs is taken as a measure of their similarity. Thus, the self is similar to the mother and both are careful about money. By contrast, the sister is quite differ-

ent, being happy rather than depressed and perceived as being more similar to the patient's ideal self than is the patient.

Kelly's therapy   This first step then leads to a consideration of how the patient might alter his or her perceptions. Personal change is difficult because change implies an alteration in the way the person sees the world, a frightening and anxiety-provoking prospect. This may be particularly so when "core" constructs are involved, those that deal specifically with perceptions of the self. The idea in this kind of therapy is to loosen the patient's theories so that new and more helpful ones can be formed. Conversation plays an important part, with the therapist challenging and adding to the patient's constructs, but Kelly advocated more active methods as well. The patient might be encouraged to "role play", being given a personality sketch of an individual and asked to act as if he were that person for a brief period:

◆ The client is to eat the kind of food they think this person would eat, read the books they would read, respond to other people in the way in which this person would respond, dream the dreams this person would dream, and try to interpret their experiences entirely in terms of this "person". It should be made clear to the client that this is a limited venture and that after a

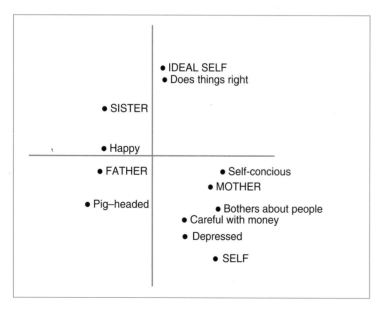

Figure 4.1   An illustration of a repertory grid analysis. (Reproduced from Rowe, D. (1988) *Choosing Not Losing*, with kind permission from Fontana Publishers)

fixed period it will come to an end and they will revert "to being themselves". It must be made clear that the fixed role is in no sense being set up as an ideal, it is merely a hypothesis for them to experiment with, a possibility for them to experience. During the short period of fixed role enactment the client sees the therapist frequently to discuss the interpretation of the fixed role, to consider the kind of experiences they are getting and to play the role with the therapist.

At the end of the fixed role enactment it is hoped that the client will have experienced behaviours from people of a kind not likely to have been elicited by their usual "self". They will have been forced into a detailed psychological examination of this imaginary person and thereby have been less centred on themselves. Above all, they may have begun to suspect that a person is self-inventing and that they are not necessarily trapped forever inside their own auto-biography and their own customary thought and behaviour. (Ref. 21, p. 14) ◆

An appealing aspect of the repertory grid technique is that it can be used to assess the progress and outcome of therapy. The distance between elements and their position relative to constructs might change, for example, so that the "self" matches the "ideal self" more closely. Furthermore, the actual constructs elicited by the grid may alter, providing further evidence of change.

Aaron Beck

Kelly's repertory grid technique provides a way of making explicit an individual's personal theories about the world. The notion of personal theories is also central to Beck's work but, unlike Kelly, Beck[23] argues that some theories are better than others, and that "erroneous" perceptions need to be altered during therapy. Just as a psychodynamic therapist would argue that no one has a perfect upbringing and that a certain amount of internal conflict is inevitable, Beck contends that everyone operates on some premises that are mistaken and that distort reality. The

problem for both the therapist and the patient is to find these premises, examine them, and to make changes if need be.

An analogy can be drawn here between the use of rules of grammar and the use of these premises. When talking, people do not consciously form their sentences. They do not have to take care to place the subject before the verb because this rule is so well learned. Similarly, when interpreting a situation, people do not consciously reflect on the rules they use in making sense of that event. But when learning a new language, it is necessary to consider what is being said very carefully, taking time to place the parts of speech in their correct order, for instance. In Beck's therapy, the patient is encouraged to consider the rules he or she uses: first, to see how premises can be self-defeating, and second, to experiment with new premises that had not been previously considered. Some of the mistaken assumptions that many people hold include:

1 In order to be happy I have to be successful in whatever I do.
2 If I make an occasional mistake it means I am inept.
3 If I don't take advantage of every opportunity I will regret it later.
4 My value as a person depends on what others think of me.

In particular, Beck has been interested in depression. This difficulty can be seen in many ways (for example, some psychologists consider it to be due to feelings of helplessness learned through lack of success in affecting the environment[24]), but Beck prefers to see it in terms of faulty premises.[25] He suggests that there is a triad of cognitive patterns which forces the person to view events in a particular way. The first component is the pattern of interpreting experiences in a negative way. Life is seen as a series of burdens and obstacles, all of which detract from the quality of life. This cognition is often associated with loss of friends, time or money. The second component involves negative self-perceptions – of being inadequate or unworthy in some way – and is often associated with self-reproach and self-castigation. The third component consists of negative views about the future, which seems unremittingly difficult and full of continuing deprivation.

Beck contends that these depressive cognitions serve to maintain the emotional difficulties in a circular fashion. If someone perceives the world in such a negative way they will not only selectively attend to depressing events but also interpret events in a negative way. The therapeutic enterprise thus becomes an attempt to question such negative views and substitute new, more helpful ways of viewing the world. If depressed people are given evidence to illustrate that they can, indeed, attain goals, or if they can be helped to re-evaluate their present performance, their depression might be lessened.[26] Results suggest that in severe forms of depression there is probably a biochemical basis, but for milder forms therapy based on this view might be more effective than chemotherapy.[27]

The problems of cures

A complex but fundamental point in psychotherapy concerns the problem of defining a successful outcome. For many physical illnesses, a patient is said to be cured when the presenting symptom is successfully treated. Similarly, some psychologists have taken removal of the presenting complaint as an indication that psychotherapy has been successful. If this criterion is used, then many patients improve without psychological care, and it has been argued that much of the improvement in patients who have received psychotherapy is due to this spontaneous remission.

Others contend that an emphasis on the disappearance of symptoms misses the point of psychotherapy. They are less interested in symptoms than in underlying difficulties and consider the quality of the therapist–patient relationship to be the important criterion of success. Rogers puts the problem in this way:

◆ [I]n my early professional years I was asking the question: How can I treat, or cure, this person? Now I would phrase the question in this way: How can I provide a relationship which this person may use for his own personal growth? (Ref. 21, p. 32) ◆

Anthony Storr, a therapist who is more closely identified with a traditional psychodynamic approach, makes a similar point:

◆ Some time ago I had a letter from a man whom I had treated some twenty-five years previously asking whether I would see . . . his daughter . . . In the course of his letter, he wrote as follows: "I can quite truthfully say that six months of your patient listening to my woes made a most important contribution to my lifestyle. Although my transvestitism was not cured my approach to life and to other people was re-oriented and for that I am most grateful. It is part of my life that I have never forgotten."

Looked at from one point of view, my treatment of this man was a failure. His major symptom, the complaint which drove him to seek my help, was not abolished. And yet I think it is clear that he did get something from his short period of psychotherapy which was of considerable value to him. A man does not write to a psychotherapist asking him to see his daughter, twenty-five years after his own treatment was over, using the terms employed in this letter, unless he believes that what happened during his period of treatment was important. (Ref. 28, p. 146) ◆

There are, however, some more objective ways of measuring the progress of therapy. One method, content analysis, categorizes the patient's statements according to certain criteria. For example, Raimy[29] divided patients' comments into three categories: (1) positive or approving self-references, (2) negative or disapproving self-references, and (3) ambivalent self-references. At the beginning of therapy most of the statements were of the second kind, indicating that the patients had negative views about themselves. As therapy progressed, there was a greater frequency of ambivalent statements. At the end of therapy, those patients who were considered to have improved gave positive self-references, suggesting a greater acceptance of themselves, while those who were considered not to have improved continued to present ambivalent or negative statements about themselves. It seemed from this study that improvement in psychotherapy was reflected in an increase in positive feelings about oneself. Thus, while it may be difficult to define what a "cure" may be for many patients in psychotherapy, there are measures that allow the progress of therapy to be monitored.

There has also been increasing interest in the processes involved in psychotherapy. Instead of concentrating on which type of therapy is most helpful, researchers have become more interested in the moment-by-moment changes which indicate progress.[30] Hill,[31] for example, argues that when therapists use self-disclosure, show approval and use paraphrasing, clients report great benefits.

Suggested reading

Two books which provide introductions to psychotherapy are Brown, D. and Peddar, J. (1979) *Introduction to Psychotherapy*, London: Tavistock, and Storr, A. (1979) *The Art of Psychotherapy*, London: Secker and Warburg. A text often used by counsellors is Egan, G. (1990) *The Skilled Helper*, Pacific Grove: Brooks Cole.

References

1. Allport, G. (1939) *Personality: A Psychological Interpretation*. Holt: New York.
2. Forer, B.R. (1949) The fallacy of personality validation: A classroom demonstration of gullibility. *Journal of Abnormal and Social Psychology* **44**: 118-123.
3. Cronbach, L.J. (1970) *Essentials of Psychological Testing*, 3rd edn. London: Harper and Row.
4. Jenkins, C.D., Rosenman, R.H. and Friedman, M. (1967) Development of an objective psychological test for the determination of the coronary-prone behaviour pattern in employed men. *Journal of Chronic Diseases* **20**: 371-379.
5. Sobel, H.J. and Worden, J.W. (1979) The MMPI as a predictor of psychosocial adaptation to cancer. *Journal of Consulting and Clinical Psychology* **47**: 716-724.
6. Eysenck, J.H. and Eysenck, S. (1976) *Psychoticism as a Dimension of Personality*. London: Hodder and Stoughton.
7. Thorp, J., Kennedy, B, Millar, K. and Fitch, W. (1993) Personality traits as predictors of trait anxiety prior to Caesarian section under regional anaesthesia. *Anaesthesia* **48**: 946-950.
8. Kahn, J.P., Kornfeld, D.S., Frank, K.A., Heller, S.S. and Horr, P.F. (1980) Type A behaviour and blood pressure during coronary artery bypass surgery. *Psychosomatic Medicine* **42**: 407-414.
9. Mathews, A. and Ridgeway, V. (1981) Personality and surgical recovery. *British Journal of Clinical Psychology* **20**: 243-260.
10. Rosenman, R.H., Brand, R.J., Jenkins, C.D., Friedman, M., Straus, R. and Wurm, M. (1975) Coronary heart disease in the Western Collaborative Group Study. *Journal of the American Medical Association* **233**: 872-877.
11. Dembroski, T.M. and MacDougall, J.M. (1982) Coronary-prone behaviour, social psycho-physiology and coronary heart disease. In: Eiser, J.R. (ed.) *Social Psychology and Behavioural Medicine*. Chichester: Wiley.
12. Mischel, W. (1973) Towards a cognitive social learning reconceptualisation of personality. *Psychological Review* **80**: 252-283.
13. Wicker, A.W. (1969) Attitudes versus actions. *Journal of Social Issues* **25**: 41-78.
14. Ellsworth, R.B., Foster, L., Childers, B., Arthur, G. and Kroeker, D. (1968) Hospital and community adjustment as perceived by psychiatric patients, their families and staff. *Journal of Consulting and Clinical Psychology, Monograph Supplement* **32**.
15. Ross, L. (1977) The intuitive psychologist and his shortcomings: Distortions in the attribution process. In: Berkowitz, L. (ed.) *Advances in Experimental Social Psychology 10*. New York: Academic Press.
16. Sullivan, H.S. (1953) *The Interpersonal Theory of Psychiatry*. New York: W.W. Norton.
17. Masson, J. (1989) *Against Therapy*. London: Collins.
18. Rogers, C.R. (1967) *On Becoming a Person*. London: Constable.
19. Truax, C. and Mitchell, K. (1991) Research in certain interpersonal skills in relation to process and outcome. In: Bergin, A. and Garfield, S. (eds) *Handbook of Psychotherapy and Behaviour Change*. New York: Wiley, pp. 299-344.
20. Whitehorn, J.C. and Betz, B.J. (1954) A study of psychotherapeutic relationships between physicians and schizophrenic patients. *American Journal of Psychiatry* **111**: 321-331.
21. Rogers, C.R. and Truax, C.B. (1967) The therapeutic conditions antecedent to change. In: Rogers, C.R. (ed.) *The Therapeutic Relationship and its Impact*. Madison: University of Wisconsin Press; © 1967 by the Board of Regents of the University of Wisconsin System.
22. Rowe, D. (1988) *Choosing Not Losing*. Fontana.

23. Beck, A. and Emery, E. (1985) *Anxiety Disorders and Phobias*. New York: Basic Books.
24. Garber, J. and Seligman, M. (eds) (1980) *Human Helplessness: Theory and Applications*. New York: Academic Press.
25. Beck, A.T., Rush, J., Shaw, B. and Emery, G. (1979) *Cognitive Therapy of Depression*. London: Wiley.
26. Loeb, A., Beck, A.T. and Diggory, J. (1971) Differential effects of success and failure on depressed and non-depressed patients. *Journal of Nervous and Mental Disease* **152**: 106-114.
27. Goldberg, D.(1982) Cognitive therapy of depression. *British Medical Journal* **284**: 143-144.
28. Storr, A. (1979) *The Art of Psychotherapy*. London: Secker and Warburg.
29. Raimy, V.C. (1948) Self-reference in counselling interviews. *Journal of Consulting Psychology* **12**: 153-163.
30. Stubbs, J. and Bozarth, J. (1994) The Dodo Bird revisited: a qualitative study of psychotherapy efficacy research. *Applied and Preventive Psychology* **3**: 109-120.
31. Hill, C. (1990) Exploratory in-session process research in individual psychotherapy: a review. *Journal of Consulting and Clinical Psychology* **58**: 288-294.

5
The Social Context

SUMMARY

The ways that people act are affected by the social and physical environment. There are some social situations in which people tend to react in undesirable ways, such as failing to help in emergencies, following unethical orders or conforming to others' views even when these are clearly mistaken. Aspects of the physical environment in psychiatric hospitals have been implicated in patient improvement. Research on physical impairments indicates that it is the ways in which health difficulties affect quality of life that are important for people with disabilities.

It has become clear that fuller understanding of such attributes as personality, memory and intelligence can be achieved by taking the social context into account. For example, an elderly person may be quite able in his or her own home but confused in a novel environment. Similarly, when an individual's IQ is considered, it is important to take not only his or her early environment into account but also the relationship with the examiner. The setting in which people act – which includes both the physical and social setting – has important influences on their behaviour. This chapter turns to some of the research that has investigated these influences. In order to understand the research bearing on this topic, it is helpful to begin by discussing three important concepts used by both sociologists and social psychologists: the ideas of norms, roles and socialization.

Norms, roles and socialization

People's beliefs about what behaviour is customary and proper in a society are termed *norms*. In different societies, different norms operate. There is, for example, a norm for children to take their father's surname in Western cultures but this is not the case in all societies. There are also differences between groups within a culture. In many factories, for example, there are norms about how quickly a worker should do his or her job. If the work is done too quickly or too slowly, sanctions might be applied against the individual. Norms change over time as well. There was a time when all medical students were expected to attend lectures in very formal clothes, but now this is not required.

Often there is a cluster of norms associated with a particular position in society. A doctor could be expected not only to be neatly dressed, but also to be technically competent, to be interested in patients, and to go out of his or her way to help in an emergency. The activities that fulfil such a cluster of norms are called a *role*. Examples of other roles are father, teacher, daughter and wife. There are several features of roles:

1 *Roles have a degree of latitude*. This means

that the norms connected with a role are not completely defined. Two people could play a role adequately in quite different ways. Although a doctor is expected to dress neatly when with patients, there is a wide variety of clothing which is acceptable; a teacher could teach in many different ways, and so on.

2 *Roles change over time*. This is another way of saying that norms change. For example, society's expectations of women have altered considerably during this century, from the expectation that they should not undertake strenuous physical and mental exercise to the belief that they are at least as competent as men.

3 *Roles are often complements*. To say that someone is a teacher implies that there are students to teach. A person cannot be a doctor unless there are patients, nor can someone be a parent unless there are children. In order for an individual to perform a role, there must be someone playing the complementary role.

4 *Different roles sometimes conflict*. An individual is likely to play many different roles in society; sometimes a student, sometimes a friend, sometimes a son or daughter. Each role has associated norms which can be in conflict. A person may be both a doctor and a husband or wife, and there are times when expectations from patients and a spouse are incompatible. Within a role there may also be conflicting expectations. Where all members of a family have the same doctor, the treatment of one member may affect others, as when a young daughter seeks contraceptive advice. It is not simply a question of what might be right or wrong in such situations, but also a problem of conflicting expectations and how these are handled.

The process of learning, understanding and fulfilling norms and roles is a vital part of social development. During this process, people become increasingly aware of others' expectations and more skilful at fulfilling them. Known as *socialization*, this learning continues throughout life. There are expectations involved in being a patient, for example, so that when someone is admitted to hospital he or she will experience a period of uncertainty until the norms are dis-

covered and the role can be enacted. When medical students enter the wards for the first time, they often report a similar sense of uncertainty until they find out what is expected of them. Thus, socialization can be seen in terms of predictability. Once a person is familiar with norms and is adept at acting roles, his or her behaviour will be predictable to others, and if everyone has the same familiarity with requirements, then the way people act will be mutually predictable. The patient will have a good idea of how the doctor will behave and the doctor will be correct in his or her expectations of how the patient will act.

Social influences

In some situations, the actions of other people can elicit behaviour which may seem unlikely or surprising. Three specific aspects are considered here. The first, termed "bystander intervention", concerns people's reluctance to intervene in emergencies. People's willingness to perform unkind and undesirable actions when asked to do so in an authoritative way forms the second topic. Third, the tendency for some people to conform to others' erroneous views, rather than to voice their own opinions, is examined.

Bystander intervention

Research into the circumstances in which people intervene to give help to others was motivated by a particularly nasty murder in New York City in 1964. A woman was killed in the street while a large number of people in nearby apartments could hear her screams and cries for help, but made no attempt to help, not even by telephoning the police. The assault took place over more than an hour and her distress was obvious. Reactions to this incident included condemnation of the residents and warnings of the imminent breakdown of society, but it also demonstrated to social psychologists that they lacked knowledge about how people react in such situations.

Usually this topic has been explored by staging incidents when someone appears to need assistance. The approach has been to recruit study participants on the basis of taking part in a psychology experiment, but they are misled as to its purpose. They might be told that the study simply involves filling out questionnaires, but it actually has an ulterior purpose. At some point the experimenter finds an excuse to leave the participants alone in the room. After some minutes, an emergency is staged – sounds of someone falling in the next room, or smoke coming from under a door. When do the participants do something about it, either trying to find the experimenter or entering the room where the incident has occurred, and when do they fail to intervene?

Diffusion of responsibility

One possible factor was suggested through interviews with the witnesses of the New York murder. Many mentioned that they had thought "someone else" would contact the police, so that there was little need for them to do so. It was as if the responsibility for helping was diffused, but since everyone made this assumption in the end nothing was done. In order to test the importance of this factor, Darley and Latané[1] led their study participants to believe that they were to take part in a group discussion about personal problems. To avoid embarrassment, they were told, each person in the study would sit alone in a private booth and talk with others through a microphone, each in turn. There would be several rounds of discussion and the experimenter said that he would not be listening in order to maintain their privacy. One group of participants was told that they would discuss their problems with one other person, a second group was told that two others would be taking part, and a third group that there would be five others. Thus, different participants thought that they were in groups of varying sizes.

In fact, there was only ever one person in the experiment. The others' voices were actually only on tape, but the participants in the study did not realize this. On the first round of discussion, one of the voices indicated that he was prone to having epileptic seizures. When it was his turn on the second round, he made a few calm comments but then he began to thrash about. It seemed that he might be having a seizure.

The experimenters reasoned that if diffusion of responsibility were an important factor in

bystander intervention, then participants who *believed* themselves to be in a large group would be less likely to leave their booth and give aid than those who believed they were part of a small group. This hypothesis was supported: 85 per cent of those who thought themselves to be the only ones listening to the seizure sought help, 62 per cent of those who thought there was one other person listening who could give aid, and only 31 per cent of those who thought there were four others. Thus, the decision to give aid was related to the number of others who were thought available to give assistance.

Of course, it could be argued that some people did not give help because they were sceptical about the genuineness of the incident. It was, after all, a psychology experiment. However, at the end of the study all participants were interviewed and none thought that the emergency was faked. Besides, there was no apparent reason why participants in the large group condition would be more sceptical than those in the small group condition. Nor was there any evidence that those who did not help were callous, uncaring individuals – at the end of the experiment when they were asked why they had not helped, they reported feeling very upset by the experience.

Interpreting the incident

Interviews with the participants pointed towards another possible reason why aid was not given. Several said they were unsure that the situation was, in fact, an emergency. There was some ambiguity in their minds about whether help was actually required. It seemed that since emergencies are very rare in most people's lives, it takes some time to make sense of what is going on before action is taken. In order to test the importance of interpretation, Darley and Latané introduced a confederate into an experiment. They reasoned that in times of ambiguity people look to the reactions of others to help them make sense of what is happening, and if this confederate was instructed not to react to an incident, the study participants would be less likely to give help.

In this experiment, they constructed three conditions. In one, the participants were left alone in a room; in a second condition two participants who were strangers to each other were left together; and in the third the participant was placed with a confederate. All were told that they were part of a market survey study and the experimenter was said to be a representative of the company. After she asked the participants to fill out several questionnaires, she indicated that she would do some work next door and would return in 10–15 minutes. They saw her go into the next room, screened from them by a curtain:

◆ While they worked on their questionnaires, subjects heard the representative moving around in the next office, shuffling papers, and opening and closing drawers. After about four minutes, if they were listening carefully, they heard her climb up on a chair to get a book from the top shelf. Even if they were not listening carefully, they heard a loud crash and a woman's scream as the chair fell over. "Oh my God, my foot . . .," cried the representative. "I . . . I . . . can't move . . . it. Oh, my ankle. I . . . can't . . . can't . . . get . . . this thing off . . . me." She moaned and cried for about a minute longer, getting gradually more subdued and controlled. Finally, she muttered something about getting outside, knocked the chair around as she pulled herself up, and limped out, closing the door behind her. (Ref. 2, p. 58) ◆

In order to ensure that everyone heard the same accident, it was recorded on tape, but they had no way of knowing this. While the accident occurred, the confederate in the third condition was instructed to look up, to stare quizzically at the curtain, shrug his shoulders and then return to the questionnaire, thus indicating that he did not consider the accident serious enough to intervene. Intervention could have been made in several ways in this study – by going into the room, by looking for help or, simply, by calling through the curtain to ask the representative if she were hurt.

The results supported the hypothesis that interpretation was significant. In the first (alone) condition, some 70 per cent of the participants intervened. When two strangers were working together, the number fell to 40 per cent. This is both a replication and an extension of the previous study. In the third (confederate) condition,

only 8 per cent of the participants made an attempt to help: by seeing someone not react to the incident they were apparently less inclined to treat it as an emergency which merited assistance.

Other studies, and studies in naturalistic settings as well, have supported the influence of these two factors. In some situations there may be little ambiguity about the meaning of an incident (as in the case of the murder) and in such cases diffusion of responsibility may be significant. In others, it may be difficult for the people involved to interpret the incident. Here the reactions of others may be important. One additional point which can be made about these studies, relevant to other work in social psychology, is that once such findings become widely known, the effect itself may no longer be present. The reactions of people who had just seen a film describing this research were compared with those of people who had not seen the film to a staged incident on the street: more of the people who had just seen the film gave assistance. Psychology can reflect back and influence society as well as provide clues about its operation.

Obedience to authority

Like the research on bystander intervention, that on obedience to authority was motivated by real-life experiences, in particular the murder of Jews during the Second World War. Milgram[3] sought to gain some understanding of why so many German officials had taken part in the Holocaust. Were they abnormal in some way, or did their claim that they were only obeying orders have any validity? Milgram was interested in the relationship between obedience and authority.

In his experiments, study participants were recruited from a wide range of age and social groups, so that his results cannot be said to apply only to particular groups such as university students. The participants were told that the experiment involved memory processes, testing the theory that people learn more quickly when they are punished for making a mistake. The participant's job was to help someone to learn some paired-associate words. For example, when the word "blue" was given, the word "box" was to be supplied. If this association was not recalled, the learner was to be given a shock by the participant and this shock was to be more intense the next time an error was made. Each participant saw the learner strapped into a chair and was then seated in front of a shock-generator. This had a total of 30 switches, labelled from 15 volts to 450 volts. The intensity of these shocks was also indicated, from "slight shock" to "danger, severe shock". The shocks were said to be painful, but not to cause any permanent tissue damage.

Actually, the learner was a confederate and the shock-generator was fake. The confederate was instructed to protest if the level was increased by the participants, then to shout and scream, and finally to fall silent. At 120 volts, for example, the learner called out that the shocks were becoming painful, and at 180 volts there were cries of "I can't stand the pain". The experimenter was to prod the participant if he baulked at giving the shocks, making such comments as "Please continue" and "The experiment requires that you continue", and saying that he would accept all responsibility for the consequences. But there was no physical coercion and no promise of greater payment. The experimental question was to see how far up the shock levels the participants would go before they refused to obey the experimenter.

Before this study, Milgram canvassed colleagues, friends and psychiatrists for their predictions of the results. They felt that only a minority of participants would continue to obey the experimenter for long and that only a tiny number would go up to the 450 volt level. You might wonder if you would agree to take part in the study at all. Nevertheless, 25 of the 40 participants went all the way to 450 volts, despite the apparent pain involved. Was this due to malevolent or sadistic personalities? It seemed not, since most showed clear signs of distress and conflict, despite their obedience.

In other experiments, the social context was shown to have an effect. When the subject and learner sat side by side, only 16 of 40 went to 450 volts, and when the subject was actually responsible for placing the learner's hand on an electric grid, only 12 out of 40. Other factors had less effect. Many of the studies were performed within the auspicious confines of Yale University

and it was thought that perhaps this may have had an influence. However, when the laboratory was transferred to an old building in the centre of the city, little difference was found.

Milgram suggested that such a situation reduces the effectiveness of the conscience. When working in an organizational context, people often suppress their own values to those of the social situation. The importance of the roles we take on in situations was illustrated by another very well-known study, in which students were asked to pretend that they were either guards in a prison, or inmates. Zimbardo[4] converted the basement of one of the buildings at Stanford University to resemble a prison, and the participants in the study wore uniforms according to their status. Originally, he planned that the experiment would continue for 2 weeks, but it had to be discontinued after only 5 days because of the behaviour of the guards. They were not allowed to use any physical violence, but they began to take their roles rather too seriously by using psychological brutality. For example by making it a "privilege" to use the toilet. Five of the prisoners had to be taken out of the study early because they were developing signs of acute anxiety and depression. Some of the characteristics of Zimbardo's study resemble the ways that some cults operate (see Box 5.1).

The relevance of these principles of obedience and role-taking to medical care has been illustrated by a study of nursing staff and their relationship to doctors. Here, the researchers were interested in whether or not nursing students would comply with an order from a doctor that should not have been obeyed according to the hospital's rules. While on the ward, the nurse received a telephone call from the ward doctor requesting her to give some tablets. There were two problems with this call. First, it was against hospital policy for medication to be given on the basis of a telephone call: the doctor should have signed the order before the drug was given. Second, the doctor requested that twice the maximum daily dosage should be given, as it was stated on the package.

When a nurse received the call, she was unobtrusively observed to see if she did, in fact, intend to give the medication (she was stopped before it was administered). Of the 22 nurses studied,

Cults

The term "cult" has come to have a very negative connotation, implying the use of coercion and deception by a charismatic leader to control, mislead and often sexually exploit individuals. Barker[5] provides a balanced and useful description of what she calls New Religious Movements in which she disputes this stereotype, finding that there is a wide variety of such movements, some of which can provide considerable benefit for many people. Nor, she argues, can generalizations be made about the type of people who are attracted to such movements. Although some movements are exploitative, others offer a certainty about the world which can appeal to someone when they feel confused about their future and who has high ideals.

Barker notes several characteristics of movements that may indicate they are potentially dangerous. These have many similarities to the prison study by Zimbardo:

- The movement cuts itself off (either geographically or socially) from the rest of society.
- A convert is encouraged to become increasingly dependent on the movement.
- The movement draws sharp boundaries between "them" and "us", "good" and "bad".
- Important decisions about converts' lives are made by others.
- The leader claims divine authority for their actions and demands.
- The movement pursues a single goal in a single-minded manner.

21 intended to fulfil the request. This result could not have been due simply to their being unaware of the inappropriate dosage, since most later said that they realized the discrepancy.[6] Milgram concluded from his work that the participants in his study were willing to apply the electric shocks because the experimenter said that he would accept responsibility for the consequences. A similar process may have been operating here. It seems that obedience to authority happens in naturally occurring situations as well as in the psychology laboratory.

These studies also indicate that people are not particularly good at predicting how they would behave in unusual circumstances. Just as you might predict that you would, of course, give help to someone who had an accident or would refuse to give apparently painful shocks in a psychology experiment, so too did another sample of student nurses predict that they would refuse to obey the doctor's orders if they were inappropriate. Of 21 nurses who were not involved in the study, all said that they would not give the medication. Assuming that these nurses were no different than the ones who participated, and there was no reason to suspect they were, it seems likely that they, too, would have complied under the circumstances.

Conformity

Another example of social influence on behaviour is provided by a series of studies performed by Asch.[7] He presented his study participants with two cards with lines on them as shown in Figure 5.1. The participants' task was to choose which of the lines shown on the right-hand card was the same length as the line on the left-hand card. On the face of it this appears an easy and

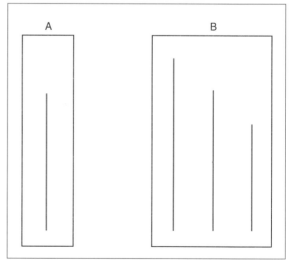

Figure 5.1 Materials similar to those used in Asch's experiments. Participants were asked to choose which line on the right-hand card is the same length as that on the left-hand card.

The ethics of deception

These studies on bystander intervention, obedience to authority and conformity involved deceiving the people in the studies. There were two kinds of deception. One kind involved the use of "confederates". These were people who had been instructed to behave in certain ways, yet participants believed they were in the experiment just like themselves. The other kind involved actively misleading participants as to the purpose of the experiment. They were told that the study was about one thing (e.g. memory processes) when actually it involved something much more powerful. Can deceptions of these kinds ever be justified?

There has been much discussion in the literature about the ethical implications of such studies. On the one hand, it is difficult to see how some of this research could have been performed in any other way. Since these studies have important social implications – we now know that ordinary people can act in very harmful ways given certain circumstances – it can be argued that deception is justified in certain cases.

On the other hand, they can have important psychological consequences for the participants – some became distressed and remained so afterwards – and many psychologists argue that such experiments bring the subject of psychology into disrepute. Perhaps you would now be unlikely to volunteer for a psychology experiment: you might be reassured to know that Milgram's experiments and many others involving deception would not be approved by a research ethics committee these days.

unambiguous task. However, Asch was able to show that under some circumstances many people would give an incorrect answer if several other people did so first.

Typically, one participant would give his or her report after four others (confederates) had given theirs. On the first few rounds of estimates, all would go well with no discrepancies. But on occasional rounds the other four would give a wrong answer. Faced with this clear discrepancy, the question was what would the participant do? To some extent, it seemed to depend on the individual. Some never conformed, others almost always. Over a large number of trials and many experiments, conformity was found on about 35 per cent of test trials. The probability of conformity could be influenced by several factors, but most especially by the presence of one other person who did not conform, where the incidence was reduced to only about 6 per cent.

It is possible to make both too much and too little of Asch's studies. Observations of the participants indicated that they were under considerable strain, suggesting that they were aware of the oddity of the situation. However, many situations in everyday life are very ambiguous, which might result in conformity. Others' responses may be important in resolving such situations, whether they be the interpretation of X-rays, the usefulness of medication for a particular patient, or diagnosis. The confederates in Asch's studies can be considered to have provided information about what kind of answer was appropriate in the situation. When, for example, diagnosis is problematic, as it often is, conformity with the opinions provided by other physicians may be significant in influencing treatment.

Most of these studies on social influences have been conducted within the laboratory and could therefore be dismissed as artificial. However, these results are similar to what happens in "real life" in many ways: often people do not respond to emergencies when they occur and this is very similar to what the experiments suggest would happen. Similarly, people are often obedient and conform in rather surprising ways in situations when someone is in authority.

Environmental influences

The research discussed so far has emphasized the influence of other people on behaviour, but some psychologists have concentrated on the effects of the *physical* environment. One issue is in the design of hospitals. During the nineteenth century, many psychiatric hospitals were built on the outskirts of cities. The idea behind this was that patients should be taken away from the stresses and strains of city life and placed in quiet, isolated surroundings. Besides serving custodial functions, these conditions were thought to be conducive to rest and recovery. Many of the hospitals were large, having 1000 patients or more. Families were not encouraged to visit (if only by the distance involved). Certain policies within these hospitals were advocated. Patients' personal possessions were taken away and hospital clothing issued. This was designed to reduce the number of reminders for the patients of their past. These measures appear harsh, but for some people at least they were based on high ideals and therapeutic intentions.

However, there was an unfortunate by-product of this treatment, in that many patients became dependent on the institution and indifferent, or even antagonistic, to leaving. They were said to be *institutionalized* and it became difficult to integrate such people back into the community. It was as if they came to consider the hospital their permanent home.

One result of this problem of institutionalization is a change in policy towards treatment procedures within existing buildings. During the 1950s and 1960s there were many attempts to minimize the difference between hospital and community. Personal possessions were allowed and more patient privacy provided. Wing and Brown[8] described how they examined three psychiatric hospitals, known as A, B and C. Hospital A was considered the most progressive, allowing most of the patients personal possessions (for example, their own clothes instead of institutional ones, their own toothbrushes, a locker to keep books, etc.) and opportunities to engage in meaningful constructive work. Hospital B shared some of these characteristics, but there were also instances of an institutional atmosphere. Not many patients, for example, possessed scissors or a mirror, and fewer baths were screened from onlookers. Hospital C was considered the least progressive, with only few activities provided, little or no privacy and few personal possessions being allowed. The staff of this hospital were also more restrictive, the patients requiring permission to leave the ward or to use the kitchen to make a drink.

Wing and Brown then took several measures of the patients' behaviour. They found that hospital C had more severely ill patients, a result that could not be attributed to condition at admission. These patients were more likely to be socially withdrawn, isolated and passive, as well as to spend much of their time "doing nothing". They were also more likely to want to stay in the hospital. There seemed to be a gradation between the hospitals, so that these observations were more common in hospital C than B than A.

Although this study was correlational, Wing and Brown's suggestion that differences in patient behaviour were due to the effects of the hospital environment was given further support when they examined the hospitals over a period of time. As physical conditions improved, so too did the clinical condition of the schizophrenic patients. In two hospitals, conditions improved and then deteriorated again: the patients' conditions showed a similar pattern. The lack of privacy and the paucity of organized activities were thought to be responsible for these effects. Other studies have implicated drab colours on the walls and large multi-occupant bedrooms as further deleterious factors. Wing and Brown[9] argued that many of the features associated with the condition of schizophrenia were due to the under-stimulation presented by these large institutions.

Changing the environment

Influenced by such research, there have been several attempts at changing the atmosphere in psychiatric hospitals over the last decades. For example, Holahan and Saegert[10] reported a study on the remodelling of a psychiatric ward. In one hospital they were able to find two nearly identical wards: in both the walls were dirty and the furniture was worn and uncomfortable. One ward was chosen for improvement. The walls were painted with bright colours and new furniture purchased. In order to create privacy, the large dormitory was divided into more personal two-bed sections and small areas of the large day ward were informally sectioned off to provide the opportunity for intimate talk. The second ward acted as a control so that the effects of the remodelling could be evaluated. Patients were randomly placed in one of the two wards and 6 months later the investigators returned.

At this later time, patients in the remodelled ward were found to be significantly more sociable with other residents, with staff and with visitors and less likely to be passive and isolated, suggesting that the differences in environment had effects on their behaviour. The researchers also took some measures of attitudes towards the ward and correlated these with the patients' activity levels. Those patients who most liked the remodelled ward tended to be those who were most active, whereas those who most liked the control ward were those who were least active (especially those who slept much of the time). Since hospital staff place a high value on social contact, these results indicate that providing bright colours and opportunities for privacy are conducive to good treatment.

Other studies have shown significant improvements in patients' behaviour by making small alterations, such as changes in seating arrangements. In one study, all the chairs were originally lined up beside one another along the walls. In order to talk, the patients had to pivot 90 degrees and it was difficult to hold a conversation with more than one person at a time. The arrangement of chairs was then altered, so that they were grouped around small tables holding magazines. As a measure of the effect of this change, the number and length of conversations between patients were recorded. As shown in Table 5.1, the new arrangement was associated with more interactions, both brief and sustained, than the old one.[11]

While these findings are suggestive, they are not conclusive. The behaviour of the patients in the altered wards may have changed not because of the character of the new conditions but because they were made to feel special simply because changes had taken place. The staff might also have felt that they were special and might have made more effort to socialize with and help patients. Nevertheless, it has become clear that improvements in the physical environment and ward policies have important effects on behaviour.

Community care

There is increasing resistance amongst those who care for people with psychiatric illnesses and severe learning disabilities against the use of large hospitals set apart from the community. Not only does this old policy seem to be counterproductive in terms of caregiving, it also stigmatizes the patients who live in the institutions. Being set apart physically makes contact with community facilities more difficult, providing less opportunity for the development of skills required to live independently. Equally, "ordinary" people rarely encounter the residents of such institutions and thus have little opportunity to begin to understand their problems. Accordingly, current policies stress the value of housing patients in smaller units sited within the community. Although there can be opposition to the provision of sheltered housing in residential communities, this may be due more to the incongruous buildings that are often constructed than to the residents themselves.[12]

Thus, research on the effects of the environment in hospitals has shown that patient improvement is strongly affected by the social and physical setting. Patients in long-stay hospitals may become institutionalized if there is a lack of privacy and opportunity to have control over their behaviour. Partly as a result of research in this area, there is now a greater emphasis on providing a more stimulating and "home-like" atmosphere.

Some researchers have taken a broader view of the effects of the environment, being concerned with how changes in living conditions can have significant effects on the health of the general population. Indeed, it has been argued that such changes are more important than medical interventions. McKeown,[13] for example, provides

Table 5.1 Number of brief and sustained interactions per day when seating arrangements in a psychiatric ward were changed as described in the text (Reproduced from Sommer, R. (1969) *Personal Space*, by permission of Prentice-Hall, Inc., Englewood Cliffs, New Jersey.)

| | Number of interactions | |
	Brief	Sustained
Old arrangement	47	36
New arrangement	73	61

evidence from various sources that the most notable improvements in health care over the last century or so are due to changes in sewage treatment, diet and housing rather than the scientific and technological advances of medicine.

Disability

The previous sections of this chapter have shown how knowledge of certain social and physical aspects of a situation can help predict how someone will behave. This section considers some aspects of disability.

Impairment, disability and handicap

It can be very useful to distinguish between these three terms because it helps us to understand the issues involved and the difficulties faced by many people in our society.[14]

- *Impairment* is the term used for the actual physical or psychological difficulty. Examples of impairments include a broken leg, loss of teeth, or a psychological phobia such an intense fear of dogs.
- *Disability* refers to the kinds of *activities* that cannot be accomplished because of the impairment. Someone with a broken leg may not be able to drive a car, someone who has lost their natural teeth may not be able to eat certain foods, and someone with a dog phobia may be unable to walk the streets unaccompanied.
- *Handicap* refers to way in which such disabilities affect social *roles*. A travelling salesman who cannot drive a car may not be able to earn a living, a person wearing dentures may be unwilling to accept invitations to dinner parties because she or he would be too embarrassed if certain foods were offered, and a person with a dog phobia may be unable to attend school because this involves the possibility of meeting a dog during the journey.

The meaning of a particular impairment or disability is unlikely to be the same for two individuals. It is possible that two people could have the same impairment and disability but not the same handicap. For one person it might mean a relatively minor change to lifestyle, but for another it could be a major adjustment. For example, a teacher could be inconvenienced by a broken leg, but it might not affect his or her livelihood, while a community nurse, who relies on self-transportation, might have to take time off work.

The medical and lay views of diseases can be very different. They can be different not only in terms of understanding the causes of the difficulty, but also in terms of severity. For example, in one study a dermatologist was asked to rate the severity of patients' psoriasis on a seven-point scale. Using the same scale, the patients themselves were asked to rate the severity of their disease: when the ratings were compared, they correlated very poorly, indicating that the dermatologist and the patients were using different criteria to make their assessments.

The patients' ratings of severity were closely related to the social effects of their disease. Questions covering the effects of their psoriasis on sexual relationships, using communal bathing facilities and going out socially correlated very well with severity from their point of view. It seemed that for the dermatologist severity involved clinical signs, whereas for the patients it involved social consequences.[15] From the medical point of view severity might be measured in terms of the size of a lesion or the extent of a growth, but from a patient's point of view it is the real and potential threat to their life routines which is important.

Social effects of impairments

It can be difficult to appreciate the important and severe consequences of major impairments on social and psychological well-being. Most students who enter medicine and the other helping professions are without significant impairments, and although many people will have relatives or friends who are impaired, it is rare to have a full understanding of the social implications.

Phillips[16] has provided an analysis of the personal experiences of people with disabilities. She argues that modern Western societies reinforce the view that people with impairments are equated to "damaged goods" – being less valuable than people who are not affected by disease or injury. Phillips interviewed several individuals with a variety of physical health difficulties, being interested in how they perceived the reactions of others. Two themes were common: difficulties in obtaining employment and difficulties in developing sexual relationships.

People with disabilities have more difficulty in obtaining employment than those without a disability. Graham *et al.*[17] measured discrimination by looking at employers' responses to two fictitious applications for secretarial jobs. The applications were matched so that that they were similar in terms of personal characteristics, qualifications and experience. The applications differed only in that one was from a "disabled" candidate and the other was not. The letter identified the person as disabled by the following addition: "I should explain that I am a person with cerebral palsy and am registered disabled. However, as I think my education and work history show, my disability has not restricted my working life". Despite the similarity in all other respects, the non-disabled applicant was 50 per cent more likely to receive an invitation to an interview. When the employers' replies were analysed, some held very paternalistic attitudes:

◆ We were interested to read your CV and work record but feel that work in this very pressurized environment with long hours and a great deal of travel and unsocial hours would not be in your interest. However we will retain your details and if anything less demanding arises we will endeavour to get in touch.   ◆

In the real world, disabled candidates would usually be aware only of the rejections and not of the unequal treatment, but Phillips quotes one candidate who recognized that his judgement of his own capabilities was often mistrusted:

❝ The thing that kills me is that I've been interviewed for jobs where the employer will say 'How are you going to do the job?' And I respond, 'Number one, if I can't do it, I'm going to tell you I can't do it.' It's like they almost don't believe that you know your own body and your own self. (p. 853) ❞

The notion that impairment means damaged goods can also mean that there are difficulties in developing sexual relationships. Many of Phillips' interviewees recounted instances where their sexual attractiveness was questioned by others, including family and friends:

❝ It got rougher when dating became a big thing because you just didn't date a blind person. And even if you could get a girl to go out with you she'd be ridiculed by all her girlfriends. Once I got this girl to go out with me. The father informs me that when I get into the house that 'No daughter of mine is going to date anyone who is less than a whole man'. And he says to me 'You're not leaving the house with my daughter'. (p. 852)   ❞

❝ I had an aunt tell me once when I was applying for a secretarial job and they asked me if I was married. My aunt said 'They probably thought that you were good to hire because they know you wouldn't get married or pregnant.' (p. 853)   ❞

Such reactions are likely to have important effects on self-esteem, a topic discussed further in Chapter 7.

Quality of life

Recently, there has been considerable interest in the notion of "quality of life", which takes not only physical health into account, but also emotional, personal and social well-being.[18] The emotional domain includes levels of anxiety, depression, sleeping disturbances and psychological adjustment to an illness. The personal domain could include ability to wash, dress and generally take care of one's hygiene, while the social domain includes the maintenance of friendships, ability to work, have satisfying sexual relationships and being able to engage in leisure activities.

While there is no objective measure of quality of life, since it is the individual's view and satisfaction which are crucial, there are many scales designed to measure these aspects of well-being. Some of the psychological scales have been mentioned in earlier chapters, such as the Hospital Anxiety and Depression Scale,[19] the General

Health Questionnaire,[20] and measures of pain (Chapter 10). Some measures of disability can be used for a wide variety of medical conditions, such as the Katz Index of Daily Living,[21] which is a scale of physical independence, and the Spitzer Quality of Life Index,[22] which involves a professional's ratings of a person's abilities in a variety of situations. Other scales are designed to measure quality of life for people with specific difficulties. For example, the Rotterdam Symptom Checklist[23] is designed to assess the impact of cancer and treatments for cancer on functioning and well-being, while the Dermatology Life Quality Index[24] is appropriate for measuring the impact of skin diseases.

Most clinical trials that examine the efficacy of different treatments now include quality of life assessments in their designs. It is important to know whether a drug, which might be clinically very efficacious, has any side-effects that interfere with quality of life. In clinical use, there might be a trade-off between clinical efficacy and social/psychological consequences.

Suggested reading

There are many books which examine specific illnesses from psychological and sociological points of view. For a more detailed look at the psychology of symptoms and illness, see Sanders, G.S. and Suls, J. (eds) (1982) *Social Psychology of Health and Illness*, London: Lawrence Erlbaum. Cherulik, P. (1993) *Applications of Environment–Behaviour Research*, Cambridge: Cambridge University Press, outlines some of the ways in which psychology can inform the way physical environments are designed.

References

1. Darley, J.M. and Latané, B. (1968) Bystander intervention in emergencies: diffusion of responsibility. *Journal of Personality and Social Psychology* **8**: 377-383.
2. Latané, B. and Darley, J.M. (1970) *The Unresponsive Bystander*. New York: Appleton-Century-Crofts.
3. Milgram, S. (1974) *Obedience to Authority: an Experimental View*. New York: Harper and Row.
4. Haney, C., Banks, W. and Zimbardo, P. (1973) Inter-personal dynamics in a simulated prison. *International Journal of Criminology and Penology* **1**: 69-79.
5. Barker, E. (1989) *New Religious Movements*. London: HMSO.
6. Hofling, C.K., Brotzman, E., Dalrymple, S., Graves, N. and Pierce, C. (1966) An experimental study in nurse–physician relationships. *Journal of Nervous and Mental Disease* **143**: 171-180.
7. Asch, S.E. (1951) Effects of group pressure upon the modification and distortion of judgments. In: Guetzhow, H. (ed.) *Groups, Leadership and Men*. Pittsburgh: Carnegie Press.
8. Wing, J.K. and Brown, G.W. (1961) Social treatment of chronic schizophrenia: a comparative survey of three mental hospitals. *Journal of Mental Science* **107**: 847-861.
9. Wing, J.K. and Brown, G.W. (1970) *Institutionalism and Schizophrenia*. Cambridge: Cambridge University Press.
10. Holahan, C. and Saegert, S. (1973) Behavioural and attitudinal effects of large-scale variation in the physical environment of psychiatric wards. *Journal of Abnormal Psychology* **82**: 454-462.
11. Sommer, R. (1969) *Personal Space*. Englewood Cliffs, New Jersey: Prentice-Hall.
12. Dalgleish, M. and Matthews, R. (1980) Living as others do. *Community Care* 26 June: 18-21.
13. McKeown, T. (1979) *The Role of Medicine*. Oxford: Basil Blackwell.
14. World Health Organization (1980) *Impairment, Disability and Handicap*. Geneva: WHO.
15. Root, S., Kent, G. and Al-Abadie, M. (1994) The relationship between disease severity, disability and psychological distress in patients undergoing PUVA treatment for psoriasis. *Dermatology* **189**: 234-237.
16. Phillips, M. (1990) Damaged goods: oral narratives of the experience of disability in American culture. *Social Science and Medicine* **30**: 849-857.
17. Graham, P., Jordan, A. and Lamb, B. (1990) *An Equal Chance? Or No Chance? A Study of Discrimination against Disabled People in the Labour Market*. London: The Spastics Society.
18. Fallowfield, L. (1990) *The Quality of Life. The Missing Measurement in Health Care*. London: Souvenir Press.
19. Zigmund, A. and Snaith, R. (1983) The Hospital Anxiety and Depression Scale. *Acta Psychiatrica Scandinavia* **67**: 361-370.
20. Goldberg, D. (1972) *The Detection of Psychiatric Illness by Questionnaire*. Oxford: Oxford University Press.

21. Katz, S., Downs, H., Cash, H. *et al.* (1970) Progress in the development of the index of ADL. *The Gerontologist* **10**: 20-30.

22. Spitzer, W., Dobson, A., Hall, J. *et al.* (1981) Measuring the quality of life of cancer patients. *Journal of Chronic Disease* **34**: 595-597.

23. Watson, M., Law, M., Maguire, G. *et al.* (1992) Further development of a quality of life measure for cancer patients: The Rotterdam Symptom Checklist (Revised). *Psycho-Oncology* **1**: 35-44.

24. Finlay, A. and Khan, G. (1994) Dermatology Life Quality Index (DLQI) – a simple practical measure for routine clinical use. *Clinical and Experimental Dermatology* **19**: 210-216.

Part II

Human Development

6

Early Social Relation-ships

SUMMARY

Even before birth, the child is influenced by and influences the parents. The newborn infant has various characteristics that elicit caring responses. By 4 weeks of age children engage in complex interactions with their parents. This relationship can be distorted by either party: for instance if the mother is insensitive to her child's needs for stimulation or if the child is developmentally delayed.

The period shortly after birth may be particularly sensitive for the formation of emotional bonds between parent and child. While cognitive development seems to be related to the quality and frequency of adult contact, adequate social development requires predictable and consistent relationships. Children appear resilient to the effects of poor relationships early in their life; isolated negative experiences have few long-term effects. Continuing adverse circumstances, on the other hand, can have a cumulative effect on the child.

Hospitalization confronts the child with both the anxiety of separation from parents and familiar surroundings and the threat of uncertainty. Being responsive to children's needs in hospital, both directly and indirectly via their parents, can alleviate anxiety.

In this second part of the book, the emphasis is on social relationships. That the newborn child can develop into a socially aware and competent individual in just a few years is intriguing. The process appears to be remarkably complex and unlikely given the amount of information that a child must learn and the range of skills which a child must master. There are both cognitive and social skills. Cognitively, a child of 5 or 6 years of age is expected to speak in an easily understandable way and to be learning about such abstractions as time, space and number. Socially, a child of 5 or 6 is expected to be able to attend school without the presence of a parent and to be making strong peer friendships.

Research in this field provides information that can be applied in detecting interpersonal problems and suggesting ways in which they might be overcome. In the delivery room, for instance, medical staff witness the first social encounter between a baby and its parents, which can be related to future patterns of interaction. Some psychologists believe that separation from the primary caregiver can markedly affect the development of a child, a belief that has clear implications for medical practice where such separations can be imposed if children are repeatedly admitted to hospital. Children in long-term care are typically involved in a greater number of social relationships than children brought up at home, and these tend to be less constant. The professional's understanding of the effects of such changes on the development of children owes much to the systematic study of these situations.

Some variables, such as the influence of specific aspects of an adult's behaviour on an infant, lend themselves to experimental study: adults can be asked to alter their behaviour systematically while the effects on the infant are recorded. Another way to study these aspects is to observe naturally occurring situations and to monitor their outcome. This type of approach underlies much of the work with infants and children in areas such as separation and long-term care, where it would clearly be unethical to produce the required conditions experimentally. To assess long-term effects, the same children would, ideally, be studied for several years, but such "longitudinal" studies are expensive and time-consuming, so that many researchers resort to a "cross-sectional" design, comparing samples of children of different ages.

The aim of this chapter is to explore the beginnings of social relationships, particularly the importance of the relationship between parent and infant. The topics which are covered here can be grouped under two headings. The first concerns social behaviour, concentrating particularly on the patterning of early relationships. In the second part of the chapter, the possibility that the quality of early relationships has long-term effects on the child is explored.

There are many other aspects of social relationships that, although not covered here, are of much interest. Most of the research mentioned in this chapter concerns the mother–child

relationship but there has been an increased interest in the father–child relationship as well. There are indications that fathers have been taking on an increased role in some aspects of child-rearing, such as getting up during the night, though not in all, such as changing or bathing the baby.[1]

The development of social behaviour

Pre-natal influences

The process of social development is often considered to begin only after birth, but the kinds of experience that the child will encounter and influence begin at conception.

There is some very interesting work on the ability of the foetus to respond to sounds and other vibrations. By observing foetal movements using ultrasonography, Shahidullah and Hepper[2] have been able to show that foetuses at 25 weeks of age respond to sounds transmitted through the mothers' abdomens, even when the mothers themselves are unable to hear the sounds. There is even evidence that the foetus is able to "learn" and has a rudimentary memory, since the responsiveness to such noises habituates over time.

The mother's state of health and social position has considerable effect on the unborn infant. Activity in the womb increases during stressful periods in the mother's life, particularly when the stressful events continue over a long period of time. Mothers who have experienced long periods of severe anxiety during late pregnancy are more likely to have children who are highly active and intolerant of delays of feeding. Crandon[3,4] gave mothers-to-be a questionnaire designed to measure anxiety and later reviewed their records for the incidence of obstetric complications. On several measures such as length of labour, use of forceps, distress and Apgar scores (which measure infants' muscle tone, heart rate, respiratory effort, etc.), those who scored highly on the anxiety questionnaire had more complications than those who had low scores.

The degree of stress that a pregnant woman

experiences may affect the date of birth. Newton and Hunt[5] studied mothers who gave birth to full-term (at least 37 weeks), moderately premature (33–36 weeks) and very premature (less than 33 weeks) infants. Although there were no significant differences between these groups in age, gravidity and parity, levels of psychological and social stress were higher in mothers of pre-term infants than full-term infants. Mothers of pre-terms were more likely to have undergone a major life event such as marital separation, unemployment of the husband, or the death of an immediate family member. Eighty-four per cent of the very premature group indicated that a major event had occurred during their pregnancy.

Abilities of the neonate

For many years, the abilities of newborns were underestimated. It was believed that infants did not begin to respond to social stimuli for several weeks after birth. However, empirical research conducted with very young children has shown that they have a wide variety of abilities. This makes much sense, since if infants were in some way biologically primed for social interaction their chances of survival would be increased. That is, both the individual and the species would be more likely to thrive if children had abilities from birth which would attract the care of adults.

Crying is one example. Bowlby[6] argued that infants are genetically programmed to cry when distressed or when out of contact from their caregivers. Three patterns of crying have been distinguished – a basic rhythmical cry, a pain cry and an angry cry – and mothers have been found to attend to these different patterns appropriately. Further, experienced women are better than inexperienced women at discriminating between different kinds of cries.

Incidentally, there is no evidence that attending to infants when they cry leads to greater demands for attention. In fact, observations suggest the opposite. Ainsworth et al.[7] observed mothers and their children at home, noting particularly the frequency and speed with which mothers attended to their infants' cries over the first year of life. The results indicated that those mothers who intervened (by picking up, touch-

ing, playing with the children) were less likely to have infants who cried frequently than mothers who ignored or responded slowly to the cries. At least until one year of age, maternal responsiveness did not reinforce the crying – rather, it reduced its probability.

Smiling and hearing are two other abilities of infants that have important social consequences. Since adults find smiles attractive, smiling may have an evolutionary advantage. It is an endogenous activity for the first weeks after birth, occurring at the rate of about 11 smiles per 100 minutes. It is present in blind infants and in all cultures, suggesting that it is innate. In addition, neonates are able to locate sounds and attend to them visually. Further, they will not only attend preferentially to human voices over impersonal clicks, but also to a female voice rather than to a male one.

An ingenious method for exploring neonates' ability to hear was developed by giving 3–day-old infants a nipple to suck. If they sucked in a particular way they could hear a tape recording of their mother's voice. If they sucked in any other way the voice of another woman, who had given birth in the same hospital at about the same time, was heard instead. Recordings of the babies' activity showed that they would, indeed, learn to suck in this particular way, indicating that they could not only discriminate between their mother's voice and someone else's, but also that they were capable of repeating behaviour which was rewarding and eliminating that which was not.[8] There is some evidence that at least part of this effect is due to prenatal experience with the mother's voice.[9,10]

The infant's appearance, particularly the eyes, may also be important to survival and social interaction. Klaus and Kennell[11] filmed mothers and their newborns shortly after birth. The mothers were given their naked babies in privacy, except for the presence of a camera and sound-recording equipment. Besides touching the baby in a fairly predictable way (first tentatively with the fingertips and later with the palm of the hand), most mothers encouraged the infant to waken and open its eyes with comments like "Let me see your eyes" and "Open your eyes and then I'll know that you love me". Several of the mothers reported that they felt closer to their children once they had achieved eye contact. Infants as young as 3 weeks look at human faces and objects resembling faces more than other stimuli. Roskies[12] describes mothers who were considering institutionalizing their children soon after birth when they found they had been affected by thalidomide. These mothers remembered the decision to keep their children within the context of an engagement of eyes.

Robson and Moss[13] conducted retrospective interviews with mothers in their third post-natal month, and concluded that a mother's feelings of attachment with her children decreased if crying, fussing and other demands did not lessen. They describe one woman in particular who was enthusiastic about her pregnancy but later wanted little to do with the child. The child did not respond to holding, smiled infrequently and showed little eye-to-eye contact. This child was later found to have suffered brain damage.

Prematurity

Thus, infants possess several attributes and abilities that increase the probability that adults will take an interest in and care for them. Neonates are able to learn quickly, are able to signal their needs and are visually attractive. When such abilities are undeveloped or lacking, as can be the case with premature children, frustration and lack of parental care may result.

In our highly technological society, many more children of very low birthweight survive in special care baby units, but this is at the expense of personal contact between parents and their babies. This has several implications, including the bonding or attachment between parents and children (as discussed below), but there is also the concern that very premature children do not develop their full potential intellectually. Most children of very low birthweight enter mainstream education, but about 10 per cent require special attention.

Recently, there has been considerable interest in enhancing the cognitive development of children born prematurely.[14] One technique involves the use of tactile stimulation therapy (known as TAC-TIC), which involves the gentle stoking of the infant's body, over the head and face, neck, upper limbs and so on, for about 20 minutes daily until discharge.[15] There is now good evidence that this simple procedure can lead to improved intellectual functioning in later life on a variety of measures.[16] It may be effective because the stroking enhances the digestive system through increased lingual lipase secretion or activity, which in turn improves the uptake of nutrients from food.

Parent–infant interaction

Most of the studies outlined above were concerned with only one participant in the parent–child dyad. However, the concept of interaction involves *mutual* responsiveness, with a sequence of behaviours. The age at which infants engage in true interactions has been variously estimated – the more recent the estimation, the younger it is thought to occur.

For example, Brazelton et al.[17] have explored the effects of a non-responsive mother on very young infants. In this study, the mothers were asked to present a still, mask-like face to their infants instead of their usual animation. Infants initially oriented and smiled, but then sobered, became quiet and looked away. Several cycles of looking, smiling and then looking away were reported. Eventually, when repeated attempts failed to achieve a response, the infant withdrew into "an attitude of helplessness, face averted, body curled up and motionless" (p.143). When the mothers returned to their more usual form of behaviour the infants, after an initial period of "puzzlement", began to smile and return to their usual cycle of interaction.

It is also the case that a handicap in the parent can affect the relationship. Brazelton also examined the effects of congenital blindness in a mother on her infant's behaviour. At 4 weeks of age the (sighted) child was very alert but would glance only briefly at her mother's eyes and would avert her face when the mother leaned over to talk. By 8 weeks the infant reacted normally with the sighted father but not with her mother. The infant still searched her face and eyes and then averted her own face. Not until some weeks later did the pair adapt successfully. Apparently, they had learned to use other modes of communication, such as the auditory, in place of the visual one.

Differences between children (temperament)

Another approach to parent–infant interaction has concentrated on individual differences between infants, examining their temperament or "behavioural style". As described in Box 6.1, temperament describes the child in terms of how he or she *acts*.

BOX 6.1

Temperament

In an extended interview, Thomas *et al.*[18] asked mothers to describe their children in terms of their behaviour in several situations. They assumed that the parents could be used as an effective source of information about their children if they were asked about current situations and if the questions were specific. Answers were validated by observing the children in different situations, and the issue of consistency was explored by observing them over a period of time.

Nine variables or dimensions were used, including *activity level* (how much the infant moves during bathing, eating, etc.), *rhythmicity* (how predictable the child's eating and sleeping patterns are), *adaptability* (how long the child takes to adjust to new situations), and *approach-withdrawal* (whether a child smiles and approaches new stimuli, such as toys, food or strangers; or whether the child cries and pulls away).

Interviews can be replaced by questionnaires,[19] where parents are given alternatives to check off as in the following item measuring rhythmicity:

When does the child wake up in the morning?
(a) The time usually varies by more than one hour.
(b) Quite often at the same time, but sometimes more than half an hour earlier or later (than usual).
(c) At the same time (within half an hour of the usual time).

Patterns of temperament can be discerned as early as 3 months and there appears to be a genetic influence at work, with the temperamental characteristics of monozygotic twins being more similar than those of dizygotic twins. There is also evidence that there is a relationship between early assessments of this sort and later behavioural and psychiatric difficulties.[20] Perhaps most importantly, this research shows that there is no one "correct" way to rear children, since each child has different requirements. A child who is unpredictable, adapts slowly and withdraws from novel situations (a "difficult child") will require a different pattern of care from one who shows high rhythmicity, adaptability and approach (an "easy child").

These ideas of temperament have been used to explore the relationships between parents and their handicapped children. The birth of a handicapped child is a very stressful event for parents, who have to make a number of adjustments to their lifestyles, relationships with grandparents and expectations for the child's future. Some parents experience such a birth as a failure and there is often a period of grieving. Because children with handicaps are often less active and responsive, parents may be more directive and less emotionally involved.

However, it may not be the type or severity of handicap that necessarily affects the parent–child relationship. Huntington *et al.*[21] used temperament questionnaires and related these to patterns of parental involvement with their handicapped children. The degree of maternal involvement was not related to the severity of the child's handicap. Rather, it was associated with temperament: the quality of her interactions with the child was higher with "easy" children, and lower with "difficult" children. They argued that interventions with such families could include outlining methods for interacting with the children in helpful ways.

Predictability

A child's predictability may be particularly important because parents who are able to anticipate their child's needs will have enhanced feelings of competence and will be able to adapt their own routines to fit the child's. By contrast, an unpredictable child could be very disruptive for the parents, who may become increasingly unsure about their abilities. This could put a strain on the relationship between parent and infant that might, in combination with further difficulties, lead to later problems.

Compared to full-term infants, predictability may be more difficult to achieve with premature infants, because they tend to be less responsive, look at their mothers less, and are more likely to break off interactions.[22] Mothers of premature infants are more likely to initiate communication and to poke, pinch and rock frequently than are mothers of full-terms, who tend to share the responsibility for interaction. Usually, as an infant matures, he or she becomes increasingly responsive and predictable, while a caregiver gains experience with a particular child and develops increased sensitivity to and skill in meeting needs. Unfortunately, this is not always the case. Parents of children who are severely mentally handicapped or who have sensory impairments may be faced with a continuing lack of predictability and responsiveness. The lack of response from children with cerebral palsy and the excess of cues from hyperactive children have been shown to affect the parent–child relationship.

Long-term effects of early experience

The effect of early experience on later development has become one of the most intensively studied aspects of psychology, stimulated considerably by the work of John Bowlby. He reviewed the research on the intellectual and social development of children who had been separated from their mothers at an early age.[23] Many of these children had been brought up in residential institutions and were considered to be developmentally delayed (especially in language), to display excessive attention-seeking, and to be unable to make close and trusting relationships with others. He attributed these effects to a lack of a continuous, warm and intimate relationship with a single mother or mother-figure. Although he later pointed out that it could be beneficial if the child could be taken care of by other adults occasionally, he repeated his point that a single bond is crucial. He also believed there was a "critical" period, such that if a child had not formed a bond by the age of

$2\frac{1}{2}$ to 3 years, the social and intellectual damage would be irreversible.

Central to his theory of *attachment* is the idea of a secure base. Parents may fulfil the needs of food and clothing, but it is equally important that they also provide a secure base from which the child can explore and develop self-reliance. For Bowlby, protection is seen as being fully as important as the more obvious biological needs. In many respects, his theory is consistent with the psychodynamic approach to personality development (Chapter 4): the infant's first relationship with a parent is seen to be critical for later development. If the parents – particularly the mother – do not provide a secure base, later development is said to be adversely affected. Trust and openness in later relationships will be much more difficult to achieve.

Ethology

Bowlby used several *ethological* studies of mother–infant behaviour to support his case. Ethological methods emphasize observation of behaviour in natural surroundings, and the observations are given an evolutionary explanation. This method of research was first used in zoology, Konrad Lorenz's descriptions of infant ducks becoming imprinted on and following their mothers soon after hatching being an example. He suggested that this response has evolutionary advantage, keeping the chicks near their mother and thus less likely to wander away.

Once an observation has been made, the researcher often attempts to manipulate the situation, systematically altering features until the important stimuli are discovered. In the case of imprinting, it seems that it is the first *moving* object that the chicks encounter that is important. Lorenz was able to arrange conditions so that the chicks became imprinted on him. Later studies indicated that they could become attached to almost any moving object (gloves, cubes) and that they will attempt to mate with these objects when mature. There seems to be a critical period involved: if the moving object is shown several days after hatching, the response is much less likely to occur. Thus, imprinting is the result of both innate and environmental factors.

The application of ethological methods to children is more complicated, since infants reared in technologically advanced societies develop in conditions very different to those in the "natural" environment, making it difficult to apply evolutionary explanations to their behaviour. Nevertheless, the emphasis on *observation* of how children behave has made this approach attractive to many psychologists.

Bowlby's theory has generated much research, probably because of its practical implications for child care. One result is the easier access given to parents while their children are in hospital. Some of his other conclusions have been less well accepted, such as his belief that it is beneficial for the child under 3 years of age if the mother is not employed outside the home. Similarly, if his critical period hypothesis is correct, this raises important questions about the possibility of successfully adopting older children who have never had the opportunity of forming a single continuous bond.

In this section four aspects of early experience are considered: first, the disruption of the parent–infant bond that may occur due to separation soon after birth; second, the effects of parent–infant separation; third, the effects of "multiple" caregiving as may occur in residential nurseries or if the mother works; and fourth, a discussion of whether any adverse effects of such experiences on the child's development can be remedied later in life.

Bonding: a critical period?

That the period immediately after birth is particularly important or "sensitive" for parent–infant bonding is based on evidence from various experimental and observational studies. The research conducted by Kennell and his colleagues[24] has been particularly influential. In an important experiment one group of women was given routine contact with their newborns: a glance at the baby shortly after birth, a short visit at 6–12 hours, and then every 4 hours visits of 20–30 minutes each for feeding over the first 3 days. This was the normal procedure at the hospital, so that this group of women and their children formed the control group. A second group of women were given this routine contact plus additional contact with their infants. They were given their naked babies to hold for one hour within the first 3 hours after birth and 5 extra hours per day over the next 3 days.

Although the mothers in each group were comparable with respect to age, socioeconomic status, ethnic background, days spent in hospital and amount of premedication, there were some striking differences in how the mothers in the two groups communicated with their children. After one month, the extended contact mothers were observed to establish more eye contact with their children during feeding and to initiate more active play with their infants than the routine contact mothers. Both groups were asked to keep diaries of their daily behaviour. Once again, the differences between the two groups suggested that the strength of the bond between the mother and the infant was related to the amount of contact shortly after birth. The extended contact mothers reported thinking about the baby more frequently and staying at home more often than the control group. They also picked up the child more frequently when it cried, soothed their children more, and were more likely to feed their children *en face* (turning the head so that it was on the same plane as the infant's).

Early contact may have some long-term effects as well. The differences between the groups still existed one year after the birth. Although about 50 per cent of the mothers in both groups had returned to work by this time, most of the control group mothers did not mention their baby when asked how they felt about this, whereas most of the extended group mothers volunteered the information that they missed their children. At 2 years, there appeared to be differences in the way the mothers spoke to their children, with the extended contact mothers asking more questions and issuing fewer commands,[25] and differences in IQ have been reported at 42 months.[26]

Although these results have not been consistently replicated, and no other team of researchers have found such long-term effects,[27] they have encouraged many obstetricians and paediatricians to make provision for early contact between the mother and her infant. Kempe and Kempe[28] have found that there is some predictive value in observing this first contact, their work indicating that the way a mother reacts to her child in the delivery room is related to the probability of later abuse and neglect (see Chapter 8). Other researchers have suggested that it may be possible to specify the optimal conditions for the establishment of the mother–infant bond. Kennell's work indicates that it is important that the mother hold her infant as soon as possible after birth. Fathers, too, seem to benefit from early contact with the newborn.

These findings on bonding also relate to the effects of pain-relieving drugs during labour. Several studies have indicated that these medications have some short-term effects, making the newborn drowsy and unresponsive.[29] By using short and simple tests on the child (such as Apgar scales) some idea of the general health and responsiveness of the infant can be gained directly after birth. Pain-relieving drugs are associated with low scores on such scales. Since these activities may be important for the bonding process, the use of these medications needs to be considered carefully.

Another cause for concern is that, in our highly technological society, premature babies are usually separated from their parents at birth. It may be days or even weeks before he or she can be held and fed by the parents. As mentioned above, premature babies are also less responsive and interactionally able, and there is often the threat of death. All of these factors may make it more difficult for parents to become bonded with their child. However, it is possible to overestimate these difficulties, and it seems that many are resolved over time. For example, Niven et al.[30] interviewed mothers of premature children some months after their children had gone home, asking them about their recall of feelings of attachment over time. The results indicated that after an initial lack of bonding at the time of the birth, feelings of attachment rose significantly over time. At the time of the birth mothers reported such feelings as:

66 I tried to keep a distance between myself and the baby at first. I tried to be professional with the baby and not to get attached (an ex-nurse). 99

In the first few post-natal days, mothers were unable to hold their children whenever they wanted, and most found this extremely distressing, or felt too frightened to risk lifting their child from the incubator:

66 I felt terrible. Other mothers could hold their babies but I couldn't. He was so fragile I thought I would break him. 99

Going home without the child was also upsetting:

66 I felt I had abandoned him. It was awful leaving him all alone in hospital. As soon as I got home I would phone and ask the nurse to give him a kiss for me. 99

66 Leaving hospital without him was the worst bit; walking out with nothing. 99

However, when the baby came home, most felt very attached to their children:

66 As soon as the baby came home I felt different. There was an instant change. I knew she was mine and nobody else's. 99

This suggests that perhaps the parent–child bond is very resilient, an issue considered later in the chapter.

Separation

A second aspect of Bowlby's theory of attachment concerns separation. Because of the need for protection, separation from the mother causes the baby distress – shown by the baby crying and attempting to locate her. Most babies show *separation anxiety* to some extent, usually between the ages of 8 and 24 months. It is most acute in novel situations. Many children also show anxiety in the presence of unfamiliar adults (*stranger anxiety*) around 8–12 months. Bowlby suggests that these are examples of attachment responses in humans that have an innate basis and serve to protect, keeping the infant close by the mother.

The importance of the experience of separation has been studied in several ways, but most notably in those circumstances where contact with a parent is lost due to parental separations or a parent's death.

Longer term separations
There has been particular concern about the effects of divorce or separation on children,

especially with the increasing divorce rate in most Western countries. The proportion of single parent families has certainly increased in the UK from 8 per cent in 1971 to 22 per cent in 1993. By the age of 16, there is currently a 1 in 4 chance that a child will have experienced the effects of a parental divorce or separation. There are now several studies which have examined the effects of such an event on children's self-esteem, school work and emotional well-being.

This research has indicated that it is not the divorce itself but the discord and disturbance that accompanies it that is most important. When comparisons are made between children whose parents are divorced and children whose parents remain unhappily married, few differences are found.[31] In a comparison between single-parent and intact families, only in those instances where there was parental conflict was the children's self-esteem adversely affected.[32]

Rutter[33] examined the relationship between the quality of parental marriage and incidence of anti-social behaviour in the children. A linear relationship was found between these two variables, such that children showing anti-social behaviour were more likely to have parents with a very poor marriage (Figure 6.1). Rutter also compared the incidence of delinquency in child-

ren who had been separated from their parents because of physical illness with those who had been separated because of family discord or psychiatric illness. The incidence of anti-social behaviour was some four times higher in the second group.[34]

There are now several long-term studies on the effects of divorce on children. One of the better known was conducted by Wallerstein.[35] Initially, 131 children between the ages of 2 and 18 years were interviewed. At the time of the separation, virtually all the children were very distressed, and most remained distressed 18 months afterwards. After 5 years, one-third of the children still showed moderate to severe depression. Although other studies have indicated a much higher level of good adjustment, there is agreement between studies that the experience of a good relationship with both parents, and an absence of continuing conflict between them, is conducive to positive outcomes.

Thus, it seems to be the meaning and circumstances of the separation which are important. The long-term effects of separation from parents due to divorce or death depends on the cause: when the parents' relationship is disturbed or quarrelsome the child may have difficulties. Perhaps early separations are best viewed as a sensitive index to the type of upbringing that might lead to later problems. Long-term discord between the child and parents or between the parents themselves is more significant than any single separation.

Multiple caregiving

A related question to the effects of separation is the issue of caregiving by several adults. Does it matter – intellectually or emotionally – if a child is looked after by many adults? This might occur if both parents work, for example, or if grandparents often care for the child. Attempts to address this issue have been made by examining naturally occurring situations in which infants have been given care by several adults. Of direct relevance to Bowlby's work are more recent efforts to extend and replicate his observations. In several reports, Barbara Tizard has explored the effects of residential nurseries for

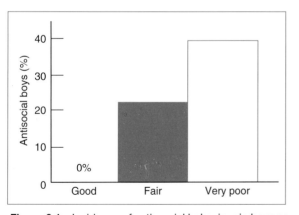

Figure 6.1 Incidence of anti-social behaviour in boys as related to the quality of their parents' marital relationship (all boys living with both natural parents). Although no children whose parents had a "good" marriage were in trouble with the law, almost 40 per cent of those whose parents had a "very poor" marriage were in trouble. (Reproduced from Rutter, M. (1971) *Journal of Child Psychology and Psychiatry* **12**: 233–260, with kind permission from Elsevier Science Ltd, The Boulevard, Langford Lane, Kidlington, OX5 1GB, UK.)

very young children (who had been taken into care) on their cognitive and social development.

Cognitive development

Tizard began by examining 65 children with an average age of 24 months. All were born full-term and none were considered to have any physical or mental handicap. The staff of these nurseries changed frequently and close emotional contact was discouraged. These nurseries were, however, much more stimulating than those studied by Bowlby. Toys, mobiles and picture books were freely available and staff were encouraged to communicate with the children.

On most measures, these children were very similar to a comparison group of working-class London children, except that they were less likely to approach strangers and their language development was slightly retarded. In further studies, Tizard has found little evidence of cognitive retardation. Tizard and Rees[36] reported their findings on the same children at 4 years of age. Some of them had remained in the institution while others had been restored to their natural mothers. Both restored and institution groups had IQs similar to the comparison group.

The children's cognitive development seemed to be related to the quality and frequency of staff contact. Tizard *et al*.[37] studied 85 children of 2–5 years of age who were being cared for in 13 residential nurseries. They found that the verbal abilities of the children were positively correlated with the frequency of informative staff talk, staff social activity and the frequency with which staff answered children's remarks. No evidence of developmental retardation was found in this sample.

Social development

These results suggest that although the quality of adult–child contact is important for cognitive and language development, it may not be necessary to have a single continuous relationship. However, some continuity of care may well be necessary for the development of trust in social relationships. In a follow-up to the earlier studies, Tizard[38] reports that at 8 years of age the institution-reared children seemed overly affectionate and "cling-

ing". It is possible that this clinging was an attempt to obtain some sort of continuity of caregiving: a response to the frequent changing of caregivers. Related to this finding is research on the effects of adoption on later development. Tizard, in keeping with many studies, reports few social and emotional difficulties in the adopted children from her sample.

Other naturally occurring situations can be used to study the importance of multiple caregiving. One situation is maternal employment, where parents arrange for their children to be taken care of by another adult during their working day. It seems that employment itself is only weakly related to children's development and behaviour. If the home environment is disrupted due to marital difficulties or if adequate provision for supervision is not made, then problems may occur.[39]

Evidence from other cultures also supports the idea that care can be given by more than one person without adverse effects. In many societies, several members of a family share the responsibility for caretaking and breast-feeding is not necessarily given by the mother alone. From an evolutionary point of view it would be advantageous for an infant to be able to form more than one bond. A sociobiological viewpoint would support the importance of the whole family in caretaking, since grandparents, older siblings and aunts and uncles would all have a greater opportunity to pass on their genes if they invested energy in the child and the child was receptive to this.[40]

Conversely, there may well be a limit to the number of caregivers who could be helpful to the child. In so far as good caregiving implies a sensitivity to a child's needs, this would require time and considerable contact. Some personal commitment on the part of the caregiver would be necessary for this. For the child – who also has a need for predictability – the different styles of interaction shown by a large number of adults may be disturbing. If only because time is required to form a relationship, it is likely that there is an upper limit on the number of people who could give satisfactory care. For cognitive development, adequate stimulation and interest is needed, and it seems likely that for good social and emotional development at least one stable relationship, with commitment on the part of the caregiver, is required.

Resilience

Another conclusion that John Bowlby drew from his review concerned the irreversibility of the effects of early deprivation. He argued that children would suffer a lasting inability to form close relationships if they had not been given the opportunity to do so before 3 years of age. Many researchers have questioned the validity of Bowlby's conclusions in this respect. They suggest that a child is not necessarily doomed to an unsatisfactory life because of an unsatisfactory childhood. Several naturally occurring situations can be used to examine the issues of the resilience of children in the face of early deprivation. It will be remembered that studies on mother–infant interaction indicated that premature infants can provide less interesting and fulfilling responses for the mother than do full-term infants. If this early experience is so significant, then differences could be expected later in life, yet few differences have been found. In one study, patterns of interaction between mothers and their premature infants proved to be poor predictors of cognitive or social ability at the age of three.[41] Similar results have been found concerning the effects of perinatal anoxia.[42]

Case studies

Perhaps the strongest evidence that early deficits can be overcome comes from several case studies (see Box 6.2), but it is always possible, of course, that the general failure to find enduring effects of early experience may be due to the insensitivity of methods currently used. Early deprivation and neglect are likely to have some long-term consequences, just as years of isolation in adulthood could be expected to affect an individual, but it appears that these consequences may have been overestimated. Children seem more resilient and responsive to change than was thought a decade ago.

A more fruitful approach may be to consider early experience within the context of later circumstances. It could be concluded from the studies of early separation on later development

> ### BOX 6.2
>
> #### Some case studies
> Koluchova[43] describes the recovery of twin boys who were totally isolated from others from 18 months to 7 years of age. They were locked in a cupboard for most of this time. When they were eventually released, they could barely walk, suffered from rickets and their IQs were in the 40s. Although they were 18 months old at the time of their incarceration, this long period of isolation would be expected to have severe long-term effects on their intellectual and emotional development if early experience were crucial. However, after 7 years of fostering in a supportive and emotionally caring home, they were found to have average IQs and average social development.
>
> Similarly, Kagan[44] describes a girl of 14 years of age who spent most of the first 30 months of her life in a small bedroom with no toys and a sister one year older than herself. When she was removed at 2 years, she was severely malnourished and retarded in height and weight. At the time Kagan conducted his interview, however, she had spent 12 years in a foster home. He reported that her IQ was within the normal range and that she gave an average performance on several cognitive tests. He noted that her interpersonal behaviour compared favourably with other adolescents.

that children who have difficulties in their first years are more likely to continue to experience difficulties as they grow, and that it is the cumulative effect that has significant consequences. This conclusion is not incompatible with the emphasis placed on mother–infant interaction earlier in the chapter. A parent and child may be able to cope with, say, a pre-term birth without undue difficulty, but further adverse experiences such as physical abnormality or unavoidable and unwanted separations may increase the risk of adversely affecting the development of the child. So, too, might difficulties in developing relationships with friends also lead to negative consequences.

Peer relationships

As children grow up they are faced with several developmental challenges, becoming more independent and developing many other relationships besides those within the immediate family. Some of these challenges are more obvious than others: major changes may occur at about the age of three, for example, when a child may be enrolled in a nursery school. The main caregiver will not always be present, and there will be many strangers to meet, both adults and peers.

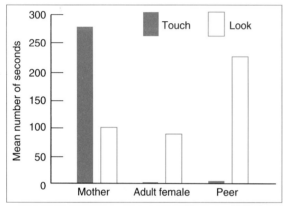

Figure 6.2 The amount of time young children touched and looked at their mother, another adult woman and another child of the same age. (Reproduced from Lewis, M. (1975) The beginning of friendship. In: Lewis, M. and Rosenblum, L. (eds) *Friendship and Peer Relations*. London: Wiley, with permission.)

However, adjustments are needed from shortly after birth, as children encounter others of their own age. Figure 6.2 illustrates some results from a study in which pairs of children between the ages of 12 and 18 months and their mothers met for the first time in a playroom. During a 15 minute period, the children rarely touched the strange adult or the other child, preferring to touch their own mothers. However, they spent much more time *looking* at the other child than at either of the adults.[45] The opportunity to play with peers is very important for children, being an integral aspect of development. Amongst the primates, the time between birth and adolescence lengthens as we go up the phylogenetic scale. This has led to the suggestion that play has

evolutionary advantages: the child has a chance to learn about social relationships and about the use and construction of tools in a relatively pressure-free environment.[46]

It has proved useful to distinguish between different types of play. When young, children are more likely to be *solitary*, being unoccupied or being an onlooker, or be engaged in *parallel* play, when they play near each other with the same materials but do not interact much. As they get older, *group* play becomes more common, when they interact together at the same activity, perhaps each adding blocks to the same tower, or actively assisting each other.

Bullying

There is increasing interest in the significance of friends in the social development of children. Poor peer relationships and the experience of being bullied are amongst the best predictors of later social and emotional adjustment. There has been a marked increase of interest in this topic in recent years, as child psychologists have found not only that it is very common but also that it can have long-term and severe effects on some children. There are a number of definitions of bullying, but all involve the abuse of power. For example, Dawkins[47] defined it as "the intentional, unprovoked abuse of power by one or more children to inflict pain on or cause distress to another child on repeated occasions". Bullying seems to occur in all schools to some extent, sometimes very frequently. In response to anonymous questionnaires, 27 per cent of boys and girls between the ages of 8 and 11 reported that they were bullied at least sometimes, 10 per cent once a week or more. Most bullying happens in the playground, and many children keep their distress to themselves.[48] As a result, programmes have been instituted in many schools, which can reduce the incidence of bullying by up to 50 per cent.

It may well be that the children who are frequently bullied are in some way vulnerable to abuse and less socially skilled. Victims tend to be less athletic, less well accepted socially and have lower self-esteem, and children with disabilities are particularly vulnerable. There are also indications that children can remember and are affected by their experiences well into adult-hood, as the following quotation given by an adult who had been blind since birth illustrates.[49]

66 I didn't realise there was anything wrong with me until I started getting picked on by kids. I used to . . . do everything that a normal kid did . . . And then when I started school, suddenly being called names! And there were lots of practical jokes. Glue in my hair, hiding my books, tripping me, stuff like that. It was rough growing up. (p. 852) 99

One method of assisting troubled children with their difficulties has been to encourage play with younger friends, a method that has met with some success. Hartup[50] describes a number of studies which illustrate the importance of peer relationships and ways in which they can be improved. In one study, children who were con-sidered socially withdrawn or isolated were divided into three groups. One group acted as a control. The other two groups were encouraged to participate in special play sessions for 4-6 weeks: for half of these children the playmates were some 15 months younger, for the other half about the same age. Exposure to children younger than the withdrawn children was par-ticularly effective in reducing isolation – perhaps the younger playmates were less threatening than the same age playmates. This study is particularly convincing because the ratings of isolation were made by people who did not know the purpose of the study (teachers) in a situation providing a good example of the children's behaviour (the classroom).

Children in hospital

Reactions to hospitalization

When children are placed in hospital, they can pass through three stages during their attempts to cope with the new environment. At first, they may show distress and protest, then misery and apathy followed, in the long term, by detachment and loss of interest in their parents. There may be some longer term reactions as well, especially if the child is required to be in hospital many times. Douglas[51] found that repeated hospital admissions were associated with a slight increase in enuresis, being most marked in children who underwent surgery. Even when social class and the reason for hospitalization are taken into account, *repeated* admissions seem to be associ-ated with later disturbances.[52]

In addition, there appears to be considerable individual variation in how children react to hos-pitalization. Although 22 per cent of children in one study showed some deterioration in their behaviour after having been in hospital (as indi-cated by their mothers), 10 per cent showed some improvement. This raises the possibility that some children may be more vulnerable to the experience than others. Can the minority of children who do show distress be predicted? Some results indicate that this might be possible. Brown[53] conducted extended interviews with mothers, took observations of the patterns of mother–child interaction and observed the children (aged 3-6 years) on the hospital wards. Those children who, at home, were prone to spend much time with the family and stayed in close proximity to them were those who showed high distress in the hospital – they were upset, laughed little and were clinging when parents visited.

Conversely, those children who were given more control over their own activities at home were likely to become involved with others on the ward and less likely to remain in bed. As in the case of other studies, the mothers' attitudes towards hospitalization were also relevant. Mothers who were anxious themselves about hospitals tended to have children who were with-drawn on the wards. Perhaps certain kinds of pleasant separations, such as having a baby-sitter or staying overnight with relatives, may prepare them for the stressful effects of hospitalization. A child coming from a secure background is less likely to be disturbed by the experience.[54]

Preparing children for hospitalization

The difficulties that children experience in enter-ing hospital can be particularly distressing, not only for the children themselves but also for parents and staff. As discussed above, repeated hospitalizations may have consequences for children's well-being. In this section, some of the research on helping children to cope with the experience is outlined. It seems that many of the principles which apply to the preparation of adults (Chapter 1) also apply to children, except that the preparatory information may need to be presented in different ways. The use of modelling via short films is also effective (Chapter 3).

Distress can be alleviated by providing emotional support for the child via the nursing and medical staff. Fassler[55] assigned children who were to have minor surgery to one of three conditions. One group was given no special information or emotional support during their stay. A second group was given extra emotional support, the experimenter reading a story to the children, giving them a set of toys to play with, and talking with them about their interests, school and family. Little mention of hospitalization was made, but the procedure of this condition ensured that the children were given some emotional support. The third group was given this emotional support, but also information concerning hospitalization; the children were given a set of toys to play with which included an operating table (providing an opportunity of talking about the treatment), they were shown a

film about a child entering hospital (similar to that discussed in Chapter 3) and their concerns and fears about their stay were discussed. Thus, this condition provided emotional support plus information.

Afterwards, each child was tested for his or her degree of anxiety. As shown in Figure 6.3, those who were given no interventions were most anxious, followed by those who were given emotional support. The most effective intervention for reducing the children's anxieties before the operation was the combination of both emotional support and preparatory information.

Helping parents

Helping parents is another effective method of reducing children's distress, since parental distress can be communicated to their children. They might be even more anxious than the child because they are more aware of the seriousness of a condition, because they have had a bad experience themselves or because they are unsure about the treatments involved.

Ferguson[56] provides an example of the importance of preparing parents as well as children. She

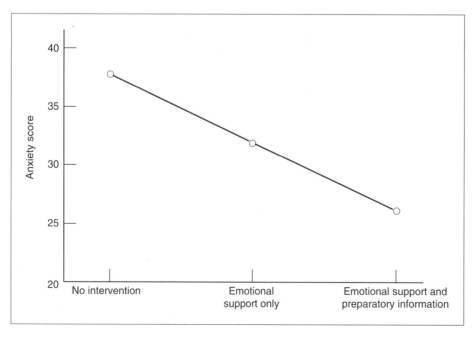

Figure 6.3 Anxiety scores for hospitalized children who had received no intervention, received emotional support, or who received both emotional support and preparatory information. (Reproduced from Fassler, D. (1980) *Patient Counselling and Health Education* **2**: 130–134, with permission.)

arranged a pre-admission home visit by a nurse for children about to have a tonsillectomy. A nurse completed the admission documents with the mother and gave her information about general hospital rules such as what to bring to the hospital, what tests to expect, the fasting requirements on the morning of surgery and what the operating room looked like. They were also told that the child would have a very sore throat after surgery and might vomit. The mothers were given the opportunity to ask questions and express concerns. A group of mothers who received no home visit comprised the control group.

Ferguson measured both mothers' and children's anxieties at admission and 10 days after release from hospital. For children of 6–7 years of age (but not younger) the pre-admission visit resulted in fewer indications of poor adjustment after discharge (e.g. difficulty in sleeping, eating, general anxiety) and mothers were less anxious during and after hospitalization.

Some research discussed earlier in this chapter has indicated that the child's family background is important, in that children from secure homes are less likely to be disturbed by the experience. Research has also indicated ways in which their difficulties could be lessened by medical and nursing staff. Ferguson took care to inform the children's mothers about hospital procedures because there is evidence that anxiety felt by the parents affects the level of anxiety in their child.[57] Skipper and Leonard[58] asked a nurse to attend some mothers when they arrived at the hospital with their children. As in the Ferguson study, the mothers were encouraged to ask questions and express their concerns. The control group mothers received the regular introduction to the hospital with little personal contact. Behavioural and physiological measures indicated a lower level of anxiety in the *children* of the experimental group mothers, and they made a more rapid recovery and experienced fewer aftereffects of their stay. The reduction of the mothers' level of anxiety was reflected in their children's recovery. Apparently, one way to help children in hospital is to help their parents make sense of the hospital routine and treatment.

The difficulties that young children experience may also be due in part to the anxiety they feel when confronted with an unfamiliar situation or unfamiliar adults. Entering hospital is a frightening experience for most children because they are not only being separated from parents but also being placed in a threatening setting. Although there is little evidence that a single hospitalization has any long-term effects, the experience is very stressful for those who are vulnerable and repeated admissions are associated with later disturbances.

A child entering hospital will meet a wide variety of adult strangers, ranging from nurses, doctors and medical students to porters and receptionists. Younger children in particular may distrust doctors, believing that they deliberately hurt patients or do not care about any hurt caused.[59] Several studies have shown that such encounters increase children's need to be close to their parents, particularly at ages between 8 months and 2 years. Yet it appears that this anxiety is strongest when an adult approaches a child, rather than allowing the child freedom to approach the adult in his or her own time. When infants are allowed to control the encounter, anxiety about strangers is much less noticeable. Thus it may be possible to reduce children's distress in hospital by allowing them some control over their encounters with medical and nursing staff. The anxiety about unfamiliar environments may be alleviated if parents are encouraged to accompany their children to hospital and to the ward: children are more willing to explore their environment if there is a "safe base" to which they can return if necessary.

Suggested reading

Smith, P.K. and Cowie, H. (1991) *Understanding Children's Development*, Oxford: Blackwell, provides a more detailed review of many of the issues covered here. For readers who are interested in the effects of premature birth, Davis, A., Richards, M.P.M. and Robertson, N. (eds) (1983) *Parent– Baby Attachment in Premature Infants*, London: Croom Helm, can be recommended. For a review of difficulties faced by children in hospital and in coping with chronic illnesses, see Eiser, C. (1990) *Chronic Childhood Disease*, Cambridge: Cambridge University Press.

References

1. Lewis, C. (1986) *Becoming a Father*. Milton Keynes: Open University Press.
2. Shahidullah, S. and Hepper, P. (1993) The developmental origins of fetal responsiveness to an acoustic stimulus. *Journal of Reproductive and Infant Psychology* **11**: 135–142.
3. Crandon, A.J. (1979) Maternal anxiety and obstetric complications. *Journal of Psychosomatic Research* **23**: 109–111.
4. Crandon, A.J. (1979) Maternal anxiety and neonatal well-being. *Journal of Psychosomatic Research* **23**: 113–115.
5. Newton, R.W. and Hunt, L.P. (1984) Psychosocial stress in pregnancy and its relation to low birthweight. *British Medical Journal* **288**: 1191–1194.
6. Bowlby, J. (1971) *Attachment and Loss: Vol. 1. Attachment*. Harmondsworth, Middlesex: Penguin Books.
7. Ainsworth, M., Bell, S. and Stayton, D. (1972) Individual differences in the development of some attachment behaviours. *Merrill-Palmer Quarterly* **18**:123–143.
8. DeCasper, A.J. and Fifer, W.P. (1980) Of human bonding: newborns prefer their mother's voice. *Science* **208**: 1174–1176.
9. Hepper, P., Scott, D. and Shahidullah, S. (1993) Newborn and fetal response to maternal voice. *Journal of Reproductive and Infant Psychology* **11**: 147–153.
10. DeCasper, A., Lecanuet, J., Busnel, M., Granier-Deferre, C. and Maugenais, R. (1994) Fetal reactions to recurrent maternal speech. *Infant Behaviour and Development* **17**: 159–164.
11. Klaus, H.M. and Kennell, J.H. (1970) Human maternal behaviour at first contact with her young. *Pediatrics* **46**: 187–192.
12. Roskies, E. (1972) *Abnormality and Normality: the Mothering of Thalidomide Children*. Ithaca, New York: Cornell University Press.
13. Robson, K.S. and Moss, H.A. (1970) Patterns and determinants of maternal attachment. *Journal of Pediatrics* **77**: 976–985.
14. Brooks-Gunn, J., Klebanov, P., Liaaw, F. and Spiker, D. (1994) Enhancing the development of low-birthweight premature infants: changes in cognitions and behaviour over the first three years. *Child Development* **64**: 736–753.
15. de Roiste, A. and Bushnell, W. (1993) Tactile stimulation and pre-term infant performance on an instrumental conditioning task. *Journal of Reproductive and Infant Psychology* **11**: 155–163.
16. Adamson-Macedo, E., Dattani, I., Wilson, A. and Carvalho, F. (1993) A small sample follow-up study of children who received tactile stimulation after pre-term birth: intelligence and achievements. *Journal of Reproductive and Infant Psychology* **11**: 165–168.
17. Brazelton, T.B., Tronick, E., Adamson, K., Als, H. and Wise, S. (1975) Early mother-infant reciprocity. In: CIBA Foundation Symposium 33, *Parent–Infant Interaction*.
18. Thomas, A., Birch, H.G., Chess, S., Hertzig, M. and Korn, S. (1963) *Behavioural Individuality in Early Childhood*. London: University of London Press.
19. Personn-Blennow, I. and McNeil, T. (1979) A questionnaire for measurement of temperament in six-month-old infants. *Journal of Child Psychology and Psychiatry* **20**: 1–13.
20. Caspi, A., Henry, B., McGee, R., Moffitt, T. and Silva, P. (1995). Temperamental origins of child and adolescent behavioural problems from age 3 to age 15. *Child Development* **66**: 55–68.
21. Huntington, G., Simeonsson, R., Bailey, D. and Comfort, M. (1993) Handicapped child characteristics and maternal involvement. *Journal of Reproductive and Infant Psychology* **5**: 105–118.
22. Brown, J.V. and Bakeman, R. (1979) Relationships of mothers with their infants during the first year of life: effects of prematurity. In: Bell, R. W. and Smotherman, W. P. (eds) *Maternal Influence and Early Behaviour*. Holliswood: Spectrum.
23. Bowlby, J. (1951) *Maternal Care and Health Care*. Geneva: World Health Organization.
24. Kennell, J.H., Jerauld, R. and Wolfe, H. (1974) Maternal behaviour one year after early and extended post-partum contact. *Developmental Medicine and Child Neurology* **16**: 172–179.
25. Ringler, N.M., Kennell, J.H., Jarvella, R., Navojosky, B. and Klaus, M. (1975) Mother-to-child speech at two years – effects of early post-natal contact. *Behavioural Pediatrics* **86**: 141–144.
26. Trause, M.A., Kennell, J. and Klaus, M. (1977) Parental attachment behaviours. In: Money, J. and Musaph, H. (eds) *Handbook of Sexology*. London: Excerpta Medica.
27. Lamb, M.E. (1983) Early mother-neonate contact and the mother–child relationship. *Journal of Child Psychology and Psychiatry* **24**: 487–494.
28. Kempe, R.S. and Kempe, C.H. (1978) *Child Abuse*. London: Fontana.
29. Aleksandrowicz, M. and Aleksandrowicz, D. (1974) Obstetrical pain-relieving drugs as predictors of neonate behaviour variability. *Child Development* **45**: 935–945.
30. Niven, C., Wiszniewski, C. and Airoomi, L. (1993)

Attachment (bonding) in mothers of pre-term babies. *Journal of Reproductive and Infant Psychology* 11: 175-185.

31. Bane, M.J. (1976) Marital disruption and the lives of children. *Journal of Social Issues* 32: 103-117.

32. Raschke, H.J. and Raschke, V. (1979) Family conflict and children's self-concepts: a comparison of intact and single-parent families. *Journal of Marriage and the Family* 41: 367-374.

33. Rutter, M. (1971) Parent-child separation: psychological effects on the children. *Journal of Child Psychology and Psychiatry* 12: 233-260.

34. Rutter, M. (1979) Parent-child separation. In: Clarke, A. and Clarke, A. (eds) *Early Experience*. London: Open Books.

35. Wallerstein, J. (1987) Children of divorce: report of a ten-year follow-up of early latency-age children. *American Journal of Orthopsychiatry* 57: 199-211.

36. Tizard, B. and Rees, J. (1974) A comparison of the effects of adoption, restoration to the natural mother and continued institutionalisation on the cognitive development of 4 year old children. *Child Development* 45: 92-99.

37. Tizard, B., Cooperman, O., Joseph, A. and Tizard, J. (1972) Environmental effects on language development. *Child Development* 43: 337-358.

38. Tizard, B. (1979) Early experience and later social development. In: Schaffer, D. and Dunn, J. (eds) *The First Year of Life*. Chichester: Wiley.

39. Ethugh, C. (1974) Effects of maternal employment on children. *Merrill-Palmer Quarterly* 20: 71-78.

40. Smith, P.K. (1980) Shared care of children. *Merrill-Palmer Quarterly* 26: 371-389.

41. Bakeman, R. and Brown, R. (1980) Early interaction: consequences for social and mental development at three years. *Child Development* 51: 437-447.

42. Corah, N.L., Anthony, E.J., Painter, P., Stern, J. and Thurston, D. (1965) The effect of perinatal anoxia after seven years. *Psychological Monographs* 79: 596 pp.

43. Koluchova, J. (1976) The further development of twins after severe and prolonged deprivation. *Journal of Child Psychology and Psychiatry* 17: 181-188.

44. Kagan, J. (1979) Resilience and continuity in psychological development. In: Clarke, A. and Clarke, A. (eds) *Early Experience*. London: Open Books.

45. Lewis, M., Young, G., Brooks, J. and Michalson, L. (1975) The beginning of friendship. In: Lewis, M. and Rosenblum, L. (eds) *Friendship and Peer Relations*. London: Wiley.

46. Tizard, B. and Harvey, D. (1977) *The Biology of Play*. London: Heinemann.

47. Dawkins, J. (1995) Bullying in schools: doctors' responsibilities. *British Medical Journal* 310: 274-275.

48. Whitney, I. and Smith, P.K. (1993) A survey of the nature and extent of bullying in junior/middle and secondary schools. *Educational Research* 35: 3-25.

49. Phillips, M. (1990) Damaged goods: oral narratives of the experience of disability in American culture. *Social Science and Medicine* 30: 849-857.

50. Hartup, W. (1989) Social relationships and their developmental significance. *American Psychologist* 44: 120-126.

51. Douglas, J.W.B. (1975) Early hospital admissions and later disturbances of behaviour and learning. *Developmental Medicine and Child Neurology* 17: 456-480.

52. Quinton, D. and Rutter, M. (1976) Early hospital admissions and later disturbances of behaviour. *Developmental Medicine and Child Neurology* 18: 447-459.

53. Brown, B. (1979) Beyond separation: some new evidence on the impact of brief hospitalisation on young children. In: Hall, D. and Stacey, M. (eds) *Beyond Separation*. London: Routledge and Kegan Paul.

54. Stacey, M., Dearden, R., Pill, R. and Robinson, D. (1970) *Hospitals, Children and their Families*. London: Routledge and Kegan Paul.

55. Fassler, D. (1980) Reducing preoperative anxiety in children. *Patient Counselling and Health Education* 2: 130-134.

56. Ferguson, B.F. (1979) Preparing young children for hospitalisation. *Pediatrics* 64: 656-664.

57. Bush, J., Melamed, B., Sheras, P. and Greenbaum, P. (1986) Mother-child patterns of coping with anticipatory medical stress. *Health Psychology* 5: 137-157.

58. Skipper, J.K. and Leonard, R. (1968) Children, stress and hospitalisation: a field experiment. *Journal of Health and Social Behaviour* 9: 275-287.

59. Brewster, A. (1982) Chronically ill hospitalised children's concepts of their illness. *Pediatrics*, 69: 355-362.

7

Developing Identity

SUMMARY

Our identity – our sense of ourselves as individuals – depends on an interplay between our innate biology and social experiences. While adolescence has been seen as a critical period in identity development, in fact identity is re-evaluated throughout our lives.

Some people develop negative views of themselves either as a result of others' reactions or through misperception of reality. This may lead some to seek plastic surgery, or develop eating disorders, in order to try to raise self-esteem, but an alternative is to develop assertiveness skills.

We all have some sense of identity, which refers to our self-concepts about a wide range of personal attributes such as gender, appearance, personality and ability. By 3 years of age, most children can correctly label their own gender, and by 7 years most understand that it is stable. Similarly, by 5 years of age children can discriminate between ethnic groups, and by 9 years have learnt that race remains constant.

Although our sense of identity begins to develop early on, it is affected by experience and cognitive development and continues to change throughout our lives. Different parts of identity are relevant to different roles. You may think of yourself as a student, a son or daughter, a friend, a customer or a lodger, depending on the context. Furthermore, identity issues change with age. In one study, individuals aged 10–18 were asked to write 20 statements about themselves, as a response to the question "Who am I?". Younger children tended to describe themselves in objective terms, such as their physical characteristics, where they live, and their possessions. Older teenagers gave responses which reflected their assessment of themselves compared to others. Occupational aspirations and ideological beliefs (for example, "I am a pacifist") began to be mentioned.[1]

A key area of identity is our valuation of ourselves, or self-esteem. Through parents, friends, teachers and the media, we learn to attach values to particular characteristics. In our society intelligence and physical attractiveness are highly valued, whereas in another societies it might be hunting prowess. The media perpetuate an association between attractiveness and goodness, and attractiveness and thinness. If a person views themselves as overweight (whether or not this is actually the case), they may then also view themselves as neither attractive nor good. Such learned linkages can lead to medical problems, such as eating disorders.

Three specific areas of identity are considered in this chapter. First, the emergence of sex role identity illustrates the interplay between biological and environmental influences in the emergence of this key aspect of the self-concept. Second, the importance of adolescence in identity development is examined. As we grow older, take on more responsibilities and seek employment, our sense of self also changes. Finally, issues concerning the self-concept of those who feel different from others, for example through being stigmatized or feeling unattractive, are considered.

Sex role identity

Roles are those activities that fulfil others' expectations. When playing the role of a student, a person is expected to turn up at lectures, to take some notes and to write exams. Most behaviour is overlaid with what is perhaps the most important role of all: the sex role. Traditionally, men are expected to be assertive and logical, women expressive and warm. There is much evidence that men and women do differ along these lines, with female medical students, for example, being more concerned with the social and psychological aspects of medicine than are their male counterparts.[2]

A notion of what behaviour is appropriate for one's own sex is learned very early. By 3 years of age, children can discriminate between different classes of toys – boys tend to choose tools and vehicles to play with whereas girls choose prams and dishes. By the age of 5, children have learned that men dominate some professions whereas women dominate others. Generally the roles that boys wish to take are those involving logical thought and objectivity whereas the positions that girls expect to take are those requiring warmth and support. One of the more interesting debates in psychology is whether these differences are due to innate, biological influences or to learned, environmental ones.

This is not only a matter of academic debate, since the views held on this issue can have far-reaching effects. For example, even though the intake of medical students has been evenly split between males and females for many years, in the UK in 1994 less than 1 per cent of consultant surgeons were female. This imbalance might be due to social reasons, such as discriminatory practices (with women being discouraged from entering surgery), career choices (see Chapter 9) or upbringing. Or perhaps women are only rarely capable of undertaking this emotionally demanding speciality due to biological reasons, as the

following extract from a letter to the *Lancet* would suggest:

◆ We live in a world where sexual equality, especially at work, prevails. However, in reality the sexes differ not only biologically but also in less tangible, more subtle ways in respect of psychological make-up (personality, attitude, temperament, emotional reaction). Such differences may become apparent and assume importance in certain occupations, of which surgery is perhaps an example.

Some aspects of surgery – for example, procedures for emergency thoraco-abdominal trauma – demand a certain attitude of mind and level of confidence, with a minimum of diffidence and hesitation and absence of any impression of panic. Such qualities may be to some extent gender dependent in favour of the male psychological constitution. There exists a sub-group of women who no doubt have these qualities and who are more likely than others to succeed in surgery. However, it is conceivable that because of innate gender differences there will tend to be fewer female surgeons overall. (Ref. 3, p. 1361) ◆

The biological viewpoint

The human embryo is initially neuter. If a Y chromosome is present, the primordial gonad differentiates into the testes, secreting hormones which promote male genital development. If these hormones are not present, the gonads develop into the ovaries. Those who hold that sex differences are innate point to these hormonal differences, suggesting that they will have effects on the development of the brain and behaviour. For example, women are slightly more adept at tasks involving the left cerebral hemisphere (verbal ability) and men at those involving the right cerebral hemisphere (spatial abilities). Second, differences in aggression have been found cross-culturally, with men tending to be more active and aggressive than women in most (but not all) societies. Third, there are several physiological differences at birth, male babies being heavier, taller, having higher metabolic rates and larger muscle to fat ratios. Fourth, there are indications that pre-natal exposure to the male hormone progestin (sometimes used to inhibit miscarriage) can have an effect on later behaviour. Reinisch and Karlow[4] studied 16 boys and 10 girls whose mothers were given synthetic progestin during pregnancy. As compared with their siblings, they were more independent, more self-assured and more self-sufficient on a personality questionnaire measure.

More evidence for the importance of hormones comes from a study on male pseudo-hermaphrodites born with a 5–alpha-reductase deficiency. Eighteen children who had female-appearing genitalia at birth were reared unambiguously as girls. At puberty, however, their male hormone levels increased naturally, and this resulted in the development of secondary sexual characteristics (a deeper voice, more hair, etc.) When studied as adults, 17 had transferred to a male gender identity and 16 to a male sex role. Their functioning seemed to depend on hormonal levels and not on previous environment.[5]

Some sociobiologists point out that, in evolutionary terms, these sex differences would be expected. Males, who have been primarily responsible for hunting, would need to be able to develop good hunting skills, such as throwing accuracy, which is dependent on spatial abilities. Women, who have been responsible for socializing children into the culture, would need to have good verbal skills.[6] These and other differences are taken to indicate that biology plays an important part in sex-typed behaviour.

The environmental viewpoint

Those who argue that sex roles are learned reject many of these arguments, believing instead that the observed differences between men and women are mainly due to parental and societal reactions to boys and girls. They, too, use evidence from several sources. Some of the gender differences in cognitive functioning which have been well documented in the past are fading in significance, a result that cannot easily be accounted for using a purely biological explanation. Cross-culturally, behaviour that is associated with men in some cultures had been found to be associated with women in others.

For example, the Mundugmor women disliked childbearing and were as fierce and angry as the men; in the Tschambuli society, the men were given to adornment and gossip while the women showed comradely solidarity, were prone to hearty laughter and were responsible for food-gathering. Both the men and the women in the Arapesh society were expected to be gentle, sympathetic and non-aggressive.[7]

Those who stress the effect of the environment have also pointed out an important aspect of statistical analysis: even when two populations are shown to differ statistically, there can be considerable overlap in scores between them. For example, one study found that girls scored higher than boys on a test of creative thinking.[8] However, the scores were not dichotomous, as shown in Figure 7.1: although the difference is statistically significant, the *practical* significance is debatable. It is not possible to predict the results on the basis of gender alone with great accuracy, since there is considerable overlap. Simply because two populations differ on average, this does not preclude similarity between them.

Parental reactions

Much of the work in this area concerns the differences in parental reactions to young boys and girls. Block[9] asked parents to agree or disagree with several statements concerning children's abilities. Parents of boys endorsed items such as "I think a child should do better than others", whereas parents of girls tended to agree with items like "I express affection by holding, hugging and kissing my child". It seemed that boys were socialized along Protestant ethic lines, with an emphasis on achievement, competition and control of feelings, whereas girls were encouraged to develop close personal ties, to talk about problems, and were given comfort and reassurance. Parents begin to describe the behaviour of their newborns along gender stereotyped lines soon after birth. Girls are described as soft and fine-featured, whereas boys are seen as better co-ordinated, hardier and larger featured.

Another test of the hypothesis that adults react to and interpret infants' behaviour according to assigned gender is to lead adults to believe that the same infant is a boy or girl and ask the adults

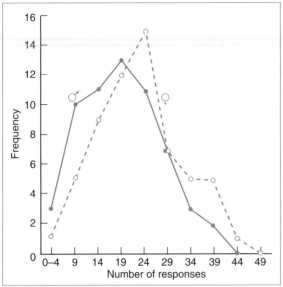

Figure 7.1 Distribution of the scores for 60 boys and 60 girls on a test for creative thinking. Although the populations differ statistically, there is considerable overlap between their results. (Reproduced from Bhavnani, R. and Hutt, C. (1972) *Journal of Child Psychology and Psychiatry* **13**: 121–127, with kind permission from Elsevier Science Ltd, The Boulevard, Langford Lane, Kidlington, OX5 1GB, UK.)

to describe and play with the child. This research strategy has been followed in several studies. In one experiment[10] 200 students were shown a videotape of a 9-month-old infant. Half of the students were told that the infant was a male, and half were told that the child was female. During the videotaped sequence, toys (a teddy bear and a jack-in-the-box) were presented to the infant and a loud buzzer sounded. The students' task was to describe the infant's responses to these events. As predicted, the ascribed gender of the child affected the descriptions. Crying was usually perceived as anger in the "male" child but as fear in the "female", and the "male" was seen as more potent and active. Apparently the expectations affected the perceptions. Other studies have shown that the time taken to respond to infants' cries[11] and the toys adults choose to give to infants are similarly affected by ascribed sex.

The different toys and reading materials actually received by children as presents have also been examined. It seems that boys are given more vehicles, sports equipment and military machines than girls, who are likely to be provided with dolls, dolls' houses and domestic toys. In a study of early school reading books, boy characters were portrayed as displaying more aggression, physical exertion and problem-solving, whereas girl characters were more likely to engage in fantasy and to be obedient.

Thus, while some psychologists have argued that the differences between men and women are due to innate, biological factors, there is much evidence implicating social influences as well. The expectations of parents and other adults during the socialization of the child are very different for boys and girls. The problem here, as in the case of intelligence, is that it is difficult to disentangle the effects of nature and nurture. By the time differences in male and female behaviours can be distinguished in children, parental and societal influences are operating. While girls as young as 12 weeks of age show greater attention to sounds than boys, parents talk to girl infants of this age more than to boys. Is it the case that mothers talk more to their female infants because the girls are more interested and responsive? Or do girls become more responsive than boys because they are talked to more often. Although adults describe and play with "male" infants differently from "female" ones, is this due only to societal expectations, or have they found such differential behaviours to be effective in the past? The studies quoted above have been very short-term: would the subjects' descriptions and behaviours change with more contact?

It is likely that both biological and social factors affect our gender identity, but once it is established it will affect our choices of behaviour and the tasks we practice. An illustration of how this can operate is provided by a study in which boys and girls (all young adolescents) were given a task which required eye–hand co-ordination (passing a loop around a curved wire in which a bell sounded if the loop touched the wire). Both boys and girls were asked to perform the tasks as well as they could, but for some the task was likened to "needlework" while for others it was described as being similar to "electronics". The label given affected the results: when the task was likened to needlework, the girls did better than the boys, but when the task was said to be similar to electronics, the boys did better than the girls.[12] This study illustrates the possibility that when one sex is better or worse than the other on certain tasks, the difference can be due to practice and cultural labels rather than innate abilities.

Valuation of sex roles

Whatever the basis for the acquisition of gender-typed behaviour, many researchers have pointed out that male roles are more highly valued in Western society than female ones. Evidence for this proposition comes from many sources. One research strategy is to ask children which sex they would prefer to be: typically, more girls wish they could be boys than vice versa, one study finding a five-fold difference. In artistic and academic work, that done by men seems to be more highly valued than that done by women. Pheterson et al.[13] showed paintings to a group of women, crediting them to either male or female artists. When asked to evaluate the paintings, the women rated the "men's" paintings higher than the "women's" on such scales as technical competence and creativity. Only when the paintings were said to have won a prize were they evaluated equally. Similar results have been found with written materials.[14]

Attribution

Success or failure at tasks also appears to have different meanings depending on the gender of the individual concerned. When attributing causes for success or failure, people often make a distinction between ability, task difficulty, luck and effort. Ability and effort are internal attributions, having to do with internal characteristics, whereas task difficulty and luck are seen to be outside the individual's control and are called external determinants. Thus, a student might blame failure in an exam to internal reasons (e.g. "I didn't work hard enough") or to external ones ("The exam was too difficult").

When this analysis is applied to achievement and gender, some differences emerge in how people account for performances by men and women. In one study, research participants read a description of a highly successful doctor. The doctor volunteered for charity work while still in training, increased the size of the practice, and was given an award as "Doctor of the Year", the youngest person ever to have received it. Half the participants were told that the physician was a man, whereas the other half were told that the physician was a woman. All were asked to suggest why this doctor was so successful. Both male and female participants considered that the "woman" physician worked harder than the man: to be equally successful, the woman would have to put more effort into her work. However, the reason why she would have to work harder was different for the males and females. The males saw the woman as having less ability than the man, whereas the females perceived a greater task difficulty for her.[15] It seems that the people in these and similar experiments had different expectations of the performance of men and women, attributing different reasons for identical performances.

Analysis of conversations

The studies described above rely on hypothetical situations rather than on actual observations of how men and women relate to one another. Perhaps a better test of the hypothesis that men and women have different status in Western society comes from analysis of conversations. A rather obvious, but important, feature of conversation is that only one person speaks at a time. A listener will usually wait until the speaker has finished before talking. There are some exceptions to this rule – interruptions – where the listener begins to talk before the speaker ends. Again, this is obvious, but it seems that interruptions are not randomly distributed between conversationalists, but are associated with status. Higher status individuals are more likely to interrupt those of lower status than vice versa. So it may be that some measure of relative status can be gained by recording how two people talk to each other and counting the interruptions.

In studies of this kind, men interrupt women more often than vice versa (96 per cent of the time in one investigation). Since in the consulting room doctors are generally considered to have more power and status than their patients, an asymmetry in interruptions could be expected and, indeed, this has been found to be the case. An important qualification to this finding, however, is that the sex of the doctor is significant. Whereas male physicians contributed some 70 per cent of the interruptions in their consultations with patients, female physicians initiated only 32 per cent, and even less when the patient was male.[16] If interruptions can be taken as a valid measure, then female doctors may either take on less status or be accorded less status by their patients than male doctors. An alternative explanation of these results is that different interviewing styles may be adopted by men and women doctors (see Chapter 11).

Mental health

These studies, conducted in both laboratory and natural settings, suggest that the situation faced by women is quite different from that faced by men. In our society at present, tasks that require logical thinking and objectivity (the traditionally masculine qualities) are more highly valued than those requiring emotional support and warmth (traditionally feminine qualities). The roles and occupations held by women tend to be less well paid and are less secure than those held by men. Some writers have connected such differences in valuation with mental health. Women are more likely to request assistance for psychiatric difficulties. They are more likely to be depressed, to suffer from suicidal thoughts and to attempt suicide, for example. Although this difference may be due simply to a greater likelihood of women expressing their difficulties (i.e. men may have as many problems but keep them to themselves), it is also possible that the higher rate of psychological difficulties occurs because feminine roles are seen as less valuable. There is evidence that levels of depression are affected by self-esteem, and the cognitive psychologist Aaron Beck (Chapter 4) suggests that women have a culturally fostered tendency to see themselves as powerless and to undervalue their achievements.[17]

It is also possible that doctors expect to find differences in symptoms depending on the gender of the patient. Some have argued that the image of men and women put across by pharmaceutical companies leads doctors to expect certain symptoms to occur more frequently in women than in men. In an analysis of medical journals, advertisements for drugs aimed at psychogenic symptoms were predominantly illustrated with women, who were shown to be emotional, irrational and complaining. Advertisements for drugs for organic illnesses, on the other hand, predominantly depicted men, who tended to be non-emotional, stoic and rational.[18] There is some evidence that such images may influence physicians' expectations of patients. In one study, clinicians were given short case histories said to be descriptions of a man (or woman) suffering from low back pain or epigastric pain. Although there are no sex differences in the prevalence of these conditions in the general population, "female" patients were said to be excessively demanding of doctors' time, to be more likely to suffer from psychosomatic illnesses, and to have complaints in which emotional factors are important.[19]

Psychological androgyny

There is an assumption in many people's minds that masculinity and femininity represent the ends of a single continuum. The ideal man might be considered assertive and instrumental, whereas women would be unassertive and passive. Women might be idealized as compassionate and expressive, while men would be low on these qualities. Women may be thought to be more dependent than men and less concerned with achievements. This model would place men and women on a single dimension: men would tend to fall at one end, women at the other.

Psychologists have questioned this traditional assumption of a single dimension, exploring the possibility that masculinity and femininity are two separate characteristics, each present in varying degrees in both men and women. In this model, an individual could score highly on either or on both masculine and feminine characteristics. One person could be both compassionate and assertive for example. Such a person would be called "psychologically androgynous" and would fall in quadrant A in Figure 7.2. Someone who was high in masculine characteristics but low in feminine ones would be termed masculine (quadrant B), and someone else who was high on femininity and low in masculinity would be termed feminine (quadrant C). Those who lie in the fourth quadrant (D) are termed "undifferentiated".

There are now several self-report questionnaires designed to measure psychological androgyny. The Bem Sex Role Inventory (BSRI),

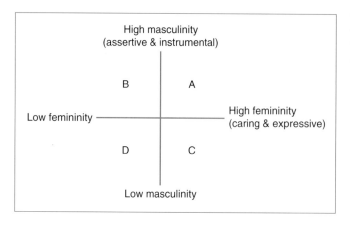

Figure 7.2 In this model of masculinity and femininity, members of either gender can possess both masculine and feminine characteristics. The quadrants A, B, C and D are explained in the text.

for example, contains 20 items on each of the masculinity and femininity scales. The individual is asked to describe how well each item describes him or herself, placing an X where appropriate. An item on the masculine scale is:

Act as a leader
Never true ———————— Always true

and one on the femininity scale is:

Affectionate
Never true ———————— Always true

One person might answer near the "Always true" end of the masculine items but near the "Never true" end of the feminine items, indicating a predominantly masculine orientation, while the opposite would be true of a feminine person. Someone who indicates that the "Always true" end of both types of items applied to them would be considered androgynous.

There is evidence that androgynous individuals are more adaptable than those who are sex-typed, showing masculine or feminine behaviours depending on their appropriateness in different situations. An androgynous man is more likely to be nurturant (e.g. to smile, talk with and touch a baby or to show sympathy and understanding to a lonely person) than a masculine one, and an androgynous woman is more likely to resist social pressures to conform than a feminine one.[20] Although there have been many criticisms of the concept of androgyny in general and the BSRI in particular, the notion that individuals can be both masculine and feminine in behaviour and that this flexibility has advantages for adjustment has gained a firm foothold in psychology.

There have been attempts to relate androgyny to the psychological health and orientation of medical students. Zeldow *et al.*[21] first gave a questionnaire designed to measure androgyny to the students during their first week at university. Eight months later, a second series of tests were given which measured the students' ability to cope with the course and their orientation to patient care. Those who originally scored high on the masculinity scale were less depressed, more confident, and more emotionally stable than low scorers on masculinity, whereas those who scored high on femininity were more likely to be satisfied with their interpersonal relationships, to consume less alcohol and to set a higher value on the interpersonal aspects of medical practice than those who scored low on femininity. Those who scored high on both scales were able both to cope with the course and to maintain caring attitudes, two attributes which are particularly important in medicine.

Identity and adolescence

While identity develops throughout life, Erikson[22] has argued that adolescence is the critical period in its formation. There are a number of reasons why a person's sense of self will change at this time. There is increasing independence from the family of origin, whose values will be reconsidered in light of increased involvement with peers and the world outside the family. There are also marked physical changes during puberty which affect sexual behaviour and body image. The period of adolescence is lengthened in technologically advanced societies, bringing for many an extended period between childhood and the self-sufficiency of adulthood. Two of the more important changes during this time involve the choice of a career and entering employment.

Choosing a career

An important way in which individuals define themselves is in terms of their intended or actual career. When first introduced to somebody, asking what they do, or are planning to do, is frequently an early question. You may recall that in the first week at university many students asked you about which course you were following, a question which serves to define you in both your own and others' eyes.

The family, peer group and the school are all influential on choice of career. Parental interest in their child's future career seems important. In one survey,[23] 81 per cent of students from an Asian background thought their parents had a great interest in their future compared to 63 per cent of white teenagers. The former had correspondingly higher aspirations than the latter. The separate effects of parental interest, peers and school are difficult to disentangle, since the type of school often depends on social background. Doctors' children, for example, often consider medicine as a career, but in addition to the direct influence from their parents, they are likely to know other professional families and receive support from their teachers and peers for their academic work.

Other sources of information are also important. Think back to when you made the decision to study medicine. What do you remember as being the most influential experiences, or sources of information? Did you have a clear idea of what to expect? When 16–year-olds with a clear idea of their future career were asked how they had made their choice, almost all mentioned the influence of friends, relatives or teachers. Six major ways in which these people affected their choice were identified.[24] They were seen as:

- sources of information about themselves, their capabilities and potential;
- sources of information about educational and occupational opportunities;

- communicators of the suitability of occupations;
- models, who had entered the particular occupation;
- agents in the acquisition of work experience; and
- facilitators in decision-making.

This has implications for careers guidance in schools. Traditional careers guidance tended to rely on "matching" theories, based on the premise that (a) people are different from each other and (b) so are jobs. The aim was to assess both in order to achieve a match with the underlying assumption was that individuals' characteristics were stable and could be measured in a reliable way. One commonly used vocational assessment tool, the Vocational Preferences Inventory,[25] asks individuals to indicate their preferences from a number of statements about work activities. People are then classified into six personality or interest types: realistic, investigative, artistic, social, enterprising or conventional. A catalogue of occupations has been developed which classifies jobs in the same way, and thus a match can be sought. Medicine is both an "investigative" and a "social" type of job.

More recently, careers guidance stresses the importance of a wider, more active view, enlarging social networks and experiences to help pupils learn more about themselves and how they react in different situations, as well as about the opportunities available. Guidance practitioners are becoming the co-ordinators of resources which can contribute to students' decision-making, such as bringing ex-pupils back into school to act as models and sources of information, organizing work placements, and seeking opportunities for pupils to develop vocational skills.

Employment and unemployment

The transition from school to work has traditionally been an important source of identity achievement. Widespread economic recession and the requirements for an increasingly skilled workforce means there are fewer jobs for those who leave school without higher qualifications. This has resulted in an increase in the numbers of students staying on in full-time education, and a growth in vocational courses designed to make young people more attractive to employers. Even so, many now experience periods of unemployment.

Avoiding unemployment by remaining a student does not necessarily confer improved psychological well-being. Among an academically able sample in their mid-twenties, who were followed up over a period of several years during the 1980s, Winefield et al.[26] found that current students had higher scores for depressed mood than both those who had completed their higher education and those who had left at age 16. Although psychological benefits might accrue later, the experience of being a student did not confer general psychological benefits on these individuals at that time. Rather, it was being in the workforce and out of the education system which resulted in improved psychological well-being. Some of the stresses involved in being a medical student or a doctor are discussed in Chapter 9.

But any job is not necessarily better than no job. The main characteristics associated with dissatisfaction and mental health problems at work have been identified as:[27]

- an uncongenial environment at work;
- unduly high work demands;
- lack of personal control over work demands and activities;
- lack of opportunities to exercise work skills;
- lack of variety in work tasks;
- lack of clarity about work tasks and inadequate feedback on performance; and
- lack of supportive, personal relationships.

Causal links between employment and mental health have been shown in a number of studies which have monitored changes in well-being over time as employment status changed. For example, young people who gained jobs became less anxious and depressed compared to those remaining unemployed.[28] This can be understood in terms of the wider functions of employment (beyond the purely financial) in providing a means of structuring time, providing a sense of identity and personal status. Those who cope best with unemployment are those with social support and a way of using their time.

Transition points appear to be particularly stressful, whether impending redundancy or job changes. The results from a major survey of employment and unemployment indicate that it is lack of certainty about employment prospects that leads to mental ill-health, rather than whether a person is unemployed or not.[29] That there are associated physiological changes has also been demonstrated. Kasl and Cobb[30] approached the management and unions of two companies who had just heard that the companies were to close. They took blood pressure measures at this initial point, then at termination of the jobs and again at 6, 12 and 24 months afterwards. Compared to a control group of workers whose employment was assured (who showed no changes over the 2–year period) the blood pressure of the redundant workers was highest just before and just after their jobs were lost and fell when a new position was found.

Self-esteem

Our sense of self-esteem – the extent to which we value ourselves and our achievements – is a central aspect of our identity. According to some psychologists, much of what we do relates to a motive to protect and enhance our sense of integrity and worth. While extremes of self-esteem may be harmful or inappropriate, a moderate to high level of self-esteem is necessary to be an effective and happy member of society. You may have experienced a rise in your pride and self-esteem when you were accepted to medical school, since it was an objective validation of your personal worth. Shame, on the other hand, implies a lowering of self-esteem, the realization that we are not all that we supposed ourselves to be. When medical students do not perform as well as they had hoped they sometimes feel ashamed of their results.

In one study,[31] medical students were asked to describe situations in which they felt proud or felt ashamed during their clinical work. Feelings of pride occurred when they believed that they had performed technical tasks well, had helped patients emotionally or demonstrated academic knowledge, as the following illustrate:

❝ I felt proud after an evening when I clerked quite a few patients and felt that I'd done quite well. I didn't really do anything specific, but felt that I was doing something useful – that I wasn't just in the way. Also felt proud because I could see that I had improved over the months of clinical work. "

" Correctly making a new diagnosis of abdominal aortic aneurysm in a patient as well as finding the presenting complaint. The fact that I was confident in my diagnosis and that it was a new diagnosis. "

On the other hand, feelings of shame occurred when they felt they had acted unprofessionally or had let patients down in some way:

" I felt very ashamed of laughing at someone during clinic because they were having a sigmoidscope examination at the time. The patient was in pain. I felt that it was very unprofessional and cruel in retrospect. "

" Going to see a very ill patient with clinical partners, causing relatives to get further distressed. Patient died later that night. My insensitivity. Our learning apparently taking priority over the last few hours of loved ones' precious time. "

These quotations also illustrate that self-esteem, although it may be fundamentally stable, fluctuates with experience. In this section, two aspects of self-esteem are discussed: the issue of stigma and ways in which self-esteem can be altered.

Stigma

We all hold stereotypes of groups of people. There are stereotypes of people with different occupations, such as psychologists and medical students, and stereotypes of people with different appearances. Some groups in a society are rejected or avoided because they deviate from norms about how people should look or behave. People with certain illnesses – such as cerebral palsy or psychiatric difficulties – are often seen to be flawed or "marked" in some way which sets them apart from others. This negative side of stereotyping is referred to as "stigma".[32]

A distinction can be made between "felt" and "enacted" stigma. Felt stigma refers to the person's expectations of negative reactions to their appearance or behaviour. This expectation can lead to avoidance (e.g. a person with psoriasis might avoid communal bathing facilities) and impression management (e.g. a person with vitiligo might use cosmetics to camouflage uneven skin pigmentation). Some authors have argued that felt stigma is much more of an issue than enacted stigma, which involves actual behavioural discrimination.

It seems that a condition becomes stigmatizing when it threatens the orderly and predictable flow of social interactions. When behaviour or appearance is unusual, we are less certain what might occur in a conversation, and this seems to be aversive for most people. Some stigmatizing conditions can be obvious (such as a facial disfigurement or a skin condition such as psoriasis). Others are hidden (such as epilepsy, mental illness or alcoholism). These conditions seem particularly important when they are persistent and are seen as central to the person's identity. For example, West[33] interviewed people about epilepsy and found several negative views about sufferers. Many believed that people with epilepsy were violent/aggressive (21 per cent), nervy (17 per cent), highly strung/unstable and withdrawn/timid (10 per cent).

One question is whether such negative views affect behaviour. Is enacted stigma common? Are people with stigmatizing difficulties treated differently than others? It seems as though they are. There are a great many studies which illustrate that people often change their behaviour, at least initially, when confronted with someone who is "different" in some way. For example, in one experiment research participants were asked to have a conversation with another individual, who was actually a confederate of the experimenters. For one group of participants the confederate entered the room in a wheelchair, apparently having had a leg amputation, while for the other group of participants the confederate entered the room as able-bodied. In both situations the confederate was instructed behave in similar ways, so that any differences in reactions were due to the perceptions and expectations of the participants. The conversations were recorded and later analysed: when talking with the person with the supposed amputation,

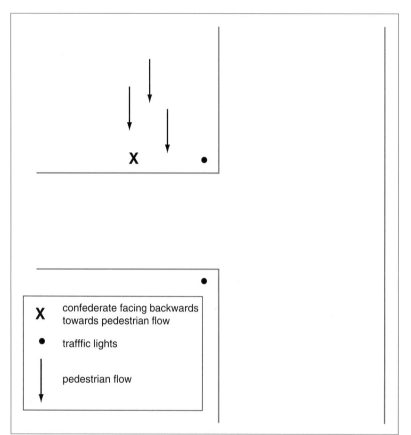

Figure 7.3 Looking downwards on the intersection, an illustration of the situation explored in a study on the effects of facial disfigurement on social distancing. See text for details.

X confederate facing backwards towards pedestrian flow

• trafffic lights

pedestrian flow

participants ended the conversation more quickly, avoided eye contact and later said that they felt more anxious.[34]

Physical marks can also result in avoidance and social distancing. Physical attractiveness has extremely important effects on others' perceptions. We live in a society which places great value on appearance, so that attractive people are often seen as having many positive traits while unattractive people are viewed less positively. This cultural view can result in a great many difficulties.

In an experiment on the effects of visible disfigurements (particularly convincing because it was performed in a real life setting), psychologists tested the hypothesis that people would avoid a person who had a noticeable facial blemish. In one condition, a confederate wore no make-up, appearing "normal". In a second condition he was made up so that there was a large blemish on one side of his face, and in a third condition it appeared that he had recently suffered an accident to the same side of his face.

The experimenters hypothesized that people would put greater social distance between themselves and the person with the blemish than the person with no blemish or the person who had suffered an accident. They tested the hypothesis in the setting illustrated in Figure 7.3. The confederate stood at an intersection with traffic lights, looking backwards towards pedestrians as they approached the intersection. Measures of physical distance were taken as the pedestrians waited for the lights to change. The question was "How close would the pedestrians stand to the confederate in the three conditions?" And "On what side would they stand – would this be random or would it be related to the side with the blemish?" The results indicated a considerable degree of distancing. There was little difference in physical distance between the conditions when the confederate wore no make-up or appeared to have had an accident, but the pedestrians stood significantly further away in the blemished condition. Furthermore, 73 per cent of the pedestrians chose to stand on the unblemished side while they waited for the lights to change.[35]

Stigma and distress

The effects of a mark depend to some extent on its visibility. Dermatological diseases such as psoriasis or vitiligo on visible areas and facial disfigurements can have significant psychological consequences.[36] Ginsburg[37] describes how people with psoriasis often feel shame and embarrassment, anxiety, lack of confidence and depression. Their condition often led to restricted social activities and sexual relationships. While it is the case that some people are able to dismiss such difficulties and get on with their lives, others become virtual hermits. For them it is the social aspects of visible conditions which are distressing, not the lesions themselves.[38,39]

When a condition is less visible, people can be very ashamed to admit to it and may take great care to conceal the difficulty. These feelings of shame are learnt from others' reactions, as discovered by Scrambler[40] in his interviews with people with epilepsy:

> It used to annoy me terribly, the shame of it really, I was so ashamed, very much so . . . My mother didn't like it either, and it's obviously rubbed off on me . . . I wanted desperately to be normal. I didn't want people to say 'Oh, see how she's an epileptic!' To me it was a terrible time and I used to suffer a lot, worrying in case I did take one, a fit. (p. 84)

Scrambler also describes how 9 out of 10 people with epilepsy interviewed indicated that they would not disclose their disease until they had become a close friend with the person involved, since:

> This is what I've found – that whenever I tell anybody that I'm epileptic they don't want to know me at all. I've had friends here: as soon as they know I'm epileptic they don't want to know me at all. (p. 83)

This reluctance to disclose is an understandable strategy in the light of the earlier evidence discussed: the psychological effects of impaired appearance or disability appear to be rooted in reality. Other people do, in fact, see those individuals differently and treat them differently.

Improving self-esteem

The basic concept outlined here is that our feelings of self-esteem are firmly rooted in both our biology and in others' reactions to us. If we are valued by others we will learn to value ourselves. Sometimes people will take steps to improve their sense of worth, in a variety of ways, sometimes through attempting to change their appearance (as in plastic surgery or through eating patterns) and sometimes by learning new personal skills (as in assertiveness training).

Plastic surgery

The concept of stigma can be used to understand something about the needs and motives of people who seek aesthetic plastic surgery. It is important to realize that, from the individual's point of view, a minor physical disfigurement can be as burdensome and damaging to self-esteem as a major one. People who are self-conscious about their appearance may go to great lengths to avoid the characteristic being exposed. For example, someone with a large nose may be constantly alert to ensure that their profile is not viewed. Surgery provides a way of removing this feeling of stigmatization, and reduces the need for constant vigilance.[41]

The likelihood of receiving treatment does not bear a direct link to the objective problem since general practitioners vary in their willingness to refer to surgery. Even the same general practitioners may treat patients who come to them with concerns about their physical appearance differently. One study found that women were more likely to be referred to a surgeon while men were often referred to a psychiatrist.[42]

There are two main types of plastic surgery – aesthetic and reconstructive. The goal of cosmetic surgery is to facilitate psychological changes, especially to reduce preoccupation with appearance. There is now good evidence that a variety of aesthetic changes are associated with positive changes in self-esteem, less anxious and depressive mood and less bodily camouflaging.[43] For example, Bradbury et al.[44] examined the effects of surgery to correct prominent ears in children between the ages of 5 and 16. Several weeks before surgery they were extensively interviewed and asked to complete questionnaires concerning their social experiences.

Twelve months post-operatively, the children were again assessed for any changes in their well-being. Over 90 per cent of the children benefited from the operation, being much more personally happy. However, there was little change in their social experiences, and some of the children did not seem to benefit. It seemed that children who were socially very isolated prior to the operation were less satisfied with the outcome.

This study also demonstrated a general principle of aesthetic plastic surgery – that there was little association between the objective severity of the prominent ears and either pre-operative or post-operative happiness. Children with the most prominent ears were not necessarily the most distressed and some children with minor prominence were very distressed. The objective degree of correction was not related to post-operative changes. However, the children's rating of prominence was highly correlated with satisfaction, thus illustrating the common finding that it is the subjective assessment which is important.

Reconstructive surgery refers to interventions that are designed to change or improve appearance, but can usually only reduce (and not eliminate) the differences between pre-operative and normal appearance. The operation may involve alteration of soft tissues (as in cleft palate), hard bony tissue (as for Cruzon or Treacher–Collins syndromes). Again, the justification for this type of intervention is on psychological and social grounds, but there is much less evidence that reconstructive surgery has a significant impact on well-being. For example, in a study[45] with children and young adolescents who received craniofacial surgery for congenital malformation, few changes were found when they were compared with a group of children from other paediatric practices. Before surgery, the craniofacial patients showed several psychosocial difficulties, but these were marginal compared to the unaffected children. One year after surgery the test scores of the patients had shifted only slightly. It may be that as these children grew further into adolescence – when appearance becomes increasingly important – greater benefits would be shown, but as yet there are few indications that this group of children suffer from their appearance unduly or that surgery has a dramatic effect on well-being.

Eating disorders

A great many explanations have been given for the development of eating disorders, but cultural preferences for a slim body shape, perpetuated through the media with associations of professional success, along with problems with self-image, are often held to be responsible for their emergence amongst adolescents. High levels of dissatisfaction with body weight have been recorded in a number of studies, with 70–80 per cent of schoolgirls being dissatisfied with their bodies and wanting to lose weight.

Anorexia nervosa usually occurs after puberty and gives rise to self-induced weight loss and amenorrhoea. It can be linked to misperceptions of body image and anxieties about lack of control over eating. The incidence of anorexia nervosa varies between different groups in a way which suggests that it is a culture- and subculture-specific difficulty.[46] For example, for schoolgirls, estimates of 1 in 250 have been obtained, rising to 1 in 100 of those at boarding school and 3.5 per cent of fashion students. It is less frequent in those who are not of white racial origin. *Bulimia nervosa* is an eating disorder closely related to anorexia nervosa of which it is often a later sequel. In bulimia, episodes of gross overeating are later purged by self-induced vomiting. Compulsive eating can be seen as a conflict between a biologically derived drive for food and a culturally derived drive for thinness.[47]

Research in the area is complicated by a number of factors. First, different diagnostic criteria have been used, undermining the comparability of studies. Some researchers have restricted their work to sufferers showing specific physical symptoms, others require a range of physical and psychological criteria to be met. Second, "cause" and "effect" can be confused, as in the finding that anorexic patients show extreme indecision when discussing the implications of growing up, or acquiring a boyfriend. It is unclear whether ambivalence about independence has contributed to the development of the anorexia, or has resulted from it. Little is known about the eating habits, communication patterns and psychological processes of those without eating disorders to provide comparison information. Third, studies of the course of the illness have used different follow-up periods and often failed to consider whether drop outs from the study differed from those remaining.

Despite these difficulties, there is some consensus about precipitating factors. These include: bereavements, family disruption, a physical illness where regain of original weight is not achieved, expectations of high scholastic achievement, and underlying depressive illness.[48] Links between eating disorders and child sexual abuse are being examined. There may be a genetic factor as well, since anorexia is more common in both members of monozygotic than dizygotic twin pairs. Many authors have argued that there is a strong link between eating disorders and a pervasive concern with others' evaluations, which is linked with low self-esteem.[49]

Sufferers often have a dread of fatness which is regarded not simply as unattractive but as loathsome, equated with social failure and deserving of condemnation. They describe a fear of losing control over their eating patterns and gaining a sense of achievement and satisfaction if they succeed in their quest for weight loss and thinness. Coupled with this, sufferers often do not see themselves as emaciated, and deny that they are ill. On the contrary, they may regard themselves as overweight: many studies show they see themselves as wider and fatter than they are objectively. For these reasons it is perhaps not surprising that people requiring professional help will conceal their determination to remain under weight, making treatment very difficult.

Bruch[50] contends that there are four key elements of treatment. First, it is essential to secure the patient's co-operation. Second, the patient's weight should be restored to normal. Third, psychological methods of treatment are often adopted, either individually or with the family to explore relationships within the family, problems with growing up, concerns about personal independence, and sexual conflicts. Finally, endocrine therapy is often required to treat persistent amenorrhoea. Progress in treatment can be measured on scales such as the Eating Disorders Inventory.[51] This scale has eight subscales which focus on the aspects identified above, such as: drive for thinness; body dissatisfaction; perfectionism; maturity fears; and interpersonal distrust. Assessing the effectiveness of treatment is

difficult since follow-up studies over long periods of at least 4 years are required.[52]

While it is widely acknowledged that physical and psychological factors interact in the development and maintenance of many conditions, eating disorders are unusual in the extent to which they are influenced by social factors. This has practical implications since it suggests that there may be scope for preventative measures of a social nature, such as discouraging the valuation of specific body shapes in the media.

Assertiveness

One aspect of our self-esteem involves our ability to deal with difficult interpersonal relationships. For a variety of reasons, we may feel that our abilities in this area are not strong and could be improved. Many people have found training in assertiveness skills can be helpful in this respect. Assertiveness emphasizes mutual respect and an acceptance of everyone's positive and negative characteristics. Dickson[53] contrasts assertiveness with *aggressive, passive* and *indirectly aggressive* behaviour. Aggressive behaviour is competitive, with the goal being to emerge as the winner, which means that someone has to lose. We show passive behaviour when we see ourselves as the victim of unfairness and injustice at the hands of others. At such times our outlook is negative, and the prospect of confrontation provokes immediate acquiescence or avoidance. Indirect aggressive behaviour is more subtle and hidden. Instead of the more obvious aggressive tactics, it becomes safer to control and manipulate rather than face confrontation and risk being rejected. We all show these types of behaviour on occasion, but they are not usually effective in resolving interpersonal issues.

Assertiveness training is usually given in small groups, with a facilitator who encourages the group members to express their feelings, beliefs and needs in a straightforward way. The training emphasizes the acceptance of responsibility for choices and behaviour, so that an assertive person is said to acknowledge needs and to make requests openly and directly. Such directness may involve the risk of rejection and refusal, but the aim is to develop a sense of self-worth which is not dependent on the approval of others. One aspect of such training programmes is to clarify the rights we all have with regard to our relationships: Dickson's list is shown in Box 7.1.

BOX 7.1

Our rights

1 I have the right to state my own needs and set my own priorities as a person, independent of any roles that I may assume in my life.
2 I have the right to be treated with respect as an equal human being regardless of my colour, race, creed, sex, age, disability.
3 I have the right to express my feelings.
4 I have the right to express my opinions and values.
5 I have the right to say "no" or "yes" for myself.
6 I have the right to make mistakes.
7 I have the right to change my mind.
8 I have the right to say "I don't understand" and to ask for more information.
9 I have the right to ask for what I want.
10 I have the right to decline responsibility for other people's problems.
11 I have the right to deal with others without being dependent on them for approval.

(Reproduced from Dickson, A. (1982) *A Woman in Your Own Right*. London: Quartet, with permission.)

Suggested reading

Sexuality issues facing young people are reviewed by Moore, S. and Rosenthal, D. (1993) *Sexuality in Adolescence*, London: Routledge. Cash, T. and Pruzinsky, T. (eds) (1990) *Body Images. Development, Deviance and Change*, London: Guilford Press, provide a comprehensive review of issues concerning disfigurement and plastic surgery.

References

1. Montemayor, T. and Eisen, M (1977) The development of self-conceptions from childhood to adolescence. *Developmental Psychology* **13**: 314-319.
2. Bean, G. and Kidder, L. (1982) Helping and achieving. *Social Science and Medicine* **16**: 1377-1381.
3. Benson, J. (1992) Surgical careers and female students. *Lancet* **339**: 1361.
4. Reinisch, J.M. and Karlow, W.G. (1977) Prenatal exposure to synthetic progestins and estrogens. *Archives of Sexual Behaviour* **6**: 257-288.
5. Money, J. and Erhardt, A.A. (1972) *Man and Woman: Boy and Girl*. Baltimore: Johns Hopkins University Press.
6. Buss, D. (1995) Psychological sex differences. *American Psychologist* **50**: 164-168.
7. Mead, M. (1950) *Sex and Temperament in Three Societies*. New York: Mentor.
8. Bhavnani, R. and Hutt, C. (1972) Divergent thinking in boys and girls. *Journal of Child Psychology and Psychiatry* **13**: 121-127.
9. Block, J.H. (1973) Conceptions of sex role. *American Psychologist* **28**: 512-526.
10. Rubin, J.Z., Provenzano, F.J. and Luria, Z. (1974) The eye of the beholder. *American Journal of Orthopsychiatry* **44**: 512-519.
11. Condry, S.M., Condry, J. and Pogatshnik, L. (1983) Sex differences: a study of the ear of the beholder. *Sex Roles* **6**: 697-704.
12. Davies, D. (1986) Children's performance as a function of sex-types labels. *British Journal of Social Psychology* **25**: 173-175.
13. Pheterson, G.I., Kiesler, S. and Goldberg, P. (1971) Evaluation of the performance of women as a function of their sex, achievement and personal history. *Journal of Personality and Social Psychology* **19**: 114-118.
14. Paludi, M.A. and Bauer, W. (1983) Goldberg revisited; what's in an author's name? *Sex Roles* **9**: 387-390.
15. Feldman-Summers, S. and Kiesler, S. (1974) Those who are number two try harder. *Journal of Personality and Social Psychology* **30**: 846-855.
16. West, C. (1980) When the doctor is a 'lady'. In: Stromberg, A. (ed.) *Women, Health and Medicine*. Palo Alto, California: Mayfield.
17. Beck, A.T. and Greenberg, R. (1974) Cognitive therapy with depressed women. In: Franks, V. and Burtle, V. (eds) *Women in Therapy*. New York: Brunner–Mazel.
18. Thompson, E.L. (1979) Sexual bias in drug advertisements. *Social Science and Medicine* **13A**: 187-191.
19. Bernstein, B. and Kane, R. (1981) Physicians' attitudes towards female patients. *Medical Care* **19**: 600-608.
20. Bem, S.L., Martyna, W. and Watson, C. (1976) Sex-typing and androgyny. *Journal of Personality and Social Psychology* **34**: 1016-1023.
21. Zeldow, P.B., Clark, D., Daugherty, S. and Eckenfels, E. (1985) Personality indicators of psychosocial

adjustment in first-year medical students. *Social Science and Medicine* 20: 95–100.

22. Erikson, E. (1968) *Identity: Youth and Crisis*. London: Faber.

23. Fogelman, K. (1979) Educational and career aspirations of sixteen year olds. *British Journal of Guidance and Counselling* 7.

24. Kidd, J. (1984) Young people's perceptions of their occupational decision-making. *British Journal of Guidance and Counselling* 12: 25–38.

25. Holland, J. (1985) *Making Vocational Choices: A Theory of Vocational Personalities and Work Environments*. Englewood Cliffs, NJ: Prentice Hall.

26. Winefield, A.H., Tiggermann, M., Winefield, H.R. and Goldney, R.D. (1994) *Growing Up with Unemployment: A Longitudinal Study of its Impact*. London: Routledge.

27. Warr, P. (1987) *Work, Unemployment and Mental Health*. Oxford: Clarendon Press.

28. Banks, M. and Ullah, P. (1988) *Youth Unemployment in the 1980s: Its Psychological Effects*. London: Croom Helm.

29. Gallie, D., Maser, C. and Vogler, C. (eds) (1994) *Social Change and the Experience of Unemployment*. Oxford: Oxford University Press.

30. Kasl, S. and Cobb, S. (1970) Blood pressure changes in men undergoing job loss. *Psychosomatic Medicine* 32: 19–38.

31. Lee-Tsang-Tan, G. and Kent, G. (1995) Emotional reactions during medical education. *Academic Medicine* 70: 343–344.

32. Jones, E., Farina, A., Hastorf, A., Markus, H., Miller, D. and Scott, R. (1984) *Social Stigma. The Psychology of Marked Relationships*. New York: Freeman.

33. West, P. (1979) An investigation into the social construction and consequences of the label "epilepsy". PhD thesis, University of Bristol. Cited in: Scrambler, G. (1989) *Epilepsy*. London: Routledge.

34. Comer, R. and Piliavin, J. (1972) The effects of physical deviance upon face-to-face interaction: The other side. *Journal of Personality and Social Psychology* 23: 33–39.

35. Rumsey, N., Bull, R. and Gahagan, D. (1982) The effects of facial disfigurement on the proxemic behaviour of the general public. *Journal of Applied Social Psychology* 12: 137–150.

36. Tobiasen, J. (1989) Scaling facial impairment. *Cleft Palate Journal* 26: 249–254.

37. Ginsburg, I. (1989) Feelings of stigmatisation in patients with psoriasis. *Journal of the American Academy of Dermatology* 20: 53–63.

38. Baugman, R. and Sobel, R. (1971) Psoriasis, stress and strain. *Archives of Dermatology* 103: 599–605.

39. Root, S., Kent, G. and Al-Abadie, M. (1994) The relationship between disease severity, disability and psychological distress in patients undergoing PUVA treatment for psoriasis. *Dermatology* 189: 234–237.

40. Scrambler, G. (1989) *Epilepsy*. London: Routledge.

41. Bradbury, E. (1994) The psychology of aesthetic plastic surgery. *Aesthetic Plastic Surgery* 18: 301–305.

42. Thomas, C.S. (1984) Dysmorphophobia: a question of definition. *British Journal of Psychiatry* 144: 513–516.

43. Pruzinsky, T. and Edgerton, M. (1990) Body image change in aesthetic plastic surgery. In: Cash, T. and Pruzinsky, T. (eds) (1990) *Body Images. Development, Deviance and Change*. London: Guilford Press, pp. 217–236.

44. Bradbury, E., Hewison, J. and Timmons, M. (1992) Psychological and social outcome of prominent ear correction in children. *British Journal of Plastic Surgery* 45: 97–100.

45. Pertschuk, M. and Whitaker, L. (1988) Psychosocial outcome of craniofacial surgery in children. *Plastic and Reconstructive Surgery* 82: 741–746.

46. Swartz, L. (1985) Anorexia nervosa as a culture bound syndrome. *Social Science and Medicine* 20: 725–730.

47. Wardle, J. (1987) Compulsive eating and dietary restraint. *British Journal of Clinical Psychology* 26: 47–55.

48. Garfinkel, P. and Garner, D. (1982) *Anorexia Nervosa: A Multi-dimensional Perspective*. New York: Brunner-Mazel.

49. Striegel-Moore, R., Silberstein, L. and Rodon, J. (1993) The social self in bulimia nervosa: public self-consciousness, social anxiety and perceived fraudulence. *Journal of Abnormal Psychology* 102: 297–303.

50. Bruch, H. (1978) *The Golden Cage*. London: Open Books.

51. Garner, D., Olmstead, M. and Polivy, J. (1983) Development and validation of a multi-dimensional eating disorder inventory for anorexia nervosa and bulimia. *International Journal of Eating Disorders* 2: 15–34.

52. Steinhausen, H.C. (1983) Follow-up studies of anorexia nervosa: a review of research findings. *Psychological Medicine* 13: 239–249.

53. Dickson, A. (1982) *A Woman in Her Own Right*. London: Quartet.

8
The Changing Family

SUMMARY

Families are systems which adapt and react to developmental changes. Changes include pregnancy, physical and mental illness, ageing and death. The family's resources and perceptions of problems are important in personal development, and therapists who work with the family network believe that an individual's difficulties are most likely to be resolved in the context of family functioning.

Although the family group is usually responsible for biological reproduction, it also plays a significant role in what can be termed "social reproduction". It is through relationships with parents and other caregivers that children acquire much of their knowledge about themselves and about the customs and expectations of society. There have been many changes in family structure over the past decades which reflect changes in customs and beliefs about child rearing.

Within each family group, there will be many rules that are shared with the larger culture, but also many which are not. Each individual family can be seen as a kind of subculture with its own set of idiosyncratic ways of coping with such events as pregnancy and birth, and such difficulties as discord and illness. There may be taboos about discussing particular topics or certain accepted ways of dealing with conflicts. Since children learn much through instruction by and observation of their parents, there is the possibility that children may grow up to use methods of coping with difficulties that are similar to those of their parents. They may come to treat their children in the way that they themselves were treated when young, or may create a marital relationship similar to that of their parents.

Psychologists who study and work with families often consider relatives not as individuals but as parts of a larger system, which adapts to and reacts to individuals' changes. The essence of a *systems approach* to families is that changes in one part of the system will have effects on all the others involved. Thus, for example, the birth of a second child affects all the relationships in a family. The parents may find that they have less time for each other and the older sibling may feel that he or she does not receive enough attention any more, becoming jealous of the new-born baby. Research in the areas of pregnancy, family discord and old age form the basis for discussion in this chapter. In all these topics, the value of understanding the family within a systems approach is clear.

Pregnancy and childbirth

One of the most important changes in a family is

the discovery of pregnancy and later birth of a child. The foetus itself is a socializing agent for its parents. Parents begin to adapt by attending antenatal clinics, preparing a cot and clothes, and informing friends and relatives. Pregnancy can raise many developmental issues for women, their partners, prospective grandparents and siblings. The careers of women doctors are particularly affected by the birth of a child. In one study, 33 per cent of women physicians reported that they had interrupted their careers for family reasons, whereas only 0.1 per cent of males had done so, and 57 per cent indicated that their career choice had been affected by their family, compared to 29 per cent of men.[1]

After the birth, all family members need to adjust their patterns of relating to each other. Not only will the parents have to adapt, but so too will previously born children. Presumably because of the increased demands on the parents, there is a marked decrease in positive interactions between the mother and earlier children, with an increase in controlling or prohibitive statements.[2]

Stress during pregnancy

As discussed in Chapter 6, the experience of stress in the mother at this time can have significant effects on the foetus. Psychological and social stressors such as unemployment and low income are also important factors affecting birthweight[3] and low birthweight, in turn, can be associated with high levels of dysphoric mood in the parents.[4]

However, not all pregnancies result in a birth. Approximately one in five of all recognized pregnancies end in miscarriage, and about one in three couples will experience this event at least once. Perhaps because it is so common, the emotional effects of spontaneous abortion on women have only recently been recognized. Many more women report grief reactions and high levels of depression after a miscarriage than do women having a planned termination. Friedman and Gath,[5] for instance, found that almost half of their sample of women showed clinically significant levels of depression 4 weeks after their miscarriage, even though the majority of miscarriages occurred during the first trimester. Most experienced a period of numbness after the mis-

carriage, and some likened the distress to that following the death of a family member. Many felt guilty and in some way responsible for the miscarriage. Other studies have shown that such difficulties can be exacerbated if there have been fertility problems in the family. There is certainly a need to provide women who experience a miscarriage an opportunity to receive support on a long-term basis.[6]

Assisted reproduction

Being unable to have a baby is emotionally difficult for most people – almost all heterosexual couples marry with the expectation that they will be able to have a child at some point. When couples cannot conceive they often report feeling shocked, angered and disappointed. Although an increasing proportion of couples are now making a positive decision to remain childless, the availability of *in vitro* fertilization (or IVF) and donor insemination programmes has made a substantial impact on many lives.

Many childless couples feel they face a number of negative stereotypes from others. Callan and Hennessey[7] asked women who were attending an IVF programme to describe comments made to them about being childless. Most claimed that they had experienced negative remarks (Table 8.1). There seemed to be the general assumption that the couple did not want children and that they were selfish and materialistic or were unwilling to accept the restrictions in having a child. Sometimes women were told that they were

Table 8.1 Percentage of women in an IVF programme reporting a variety of comments from others (Reproduced from Callan, V. and Hennessey, J. (1988) *Journal of in Vitro Fertilization and Embryo Transfer* **5:** 290–295, with permission.)

Comments	Percentage
Don't you want children? You're selfish, vain, greedy	39
You're better off without children	26
When are you starting a family? Why aren't you pregnant yet?	18
It's all in your mind, relax, take a holiday, you're trying too hard	13
I'd hate to be like you	10

lucky to be childless; on other occasions they were seen as unhappy and unfulfilled.

Women undergoing IVF treatment report a number of stressors. Waiting seems to be a significant source of stress – waiting for an appointment, waiting for treatment and waiting for results are all important. There is also some evidence that males can suffer as well. Stress has negative effects on sperm count, motility and morphology. In one study,[8] the quality of semen samples given by men was assessed at two points – during the pre-IVF workup, when difficulties were first being identified, and then after ovum aspiration, when a sample was needed to inseminate the eggs. Sperm density, total sperm count and sperm motility were all lower in the second sample presented for IVF, suggesting that the stress imposed through the IVF procedure was associated with a reduction in sperm quality.

On the other hand, it is possible to believe that infertility problems can be more debilitating than they actually are. Callan[9] compared the levels of well-being of three groups of women: mothers; women who were voluntarily childless; and women who were involuntarily childless and attending an IVF programme. He found that there were many similarities between the groups of women. Across various indices of happiness, all were generally similar. While the infertile women rated their lives as being less interesting, emptier and more disappointing, they were more pleased than other women with opportunities for relaxing activities, time to themselves and independence. They also reported more loving marital relationships.

Theory of reasoned action

Success rates for IVF can be low, so that many couples will experience repeated failures in their attempts to have a child. It is not clear why some couples who have objectively high chances of a successful attempt leave the IVF programme, while others wish to have as many attempts as possible despite the financial costs and having medical histories which suggest a low likelihood of success.

One approach which has been used to understand this difference is based on the "theory of reasoned action". Developed by Ajzen and Fishbein,[10] the theory states that a person's intention to perform a certain act in the future depends on three main factors: first, the person's attitude (positive or negative) towards the act (in this case towards continuing on the programme); second, the person's view of social norms about the action (in this case whether a woman believes that others around her such as her partner, family and friends think that continuing on the programme is a good idea); and, third, the person's beliefs about the outcome of the action (in this case whether further attempts will be successful).

In order to test this theory, women who had experienced at least one IVF attempt were asked to indicate their beliefs along these three dimensions. When those who intended to stop were compared with those who intended to continue, the best predictor of behaviour was the belief that friends and family would not pressure them to continue and that further attempts would be unlikely to succeed. Many background variables, such as the number of previous IVF treatments, length of infertility and level of education, were unrelated to the intention to stop or continue.[11]

Parenting

There has also been interest in the quality of parenting amongst women who have given birth through assisted reproduction. This is an important area of research since it may tell us much about the role of genetic ties in family functioning. Golombok et al.[12] compared four groups of families, whose children (1) were born through IVF (in which children are genetically related to both parents); (2) were born through donor insemination (where the genetic tie is with the mother alone); (3) had been adopted at birth; and (4) were conceived naturally. All of the children were between 4 and 8 years of age.

Through a variety of interview and questionnaire methods, they found that there were few differences on any of the measures of children's emotional well-being across groups. Genetic closeness was not related to how well the children developed emotionally. Contrary to the concern that the new reproductive technologies would have a negative effect on family functioning, the quality of parenting in families with a child conceived by assisted conception was superior to that shown by families who did not require assistance. On measures of mother's warmth to, and emotional involvement with, the child and both parents' quality of interaction with the child, parents whose children were conceived through assisted reproduction scored more positively. The adoptive mothers and fathers were very similar in quality of parenting to the parents of children conceived by assisted reproduction. From this study, at least, it seems that the quality of the parent–child relationship is not associated with genetic similarity.

Antenatal classes

One way in which many prospective parents prepare for the changes involved in the birth of a child is attendance at antenatal classes. Such classes typically provide a range of information about the mechanics of birth, ways of coping with labour pain and what might be expected during the post-natal period. Breathing and relaxation exercises are encouraged and information about analgesics given. Typically, a series of 5–8 weekly sessions are arranged, usually in small groups, which gives an opportunity for discussion and some sharing of concerns.

There is some evidence that attendance at such classes is helpful, but methodological problems are common in studies in this area. Participation in pre-natal classes is highly related to socio-economic status (those of the higher social classes being much more likely to attend), making it difficult to specify the reasons for any differences between those who have attended and those who have not.[13,14] There are, however, a few studies which have attempted to take socio-economic and other demographic factors into account. For example, Hetherington[15] compared 52 couples who attended classes and matched them on a number of variables (age, race, parity) with couples who had a child at about the same time but who did not attend classes. The prepared couples were found to be less likely to require technological assistance (the use of forceps or caesarian sections) and to require less analgesia and anaesthesia. Many of the couples attributed their satisfying birth experiences to the classes and felt that using methods taught to them during the classes had helped them to achieve this.

It may be that any positive effects of classes are due to an increased sense of mastery or self-efficacy. If women are able to use the coping methods taught in the classes during the actual birth, they will feel a greater sense of perceived control over what happens to them. The woman's partner may be particularly important in this respect, especially if the partner provides support in the use of coping strategies.[16]

Therapeutic terminations

In order to assess the effects of therapeutic terminations on women's well-being, it is important to take several factors into account. First, whether or not the pregnancy was wanted – not all women who have an abortion have unwanted pregnancies (e.g. those whose pregnancies are terminated for genetic reasons), and not all women with unwanted pregnancies seek an abortion; and second, whether a request for abortion is refused. In answering questions about the effects of abortion, women (and their children) whose requests had been turned down as well as those whose requests had been granted need to be studied.

Early reports on abortion often employed no control groups, relying mainly on clinicians' observations. Longitudinal studies suggest that early termination of pregnancy has little long-term adverse effect on most women. Nevertheless, it has great emotional significance at the time and few women find the decision an easy one.[17] Women who have terminations due to diagnosis of genetic abnormality seem to be particularly "at risk". Donnai et al.[18] interviewed 12 women who had a termination for this reason. All showed strain at the time of the interview, while emotional recovery was considered to be good for 7 of the women, fair for 3 of the women and poor for the remaining 2 women at 7 and 10 months after termination. The findings led the authors to change their clinical practice in dealing with genetically related terminations, ensuring that a health visitor contacts the women while in hospital and offers future support.

In a long-term study (over 15 years), children of women whose applications for abortion were refused were compared with children of the same sex born in the ward at about the same time. The mothers were matched for age, parity and social class. The initially unwanted children were more likely to have an unmarried mother, to be born into a family where divorce occurred, and to do less well at school than the wanted children. There was also evidence that they were more likely to have psychosomatic symptoms (headaches, stomach aches, etc.) and to be referred to a school psychiatrist.[19] However, there were several other measures on which no differences were found: many of the unwanted children had satisfactory intellectual achievement and social adjustment, for example.

Several factors seem to affect the decision whether or not to provide an abortion. Religious and moral beliefs, rape, the possibility of a handicapped child and danger to the mother's physical or mental health are all relevant. It is also possible that an abortion is sometimes granted as a reward for conscientious contraceptive use or refused on the basis of irresponsibility. These possibilities were tested by giving people short case histories of women who had become pregnant and wanted an abortion. In order to give the experiment some real-life validity, the study participants were asked to imagine that they were members of a panel which considered abortion applications. They were asked to read the case histories and to indicate whether they were in favour of or against granting the request. The histories were systematically varied in content: some women were said to have a casual relationship with the father while others had a steady and involved one, and some women were said to have become pregnant because of lack of preparation (forgetting to take contraceptives on a camping trip) while others had become pregnant because the method had failed.

The panellists were more strongly in favour of granting an abortion when the conception was due to a failure in the method than when it was due to a failure of the person to use the method consistently, and when the relationship was steady than when it was casual. These results are interesting, because they indicate that the panellists were more likely to confer motherhood on those women who were less able to plan their pregnancy and less likely to have the emotional support of the father. It was as if requests were withheld in order to punish inconsistent use of

contraceptives and the less socially acceptable behaviour of having several sexual partners.[20]

Family discord

The increasing divorce rate has made conflict within the family an area of concern. It is not clear if this increase is due to more marriages breaking down, to more broken marriages ending in divorce (due to the relaxation in divorce laws and the lessening social stigma) or to a combination of these factors. Divorce is more likely for couples who marry after a short courtship, who marry because of pregnancy or who come from different social and economic backgrounds. Although divorce is a stressful and unhappy time, it has been pointed out that it can have positive effects. Since most people marry again afterwards, the act of divorce can be seen as an indication that the people involved are looking for a fuller and more satisfying relationship than they were experiencing previously. Some of the effects of divorce on children are outlined in Chapter 6.

Perhaps a more useful way of considering marital conflict is not in terms of whether it results in divorce but rather how the conflicts are managed. It has been argued that all relationships involve a degree of conflict and that some level of discord should be accepted as an inevitable part of every relationship. According to this view, it is the ways in which couples deal with their disagreements that is important.

Violence in the family

The incidence of violence in the family is difficult to ascertain. One difficulty concerns visibility. It is likely that only a small proportion of violent incidents are recorded by the police or by doctors. Another problem is definition: does violence mean purely physical abuse, or does it also include emotional neglect?

Many parents use some form of physical punishment towards their children, often at a very early age. One-quarter of the mothers (outpatients at a medical clinic) had begun to use "spanking" as a punishment before their children were 6 months of age.[21] In another study of university students, more than half reported actual or threatened use of violence from their parents.[22] Gelles[23] conducted in-depth interviews with husbands and wives: about 60 per cent had used physical aggression during a marital conflict.

More important than incidence, perhaps, are the attempts to understand – rather than simply condemn – violence in the home. Until comparatively recently, parents were considered to have every right to treat their children as they saw fit. Only over the past 100 years in Western society has the abuse and exploitation of children been made illegal, and there is continuing research on the effects of physical abuse towards children. For example, Salinger et al.[24] found that children aged between 8 and 12 years who had suffered abuse in the home had lower status amongst their peers, were more aggressive and less co-operative than children who had not been abused.

There may be some continuing ambivalence about violence towards wives. In one study, people were given a fictitious description of a man and a woman fighting. The violence escalated and ended in the woman becoming unconscious. As a measure of how acceptable violence was between these couples, they were then asked how severely the man should be punished. Half were told that the couple were husband and wife, the other half that they were not married. Less severe punishments were recommended for the man when he was married to the woman, indicating a greater acceptance of violence within a marital relationship than outside it.[25]

Precipitating factors

Studies on the characteristics of people who use violence against children have come to different conclusions. Some researchers (but not all) have found child abuse to be most prevalent in the lowest social classes. Child abuse is associated with such social conditions as low income, poor housing and unemployment. According to this viewpoint, the environment places stress on the individual, violence being one possible result. The suggestion is that anyone could become an abusive parent given such circumstances. But here again there is the problem of visibility: abuse may indeed be more prevalent in such conditions

or it may simply be more likely to be detected. Social and community workers visit families whose economic plight is apparent more frequently, making evidence of abuse visible and more likely to be reported. Others have argued that violence is due to personality disturbances – there is a higher rate of divorce, separation and minor criminal offences in abusive families, and depression in the mother is commonly found. She is also likely to have had her first child when very young.

Another suggestion is that abuse is triggered by difficult children. Although only 7 per cent of live births are premature, approximately 25 per cent of abused children are born prematurely. Perhaps these infants are more difficult to rear because they fuss and cry more than full-term infants and give fewer rewards to their parents. Prematurity is also associated with young mothers who are under stress. Perhaps these women, because of their relative social immaturity, have greater difficulty in coping with their infants' demands.

Another possible reason for this link between prematurity and abuse is failure of early bonding (see Chapter 6). Since the parents have only limited access to the child for the first weeks, the attachment between them may be weaker than usual. Relevant to this, Lynch[26] studied the relationship between ill-health and child abuse. She used the siblings of abused children as the comparison group, reasoning that they were similar to each other in many ways and that the personalities and social circumstances of the parents would be relatively stable. She found several differences between the siblings, including a higher incidence of abnormal pregnancies and deliveries and, important for the bonding hypothesis, a greater likelihood of separation between mother and child for the first 48 hours after birth and over the next 6 months. A later study indicated that abused children were twice as likely to have been in a special care nursery after birth than a comparison group.

Receiving or witnessing violence as a child could also be a relevant factor. Perhaps the use of violence as a way of resolving conflicts is learned as a child and serves as a model for resolving conflicts in later life. Gelles[23] interviewed 43 women who had suffered violence from their husbands: 40 reported that they had been the victims of violence as children, and 25 reported that they had witnessed their parents being violent to one another. In a larger study, over 80 per cent reported that their husbands' parents had used violence, either towards their children or between themselves.[27]

In the absence of comparison groups in many studies, it is not possible to say how high these figures are in comparison to the rest of the population. Most abused children do not become abusive parents.[28] Nevertheless, it seems possible that as children grow they learn ways of coping with conflict from their parents. Several investigations have attempted to correlate ways of coping experienced as a child with favoured methods as adults. Owens and Straus[29] found such associations. Those who observed and received violence as children were more likely to have committed violence themselves as children and were more likely to approve of violent behaviour as adults.

An important qualification is needed here, however. In many studies, an individual's own reports of past events are relied upon to give a picture of upbringing. There are two main reasons why this might be inadequate. First, there is the problem of *memory*. People may be more likely to remember their parents engaging in violence if violence has recently occurred in their own homes. Second, there is the question of *social desirability*. People might be more willing to admit to violence from their own parents if they have committed violence themselves.

Prediction

The lesson from these studies is that there does not seem to be any one factor that is unique to violent families. While, as a group, abusive parents have been found to differ from non-abusive, there is much overlap between the two populations, so that there is no one factor that can be pinpointed as being solely responsible. Many parents who use violence come from deprived backgrounds, but not all with such childhood experiences become abusive. Similarly, many battered children are premature, but only a minority of premature children are battered.

This has two implications. First, abuse might be more appropriately considered as lying along a continuum that includes nutritional and emotional neglect as well as physical abuse, so that it is a question of degree rather than of kind. Second, it may be more fruitful to consider violence as a result of many factors, several of which in concert can make it more probable. The cumulative effects of prematurity in the child, youthfulness in the parents, social and economic stresses, personality and past experience with violence, may all contribute.

There has been particular interest in testing the possibility that abuse could be predicted from observations of the interactions between babies and their parents soon after birth. The idea is to take several measures which seem to be related to abuse and then follow the families over the next several years. Initial measures have included social and demographic indicators (e.g. age of the mother and income) and patterns of interaction (e.g. parents' care of the newborn). Outcomes have included reports to local child abuse registers, reviews of medical records and failures-to-thrive. Although such predictors are far from perfect, it does seem that much greater than chance prediction can be achieved.[30]

Prevention

Where prediction is possible, interventions become more feasible. Several attempts have been made to prevent child abuse. There is a statistical problem in evaluating the effectiveness of intervention programmes because of the low number of children who are actually physically harmed, but there are some encouraging results.

In one study an attempt was made to strengthen the bond between mother and child by increasing their early contact with one another. Mothers were randomly assigned to either a control group, in which the mothers had 20 minutes of contact for feeding every 4 hours in the first 2 days post-partum, or they were assigned to a "rooming-in" group, in which the child and mother had an additional 6 hours together for each of these first 2 days. Although the children in these two groups did not differ in the frequency with which they visited the hospital for out-patient care or were ill, at least some were treated differently by their parents. Of the

277 children in the study, no rooming-in children were considered to have experienced abuse, neglect or non-organic failure to thrive, whereas nine control group children were considered to have suffered these conditions. Five of this group eventually died. These researchers concluded that mothers who were given close and extended physical contact with their newborn infants were less likely to abuse or neglect their children than women given more limited exposure.[31]

In another study, three groups of mothers were followed up after the birth of their child. One group consisted of mothers not considered at risk on the basis of labour room and post-partum observations. A second group of "at risk" mothers was given comprehensive paediatric follow-up by a physician and a health visitor, and a third group, similar to the second, was given no such assistance. In this latter group of 50 families, five children were later hospitalized for treatment of serious injuries whereas none of the high-risk intervention group nor of the low-risk group required such hospitalization.[32] In some hospitals all parents who may have difficulty in forming attachment bonds because of the baby's need for special care are seen by a social worker and given the opportunity to discuss practical and social problems.

Prediction and prevention of violence between adults may be more difficult to achieve, partly because of the greater reticence to interfere with adult relationships and partly because of practical considerations – it may be very difficult to elicit the co-operation of both partners. Attempts to prevent the re-occurrence of marital violence include the establishment of battered women's refuges. They provide a much needed safe place for women: several studies have indicated that many women return to a violent home because they have "nowhere else to go".

Sexual abuse

Awareness of the prevalence and severity of the sexual exploitation of children has increased markedly over the past several years. A commonly used definition of abuse is that it involves (a) forced or coerced sexual behaviour imposed on a child, and (b) sexual activity between a child and a much older person, whether or not obvious coercion is involved. A common definition of "much older" is 5 or more years.[33]

The proportions of people who have been abused during childhood is much higher than previously imagined. Reported rates range from 6 per cent to 62 per cent for females, and from 3 per cent to 31 per cent for males. There are several reasons why such widely differing results have been obtained. First, studies have been conducted in a variety of ways, ranging from in-depth and confidential interviews to anonymous questionnaires, and with various populations, such as samples of the general population or from medical and psychiatric clinics. Another factor affecting reported prevalence is the criteria used to define abuse, where there is much controversy. Some researchers have used very strict criteria, such as intercourse, while others have used less restrictive criteria, such as exposure.

Effects of abuse

Whatever the true prevalence, there is no doubt that sexual abuse can have severe and long-lasting effects. Initial effects include sleep and eating disturbances, fears and phobias, depression, anger, guilt and shame. Children often blame themselves for the abuse, a reaction that may be encouraged by the perpetrator. There can also be physical symptoms indicative of anxiety and distress, inappropriate sexual behaviour, and disturbances in social behaviour, such as running away from home, truancy and delinquent behaviour. Certainly, the possibility of abuse should be considered for children who show sudden changes in such behaviour.

Abuse has been shown to have a number of longer term effects. The kinds of disturbances outlined above may persist for years if unrecognized for what they are. Long-term effects include continuing eating disturbances and sleeping difficulties, but depression is the most commonly reported symptom. Sexual abuse which involves physical contact is associated with a higher level of depression and a greater number of depressive episodes, and women who have been abused are more likely to have been hospitalized for depression. Other studies have shown that people who have been sexually abused are more likely to be self-destructive (through attempted suicide, drug abuse or self-mutilation), to have low self-esteem and to have hesitations about developing sexual relationships. Factors which appear to exacerbate such reactions include multiple incidents, abuse by someone within the family rather than by someone outside it, the presence of force, and disbelief or lack of comfort when the abuse is disclosed.[33]

These effects can be attributed to four types of trauma-causing factors, called traumatic sexualization, stigmatization, betrayal and powerlessness. *Traumatic sexualization* refers to the process in which a child's sexuality is shaped in a way which is inappropriate for his or her developmental stage, so that sexual behaviour develops at a young age and can become a way of obtaining rewards or being accepted by others. *Stigmatization* refers to the negative connotations that are communicated to the child about the experience. Shame and guilt may become incorporated into the child's self-image, reactions which may be reinforced if others blame the child or react with shock after disclosure. *Betrayal* refers to the reaction when children find that someone who they have depended upon has caused them harm, and *powerlessness* can result when the child finds that he or she is incapable of changing the situation. This might be particularly important when the abuser is authoritarian or threatening, or if the child is not believed. Interventions designed to help abused children seek to address these factors.

Prevention

Many of these reactions can be found in people who have undergone a variety of traumatic events (such as physical assault in the street, witnessing a traumatic event, being in combat). This area will be discussed further in Chapter 9, where post-traumatic stress disorder is explained, but it is helpful to provide a brief description of preventive interventions which have been used in this area here.

Programmes have been designed to alert children, parents and professionals to the possibility of abuse. Most efforts to reach children have several common and basic themes, including education about what sexual abuse is, the broadening of awareness of who potential abusers might be (including people who children know

and like), and encouragement to tell someone if an abusive attempt occurs. A central issue here is that child abuse education is not the same as sex education, since it has much more to do with personal safety, assault prevention and empowerment. Since boys as well as girls are subject to abuse, such programmes have been aimed at both sexes.

Preventive education aimed towards parents is also important, since they have a central role in protecting children. The hope is that by sensitizing parents to the possibility of abuse, the incidence might decline and detection rates might increase. Yet few parents raise the possibility with their children. It seems that parents are often concerned that they could frighten their children unnecessarily by discussing the possibility with them but, paradoxically, most parents warn their children about being kidnapped, a much less likely possibility. Perhaps some reasons for this reluctance are embarrassment and possible reminders of previous incidents in their own lives.

It may be useful to at least target parents of children who might be particularly vulnerable to abuse. Such children include those who have been abused previously, children with disabilities or emotional problems and families in which there is a stepfather, which is one of the common factors associated with sexual abuse.

Help for abusers

There is also the issue of help for the perpetrator of the abuse. Punishment without rehabilitation runs the risk that the abuse will continue and places other children at risk. It has been argued that there are four important questions to be answered: first, why a person would find relating sexually to a child emotionally gratifying; second, why a person would be capable of being sexually aroused by a child; third, why more normal sexual interests have not developed; and fourth, why a person would not be deterred by the social constraints and inhibitions against abuse.

Perhaps because of previous experience of sexual abuse themselves, adults who abuse children may be unable to form emotionally mature relationships with other adults. There may be low self-esteem, or perhaps it is a way of asserting dominance over another, but in some way the relationship meets the adult's needs. Feminist theories place much emphasis on the ways that victims are often blamed in our society and that this can serve as a justification for abuse in the minds of perpetrators. Alcohol consumption, which may serve as a direct physiological disinhibitor, is frequently associated with sexual abuse.[34]

Interventions with abusers often take these aspects of development into account, but there is often a difficulty in helping them to understand and appreciate the effects of their behaviour on children. It seems that many perpetrators minimize the consequences of their actions. Attempts to alter attitudes and beliefs about the effects of abuse have included the showing of videotapes of survivors talking about their feelings and reactions, but this is not always successful. Therapeutically managed confrontation of the perpetrator by the victim can be successful. In one case, therapists enlisted the co-operation of a woman who had been abused by her stepfather. After much support, she was able to confront him, a process which was important in the emotional development of both people involved.[35]

Family therapy

Helping people with their psychological and interpersonal difficulties can take many forms. Some of these were discussed in Chapters 2 and 3. There, the emphasis was on treating the individual independently from his or her family group. Although the patient's relationships within the family might be discussed, parents or spouses would not usually be invited into the consulting room.

Family therapists take a different view. A basic tenet of family therapy is that an individual's difficulties cannot be considered or treated adequately unless all of the immediate family (and sometimes a larger network of relatives) is seen in therapy. There are several advantages to such an approach. It provides an opportunity to observe how members of a family actually relate to one another. Rather than relying on one individual's view of what happens in the family, the therapist is able to see the patterns of interaction.

Also, the therapist is able to act as a kind of referee, encouraging the family members to consider how they are relating to each other and exploring the nature of their conflicts. It may be possible to help members of the family explain their points of view more clearly. Having someone present who is not punitive and who will provide support if necessary may make it easier for children to articulate their concerns, for example.

An important advantage of family over individual therapy concerns the problem of generalization. Many therapists consider psychological difficulties to be evidence of trouble in relationships. In the therapeutic relationship, the patient is given the opportunity to discover the problems inherent in his or her usual ways of relating to people. However, if this person is then required to return to a family in which difficulties remain, it may be harder to put into practice what has been learnt. By helping the whole family together, this problem is reduced.

There are different types of family therapy. Some therapists place emphasis on the need for families to have strong boundaries. Families exist to perform certain tasks – such as nurturance, regulation of behaviour and socialization of children. Parents, for example, might be seen as the primary decision-makers and ought not to disagree between themselves in front of the children, or one parent ought not to form alliances with a child against the other parent, since this would result in confusion for the child. In this type of approach, the aim might be to strengthen the parental alliance.[36]

Other therapists prefer to help families to develop their own ways of relating to each other, ways which are suitable for them. In this type of approach, the aim might be to encourage the family members to try out various solutions to their problems, but the final way of relating is their choice. Families differ in the extent to which changes in one part of the system affect everyone. In some families, a joyous occasion for one person is experienced as a joyous occasion for all. Perhaps a child does particularly well at school, and the achievement would be seen as a family accomplishment, not just the child's. The sense of the family as a unit – its *cohesiveness* – would be very strong. In the extreme, the family might be termed "enmeshed". In other families, the members might be much more independent, so that a change for one person would not involve a systemic change. For such a family a child leaving home, for example, would not be seen as a major event, because it affects only one individual. Such a family would be considered low in cohesion or "disengaged".

Families also differ in the extent to which they adapt to changes. Children are born, become increasingly independent, and eventually hope to leave home. These events require considerable adjustment for all concerned, but in some families such changes are resisted. Perhaps the parents will attempt to discourage their children from becoming independent because that would pose a threat to their roles as parents. Or perhaps a single parent might seek to develop another adult relationship, but the children might be very negative about this because it seems to threaten the parent–child relationship. The extremes of *adaptability* are termed "rigid" and "chaotic".

Applications of family therapy

Whatever the approach taken, a family therapist would be interested in the ways a family adapts (or fails to adapt) to changes. These might be changes of a maturational kind (as in the growth of independence of an adolescent), or changes in physical or mental health.

Helping families cope with changes in physical health

The basic tenet of family therapy – that changes in the circumstances of one family member change the way a family functions – can be applied to the adaptations that physical illness requires. Clearly, if a parent becomes progressively more ill, such as developing multiple sclerosis, the rest of the family will have to make many adaptations. If the breadwinner becomes ill, for example, a partner may need to gain paid employment, thus altering his or her ability to spend time with the children. The child might become frightened or have difficulties in school.

Similarly, when a child is admitted to hospital, especially for a life-threatening procedure, the disruption for the entire family can be profound. Hare *et al.*[37] discuss the ways in which a family

can be affected by paediatric bone marrow transplantation, in which the bone marrow of a sibling is used to help a patient's efforts to overcome cancer. They note that the ability of a family to cope with such a procedure depends not simply on the event itself but also the family's resources and their perceptions that the stress can be dealt with within the existing system. If the resources are not adequate to the task, some changes in the system will be required.

When a transplantation is a possibility, the family has to be concerned with the well-being of the donor as well as the patient. The parents may not be in full agreement about the desirability of the transplant: they have their relationship to consider. The healthy sibling may be aware of this yet be unable to express his or her views clearly. Such a balance of needs may have many long-term effects, regardless of the success of the transplant.

Helping families cope with changes in mental health

There is considerable evidence about the importance of the family in the re-emergence of psychiatric difficulties, such as schizophrenia. Current thinking about schizophrenia is that it is biologically based (some people are more susceptible than others) but that biological factors interact with stressors in the environment. Since patients, once they leave hospital, often live at home with their families, the home may exacerbate the difficulties if the family environment is primarily negative, unpredictable and stressful.

Brown *et al.*[38] were interested in factors associated with relapse in schizophrenic patients after they left hospital. They took several measures including prior behavioural disturbance, impairment at work and the support the patients would receive once they were discharged from hospital. As a measure of support, they interviewed a key relative soon after the patient entered hospital, being especially interested in the number of critical and hostile comments made by this relative about the patient and the illness. This latter factor is known as expressed emotion, or EE:[39] families who score highly on EE often believe that the patient can control the symptoms (if only he or she wished to do so).[40] When the relapse rates were later considered, this variable turned out to be the best single predictor: 58 per cent of patients whose relative expressed several negative comments relapsed, but only 16 per cent with relatives who expressed few negative comments. Indicators of previous behavioural disturbance had little predictive power.

Leff *et al.*[41] tested the possibility that if members of a patient's family were included in therapy, the probability of relapse would be reduced. In all of the families chosen, there was much expressed hostility, so that a high relapse rate would be expected. One half of the families were assigned to the routine care group, which consisted of the typical out-patient care for the patients themselves. The other half were given a family-based treatment package, which included information about schizophrenia, involvement with a self-help group where the relatives could get together to discuss their difficulties, and family therapy. While 50 per cent of the routine care patients later relapsed, only 9 per cent of those whose families were involved in their treatment suffered a relapse. This difference was maintained at a follow-up conducted 2 years later. The conclusion of these and similar studies[42] is that stress reduction in the home environment is the key to effective intervention.

Thus, family therapy concentrates upon the relationships between family members. Instead of considering an individual's problems in isolation, difficulties are seen to be a family problem: even if one person has been diagnosed as ill in some way (for example, suffering from cancer or from schizophrenia), the illness will affect the whole family. The way the *family* reacts, and not just the individuals within it, will affect recovery.

Old age

The process of adjusting to old age is a particularly important one, both for the individuals themselves and for their families. Coupled with an increased vulnerability to disease, there is a loss of power and control. Retirement has more than financial implications, since it can also result in a decrease in self-esteem, social support and satisfaction with life. In modern Western society, youth is associated with promise and worth, whereas old age is considered less positively. This is in contrast to some other cultures, where old age represents wisdom and leadership. Older people are often considered to be less competent than the young, so that failure may be attributed to lack of ability in the elderly but lack of effort on the part of the young.[43] This section discusses some of the research on the problems that elderly people have in making such adjustments.

Defining old age

Although chronological age is usually the way we decide whether a person is elderly, many of the important features of old age are masked by this measure. The range of physical and social capabilities of elderly people is wide, so that chronological age does not provide a good criterion for predicting how a person will behave. Although many cognitive and physical differences have been found between older and younger people, these differences are due in part to other factors besides age itself.

Most significantly, different generations have very different life experiences. Younger people have more practice and experience in many of the tasks used by psychologists, such as IQ tests. The young are more likely to engage in tasks, such as driving a car, which gives them practice in reaction times: when the elderly are given practice in such tasks they approach the young in speed. Overall lower scores of older people can be attributed to less experience with the type of tests used rather than to lower intelligence or ability. Correlations between chronological age and various psychological, social and physiological measures have generally been low.

Problems faced by elderly people

These results are important because views of the ageing process can have significant effects on how elderly people are treated. A doctor or nurse who considers ageing to be due primarily to physiological deterioration may be less likely to recommend training programmes, for example. Yet such problems as incontinence respond well to techniques of behaviour therapy.[44] Those who take a biological view might also be less likely to allow elderly patients to take responsibility for their decisions or to encourage independence. Barton *et al.*[45] observed residents and staff in a nursing home, paying particular attention to how the staff reacted to indications of independence in the residents. Residents who attempted to look after themselves were likely to receive responses which discouraged self-reliance, whereas praise was given if the residents accepted assistance.

Such practices may have important consequences for the welfare of elderly people, dissuading them from relying on and practising their own skills and abilities. In a particularly telling study on this issue, nursing home residents were divided into two groups. Some residents were told that many of the features of their living conditions were their own responsibility. For example, they were each given a plant to care for, they were encouraged to review how the home was run, and to comment upon the complaints procedure. By contrast, the residents in the other group were not encouraged to look after themselves to any degree, being told that the staff were responsible for their care. They, too, were each given a plant but were informed that the staff would water it, and so on. After 3 weeks, self-report questionnaires indicated that the first group were more active and happier than the second, and these reports were supported by nurses' observations. Strikingly, 71 per cent of the group who were told that they would be given almost complete care showed some deterioration over the period of the study, whereas 93 per cent of the self-reliant group showed improvement.

Eighteen months later, the researchers returned to the nursing home. They found that 30 per cent of the staff-reliant group had died by this time, but only 15 per cent of the self-reliant group had passed away. Although the numbers were small, the results could not be accounted for by such variables as their overall health status when the study began. The conclusion reached was that the debilitated condition of elderly people living in institutions can be due to the environment in which they live. Without the opportunity and encouragement to make decisions about their lives, deterioration may result.[46]

As a group, elderly people show a diminished ability to adjust to change. Particular care is therefore needed when adjustments are required, such as a change of residence. Several studies have indicated that the mortality rate is excessively high when elderly people are rehoused or transferred from one hospital ward to another. In one study, elderly patients who were moved from one hospital to another were compared with those who remained. The patients were matched on several relevant variables, including age, sex, length of hospitalization and organic and functional illness. When their mortality rates were compared for the first 4 months after transfer, the group of patients who had been moved showed an incidence of death four times higher than those who had stayed.[47]

Dying

Much has been written about the ways that people cope with their own death. Most of this work has come from doctors and nurses who are intimately involved with people who are terminally ill, relying on their observations of patients and their relatives. Kubler-Ross[48] has had a considerable impact with her contention that terminally ill people pass through five stages. The first reaction is often *denial*, a refusal to believe that death is imminent. This stage is characterized by statements such as "No, not me, it can't be true" and may be coupled with isolation from others. Denial often recurs throughout the coping process.

The second stage is characterized by *anger*, envy and resentment. Anger is often directed towards both staff and relatives, which may make it difficult for them to cope if it is taken personally. When anger does not prove effective, the third stage of *bargaining* is entered. It is seen as an attempt to postpone death by looking for a reward for good behaviour. In the hope that doctors will take better care, offers to leave the body to science may be given, for instance. Fourth, and when death seems inevitable, *depression* is commonly experienced. Death involves more than the loss of one's own life, it also involves the loss of family, friends and plans for the future. This period is characterized by sadness and crying, and Kubler-Ross stresses the importance of allowing patients to work through this stage, rather than giving encouragement and reassurance that they will recover. Patients may need assistance in talking over their feelings.

Finally, she believes that, given time and help, people come to the stage of *acceptance* when they realize that the struggle is over and that it is time to die. This stage is characterized by silence and an increasing wish to be detached from others.

Other writers have taken issue with Kubler-Ross, contending that terminally ill people do not go through stages in any set order but may show any reaction at any time. It seems from their observations that denial, anger, bargaining, depression and acceptance are not stages but reactions that occur and re-occur throughout the illness.

Family and professional reactions

There is agreement, however, on the importance of considering not only the patient but also his or her family. On the one hand, their reactions are important for the patient. The spouse's ability to cope with financial and personal affairs may make it easier or more difficult for the patient to accept death. Kubler-Ross also points out that the reactions of friends and family may not be compatible with those of the patient: if they continue to deny death, it would be difficult for the patient to talk with them. On the other hand, the patient's family have needs in their own right and they, too, often cope in similar ways to the ill person him or herself. It is not uncommon for them to have feelings of anger and resentment towards the patient because of "desertion" and feelings of guilt for not noticing the illness sooner. The family is sometimes angry at medical staff since they can be seen as somehow responsible, coupled with envy because they are able to care for the patient. Sometimes the family withdraws from the patient, leaving him or her isolated.

It may also be difficult for nursing and medical staff to cope with the complexity of emotions shown by patients and their families, and it has been argued that the difficulties can be compounded by the staff's own feelings about death. Some writers contend that an important reason for entering the medical profession is to cure people, and that an inability to do so is a sign of failure, when "nothing else can be done". There is evidence that, indeed, terminally ill people receive poorer care than those who are recovering. Leshan[49] measured the time between the time that nurses received a bedside call from patients to their response. The nurses took longer to answer the calls from the terminally ill than from those less seriously ill, even though they were unaware of this difference in their response times. Another study indicated that those patients who had declined the most were moved the greatest distance from the nursing station.[50]

A terminal prognosis

There has been much discussion about whether patients and their relatives should be told of a terminal prognosis. Practising physicians disagree about this but, generally, the more recent the study the greater the proportion who favour informing. A generation ago, 60–90 per cent of doctors were found to be against it, whereas more recent studies have indicated that most are now in favour of giving this information.

The decision seems to be influenced by several factors. One possibility is a general reluctance to transmit bad news: there is a reticence in people to give this kind of information, particularly if the news is to be given personally.[51] Another factor involves the patient's personality. "Calm" patients are more likely to be told than "emotional" ones, although there is actually little evidence that personality patterns can be used to predict the individual's response to terminal illness with any consistency. A third factor concerns the patient's family circumstances. Although 67 per cent of the physicians in one study said that the patient should be told, 37 per cent reported that when their wishes were in conflict with the family's, the latter's wish should be honoured.

Skirting mention of the terminal illness has consequences as much as open discussion, although the consequences will be different. Some have argued that keeping the information from patients can mean that staff have to guard against disclosure (distancing them from their patients) and that this can result in suspicion and mutual pretence. Behind the decision not to inform lies the assumption that patients will not be able to discern the deception, an assumption which may not be warranted: patients seem very sensitive to the non-verbal cues given by staff.[52] Open awareness, on the other hand, can be seen to facilitate communication, giving the patient an opportunity to die as he or she would like, to reconcile long-standing misunderstandings with friends and family, and to help make plans for the bereaved.

Perhaps the more appropriate question is not "What do you tell the patient?" but rather "What do you allow the patient to tell you?".[53] Listening to a terminally ill person and observing the extent to which each individual attempts to gain information may provide the surest clues as to appropriate action. The attitudes that the caregiving staff have towards death are therefore critical, in that patients may not be able to discuss the possibility of death with those who are uncomfortable and avoid the topic. Some further points about breaking bad news are made in Chapter 11.

The care of people with terminal illness has changed in recent years. An increasing awareness of their difficulties has helped define the responsibilities of the caregivers. The idea of "safe conduct" has been suggested as the caregivers' role, requiring commitment not only to control pain, but also to approach the patient with acceptance, candour, compassion and mutual accessibility. An important development is the hospice, an environment in which openness about death is encouraged. Children and pets are welcome, and drugs such as heroin and alcohol are available. The needs of the whole family are considered and not just those of the patient. By comparing the experiences of terminally ill people who are dying in such specialized palliative care units rather than in general hospitals, an estimate of the improvements in quality of life can be made.[54]

Bereavement

Generally, the term bereavement is used to refer to reactions after the death of a friend or relative. But it can also be used as a more general term, to describe the reactions after a wide variety of losses, such as the reactions of a child who has to move school, the move away from the parental home, the amputation of a limb or the loss of a pet. Bereavement reactions such as numbness, disbelief and preoccupation with the lost object or person may occur after any event which involves the loss of security and routines.[55]

The adjustment required of bereaved people can be considerable. The number of consultations with general practitioners increases sharply after the death of a relative, one study showing a seven-fold increase in prescriptions for sedatives and another an increase in suicide. Many widowed people report that their children show behaviour problems, and these difficulties have been found to be associated with poor adjustment in the parent.[56] An increase in physical symptomatology has also been found by several researchers, with something like a 40 per cent increase in mortality rates in the first 6 months following a spouse's death.[57] Although there are several possible explanations for these findings,[58] including a reduction of immunocompetence,[59] many researchers have argued that the most important is the "broken heart" suffered by the survivor.

Difficulties in adjustment

Bereaved people frequently show periods of somatic distress (loss of appetite and initiative) and preoccupation with images of the person or object which has been lost. These reactions are considered to be part of normal grief and to be signs of deeper difficulties only when they are not resolved. In an attempt to determine significant factors, Parkes[56] interviewed the surviving partner 3 weeks, 6 weeks and 13 months after the death. The following factors were identified as being associated with a poor adjustment after a bereavement: low economic status, multiple life crises, severe distress, yearning, anger and self-reproach, and short terminal illness with little warning of the death. The significance of this last factor has been given further support in another study that indicated that the risk of mortality in the bereaved was twice as high if the death occurred suddenly without the opportunity to prepare for it.[60] This result suggests that grieving begins before the death of a relative and that the shock may be lessened if there is an opportunity to begin to adjust beforehand. Perhaps adjustment is easier when there has been the opportunity to say good-bye.

The distressing effects of miscarriage were mentioned earlier in the chapter, but the effects of death are illustrated in the case of stillbirth or neonatal death. Although about 1 in 70 babies dies at or around the time of birth, it is only recently that the extent of the family's grief has been recognized. [61,62] Difficulties can persist for many years. There is a lack of facilities in maternity hospitals for the women involved and, as a result, they are often sent home soon afterwards without further support. [63]

Several approaches have been taken to help families with their grief. Perhaps one of the most important advances in this area is that parents can benefit greatly if they are given an opportunity to spend time with and have a photograph of their dead child. [64] This seems to be related to more positive adjustment since the presence of memories is related to attachment, acceptance of the reality of the loss and ability to work through the grief. [65] It does not seem useful to recommend that the parents try for another child immediately since this signals a lack of understanding of the depth of the loss.

BOX 8.1

Tasks of mourning

Worden described four tasks that need to be accomplished during the process of mourning for a loss.

1 *Accepting the reality of the loss.* A bereaved person may find the reality of the loss too painful to contemplate and so may use denial to protect themselves. This can be explicit, but is more likely to be rather more subtle, such as keeping the deceased person's belongings "for when they return", or by minimizing the significance of the loss.

2 *Experiencing the pain of the loss.* Worden argues that people can employ a variety of strategies to avoid painful thoughts and feelings but that they need to *feel* the pain of the loss in order to adjust.

3 *Adapting to a world without the deceased person.* This involves taking on the domestic and work-related roles that the deceased person previously filled.

4 *"Letting go" of the deceased person.* Finally the bereaved person needs to withdraw emotionally from the previous relationship, investing their emotional needs in others.

Although painful, most people eventually come to terms with the death of a relative. In the case of sudden or unexpected losses this process may be more difficult and protracted, when professional help may be required. Box 8.1 outlines the tasks of mourning which Worden[66] suggests are necessary if a person is to adapt to the loss. Bereavement counselling and bereavement therapy seek to help the individual work through these tasks.

Suggested reading

The *Journal of Reproductive and Infant Psychology* includes articles which are concerned with the psychological aspects of pregnancy and birth. Monach, J. (1993) *Childless: No Choice. The Experience of Involuntary Childlessness*, London: Routledge, reviews the literature on the effects of infertility. For an introduction to family therapy, J. Burnam's (1986) *Family Therapy*, London: New York/Routledge, can be recommended. A helpful book on grief and bereavement is Worden, J. (1982) *Grief Counselling and Grief Therapy*, London: Tavistock. Sympathetic and comprehensive overviews of the issues involved in child sexual abuse are given by Doyle, C. (1994) *Child Sexual Abuse - a Guide for Health Professionals*, London: Chapman and Hall, and by Finkelhor, D. (1986) *A Sourcebook of Child Sexual Abuse*, London: Sage.

References

1. Brotherton, S. and LeBailly, S. (1993) The effect of family on the work lives of married physicians: What if the spouse is a physician too? *Journal of American Medical Women's Association* **48**: 175–181.
2. Dunn, J. and Kendrick, C. (1980) The arrival of a sibling. *Journal of Child Psychology and Psychiatry* **21**: 119–132.
3. Stein, A., Campbell, E., Day, A., McPherson, K. and Cooper, R. (1987) Social adversity, low birth weight ad preterm delivery. *British Medical Journal* **295**: 291–293.
4. Aradine, C. and Ferketich, S. (1990) The psychological impact of premature birth on mothers and fathers. *Journal of Reproductive and Infant Psychology* **8**: 75–86.
5. Friedman, T. and Gath, D. (1989) The psychiatric consequences of spontaneous abortion. *British Journal of Psychiatry* **155**: 810–813.

6. Garel, M., Blondel, B., Lelong, N., Bonenfant, S. and Kaminski, M. (1994) Long term consequences of miscarriage: the depressive disorders and the following pregnancy. *Journal of Reproductive and Infant Psychology* **12**: 233-240.

7. Callan, V. and Hennessey, J. (1988) Emotional aspects and support in in vitro fertilization and embryo transfer programs. *Journal of in Vitro Fertilization and Embryo Transfer* **5**: 290-295.

8. Harrison, K., Callan, V. and Hennessey, J. (1987) Stress and semen quality in an in vitro fertilization program. *Fertility and Sterility* **48**: 633-636.

9. Callan, V. (1987) The personal and marital adjustment of mothers and of voluntarily childless wives. *Journal of Marriage and the Family* **49**: 847-856.

10. Ajzen, I. and Fishbein, M. (1980) *Understanding Attitudes and Predicting Social Behaviour.* Englewood Cliffs, New Jersey: Prentice-Hall.

11. Callan, V., Kloske, B., Kashima, Y. and Hennessey, J. (1988) Toward understanding women's decisions to continue or stop in vitro fertilization: The role of social, psychological and background factors. *Journal of in Vitro Fertilization and Embryo Transfer* **5**: 363-369.

12. Golombok, S., Cook, R., Bish, A. and Murray, C. (1995) Families created by the new reproductive technologies: Quality of parenting and social and emotional development of the children. *Child Development* **66**: 285-298.

13. Beck, N.C. and Siegel, L.J. (1980) Preparation for childbirth and contemporary research on pain, anxiety and stress reduction: a review and critique. *Psychosomatic Medicine* **42**: 429-447.

14. Nelson, M.K. (1982) The effect of childbirth preparation on women of different social classes. *Journal of Health and Social Behaviour* **23**: 339-352.

15. Hetherington, S.E. (1990) A controlled study of prepared childbirth classes on obstetric outcomes. *Birth* **17**: 86-91.

16. Copstick, S.M., Taylor, K., Hayes, R. and Morris, N. (1986) Partner support and the use of coping techniques in labour. *Journal of Psychosomatic Research* **30**: 497-503.

17. Hardy, J.A. (1982) Psychological and social aspects of induced abortion. *British Journal of Clinical Psychology* **21**: 29-41.

18. Donnai, P., Charles, N. and Harris, R. (1981) Attitudes of patients after "genetic" terminations of pregnancy. *British Medical Journal* **282**: 621-622.

19. Blomberg, S. (1980) Influence of maternal distress during pregnancy on post-natal outcome. *Acta Psychiatrica Scandinavia* **62**: 405-417.

20. Allgeier, E.R., Allgeier, A. and Rywick, T. (1979) Abortion: reward for conscientious contraceptive use? *Journal of Sex Research* **15**: 64-75.

21. Korsch, B.M., Christian, J., Gozzi, E. and Carlson, P. (1965) Infant care and punishment. *American Journal of Public Health* **55**: 1880-1888.

22. Straus, M.A. (1971) The social antecedents of physical punishment. *Journal of Marriage and the Family* **33**: 658-663.

23. Gelles, R.J. (1974) *The Violent Home.* Beverly Hills: Russell Sage.

24. Salinger, S., Feldman, R., Hammer, M. and Rosario, M. (1993). The effects of physical abuse on children's social relationships. *Child Development* **64**: 169-187.

25. Straus, M.A. (1976) Sexual inequality, cultural norms and wife-beating. *Victimology* **1**: 54-70.

26. Lynch, M.A. (1975) Ill health and child abuse. *Lancet* **2**: 317-319.

27. Roy, M. (1977) *Battered Women.* New York: Van Nostrand.

28. Langeland, W. and Dijkstra, S. (1995) Breaking the intergenerational transmission of abuse: Beyond the mother-child relationship. *Child Abuse Review* **4**: 4-13.

29. Owens, D.J. and Straus, M. (1975) The social structure of violence in childhood and approval of violence as an adult. *Aggressive Behaviour* **1**: 193-211.

30. Leventhal, J.M. (1988) Can child maltreatment be predicted during the perinatal period: Evidence from longitudinal cohort studies? *Journal of Reproductive and Infant Psychology* **6**: 139-161.

31. O'Connor, S.M., Vietze, P.M., Hopkins, J.B. and Altemeir, W.A. (1977) Post-partum extended maternal infant contact. *Pediatric Research* **11**: 380.

32. Lynch, M.A., Roberts, J. and Gordon, M. (1976) Child abuse: early warning in the maternity hospital. *Developmental Medicine and Child Neurology* **18**: 759-766.

33. Finkelhor, D. (1986) *A sourcebook of child sexual abuse.* London: Sage.

34. Araji, S. and Finkelhor, D. (1986). Abusers: A review of the literature. In: Finkelhor, D. (1986) *A Sourcebook of Child Sexual Abuse.* London: Sage.

35. Valente, M. and Borthwick, I. (1995) Sexual abuse: Using survivors' experience to confront denial. *Child Abuse Review* **4**: 57-62.

36. Minuchin, S. (1974) *Families and Family Therapy.* London: Tavistock.

37. Hare, J., Skinner, D. and Kliewer, D. (1989) Family system approach to bone marrow transplantation. *Children's Health Care* **18**: 30–36.

38. Brown, G.W., Birley, J. and Wing, J. (1972) Influence of family life on the course of schizophrenic disorders. *British Journal of Psychiatry* **121**: 241–258.

39. Kuipers, L. and Bebbington, P. (1988) Expressed emotion research in schizophrenia: theoretical and clinical implications. *Psychological Medicine* **18**: 893–909.

40. Brewin, C., MacCarthy, B., Duda, K. and Vaughn, C. (1991) Attribution and expressed emotion in the relatives of patients with schizophrenia. *Journal of Abnormal Psychology* **100**: 546–554.

41. Leff, J., Kuipers, L., Berkowitz, R. and Sturgeon, D. (1985) A controlled trial of social intervention in the families of schizophrenic patients: two-year follow-up. *British Journal of Psychiatry* **146**: 594–600.

42. Tarrier, N. (1989) Effect of treating the family to reduce schizophrenia: a review. *Journal of the Royal Society of Medicine* **82**: 423–424.

43. Reno, R. (1979) Attribution for success and failure as a function of perceived age. *Journal of Gerontology* **34**: 709–715.

44. Mandelstam, D. (1980) *Incontinence and its Management*. London: Croom Helm.

45. Barton, E.M., Baltes, M. and Orzech, M. (1980) Etiology of dependence in older nursing home residents during morning care: the role of staff behaviour. *Journal of Personality and Social Psychology* **38**: 423–431.

46. Rodin, J. (1986) Aging and health: Effects of the sense of control. *Science* **233**: 1271–1276.

47. Killian, E.C. (1970) Effects of geriatric transfers on mortality rates. *Social Work* **15**: 19–26.

48. Kubler-Ross, E. (1970) *On Death and Dying*. London: Tavistock.

49. Leshan, L. (1964) In: Bowers, M., Jackson, E., Knoght, J. and Leshan, L. (eds) *Counselling the Dying*. New York: Thomas Nelson.

50. Watson, W.H. (1976) The ageing sick and the near dead; a study of some distinguishing characteristics and social effects. *Omega* **7**: 115–123.

51. Tesser, A. and Rosen, S. (1975) The reluctance to transmit bad news. In: Berkowitz, L. (ed.) *Advances in Experimental Social Psychology*. London: Academic Press.

52. Teasdale, K. and Kent, G. (1995) The use of deception in nursing. *Journal of Medical Ethics*, **21**: 77–81.

53. Saunders, C. (1969) The moment of truth: care of the dying person. In: Pearson, L. (ed.) *Death and Dying*. Cleveland: Case Western Reserve University Press.

54. Viney, L., Walker, B., Robertson, T., Lilley, B. and Ewan, C. (1994) Dying in palliative care units in hospital: a comparison of the quality of life of terminal cancer patients. *Journal of Consulting and Clinical Psychology* **62**: 157–164.

55. Archer, J. and Winchester, G. (1994) Bereavement following the death of a pet. *British Journal of Psychology* **85**: 259–271.

56. Parkes, C.M. (1975) Determinants of outcome following bereavement. *Omega* **6**: 303–324.

57. Parkes, C.M., Benjamin, B. and Fitzgerald, R. (1969) Broken heart: a statistical study of increased mortality among widowers. *British Medical Journal* **1**: 740–743.

58. Stroebe, W., Stroebe, M., Gergen, K. and Gergen, M. (1982) The effects of bereavement on mortality: a social psychological analysis. In: Eiser, J.R. (ed.) *Social Psychology and Behavioural Medicine*. Chichester: Wiley.

59. Bartrop, R.W., Luckhurst, E., Lazarus, L., Kicoh, L. and Penny, R. (1977) Depressed lymphocyte function after bereavement. *Lancet* **1**: 834–836.

60. Rees, W.D. and Lutkins, S. (1967) Mortality of bereavement. *British Medical Journal* **4**: 13–16.

61. Oglethorpe, R. (1983) Stillbirth: a personal experience. *British Medical Journal* **287**: 1197–1198.

62. Forrest, G.C. (1983) Mourning perinatal death. In: Davis, J.A., Richards, M. and Robertson, N. (eds) *Parent–Baby Attachment in Premature Infants*. London: Croom Helm.

63. Lovell, A. (1983) Some questions of identity: late miscarriage, stillbirth and perinatal loss. *Social Science and Medicine* **17**: 755–761.

64. Forrest, G.C., Standish, E. and Baum, J. (1982) Support after perinatal death: a study of support and counselling after perinatal bereavement. *British Medical Journal* **285**: 1475–1479.

65. Murray, J. and Callan, V. (1988) Predicting adjustment to perinatal death. *British Journal of Medical Psychology* **61**: 237–244.

66. Worden, J. (1982) *Grief Counselling and Grief Therapy*. London: Tavistock.

9
Adjustment to Life Events

SUMMARY

Everyone must make adjustments in order to cope with life changes. The term stress has been used to refer to both the physiological reactions to the event and to the event itself, but a more adequate definition also takes the person's appraisal of the event into account.

The amount of change recently experienced by an individual – particularly adverse change – is related to the incidence of physical illness. This may be due to changes in the immune system. The experience of severely threatening life events is also associated with the onset of psychiatric illnesses. Illness itself causes stress, compounding the problem. Victims of unpredictable and uncontrollable events such as assault and natural disasters may need assistance to overcome post-traumatic stress.

Methods for buffering the effects of stress are effective because they modify the individual's perceptions of his or her ability to cope. Stress inoculation training involves both a reappraisal of situations and provides new strategies for reacting to them. Giving patients a measure of predictability and control over their care may give them time to prepare for what is to come, and social support is important for the maintenance of self-esteem and hope for the future in the face of adversity.

This second part of this book is concerned with the ways that people develop throughout their lives. Important aspects of this process are predictability and control: as an individual develops, he or she learns how to predict and how to influence the daily events of life. When circumstances change, however, a person must make adjustments in order to understand this novel situation and learn new ways of behaving within it. Adjustments are particularly evident when major events occur, such as the birth of a child, but even minor, everyday events ensure that life is a constant process of adaptation.

Defining stress

The adjustments required by the changes can be said to place the person under *stress*, a concept that has been used in several different ways.

A physiological approach

Selye[1] concentrated on the way the organism adapts to events. According to his model, the organism is weakened by prolonged or recurrent stresses since, over time, there is a decreasing ability to adapt. As the person is constantly knocked out of a homoeostatic balance, the adjustments become progressively more difficult to make.

Much research supports the idea that different systems in the brain respond to different kinds of stressful experiences.[2] The pituitary adrenal-cortex system is activated by conditions where the organism is helpless, being linked with depression and loss of control. The sympathetic adrenal-medullary system is mobilized when the organism retains control over a challenge and is associated with the release of catecholamines and sympathetic nervous system reactions. A third system, the hypothalamic-pituitary sex steroid axis, is related to the degree of persistence in attempting to control stressors.

Of much interest is the eventual effect of stressors on health. Neuroendocrine changes can induce physiological abnormalities which eventually lead to pathology if neuroendocrine feedback controls are overridden. Heightened steroid release may be associated with susceptibility to depression and infections (perhaps through changes in the immunological system), while the stimulation of catecholamines may be linked with high blood pressure and sudden cardiac death.[3]

An environmental approach

Another approach to stress has concentrated on the events themselves rather than the organism's responses to them. Some events are considered to be intrinsically more stressful than others. The rate of psychological and somatic distress following natural disasters and severe accidents is very high and it would seldom make sense to equate the loss of a spouse with, say, a change in residence.

One way of studying life events that has gained considerable popularity is based on the idea that adjustment is related to both the number and severity of experienced changes. Much of this research has been based on the kinds of ideas used by Holmes and Rahe.[4] Originally, they chose 43 events which they considered to be relatively common, shown in Table 9.1. They asked a sample of people to rate each event for the degree of adjustment that would be required, so that their relative importance could be ascertained. Some events, such as the death of a spouse or divorce were rated highly, while others such as a vacation or minor violations of the law were given low values. The ratings shown in Table 9.1 are called Life Change Units (LCUs). The death of a spouse was considered to be twice as stressful as marriage, which in turn was seen to be twice as stressful as a change in living conditions. This has been termed the Social Readjustment Rating Scale (SRRS). Organized into a questionnaire format – the Schedule of Recent Experiences (SRE) – the list provided a means whereby people could check off events they had experienced over the previous 6 months or year.

One problem with this approach is that the same stressors can produce quite different reactions in different people. While a divorce might be very stressful and emotionally difficult for one partner, it might be liberating for the other. The Holmes and Rahe approach assumes that all change, because it requires adjustment, results in stress. Many of the events on their scale can be happy and positive occasions. It now seems that it is mainly events which are experienced as negative and which imply some long-term threat that result in stress.

An interactional approach

Although both the physiological and environmental approaches provide insights into the process of adjustment, neither, on its own, can provide a full account. Both fail to take the *meaning* of events into consideration. It is difficult to see how either the physiological or the environmental approach could themselves

Table 9.1 The Social Readjustment Rating Scale (SRRS) (Reproduced from Holmes, T. H. and Rahe, R. H. (1967) *Journal of Psychosomatic Research* **11:** 213–218, with kind permission from Elsevier Science Ltd, The Boulevard, Langford Lane, Kidlington, OX5 1GB, UK.)

Rank	Life event	Mean value
1	Death of spouse	100
2	Divorce	73
3	Marital separation	65
4	Jail term	63
5	Death of a close family member	63
6	Personal injury or illness	53
7	Marriage	50
8	Fired at work	47
9	Marital reconciliation	45
10	Retirement	45
11	Change in health of family member	44
12	Pregnancy	40
13	Sex difficulties	39
14	Gain of new family member	39
15	Business readjustment	39
16	Change in financial state	38
17	Death of a close friend	37
18	Change to different line of work	36
19	Change in number of arguments with spouse	35
20	Mortgage over £10 000	31
21	Foreclosure of mortgage or loan	30
22	Change in responsibilities at work	29
23	Son or daughter leaving home	29
24	Trouble with in-laws	29
25	Outstanding personal achievement	28
26	Wife begins or stops work	26
27	Begin or end school	26
28	Change in living conditions	25
29	Revision of personal habits	24
30	Trouble with boss	23
31	Change in work hours or conditions	20
32	Change in residence	20
33	Change in schools	20
34	Change in recreation	19
35	Change in church activities	19
36	Change in social activities	18
37	Mortgage or loan less than £10 000	17
38	Change in sleeping habits	16
39	Change in number of family get-togethers	15
40	Change in eating habits	15
41	Vacation	13
42	Christmas	12
43	Minor violations of the law	11

adequately explain why different people can have very different reactions to the same event. A more attractive option to understanding adjustment to life events would not only take environmental and response factors into account but also provide an indication of how personal meanings and coping strategies affect individual responses.

The important aspect of this analysis involves cognition: the person's appraisal of the demand is crucial for the understanding of stress. There may, for example, be the external demand of an exam, but if the student does not perceive the demand as being important, or feels well prepared, there will be little stress. Hunger may become stressful if there is no food about and it seems difficult to obtain, but not if a simple trip to the refrigerator will relieve it.

The interactional model also includes the ways that individuals attempt to cope with or adjust to the demands. Attempts to cope can involve either direct action or can be palliative. *Direct action* involves taking active steps to minimize the stress and is most appropriate when the situation can be anticipated or changed. Studying for an exam or asking about the effects of an operation would be examples of such preparation. Another response would be to attempt to avoid or escape from the source of the problem, which may be possible in physically stressful situations but more difficult in psychologically disturbing ones.

While direct action strategies involve attempts at mastery over stressful demands, *palliative* strategies are more emotion-based, and involve moderating the distress evoked by the events. Palliative strategies include the use of drugs such as alcohol or tranquillizers, or could be more psychological, such as the use of denial or distraction. These strategies could be most appropriate when there is little possibility of changing the nature of the stressor.

These three aspects – demand, appraisal and response – provide a useful way of defining what psychologists mean by the term stress: stress is said to occur when there' is an *imbalance* between the demand and ability to cope with it. But it is the *perceived* demand and the *perception* of capability to cope which are important here.[5]

It follows from this definition that it would be possible to reduce stress in several ways. These can include:

1 reducing the actual demands (for example, reducing the number of hours worked);

2 altering appraisals of demands (for example by changing the ways that people interpret situations);

3 increasing the number and effectiveness of coping methods (for example, teaching relaxation skills); and

4 increasing confidence in the ability to use coping methods (for example, providing evidence that coping methods can be used successfully).

The aim of this chapter is to discuss the research on adaptation to life events, using this transactional model as a basis for exploring the links between stress and illness, the stresses involved in medicine, and ways of helping people to cope with the demands made upon them. Much of this work can be characterized as *psychosomatic* research, which involves the exploration of the relationship between psychological and physiological mechanisms in the onset of disease and illness. Some researchers have concentrated on the physiological approach, others have used the environmental one and yet others have been more concerned with the ways that people appraise their situation. One theme is the importance of control: when people believe that they are able to exert control over what happens to them they are less likely to feel under stress.

Life events research

Research relating the experience of life events to illness has concentrated on their effects on physical well-being and emotional distress.

Physical illness

The Schedule of Recent Experiences developed by Holmes and Rahe has been used in several studies on physical illness. For example, the incidence of such events in physicians' lives has been examined. Doctors were asked to fill out the questionnaire for the previous 18 months and were divided into three groups according to the number of LCUs they reported: high, moderate or low. Nine months later, the physicians were

contacted again and asked about their illnesses. LCU and significant health problems were, indeed, related to each other: 49 per cent of the high LCU group reported illnesses, 25 per cent of the moderate group, but only 9 per cent of the low LCU group.

One might also expect that the seriousness of illnesses would also be related to the number and severity of life events. In order to test this hypothesis, Wyler *et al.*[6] asked surgical, psychiatric and gynaecological patients to check off life events which had occurred during the previous year. Each patient's diagnosis was coded for seriousness, so that the researchers could test the strength of the relationship between seriousness and LCUs experienced. They did in fact find a correlation between these variables for chronic diseases such as diabetes and hypertension, but not for acute illnesses.

Difficulties with life events research on physical illness

Although there are many studies which have found similar results, caution is required in several respects. First, many of the studies have been retrospective, relying on memory for the incidence of events and sometimes for the incidence of illness. As shown in the chapter on memory, retrospective data are not always reliable and the possibility that patients look for reasons for their illness in life events cannot be overlooked. Perhaps people who are likely to remember life events are also those who remember illnesses, so that the correlations may simply reflect differences in recall. This problem could be overcome to a large extent if prospective studies were undertaken and if medical records could be consulted. Perhaps the investigator could give the questionnaire to a group of people and then return later to collect evidence of physical illness.

A further point is that the Schedule of Recent Experiences does not distinguish between positive and negative life events: stress is assumed to occur whether events are welcome or unwelcome, since all require adjustment. According to the transactional model of stress, however, the person's appraisal of environmental demands is seen as being crucial, so one might expect that negative experiences would have more severe effects than positive ones. This viewpoint has been receiving greater support in recent years as the evidence mounts that only experience of negative life events is associated with subsequent illness.[7]

Another reason why attributing causality is problematic has to do with the distinction between *disease* and *illness behaviour*. The incidence of symptoms in the general population is actually very high, with most people having some sign of disease much of the time. There is some evidence that life events make people more aware of their health status and more likely to consult their doctors.[8] Many of the events could have a demoralizing effect on people, making them less able to cope with their symptoms and more prone to seek medical help. In seeking this assistance, undiagnosed conditions may become more visible.

However, a series of studies in which people volunteered to be infected by the common cold virus support the existence of a link between the experience of life events and physical illness. They were first given a physical examination and judged to be in good health and then asked to complete scales designed to measure the experience of recent life events (including the negativity of the events) and their health practices (e.g. smoking, alcohol intake, exercise, etc.). All volunteers were then either given a placebo or were "virally challenged" through exposure to common cold viruses. Because they were kept in quarantine, their diet and behaviour could be controlled and monitored.

The results showed that those who had initially reported many negative life events were more likely to show symptoms of infection than those who reported fewer. They were more likely to have a raised temperature (as shown in Figure 9.1) and more likely to have a runny nose.[9] Several such studies have shown a consistent relationship between stress and infection, and there is now some work which seems to explain this link.

Effects of stress on the immune system

A wide variety of stressful situations – such as bereavement, marital discord, job loss and other chronic threats – have been related to changes in the immune system.[10-12] The argument is that stress impairs immunological functioning and makes the person more vulnerable if exposed to an infectious agent. It is possible that cortisol and the catecholamines, which are released under stress, have an immunosuppressant capacity.[13]

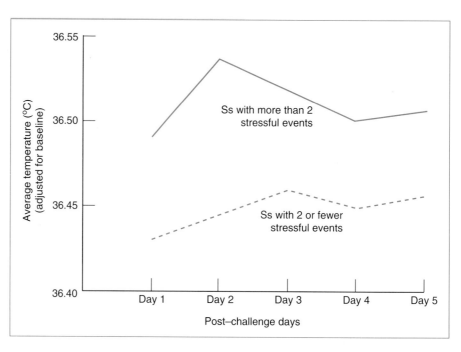

Figure 9.1 Average post-challenge daily temperatures for volunteers infected with the common cold virus. There is a clear difference between subjects who have had more than two recent stressful events in their lives and those with just two or less than two. (Reproduced from Cohen, S., Tyrrell, D. and Smith, A. (1990) *Journal of Personality and Social Psychology* **64:** 131–140. Copyright © 1993 by the American Psychological Association. Reprinted with permission.)

Some studies have examined immuno-competence directly. In one project,[14] blood samples were taken from first-year medical students on two occasions, a month before their exams (to provide a baseline) and then during the exam week. The Holmes and Rahe SRE and a scale to measure the students' loneliness was administered at baseline and the blood samples were assayed for natural killer cell (NK) activity (one indicator of the cellular immune response) on both occasions. There was a significant decrease in NK activity from the first to the second blood sample, suggesting that the students were more vulnerable to disease during the examination week than a month before. The students who reported that they felt lonely had lower NK activity than students who did not report loneliness and, most importantly for the validity of the SRE, students who had experi-enced many life events had lower NK activity than those who had experienced only a few. These results suggest that there may be a causal link between the experience of stressful life events (such as medical school examinations) and vulnerability to disease.

Unfortunately, no measures of changes in the use of drugs or alcohol, amount of sleep or diet were taken in this study, so it is not possible to say if changes in NK activity were mediated by these factors. In fact, it is difficult to control for all the factors which might affect the immune response in humans, so that it can be preferable to use other species for study, whose physical environment can be controlled and monitored more easily and accurately. One example of such a study involved giving electric shocks to rats. Although there are ethical issues involved in the use of animals for our benefit (see Box 9.1), this

---

BOX 9.1

The ethics of animal research

The use of animals in teaching and research is controversial. Everyone would agree that animals should be treated with respect and not abused or caused unnecessary pain. There are many guidelines and restrictions on how they should be housed, fed and if necessary killed. However, there are important dis-agreements about the situations in which animals can be legitimately used for the benefit of mankind.

Those who disagree with the use of animals put forward two main arguments. One con-cerns the rights of animals. The argument here is that animals have as much a right to live a pain-free life as do humans. They have mem-ories, use tools, communicate with one another and some have rudimentary cultures. Since, on a basic level, we share most of our DNA with animals, particularly primates, they are not so very different from us and so share many of the same rights as us. According to this position, it is morally wrong to inflict pain on a sentient being under any circumstances. To do so is to be guilty of "speciesism".[15] The other argument concerns the consequences of research. The demonstration of a biological process in an animal cannot necessarily be generalized to humans. In the examples given in this chapter, for instance, researchers have modelled the effects of stressors such as bereavement or job loss by giving inescapable electric shocks to rats. On the face of it, these are very different processes.

Although they agree that using animals for teaching or research has important moral implications, those who support the use of animals have quite different beliefs. They counter the "speciesism" point by arguing that we, as humans, have a greater moral obligation to further the interests of our own species than those of other species. Overriding the rights of animals can be justified if there are positive consequences.[16] Experiments with animals have provided us with much infor-mation and the opportunity to test technical means to relieve human suffering. Many experi-mental medical techniques have been found to have adverse effects on animals: would we, as a society, prefer to use adults and children in clinical trials before animal testing?

study illustrates how important research can be conducted with other species.

In this research, groups of rats were run in pairs in two separate cages. Both received a session of 80 electric shocks, but the animals in each pair were treated somewhat differently. One animal in each pair could terminate the shocks by turning a wheel in its cage, but the other animal could not do this: its shock would terminate only when the other in the pair turned the wheel. This is called a "yoked" design. Thus, the only difference between the groups was that one rat in each pair had control over the termination of shocks, while the other had no such control. This is a psychological difference, because the intensity, duration and pattern of the shocks were identical. In order to control for the possibility that simply being in the cage had some effects on the immune system, a third group of rats was also included, but they did not receive the electric shocks in this way.

Blood was later collected and lymphocyte proliferation measured. It was found to be different between the three groups. The rats who experienced inescapable shocks showed a significant degree of immunosuppression, but this was not the case for the other two groups. The immune systems of the rats who were able to escape the shocks and the rats who did not receive any shocks were not compromised. Thus it was the experience of lack of control which was important, not the experience of the shocks themselves.[17] Other studies[18] have shown that when rats are injected with cancerous cells, tumours are more likely to grow if the rats are subsequently subjected to inescapable shocks than escapable ones.

Furthermore, it seems that experience when an animal is young can also affect ability to reject tumour cells. The idea that the types of experiences people have when they are young have significant effects on their later well-being is discussed in several places in this book. This principle may also hold in the case of susceptibility to disease. In a very interesting study, Seligman and Visintainer[19] gave escapable or inescapable shocks to rats when they were only 27 days old. At 90 days they were implanted with cancerous cells: to simplify somewhat, those given inescapable shocks early in their lives were more likely to develop tumours.

This area of research is exciting for two reasons. First, it helps us to understand better the relationship between stress and illness. But second, and of more practical importance, it shows that social and psychological factors are important in the onset of disease. The idea here is that when animals (and people) feel helpless to change their environment and helpless to change or avoid negative events, they are more vulnerable to the development of disease. This provides another avenue of intervention: if people can be given an increased sense of control over what happens to them, then their physical health may benefit. There has been much interest in the possibility that people infected with HIV may be less likely to go on to develop AIDS if they can develop the needed psychological resources and coping methods.[20] While it is a mistake to conclude that "peace of mind" or a "positive frame of mind" will lead to a halt to the progression of a disease, the feeling of control is likely to prove very significant.[21,22]

Psychiatric illness

Not only can negative life events lead to physical illnesses, they can also trigger psychiatric difficulties. Some of the more important studies in this area have been conducted by Brown and his colleagues, who were interested in the onset of depression and of schizophrenia. Clinical depression is a very serious difficulty. Although most people experience times when they feel very "down", have trouble sleeping and lose interest in their usual activities, these difficulties become much more severe and chronic in clinical depression. There may be thoughts about suicide and a pervasive negative outlook on life, personal capabilities and the future. Schizophrenia is another debilitating psychiatric illness, whose characteristic symptoms involve thought disturbances in content (e.g. delusions) or form (e.g. incomprehensible statements without meaningful relationships), perhaps with associated hallucinations.

Brown compared samples of "healthy", "normal" subjects who were randomly chosen from the population (to serve as comparisons) with groups of psychiatric patients. He conducted extended personal interviews with each person, being careful to date events and verifying them whenever possible.

Depression

In the study of depressed women,[23] the reports of life events given by clinically depressed patients were compared with a community sample of women. It was only those experiences which implied a long-term threat of some kind, such as the loss of a trusted friend or spouse, learning that a husband was seriously ill, or the necessity of making an important decision, which distinguished between the two groups of women. Some 59 per cent of the patients had experienced such a severe life event within the 9 months preceding the onset of depression, while only 26 per cent of the community sample (some of whom were considered to be clinically depressed although they had not sought assistance) gave comparable reports. This indicated that severe events which had long-term negative implications were associated with depression. Brown argued that these events were causally related to depression, in that they often preceded the time when patients were beginning to feel a need for psychiatric help.

Further research has tended to confirm that that there are three types of provoking factors: (1) loss of attachment figures or loss of significant activities such as employment or child-rearing, (2) disappointments or loss of cherished ideals or beliefs, and (3) failures which result in the loss of self-esteem. All three types involve uncontrollable events which negatively affect the person's sense of social significance.

Vulnerability

But this is only one aspect of his contribution. Brown also wanted to provide an explanation of why only some of the women who underwent stressful life events became depressed. Brown found that loss of the mother before the age of 11, lack of intimacy with a husband or partner, having three children at home under the age of 14, or lack of paid employment made the women vulnerable to the provoking effects of life events. In one or more of these circumstances, the individual may be less likely to believe that she will be able to cope with life's problems or to be able to resolve the present difficulties. On the other hand, if the individual had a secure childhood, had an intimate tie and was in paid employment, the experience of a major event is unlikely to provoke depression.

Thus, the argument is that experiencing severe life events is not in itself sufficient to bring on depression. Nor is vulnerability by itself enough. Rather, it is the combination of provoking events and vulnerability factors that is significant. Table 9.2 illustrates some of these data, giving in percentages the proportion of women who were depressed in the presence or absence of life events. For example, 32 per cent of the women who experienced a severe event without an intimate relationship became depressed, but only 10 per cent of those who had such a tie.

Table 9.2 Percentage of women who were depressed and who had a severe life event and either lack of intimacy or three children at home under the age of 14 (Reproduced from Brown, G. W. and Harris, T. (1978) Social origins of depression. *Psychological Medicine* **8:** 577–588, with permission of Cambridge University Press.)

Severe event or major difficulty	Lack of intimacy with husband/partner		At least 3 children aged under 14 years	
	Yes	No	Yes	No
Yes	32%	10%	43%	17%
No	3%	1%	0%	2%

Schizophrenia

In his studies of acute schizophrenia, a different mechanism was suggested. Here, Brown argued that life events trigger the onset of symptoms in those people already likely to suffer, rather than being responsible for the formation of the condition. The illness is said to be "brought forward" in time due to these events (which could be quite minor). Interviews with schizophrenic patients and their relatives indicated a higher incidence of events in the 3 weeks before onset than in a sample of people chosen from the general population. Although the schizophrenic episodes seem to have been triggered by the events, the events themselves were not considered to be sufficient cause: long-term tension in the home appeared to be associated with the probability that people would become disturbed after such changes.

Further support for Brown's conclusions on psychiatric illness has been provided by other workers using somewhat different research designs. But stressful life events occur fairly commonly and only a small proportion of people become clinically depressed, so it appears that other factors are also important in the aetiology of psychiatric illness. Brown seems to have identified some of these, the vulnerability factors. Additionally, genetic influences are likely to be relevant. Prospective studies will provide a better estimate of the significance of the link between life events and psychiatric illness.

Stressful effects of illness

Illness can have a variety of effects on people, depending on their severity and chronicity. Even relatively minor diseases can have significant effects on performance, which may have significant implications when, for example, a student is taking an examination. However, it is the effects of major illness which are of more clinical concern, where both depression (through loss of normal functioning) and severe anxiety (through perceptions of danger) are common. Depression is a common response to chronic illnesses. Devlin et al.[24] found that 25 per cent of patients who underwent surgery for anorectal cancer had psychiatric difficulties with depression. This was associated with loss of sexual relationships (due to embarrassment and fear of spillage). A hysterectomy in a young woman is often followed by depression, and the loss of a limb through amputation has been compared to the loss of a friend or spouse through death.[25] Both involve a process of grieving.

Breast cancer is a particularly stressful disease that has implications for women's sexual identity and self-confidence as well as their physical health. Renal dialysis, although often considered to be a life-saving development, also poses many problems for patients and disabling levels of anxiety and depression have been found in many dialysands. Nichols and Springford[26] found that patients have many difficulties that go unrecognized by medical staff. Although staff expect patients to feel physically well between sessions, this was not the case for 44 per cent of the sample. Additionally, 60 per cent of the patients said that they "felt no good as a parent" and 50 per cent that they were "spoiling their spouses' lives". Nineteen per cent reported suicidal wishes. Indeed, survival by dialysis has been likened to a terminal illness, with a slow, progressive multisystem failure and growing weakness and discomfort. These studies illustrate the circularity of stress and disease: the illness may be due in part to stress and the illness, in turn, results in the need for further adjustment.

There is also the effect of illness on the patient's friends and relatives, who may carry a considerable burden of caregiving. Such burdens may be increasing with the increasing emphasis on treating patients at home, rather than in hospital. When caring for cancer patients, giving emotional support, providing transportation and doing extra household tasks are noted as most time-consuming, and these increase with increasing patient dependency.[27] Caring for people who are dementing usually results in many difficulties. Caregivers are most likely to be depressed if they feel a loss of control, if they feel unable to cope with the impact of caregiving and if there is no perceived hope for the future.[28] Such difficulties can be translated into changes in the immune system, thus leaving caregivers themselves more open to the development of disease.[29]

Hospitalization

Part of the stress involved in illness can be related to factors of uncertainty and unpredictability in medical care. In hospital, there are other events occurring besides the operation and the associated pain. A scale similar to the Holmes and Rahe scale has been used to assess the degree of adjustment involved in being in hospital.[30] It was developed by asking patients to rank events they had experienced when in hospital from most stressful to least stressful. These events fell into several categories, such as unfamiliarity of surroundings and loss of independence. Interestingly, many of the most highly ranked events were concerned with the incidental aspects of being in hospital – having strangers sleep in the same room and having to eat at different times than usual. This scale has been given some validation by a later study: those patients who reported that they had experienced many of the events on the scale were observed to show the largest changes on cardiovascular measures.[31]

Observing the illnesses and deaths of other patients has an adverse effect on many people. Bruyn *et al.*[32] examined patients' reactions to death and emergencies in a coronary care unit. Of the 29 patients studied, 17 witnessed such an event, and their blood pressure and anxiety levels were compared with those of the remaining 12 patients who did not. Thirteen of the 17 patients showed abnormal physiological responses, and over half became more anxious, compared to only one of the 12-patient comparison group. These studies reflect the problem of iatrogenic illness (illness caused by the process of medical care itself) which is a topic considered in the final chapter.

Post-traumatic stress disorder (PTSD)

The notion that involvement with serious events, from accidents and assaults through to disasters and wars, can have a significant psychological consequences has received much support in recent years. Such events are usually uncontrollable, unpredictable and physically dangerous. This area of research was stimulated by the reports of American soldiers who served in Vietnam during the 1960s and 1970s. Some claimed to be severely incapacitated by what they saw and did during the war, so much so that they were unable to work, sleep or readjust to civilian life. Much further research has been conducted with people who had close contact with major disasters, such as the Mount St. Helens eruption in Washington, the King's Cross fire in London or other large-scale tragedies which resulted in the loss of many lives. However, it has become clear that this set of difficulties can also occur when only one individual is harmed in some way, such as in a personal assault or rape[33] or a motor vehicle accident.[34]

It seems that some people are less affected by their experiences than others. While one person might be severely incapacitated, another might be able to cope with less difficulty. Most people who experience such powerful emotional reactions recover within a few weeks or months. However, approximately 5 per cent will develop a more entrenched and chronic reaction known as post-traumatic stress disorder. There are four typical characteristics of PTSD:

1 The person has experienced an event that would be markedly distressing for almost anyone, such as a serious threat to one's own life or physical integrity, or seeing someone seriously injured or killed as a result of an accident or physical violence.
2 The traumatic event is persistently re-experienced through intrusive memories, recurrent dreams or intense distress when confronted with events which resemble the trauma.
3 The person persistently avoids anything which reminds him or her of the trauma.
4 The person experiences persistent symptoms of increased arousal, such as difficulty in falling or staying asleep, inability to concentrate, irritability or outbursts of anger, and hypervigilance.

If such symptoms persist for more than a month, a formal diagnosis of PTSD would be made.

It is important to emphasize that the individual does not have to be physically harmed him or herself. Seeing the effects of damage on others can also be traumatic. There are several studies on the effects of professionals working with victims, such as firefighters or the police who helped after the downing of the TWA airliner at Lockerbie. Medical staff and medical students can also be affected by their experiences. After the tragedy at the Hillsborough football ground in Sheffield in 1989, when 96 people died, staff and students were asked to complete questionnaires about their contact with the deceased and with relatives and the extent of any subsequent psychological difficulties. Approximately one medical student in eight at the Medical School was considered to have had a high level of involvement (either through being at the ground at the time, helping relatives afterwards or working at the hospitals when the victims arrived), and these students scored higher on questionnaires of distress and PTSD than students who had low levels of involvement.[35]

Interventions for PTSD

One explanation for the cognitive and emotional reactions described above is that the experience of such events forces us to reconsider some of the basic assumptions we make about our life. Most of us, most of the time, assume that the world is essentially a benign, predictable place, in which a severely negative event is unlikely to happen to us personally. Although such events do occur, by and large we believe that they happen to other people. This is generally a useful and accurate assumption to make, but when a dangerous and unpredictable traumatic event does occur, people are forced to reconsider this fundamental belief. Such readjustments can result in considerable emotional turmoil, as people attempt to integrate the experience with their previously held assumptions.[36]

After such experiences, people often feel the need to talk, many times, about what has happened to them. It seems necessary for victims to have others who are willing to listen and who are emotionally supportive. Victims who have people available at the time of the crisis seem to be less likely to suffer the intrusive images and thoughts which are characteristic of PTSD. For example, Joesph et al.[37] asked survivors of the Jupiter disaster (when an oil tanker collided with a cruise ship in the Mediterranean Sea), to indicate the amount of interpersonal support they received afterwards. Those who indicated that they had later contact with other survivors, received emotional support and had the opportunity to confide their feelings at the time were less likely to report PTSD symptoms 18 months later. Such research suggests that people may be helped if formal attempts are made shortly after a disaster to provide counselling.

"Psychological debriefing" is the term used to describe programmes which are provided for groups of victims of such events. These programmes seek to (a) provide an opportunity for people to share their experiences with others and (b) normalize the emotional and cognitive reactions by illustrating that others also have these reactions. The aim is to reduce the likelihood that the reactions will become chronic. Although debriefing groups are now often provided for victims and heath care workers after

PTSD after medical procedures

Many people will become a victim of some kind at some point in their lives. Although few will be involved in a major disaster, many will be the victims of assault, rape or burglary. These events can have similar consequences to larger-scale traumas, with re-living of the events, feelings of vulnerability, avoidance of situations which are reminders of the event, difficulty in sleeping and inability to concentrate. Shalev et al.[39] describe cases of patients who reported symptoms of PTSD after experiencing medical emergencies or invasive medical tests. For example:

◆ Mr. E had been scheduled for an elective heart catheterization. Having been prepared for the intervention, Mr. E was cooperative and in good humour during its first phase, talking to his cardiologist and being kept aware of the progress of the procedure. Suddenly a dramatic change occurred, the memories of which, he would say later, "have been etched into my brain like a disk which is played back endlessly". While talking to his cardiologist he suddenly observed panic in his physician's face and heard him shouting. He recalls having observed a flat EEG signal on the monitor and having noticed that everyone around became agitated and was preparing to administer cardiac shock. He remembers having felt the electrodes on his chest followed by the most unimaginable excruciating pain in all parts of his body.

During the weeks following the catheterization, Mr. E progressively developed a psychological state characterized by hyperarousal, difficulty in falling asleep, repeated flashbacks, difficulty concentrating, restlessness and avoidance of cues relating to his catheterization. He had frequent nightmares in which he was back in the operating room and the entire scene was recurring. (p. 248)   ◆

disasters, there is much research to be done in this area.[38]

Becoming a doctor

The process of learning, understanding and fulfilling norms and roles is a vital part of social development. Although the term *socialization* is usually applied to children, it continues throughout life. There are expectations involved in being a patient, for example, so that when someone is admitted to hospital he or she will experience a period of uncertainty until the norms are discovered and the role can be enacted. Medical training is the process of becoming socialized into medicine. Students do not only learn the technical side of doctoring, but also the ways to behave towards patients and staff, how to dress and how to act in a professional manner. When they enter the wards for the first time, medical students often report a sense of uncertainty until they find out what is expected of them.

Stress of being a medical student

Homesickness

Homesickness provides a good example of how processes begun in childhood continue into adulthood. As discussed in Chapter 6, attachment theory concerns the ways in which children become attached to their caregivers and then as they grow up gradually move away from them physically and emotionally. Going to school, developing friendships and the independence of adolescence are steps along this process.

Leaving home for university is a further step, but one which can be difficult for many students. Most people suffer a degree of homesickness when they come to university, with episodes of depressed mood, anxiety and absent-mindedness. In perhaps 10–15 per cent this can be continuous and very distressing. This is similar to a grieving reaction, in which there can be a preoccupation with thoughts about home, sleeping and eating disturbances and feeling withdrawn from others. For most students the reactions gradually decrease as they adapt to the loss of their familiar and secure home environment, but for some the experience worsens and

deteriorates.[40] Perhaps it is most important to know that these are common reactions, will often become less frequent over time, and that university counselling services are skilled and more than willing to give assistance.

Academic and clinical concerns

The stresses experienced by medical students vary over time. Initially, many students need to adjust from the position of being top of their class at school to being just one of many very bright and able people. There can be fears of new academic demands (not only the amount to learn, but also the uncertainty about what needs to be covered), lack of feedback, and concerns about letting parents down. The approach of written examinations is associated with increasing anxiety,[41] but oral examinations are regarded as particularly stressful forms of assessment, more stressful than initial interviews to medical school.[42]

During the clinical years, concerns about dealing with patients and senior staff tend to take precedence over academic concerns. Firth[43] explored the sources of stress in clinical students by asking them to "describe a real event which has occurred in the past month in your role as a medical student, and which has been stressful to you". Some of the results are shown in Table 9.3. It is interesting to note that almost as many students complained of having too little responsibility as having too much. Firth also asked the students to complete the General Health Questionnaire,[44] which is designed to measure the amount of distress experienced: 31.2 per cent of the students scored above the threshold on the questionnaires (the threshold score indicates that the person might be in need of some psychological assistance). Further, many students were drinking much more alcohol than is recommended.

Table 9.3 Percentages of students reporting stressful experiences (Reproduced from Firth, J. (1986) *British Medical Journal* **292:** 1177–1180, with permission.)

Stressful experience	Percentage
Relations with consultants	34
Too much responsibility	29
Too little responsibility	28
Talking with terminally ill patients	25

When on the wards many students find their lack of experience frustrating and emotionally upsetting. They may find that learning to perform physical examinations on patients makes them feel guilty and invasive. Students may also feel helpless because of their lack of expertise. These feelings can be particularly acute when dealing with young or vulnerable patients and can be illustrated by the following quotations:

66 Meeting a chronic schizophrenic girl of my own age who seems to have so little going for her in her life. Her mother can no longer cope with her and she rarely is visited by any of her family. I feel I can identify with her at her more lucid times and that she can be an extremely likeable person. The thought that there is so little to offer this girl is upsetting, frustrating and it gives me a feeling of helplessness. With other chronic patients I have met I have been able to accept their situation but being able to identify with this girl makes this a problem for me. 99

66 Talking to and checking in a terminally ill patient one day. Tending to his incontinence. Next day seeing the patient within half an hour of his death on the ward. I was unhappy that anyone should die in such a distressed and uncomfortable manner, and in such noise and impersonal surroundings. There seemed to be no dignity, or peace, in dying in hospital. (Ref. 45, p. 10-11) 99

Doctoring

After qualification, other types of stress become more significant. Although doctoring can be seen as a "good" job, there is evidence that it is a particularly stressful occupation, with physicians having a higher incidence of drug abuse, alcoholism and divorce and suicide than the general population.[46] Work overload is the major difficulty, but dealing with death, relationships with senior doctors and mistakes which are attributed to personal failings are also important.[47] Sleep deprivation, particularly during the qualifying year, is associated with decrements in reasoning ability and an increase in irritability.[48] When

newly qualified doctors were asked, "Do you think your hours of duty are so long as to impair your ability to work with adequate efficiency?", 37 per cent reported that this was "often" or "always" the case.[49]

Other studies have shown that, within medicine, some specialities are more stressful than others. A comparison was made of the incidence of coronary heart disease in highly stressful medical specialities (general practice and anaesthetics) with that in low-stress ones (pathology and dermatology). Questionnaires were sent to 1000 physicians in each group, and a respectable response rate of 65 per cent was achieved. Coronary disease was some three times more prevalent in general practitioners and anaesthetists than in dermatologists and pathologists.[50]

"Burnout" has become a popular term. It is usually seen as having three components: emotional exhaustion (tiredness, irritability, high alcohol consumption), depersonalization (treating patients and other people as though they are objects), and low productivity accompanied by feelings of low achievement.[51,52] Perhaps it is these feelings which lead to high levels of anxiety and depression in some groups working in the health services.[53]

Personal issues

There can also be related interpersonal difficulties. One important issue is sexual harassment. Lenhart et al.[54] surveyed members of the American Medical Women's Association, finding that a majority of respondents reported some form of unwanted sexual attention within the previous year. As shown in Figure 9.2, although overt sexual assault was not reported, there were numerous instances of sexual comments and unwanted touching.

Women and men may make different career choices. While marriage and parenting were related to a greater number of hours worked and higher income for men, the opposite has been found for women: their careers were often slowed by family commitments.[55] There may also be career conflicts between male and female doctors who marry each other. In such relationships, 73 per cent of the men had higher earnings than their partners, and in only 16 per cent was

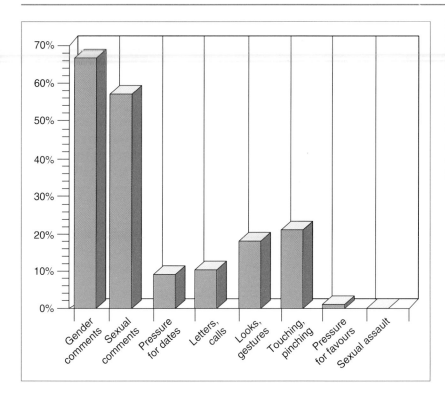

Figure 9.2 Percentages of women doctors reporting different types of unwanted sexual attention within the previous year. (Reproduced from Lenhart, S. *et al.* (1991) *Journal of American Medical Women's Association* **46:** 121–125. Copyright © 1991 American Medical Women's Association. Reprinted with permission.)

the converse the case. It seem that male careers are given priority in such relationships.

Because doctors may need to move from city to city to pursue their careers, spouses and partners may be required to leave their sources of emotional support and have their own career plans interrupted. Female partners of male doctors have indicated a great deal of burden in rearing families almost single-handed.[56,57] Although these professional and personal difficulties may be upsetting, there are many ways in which doctors and their families cope with them. Some of these are outlined below.

Coping with stress

The theme of this part of the book has been adjustment to change – the learning of ways of coping with new situations throughout life. If the stresses involved in such changes as the birth of a child, bereavement and working as a doctor can be moderated or buffered in some way, then the negative psychological and physiological

responses involved may be reduced. Drugs are often used by the medical profession to help their patients and sometimes themselves to cope with their difficulties. Areas of research that point to alternative psychological approaches to coping with stress are considered in this part of the chapter.

Lazarus and Folkman[58] distinguished between problem-focused and emotion-focused coping strategies. Problem-focused coping refers to problem-solving actions or efforts aimed at managing the demands of a situation, while emotion-focused strategies aim to manage the emotional responses to demands. Examples of problem-solving strategies can include gathering information about the stressor, planning what to do in a situation and time management[59] (see Box 9.3). Some emotion-focused strategies include venting anger, distraction or denial. People tend to use problem-focused strategies when they believe that something constructive can be done to relieve the stress, while emotion-focused methods are more likely to be used when they believe that events are not controllable.

BOX 9.3

Time management

The key point about time management is that time is our most precious non-renewable resource. Thus, we should try to use it as effectively and efficiently as possible. Here are five essentials:

1 *Get organized*. Being disorganized is stressful and causes mental overload. Try to:
   - keep on one task, rather than switching between tasks. Give it your *full* attention,
   - avoid distractions,
   - minimize nag factors – never allow important tasks to become urgent
   - make notes of what you have to do rather than rely on memory, and
   - maintain a tidy and organized working environment.
2 *Maintain an overview of your work*. What is your job? What are you at university for? Take an overview of the course, perhaps marking deadlines on a year planner. Then take a tactical view, asking whether what you do on a day-to-day basis is consistent with the overall aims. This involves three steps:
   - Use a "to-do" list to help you to remember what the tasks are
   - Prioritize each task you need to do – A, B or C

   - Cross off the tasks as you do them.
3 *Managing interruptions*. Educate others not to interrupt you when you have planned to work, and educate yourself not to be tempted by distractions. We have a tendency to interrupt unpleasant tasks with interesting ones. Instead, reward yourself when you complete an unpleasant job. In general:
   - Keep your door closed
   - Be assertive
   - When interrupted, decide whether it is important. Don't be a martyr to others' needs
   - Set time limits and stick to them.
4 *Pace yourself*. It is easy to panic, thinking that there is so much to do that you'll never get it done. Spend some time planning your tasks, rather than jumping right in. Work during your best times of the day.
5 *Set some personal objectives*. Write down four resolutions that you will institute over the next 2 days. For example, to clear your desk or to close your door while working. If you take only one change away from reading this outline on time management it will have been worth while.

Cognitive approaches

The model of stress outlined earlier in the chapter indicated that stress involves not only demands from the environment but also individuals' perception or appraisal of these demands. The way people react depends in part on their beliefs, values and attitudes about the event. Although it is true to say that some events are inherently stressful for humans (e.g. prolonged lack of sleep), many researchers have argued that in most everyday situations the "cause" of the stressful response lies within the perceptions of the individual. This is not to say that these perceptions are wrong, but that they reflect belief systems. The implication is that if these beliefs can

be altered then the events will result in less stress.

Some researchers have noted that defence mechanisms can be effective. Denial is a common initial response to the possibility of one's own or a relative's death and may assist people in eventually coming to terms with the fact. Evidence that denial can be effective in reducing stress responses is given by a study of people whose children were dying of leukaemia. Parents who denied the fatal significance of the disease showed lower levels of cortical stress hormones than those parents who recognized the implications.[60] Children, too, can benefit from such strategies.[61] It will be remembered from Chapter 1 that although it was generally beneficial to inform patients explicitly of the procedures and consequences of surgery, certain patients showed somewhat worse outcomes. Perhaps these patients were using denial or distraction in order to cope, and these mechanisms were overridden by the information.

Stress inoculation training

A procedure for providing alternative ways of coping with stress is called "stress inoculation". This approach is based on the notion that people have difficulty in coping with change because they do not have an adequate repertoire of coping strategies available. Rather than encouraging denial of stressful events, attempts are made to provide new skills.

Stress inoculation training involves attempts to encourage adaptive rather than maladaptive self-instructions through three phases: education, rehearsal and application. The educational phase is designed to give the individual a framework for understanding the nature of responses to stressful events. The ways that interpretations of a situation can serve to increase physiological arousal and exacerbate the situation are discussed. To take an example of this approach, Novaco[62] described a programme with patients who commonly reacted with anger to frustrating events. When provoked, these patients would say to themselves things like: "Who the hell does he think he is: he can't do that to me" or "He wants to play it that way, okay, I'll show him". By discussing these self-instructions, the patients were led to see the possibility that their emotional reactions to the situations were influenced by their cognitive appraisals.

The second phase – rehearsal – involves the exploration of alternative self-statements. Instead of maladaptive ones, adaptive responses are encouraged. In Novaco's study, the patients were asked to analyse the situations in which they found themselves uncontrollably angry, looking for the events that triggered the anger and reflecting on alternative self-instructions they could have used. Instead of "He thinks I'm a pushover; I'll get even", the patients were encouraged to instruct themselves to "Stay calm. Just continue to relax", and "Don't assume the worst or jump to conclusions". In both imagination and role play, the patients were asked to congratulate

themselves when they successfully coped with their anger. An important point about this programme was not that it sought to inhibit anger itself. Rather, it gave the patients a greater repertoire in their coping reactions and encouraged more socially acceptable ways of expressing themselves.

The third phase involves application of these new self-instructions. By asking the patients to keep diaries of their experiences outside the training sessions, Novaco was able to show that the programme was successful in real life. Encouraging an awareness of the importance of interpretations and providing alternative strategies for coping with situations enabled the patients to adjust to events more effectively. Similar programmes have been used with cardiac catheterization patients (Chapter 3) and in the control of pain (Chapter 10).

Predictability and control

A recurring theme throughout this book is that people have a strong need to be able to predict what will happen to them. The frequency with which patients complain that they are not given enough information about their care, the problems that parents may encounter if their child behaves in an unpredictable way and the extra difficulties faced by a bereaved person if a relative's death is sudden and unexpected are all examples of the importance of this need.

In Chapter 1 it was shown that giving people information about their impending operation reduced their anxiety. Positive benefits are also achieved by preparing patients for a change in their care while they are in hospital. In this small-scale experiment, 14 patients who were to be transferred from coronary care units to ordinary wards were randomly assigned to one of two groups. Seven were given a routine transfer, while the other seven were given extra preparation (being told when the transfer would occur, what the new ward would be like) and a member of the coronary care unit staff visited the patients in the new setting. The researchers measured the incidence of complications in these two groups: five of the first group but only one of the second group had medical complications in the novel setting.[63]

One reason why predictability is important is that it allows people to exert some control, if not over the situation at least over their responses to it. The studies with rats who were given escapable or inescapable shocks mentioned earlier in the chapter is an illustration of this, but the same principle has also been illustrated in studies with humans who have to deal with real-life situations, as in an experiment with dental patients undergoing treatment. Some patients were given only the routine care usually found during a dental appointment, with the dentist simply performing the work with few comments. Another group of patients were given more control over the dentist's behaviour through the use of "stop signals": they were told that if they wanted a rest or wanted the dentist to stop, they could raise an arm. A third condition was designed to increase the predictability of the situation. Here, the dentists gave a running commentary of their work as they performed it – what they were doing, when some discomfort might occur, and when there would definitely be no pain. When the patients were interviewed after the appointment, 50 per cent of those in the routine care condition reported that they had felt some pain, compared to 15 per cent of those given a stop signal (which was rarely used) and 22 per cent of those given the commentary. Being able to predict or control the situation reduced discomfort.[64]

Social support

The notion that fulfilling and intimate relationships with others assist in coping with changes has a long history. In this century, Durkheim – often considered the father of modern sociology – noted that suicide rates among married people were much lower than those among people who had been divorced or who had never married. He attributed this difference to a protective effect engendered by close relationships: life may not seem so stressful if there is at least one person with whom we can talk. It seems that having good friends is good for both physical and emotional well-being.

Nuckalls et al.[65] reviewed the records of mothers for the incidence of complications during pregnancy and delivery (e.g. high blood pressure, prolonged labour), the extent to which they experienced life changes, and the degree of psychosocial support felt by the women (as measured by their marital happiness, friendships and confidence in the support they would be given by their families). Amongst mothers who had high life-change scores both before and during pregnancy, 91 per cent of those with low social support had one or more medical complications, but only 31 per cent of those with high social support. In the absence of stressful events, no relationship between support and complications was found.

In a longitudinal study, over 4700 adults were initially interviewed. They were asked about several aspects of their lives, including socioeconomic status, social contacts and the number of preventative measures they took to safeguard their health. Nine years later, the investigators managed to follow up 96 per cent of the sample. Those adults who reported close contact with others at the initial interview were much less likely to have died 9 years later by a factor of 2.3 in the case of men, 2.8 for women.[66] This association held even when such variables as socioeconomic status, smoking habits, obesity, alcohol intake and physical activity 9 years earlier were taken into account.

Having good friends is also good for emotional functioning. Brown's retrospective study on the high incidence of depression without a confidant supports this idea, and there are some prospective studies as well. Henderson[67] examined a cross-section of the population in Canberra. Residents were interviewed a total of four times over a one-year period. All were considered to be psychologically healthy at the time of the first interview. At each subsequent interview, measures of social support, experience of negative life events and psychiatric disorder were taken. The hypothesis that lack of adequate social relationships was associated with the onset of neurosis was supported, but only in the presence of adverse life changes. As Brown's work indicated, it is the combination which is significant, and not one or the other independently.

A very interesting line of research on these issues has been conducted by Pennebaker. He argues that we are able to come to terms with traumatic events more easily and quickly if we discuss our feelings and experiences with other people, a view which is consistent with the research on PTSD mentioned earlier in the chapter. He has noted that people who have been victims of family or sexual abuse, who have been bereaved or have other negative experiences are often reticent to talk about their feelings. People may attempt to avoid thinking about aspects of their experience because of the emotional pain or may be ashamed about their feelings. Such inhibitions may actually make the psychological resolution of difficulties less likely and lead to health problems. A survey of spouses of suicide and accidental-death victims indicated that those who were most likely to become ill in the year following the death were ones who had not confided in another about their experiences.[68]

In a series of studies, Pennebaker has explored the possibility that if people are encouraged to speak about their problems they can come to a resolution more readily. It may not even be necessary to actually speak to another – merely writing about a traumatic event seems to be helpful emotionally[69] and can have positive effects on the immune system.[70]

Suggested reading

Nichols, K.A. (1993) *Psychological Care in Physical Illness* (2nd edn), London: Chapman and Hall, considers the difficulties in coping with many conditions, especially renal dialysis. Steptoe, A. and Appels, A. (1989) *Stress, Personal Control and Health*, Chichester: Wiley, provides several chapters that review many of the topics covered in this chapter, while Adler, N. and Matthews, K. (1994) Health psychology: why do some people get sick and some stay well? *Annual Review of Psychology* **45**: 229–259 review recent research on the relationship between stress and illness.

References

1. Selye, H. (1956) *The Stress of Life*. New York: McGraw-Hill.
2. Henry, J.P. (1982) The relation of social to biological processes in disease. *Social Science and Medicine* **16**: 369–380.
3. Steptoe, A. (1984) Psychophysiological processes in disease. In: Steptoe, A. and Mathews, A. (eds) *Health Care and Human Behaviour*. London: Academic Press.
4. Holmes, T.H. and Rahe, R. (1967) The social readjustment rating scale. *Journal of Psychosomatic Research* **11**: 213–218.
5. Cox, T. (1978) *Stress*. London: Macmillan.
6. Wyler, A.R., Masuda, M. and Holmes, T. (1971) Magnitude of life events and seriousness of illness. *Psychosomatic Medicine* **33**: 115–122.
7. Dohrenwend, B.S. and Dohrenwend, B. (1978) Some issues in research in stressful life events. *Journal of Nervous and Mental Disease* **166**: 7–15.
8. Rundall, T.G. (1978) Life change and recovery from surgery. *Journal of Health and Social Behaviour* **19**: 418–427.
9. Cohen, S., Tyrrell, D. and Smith, A.(1993) Negative life events, perceived stress, negative affect, and susceptibility to the common cold. *Journal of Personality and Social Psychology* **64**: 131–140.
10. Kiecolt-Glaser, J., Cacioppo, J., Malarkey, W. and Glaser, R. (1992) Acute psychological stressors and short-term immune changes: What, why, for whom and to what extent? *Psychosomatic Medicine* **54**: 680–685.
11. Herbert, T. and Cohen, S. (1993) Stress and immunity in humans: a meta-analytic review. *Psychosomatic Medicine* **55**: 364–379.
12. Zakowski, S., Hall, H. and Baum, A. (1992) Stress, stress management, and the immune system. *Applied and Preventive Psychology* **1**: 1–13.
13. Jermott, J. and Locke, S. (1984) Psychosocial factors, immunologic mediation, and human susceptibility to infections: How much do we know? *Psychological Bulletin* **95**: 78–108.
14. Kiecolt-Glaser, J.K., Garner, W., Speicher, C., Penn, G., Holliday, J. and Glaser, R. (1984) Psychosocial modifiers of immunocompetence in medical students. *Psychosomatic Medicine* **46**: 7–14.
15. Singer, P. (1979) *Practical Ethics*. Cambridge: Cambridge University Press.
16. Gray, J. (1987) The ethics and politics of animal experimentation. In: Beloff, H. and Coleman, A. (eds) *Psychological Survey 6*. Leicester: The British Psychological Society.
17. Laudenslager, M., Ryan, S., Drugan, R., Hyson, R. and Maier, S. (1983) Coping and immunosuppression: Inescapable but not escapable shock suppresses lymphocyte proliferation. *Science* **221**: 568–570.
18. Visintainer, M., Volpicelli, J. and Seligman, M. (1982) Tumor rejection in rats after inescapable or escapable shock. *Science* **216**: 437–439.
19. Seligman, M. and Visintainer, M. (1985) Tumor

rejection and early experience of uncontrollable shock in the rat. In: Brush, F. and Overmier, J. (eds) *Affect, Conditioning and Cognition*. Hillsborough: Erlbaum.

20. McCutchan, J. (1990) Virology, immunology, and clinical course of HIV infection. *Journal of Consulting and Clinical Psychology* **58**: 5-12.

21. O'Leary, A. (1990) Stress, emotion and human immune function. *Psychological Bulletin* **108**: 363-382.

22. Gorman, J. and Kertzner, R. (1990) Psychoimmunology and HIV infection. *Journal of Neuropsychiatry and Clinical Neurosciences* **2**: 241-252.

23. Brown, G.W. and Harris, T. (1978) *Social Origins of Depression*. London: Tavistock.

24. Devlin, B.H., Plant, J.A. and Griffin, M. (1971) Aftermath of surgery for anorectal cancer. *British Medical Journal* **3**: 413-418.

25. Parkes, C.M. (1975) Psychosocial transitions: comparison between reactions to loss of a limb and loss of a spouse. *British Journal of Psychiatry* **127**: 204-210.

26. Nichols, K.A. and Springford, V. (1984) The psycho-social stressors associated with survival by dialysis. *Behaviour Research and Therapy* **22**: 563-574.

27. Oberst, M., Gass, K. and Ward, S. (1989) Caregiving demands and appraisal of stress among family caregivers. *Cancer Nursing* **12**: 209-215.

28. Morris, R., Morris, L. and Britton, P. (1988) Factors affecting the emotional well-being of the caregivers of dementia sufferers. *British Journal of Psychiatry* **153**: 147-156.

29. Kiecolt-Glaser, J., Dura, J., Speicher, C., Trask, O. and Glaser, R. (1991) Spousal caregivers of dementia victims: longitudinal changes in immunity and health. *Psychosomatic Medicine* **53**: 345-362.

30. Volicer, B.J., Isenberg, M. and Burns, M. (1977) Medical-surgical differences in hospital stress factors. *Journal of Human Stress* **3**: 3-17.

31. Volicer, B.J. and Volicer, L. (1978) Cardiovascular changes associated with stress during hospitalisation. *Journal of Psychosomatic Research* **22**: 159-168.

32. Bruyn, J.G., Thurman, A., Chandler, B. and Bruce, T. (1970) Patients' reactions to death in a coronary care unit. *Journal of Psychosomatic Research* **14**: 65-70.

33. Jackson G. (1991) The rise of post-traumatic stress disorders. *British Medical Journal* **303**: 533-534.

34. Green, M., McFarlane, A., Hunter, C. and Griggs, W.

(1983) Undiagnosed post-traumatic stress disorder following motor vehicle accidents. *Medical Journal of Australia* **159**: 529-534.

35. Kent, G. and Kunkler, A. (1992) Medical student involvement in a major disaster. *Medical Education* **26**: 87-91.

36. Creamer, M., Burgess, P. and Pattison, P. (1992). Reaction to trauma: a cognitive processing model. *Journal of Abnormal Psychology* **101**: 452-459.

37. Joesph, S., Yule, W., Williams, R. and Andrews, A. (1993) Crisis support in the aftermath of disaster: A longitudinal perspective. *British Journal of Clinical Psychology* **32**: 177-185.

38. Bisson, J. and Deahl, M. (1994) Psychological debriefing and prevention of post-traumatic stress. *British Journal of Psychiatry* **165**: 717-720.

39. Shalev, A., Schreiber, S., Galai, T. and Melmed, R. (1993) Post-traumatic stress disorder following medical events. *British Journal of Clinical Psychology* **32**: 247-253.

40. Fisher, S. and Hood, B. (1987) Stress of transition to university. *British Journal of Psychology* **78**: 425-441.

41. Kent, G. and Jambunathan, P. (1989) A longitudinal study of the intrusiveness of cognitions in test anxiety. *Behaviour Research and Therapy* **27**: 43-50.

42. Arndt, C., Guly, U. and McManus, I. (1986) Preclinical anxiety: the stress associated with a viva voce examination. *Medical Education* **20**: 274-280.

43. Firth, J. (1986) Levels and sources of stress in medical students. *British Medical Journal* **292**: 1177-1180.

44. Goldberg, D. (1972) *The Detection of Psychiatric Illness Questionnaire*. London: Oxford University Press.

45. Firth-Cozens, J. (1987) The stresses of medical training. In: Payne, R. and Firth-Cozens, J. (eds) *Stress in Health Professionals*. Chichester: Wiley, pp. 3-22.

46. Richings, J., Khara, G. and McDowell, M. (1986) Suicide in young doctors. *British Journal of Psychiatry* **149**: 475-478.

47. Firth-Cozens, J. and Morrison, L. (1989) Sources of stress and ways of coping in junior house officers. *Stress Medicine* **5**: 121-126.

48. Asken, M.J. and Rahan, D.C. (1983) Resident performance and sleep deprivation. *Journal of Medical Education* **58**: 382-388.

49. Wilkinson, R., Tyler, P. and Varey, C. (1975) Duty hours of young hospital doctors: effects on the quality of their work. *Journal of Occupational Psychology* **48**: 219-229.

50. Russek, I. (1962) Emotional stress and coronary heart disease in American physicians, dentists and lawyers. *American Journal of Medical Science* **243**: 716-725.

51. Maslach, C. and Jackson, S. (1982) Burnout in the health professions: A social psychological analysis. In Sanders, G. and Suls, J. (eds) *Social Psychology of Health and Illness*. London: Erlbaum, pp. 227-251.

52. Mayou, R. (1987) Burnout. *British Medical Journal* **295**: 284.

53. Caplan, R. (1994) Stress, anxiety, and depression in hospital consultants, general practitioners and senior health service managers. *British Medical Journal* **309**: 1261-1263.

54. Lenhart, S., Klein, F., Falcao, P., Phelan, E. and Smith, K. (1991) Gender bias against and sexual harassment of AMWA members in Massachusetts. *Journal of American Medical Women's Association* **46**: 121-125.

55. Uhlenberg, P. and Cooney, T. (1990) Male and female physicians: family and career considerations. *Social Science and Medicine* **30**: 373-378.

56. Elliot, F. (1979) Professional and family conflicts in hospital medicine. *Social Science and Medicine* **13A**: 57-64.

57. Brett, J. (1980). The effect of job transfer on employees and their families. In: Cooper, C. and Payne, R. (eds) *Current Concerns in Occupational Stress*. Chichester: Wiley, pp. 99-136.

58. Lazarus, R. and Folkman, S. (1984) *Stress, Appraisal and Coping*. New York: Springer.

59. Fontana, D. (1993) *Managing Time*. Leicester: British Psychological Society.

60. Wolff, C.T., Hofer, M. and Mason, J. (1964) Relationship between psychological defenses and mean urinary 17-hydroxy corticosteroid excretion rates. *Psychosomatic Medicine* **26**: 576-591.

61. Weisz, J., McCabe, M. and Denning, M. (1994) Primary and secondary control among children undergoing medical procedures: adjustment as a function of coping style. *Journal of Consulting and Clinical Psychology* **62**: 324-332.

62. Novaco, R. (1975) Anger control: *The Development and Evaluation of an Experimental Treatment*. Lexington: Heath.

63. Klein, R.F., Kliner, V., Zipes, D., Troyer, W. and Wallace, A. (1968) Transfer from a coronary care unit: some adverse responses. *Archives of Internal Medicine* **122**: 104-108.

64. Wardle, J. (1983) Psychological management of anxiety and pain during dental treatment. *Journal of Psychosomatic Research* **27**: 399-402.

65. Nuckalls, C.B., Cassel, J. and Kaplan, B.H. (1972) Psychosocial assets, life crises and the prognosis of pregnancy. *American Journal of Epidemiology* **95**: 431-444.

66. Berkmal, L.F. and Syme, S. (1979) Social networks, host resistance and mortality. *American Journal of Epidemiology* **109**: 186-204.

67. Henderson, S. (1981) Social relationships, adversity and neurosis. *British Journal of Psychiatry* **138**: 391-398.

68. Pennebaker, J. and O'Heeron, R. (1984) Confiding in others and illness rates among spouses of suicide and accidental-death victims. *Journal of Abnormal Psychology* **93**: 473-476.

69. Pennebaker, J. and Beall, S. (1986) Confronting a traumatic event: Toward an understanding of inhibition and disease. *Journal of Abnormal Psychology* **95**: 274-281.

70. Pennebaker, J., Kiecolt-Glaser, J. and Glaser, R. (1988) Disclosure of traumas and immune function: health implications for psychotherapy. *Journal of Consulting and Clinical Psychology* **56**: 239-245.

Part III

Doctor–Patient Communication

10
Pain

SUMMARY

An understanding of the topics covered in this chapter – pain and placebos – relies on an appreciation of the interdependence of psychological and physiological factors (mind and body). The magnitude of an injury does not always predict the amount of pain experienced since there are emotional and evaluative reactions to injuries. Responses to pain are affected by personality, cultural variables and family background. Measurement is difficult, but since pain is a private experience, self-report measures may have most validity.

There are many psychological approaches to reducing pain, including behavioural approaches, in which people in chronic pain are rewarded for activity, cognitive techniques, which involve distraction and changing interpretations of discomfort, and hypnosis. Several theories have been used to explain placebo effects, and there is evidence that they operate through the release of endorphins.

This third section of the book considers fields of study that are of direct relevance to medicine, including pain, the doctor–patient consultation and the influence of social and psychological factors on compliance. In this chapter, research on pain and the placebo effect is covered. Like the discussion of stress given in the previous chapter, these are areas where the distinction between psychological and physiological processes is far from clear.

The puzzle of pain

It is possible to consider pain in terms of pain receptors and neural pathways by tracing the neural connections between an injured site and the brain. However, relying solely on this kind of explanation of pain would assume that there is a good, perhaps even a one-to-one, relationship between the magnitude of tissue damage and the person's experience of pain. There is strong evidence that this is not always so.

Much of the impetus for modern research into the experience of pain was provided by the American anaesthetist, Beecher. While treating soldiers in the Second World War, he was struck by the lack of correspondence between their reports of pain from injuries sustained on the battlefield and reports from civilians having less traumatic injuries and operations during peacetime. The surprising observation was that only a minority of the soldiers requested pain relief for what were often severe wounds, with about 60 per cent reporting either slight pain or no pain at all. By contrast, almost all civilians requested analgesics for similar injuries. Beecher at first considered the possibility that there were some social inhibitions about reporting pain even if the soldiers felt it, but this was not an adequate explanation because they were willing to voice their complaints about the relatively slight pain involved in injections. He concluded that it was not necessarily the magnitude of an injury that was significant in the experience of pain but, rather, the circumstances in which it occurred.[1]

Childbirth provides another example. Although there are large individual differences in the levels of pain experienced during childbirth, it would be expected that there would be some correlation between obstetric measures and women's self-reports about how painful labour had been. However, neither amount of bleeding, labour time nor the weight, head circumference and presentation of the foetus have been found to be associated with how women describe their delivery.[2]

The puzzle of pain is complicated further by observations about *when* it occurs. From a biological view, no pain would be expected when there is no injury, and every injury should result in pain. However, there are some reports of quite severe injuries being suffered with little pain, as in some religious ceremonies in India where large steel hooks are inserted into the back muscles. At the height of the ceremony, the participants are suspended by these hooks, but they seem to tolerate these injuries with little discomfort.[3] Conversely, there are occasions when people experience pain without recent injury, as in phantom limb pain. Patients sometimes complain of pain which is located in the leg or arm which has been amputated, pain that is persistent, long-term and difficult to relieve. In a large proportion of patients who complain of abdominal and gastrointestinal pain, no organic basis for their discomfort can be found, yet it is clear that they are in considerable distress.

Reacting to pain

One fundamental problem with most of these studies is that pain is a private experience, one that cannot be felt by anyone other than the individual involved. A number of studies[4] have indicated that there can be wide differences between how observers estimate another's pain and the person's actual experience. People vary in their willingness to express pain as well as in their sensitivity to it. For example, patients who score high on the extroversion scale of the Eysenck Personality Inventory (see Chapter 4) are more likely to express discomfort, while high scores on the neuroticism scale are associated with heightened sensitivity. There are also cultural differences in how inhibited people are in expressing their pain, suggesting that as children grow up they learn how much (or how little) they should complain about discomfort.[5]

There is experimental evidence to support the possibility that we adapt the degree to which we express pain depending on others' reactions. In one study,[6] research participants were persuaded to undergo several electric shocks. They were asked to rate the intensity of each shock on a scale of 1 to 100. Half the participants were given the shocks with a confederate who was instructed to give ratings about 25 per cent below theirs. The confederate thus acted as a tolerant model whose apparent discomfort was less than the participants'. The other half of the participants were given the shocks with the confederate acting only as an observer, so they were not exposed to a person who gave low ratings. When the shock intensity ratings for the two groups were compared, those exposed to the tolerant model gave lower ratings than those not so exposed.

Reactions to painful stimuli seem to "run in families" and a similar learning process may be occurring here as in the laboratory. Apley[7] compared two groups of families – those who contained children who complained of abdominal pain with no discernible organic origin and those with children who did not make such complaints. When he assessed other members of the families besides the children, he found that they, too, were much more likely to make similar complaints. He argued that this difference between the groups was due to a combination of heredity and environment, with the possibility that parents unwittingly reinforce or reward children for their complaints by giving them small presents when they complain of abdominal pains.[8]

Apley also noted that the children's complaints were often associated with stressful events, such as beginning school or the birth of a sibling. There may be a particularly important relationship between the experience of stressful events (especially those which imply a long-term and severe threat, such as the death of a relative or loss of employment) and the onset of abdominal pain. Creed[9] interviewed appendectomy patients after their operation. Some 59 per cent had experienced such an event in the months prior to the onset of pain. This compared with only 31 per cent of a non-patient community sample, so the finding is consistent with the work discussed in the previous chapter which related stressful events and illness. However, in some appendectomy patients the appendix is found not to be acutely inflamed at operation, even though the symptoms mimic those of appendicitis. Only 25 per cent of the acutely inflamed patients in this study had experienced such an event, compared to 59 per cent of the rest. In most cases the event had occurred within 9 weeks of the operation. Similarly, Craig and Brown[10] compared patients who were found to have an organic cause for gastrointestinal pain with those whose pain was diagnosed as psychogenic or functional (i.e. without an organic basis): 23 per cent of the former group but 67 per cent of the latter had experienced a major event or difficulty recently.

Thus, there are several reasons to believe that a straightforward anatomical model of pain is inadequate. Pain can occur when there has been no recent injury (as in phantom limb pain) and some patients report little pain after severe injuries (as in Beecher's Second World War soldiers). These observations could be due in part to differences in how willing people are to express their pain, but this does not appear to be the whole story. We learn to express or inhibit complaints in keeping with cultural and family norms, and the experience of stressful life events can be associated with the onset of abdominal pain.

Gate Theory

The best known modern theory of pain is Melzack and Wall's "Gate Theory".[11] Briefly, they suggest that pain involves not only physical sensations but also emotional and evaluative reactions to these sensations. They argue that signals from an injured site run to the dorsal horn of the spinal cord which in turn acts like a gate between peripheral fibres and the brain. The gate is opened (i.e. the dorsal horn cells are excited) by small fibres running from the site of stimulation and is closed by other, larger fibres from the same site. But the gate is also affected by fibres from the reticular system of the brain, which can serve to inhibit or excite the dorsal horn cells. The reticular formation is also affected by cortical activity, so that past experiences, anxiety, attention and the meaning of the situation influence the opening and closing of the gate.

Melzack and Wall make a distinction between three components which contribute to the experience of pain. The first component is the *sensory-discriminative*, which involves the sensory information received by the individual. Such information includes the location and magnitude of the injury. The second is the *affective-motivational* component, which provides the motivation to act as a result of this information. The third, *cognitive-evaluative* component is affected by past experiences and expectations. Taken together, these components interact to determine how much distress a person feels and how he or she will react to the distress.

Melzack and Wall use this model to account for many of the above observations. They argue that the sudden loss of a limb through amputation removes not only the excitatory fibres running from the site of the injury but also the inhibitory ones, so that the gate may remain permanently open. This could explain why people who have phantom limb pain may feel the discomfort involved in the injury which led to the amputation rather than the amputation itself. For the Second World War soldiers seen by Beecher, being injured on the battlefield had positive connotations, in that it meant that they would be rested away from the fighting and unlikely to be killed. For the civilian patients, a similar injury was life-threatening and a disruption to their normal routine. In the first situation the gate would be closed, in the second opened wide.

The important point about the gate model is that the emotional and evaluative reactions to an injury affect the experience of pain. This raises the possibility that a wide range of treatment programmes could be used when dealing with patients who are troubled by pain. For example, discomfort could be alleviated by supporting patients emotionally or by helping them reinterpret their sensations. Gate Theory also makes it clear that there is no strict distinction between organic and functional pain, since every pain has both somatogenic and psychogenic components, although one or the other may predominate for any individual in a particular situation.

Problems of pain research

Two important considerations in pain control research must be mentioned before methods of relieving suffering are outlined. The first problem concerns measurement. *Physiological* measures, such as the level of corticosteroids in the blood, heart rate or respiration rate, are useful but there is often little relationship between different physiological assessments. Corticosteroid level is not always related to heart rate, for example. The second concerns the context in which research is performed: methods for pain control which are developed within the laboratory may or may not be applicable to clinical care.

Measurement

A large number of measures of pain have been developed, but are mainly of two types – self-report and behavioural. In this chapter the concern is with the amount of pain experienced or shown behaviourally, but a clinician or researcher would often be equally interested in how pain levels affect quality of life, such as a person's ability to work, engage in leisure activities' and social relationships.[12] Some of these issues are discussed in Chapter 5 under Disability.

Self-reports

Self-report measures, although they suffer from the fundamental problem that the expression of pain may not correspond exactly to feelings of pain, are widely used. Perhaps the most popular is the simple Visual Analogue Scale (VAS). As illustrated in Figure 10.1, the patient is asked to place an "X" on a 10–cm line, between the extremes of "I have no pain at all" and "My pain is as bad as it possibly could be". Then it is a simple procedure to measure the distance from one end to give a numerical score. For example, Rosen[13] asked women in the first stage of labour to indicate on the VAS the amount of pain they felt as their contractions grew stronger: their pain scores paralleled cervical dilation.

The VAS provides a single score of severity, being intended to include the sensory, emotional and evaluative components of pain. A method which is designed to measure each of these components separately is the McGill Pain Questionnaire (MPQ). The patient is asked to choose adjectives from a total of 20 lists which best describe the pain. Some lists refer to sensory aspects, others to the emotional and evaluative ones, as shown in Table 10.1. Within each list the adjectives are rank ordered, so that a choice of, say, "pounding" would be given a higher score than "flickering" or "quivering". Patients with some kinds of pain (e.g. the acute pain after an episiotomy) tend to score high on the sensory lists, while others (e.g. with chronic pain) score high on the affective lists. Table 10.1 indicates the adjectives often chosen by women who have just given birth[14] and patients with toothache.[15] Thus, this approach is much more subtle than the VAS and can assist the doctor in tailoring treatment to the individual's needs.

There are also a number of assessments specifically designed for children, who may not be able to express themselves in the same way as adults. Some scales use a series of faces showing varying levels of distress, and a "pain thermometer" has also been developed.[16]

No pain at all ———————————————————— Pain as bad as it could be

Figure 10.1　The Visual Analogue Scale is used by asking patients to place an "X" somewhere on the line between the extremes which corresponds to their experience of pain.

Table 10.1 Some of the lists of adjectives from the McGill Pain Questionnaire. Patients are asked to choose those words which best describe their pain. Adjectives marked by * indicate words often chosen by women to describe labour, those by ** words chosen by patients to describe toothache (Table originally published in Kent, G. (1984) *The Psychology of Dental Care*. Bristol: John Wright.)

Sensory		Affective	Evaluative
Flickering	Sickening**	Tiring	Annoying**
Quivering	Suffocating	Exhausting*	Troublesome
Pulsing			Miserable
Throbbing**			Intense*
Beating			Unbearable
Pounding*			

Cognitive assessments

The measurement of the *cognitions* associated with pain is becoming increasing useful and important. In keeping with Gate Theory, the argument is that the experience of pain depends largely on how people interpret their sensations and their concerns about how they could deal with discomfort. Accordingly, it would be important to assess what patients say to themselves when they encounter a potentially painful situation. This seems to be particularly important in chronic pain, where the patient's beliefs about how well he or she can cope are critical.

For example, Philips[17] asked a large group of chronic pain patients (with an average of 6 years' discomfort) to indicate which of a list of thoughts, feelings and attitudes occurred to them at the onset of a severe pain attack. One group of attitudes concerned positive coping responses (such as "I'm trying to relax to bring this pain under control" and "I'll just have to act as natural as I can"). However, the majority of beliefs involved maladaptive cognitions, such as "I wish I didn't have to do anything to-day", "I wonder if they will ever find a cure for my pain" and "I can think of nothing other than my pain". These were cognitions which supported a passive and avoidant response, where the expectation of being able to exert control over the level of pain is low.

Behavioural measures

Another way of measuring pain would be to monitor the patient's behaviour. Darwin sug-

gested that facial expressions are largely genetically determined and people from different cultures throughout the world show similar expressions for anger, fear and pain. It has been suggested that virtually all forms of pain involve particular facial configurations including lowering of the brow, eye narrowing and closing and wrinkling of the nose. Often, facial expressions are most obvious at the onset of pain and decline afterwards. However, when people in our culture believe themselves to be watched they show fewer indications of pain, so that unobtrusive observation may give results different from those of overt observation.[18] Other nonverbal signs such as low activity levels, guarding and grimacing or tightening of the muscles, form important aspects of the assessment of chronic pain.[19]

Alternative measures involve the amount of analgesia given or requested. In several studies, patients' requests for analgesia have been used to assess pain but, as outlined above, people vary in the amount of discomfort they are willing to tolerate before complaining. Another possibility would be to note the amount of analgesic given by staff. Nurses, for example, could be expected to be very able at recognizing the signs of pain due to their wide experience. Bond and Pilowski[20] took self-report measures of pain using the VAS, and then monitored patients' requests for analgesics and the responses of the nursing staff. They found that the perception of pain did not always result in a request for medication, requests when made did not always lead to administration by staff, and the strength of the medication administered was not proportional to pain levels. The gender of the patient seemed particularly relevant, as shown in Table 10.2. Nursing staff were much more likely to take the initiative in administering analgesics with female patients and more likely to refuse requests from males. Perhaps cultural expectations were operating here: the nurses may have believed that men should be able to tolerate more pain than women.

These difficulties with the measurement of pain illustrate the complexity of the phenomenon. Physiological, self-report and behavioural measures do not always correlate particularly well and this presents problems for pain control research. Since pain itself is open to so many

Table 10.2 Pattern of administration of analgesic drugs to men and women in radiotherapy wards. Drugs requested and given during one week (Reproduced from Bond, M.R. (1979) *Pain*, with permission of Churchill Livingstone.

	Men	Women
Number of patients	15	12
Number of occasions drugs given at patient's request	23	28
Number of occasions drugs given on initiative of nurses	1	22
Number of occasions on which nurses refused patient's requests for drugs	18	0

influences it is not surprising that measuring techniques are similarly affected.

Clinical versus laboratory pain

A second problem with research in this area concerns the use of laboratory versus "real-life" situations. Whereas experimentally induced pain is short-lived and can be controlled by the subject, clinical pain is often persistent, beyond the patient's control, and accompanied by high levels of anxiety. In the laboratory, pain is induced by stimuli that are novel to the subject (e.g. electric shock, the application of a tourniquet or immersion of a hand into ice-cold water for long periods), whereas patients often have prior experience with clinical pain, either personally or through observation of others. Given that the meaning of painful stimuli is very different in the two situations, results found in the laboratory may not always be relevant for clinical populations. Certainly, laboratory tests do not predict post-operative need for analgesia with any reliability.

In summary, then, there are several problems of measurement in conducting research on pain. Physiological, self-report and behavioural measures can all be used, but each has its drawbacks. They do not always correspond with each other (a patient may score high on a self-report index but low on a behavioural one, for example) and they are open to cultural and contextual influences.

The alleviation of pain

Surveys of the general population have indicated that a great many people routinely experience some form of discomfort. When Crook *et al.*[21] telephoned a large group of randomly selected households on general practitioner lists, they found that 16 per cent of individuals had experienced pain within the previous 2 weeks. Eleven per cent had persistent pain, commonly back pain. Such results indicate that any interventions which succeed in reducing pain and pain-related disabilities would be of benefit to a great many people.

Labelling experience as painful

In order to understand the pain-control techniques discussed below, it is important to remember that pain involves sensory, emotional and cognitive components. Although these interact, Gate Theory suggests that learning affects the emotional and cognitive components. The experience of pain depends on the cognitive labels placed on sensations. As a demonstration of this principle, participants were asked to report the amount of distress they experienced while their hand was immersed in very cold water (2°C), being told about the sensations the immersion would give (i.e. coldness, tightness of the skin, numbness). One group of participants was told that the experience would be "painful", whereas the other group did not receive this pain label warning. Even though the procedure was the same, the emotional and evaluative interpretations of the ice water were manipulated.

The results indicated that those given no "pain" warning were less distressed and actually showed higher hand temperatures, differences showing up during the latter half of the 6–minute experiment. Although both groups had similar expectations about sensations, the way this information was processed was different, having both physiological and psychological effects on their ability to tolerate the experience.[22]

There are also some clinical situations in which direct warnings about pain are unhelpful. The word "pain" serves as a label for sensory information, so that a patient may come to interpret (and feel) sensations as painful. Beales[23] describes how children attending a hospital casualty department would rarely present with pain. When a bandage covering a skin lesion was removed, however, the unpleasantness of the lesion was emphasized by the staff through such remarks as "Oh dear, you have got a mess there, haven't you", and when treatment was about to commence the children were told to anticipate pain by such comments as "I'll try not to hurt too much". When such remarks were made, the children's distress typically increased.

Thus, there is evidence that learning and experience affects the cognitive and emotional components of pain. Several psychological techniques for alleviating pain and helping people to cope with the pain they feel are discussed below. They involve providing new learning experiences in order to modify the perception of pain. Alternate or complementary methods such as acupuncture are not considered here, although this latter technique is receiving increasing attention and acceptance[24] and may be effective because it involves the release of endorphins.[25]

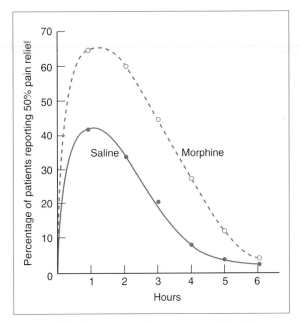

Figure 10.2 Percentage of patients reporting 50 per cent pain relief over a 6-hour period from 10 mg morphine sulphate or sterile saline. (Reproduced from Houde, R.W., Wallerstein, S.L. and Rogers, A. (1960) *Clinical Pharmacology and Therapeutics* **1**: 163–174, with permission.)

Pharmacological techniques

Perhaps the most obvious method of pain relief involves the blocking of neural transmission. Novocain, for example, is an effective analgesic because it blocks nerve conduction from the injured site. The operation of the opiates, such as morphine, is much harder to specify. It is difficult to state precisely what sites are responsible for its analgesic properties, although sites appear to exist in the midbrain and spinal cord.

It seems that morphine acts partly by changing the patient's attention to or consciousness of the sensory input. For instance, the percentage of cancer patients who reported at least 50 per cent pain relief from morphine or saline solution is shown in Figure 10.2. All patients had chronic pain due to their disease, the majority from bone metastases. The evaluations of effectiveness were conducted "double blind" (i.e. neither the person who administered the drug nor the person who evaluated its effectiveness knew which patients were receiving morphine and which saline

solution) and measures were taken at hourly intervals. There was a substantial response to the saline solution and the time–effect curve mimicked that of morphine, suggesting that some of the effect of morphine may be due to placebo effects as discussed in more detail later in this chapter.

Personality traits are related to patients' reports of the effectiveness of analgesics. Typically, patients report relief from pain shortly after administration of an analgesic. The pain then slowly increases until the next administration. However, such a picture does not take personality differences into account, as shown by Figure 10.3, where the pain scores of patients given pentazocine for lumbar disc disease are illustrated. Those who scored high on the neuroticism and extroversion scales of the Eysenck Personality Inventory (EPI) gave consistently higher reports of pain and were strongly affected by the analgesic, whereas medication seemed to have less effect on those patients who scored low on the EPI.

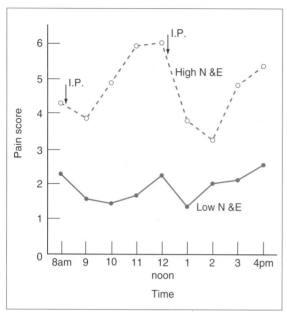

Figure 10.3 Pain relief following injection of pentazocine in patients with high neuroticism and extroversion (N and E) scores (upper curve) and those with low scores (lower curve). (Reproduced from Bond, M.R., Glynn, J.P. and Thomas, D.G. (1976) *Journal of Psychosomatic Research* **20**: 369–381, with kind permission from Elsevier Science Ltd, The Boulevard, Langford Lane, Kidlington, OX5 1GB, UK.)

Behavioural approaches

Thus far in this chapter, most emphasis has been on acute pain, such as that resulting from an injury or an operation. The psychological effects of acute pain are quite different from those of chronic pain, with anxiety being a common re-action to the former, depression to the latter. Chronic pain may begin with a specific injury, but prescribed treatments do not always provide relief and the patient may suffer for years without comfort, losing sleep and curtailing activities. For such people, chronic pain can become the most important feature of their lives, so that com-plaints, inactivity and requests for analgesics become increasingly frequent.

It has been argued that such "pain behaviours", like other kinds of behaviour, are shaped and maintained by rewards such as attention and sympathy. There is evidence that people whose spouses are very solicitous – in the sense of being very comforting when they complain about pain – give higher ratings of discomfort and are less active than those whose spouses are less

tolerant of their pain complaint.[26] Spouses who make such comments as "You sit down, I know it hurts you to do that, I'll do it for you" might actually exacerbate the difficulty by decreasing patients' sense of control and self-efficacy.[27]

The resulting idea is that if pain behaviours are increased by social reinforcements, then they could be reduced if activity and accomplishment were rewarded instead. The goal of chronic pain management programmes is to reduce the pain behaviours and increase well-being. Thus, posi-tive reinforcement is made contingent on activity rather than illness. Bonica and Fordyce[28] used this operant approach. They have reported a study in which 36 patients who had difficulty with chronic pain were no longer given reinforce-ments for their "pain behaviour". Instead of receiving analgesics on request, the patients were given medication at fixed time-intervals. Rewards were given for increases in activity and exercise. Over a period of some months, activity levels increased while medication intake and subjective reports of pain decreased. When asked, the patients rated their pain as being less intense and as causing less interference with daily activities. Further, these results were maintained some 22 months later. Although there was no control group in this study and there was considerable screening of patients, the lack of previous success with more traditional treatments makes the results encouraging.

In such studies, patients are encouraged to make small and gradual improvements in their activity, using the idea of shaping discussed in Chapter 3. An example of this approach is pro-vided by a case study of a patient with chronic low back pain. Many patients with low back pain find it difficult to sit or stand in one position for any period of time, resulting in frequent shifting from standing to sitting. For this patient, shaping was used to increase the ability to stand or sit still for extended periods of time. At first, she was rewarded for performing an easily achievable tasks (such as walking, with the arms swinging at the sides), being given much social encour-agement and reinforcement. Gradually the tasks became increasingly difficult, so that over a number of therapy sessions she was able to stand and sit for several minutes much more comfort-ably.[29] Additional behavioural intervention, relaxation training, has been tried with such patients, further increasing activity and reducing analgesic use. This applicability of behavioural treatments to pain relief illustrates the multifactorial nature of pain and the interdependence of behavioural and physiological variables.

Cognitive techniques

Cognitive techniques for alleviating pain encourage the individual to modify his or her evaluations of the sensory information. One way of doing this is through distraction, where the patient is encouraged to shift attention away from the wound or procedure. This approach is particularly helpful when there is only a brief period of stimulation, such as in drilling during a dental restoration, and in casualty departments, as when a wound is sutured. In the study of children attending a casualty department mentioned earlier, Beales[23] describes how nurses would successfully hide sutures from the children's sight and engage them in conversation. The children often gave no indication of pain until the doctor commented after a first suture "There, you didn't feel that, did you?", thus interfering with attempts at distraction, focusing the child's attention on the lesion and the procedure, and labelling it as painful. In all cases, the children indicated pain as each subsequent suture was made.

Whereas distraction aims to shift the patient's attention away from any discomfort, a second method aims to encourage the patient to interpret and evaluate information in less distressing ways. Langer *et al.*[30] applied some of these techniques to surgical patients. They were assigned to one of two groups: one group of patients were given examples of how perceptions about a noxious event influences how that event is experienced. They were taught to use selective attention, being encouraged to focus on the positive aspects (e.g. the improvement in health) that the treatment would bring. Compared to patients who were not given such instructions, the experimental group had fewer requests for sedatives, spent less time in hospital (an average 5.6 days compared to 7.6 days in the comparison group patients) and showed less anxiety and greater ability to cope as evaluated by nurses.

Cognitive–behavioural approaches

More recently, psychologists and others working in pain clinics have integrated the behavioural and cognitive approaches, finding that a combination of these techniques can be very effective. As outlined earlier, patients who experience chronic pain often have maladaptive cognitions, especially the view that control of the pain is out of their hands and that they are reliant on professionals to provide relief. Some psychologists working in chronic pain clinics argue that such beliefs lie at the heart of the chronic pain problem: as long as patients hold on to such beliefs, the argument goes, they will see no purpose in taking active steps to control their discomfort.[31,32]

According to this approach, the behavioural techniques used by Bonica and Fordyce are effective because they demonstrate to the patients that they can, indeed, regain control over their pain and over their lives. Their sense of self-efficacy is increased when activity, rather than pain complaints, is rewarded. The aim of cognitive–behavioural interventions is to alter such beliefs so that the patient comes to believe that they, and not professionals, can affect the discomfort.

Maladaptive beliefs are challenged in two ways – through education and through encouraging patients to be more active. A study by Peters *et al.*[33] used this approach with patients who had chronic non-malignant pain that had lasted for at least 6 months duration. Initially, they assigned one group of patients to the routine care given at the hospital. A second group was treated on an in-patient basis and a third group as out-patients. These two latter groups were given several cognitive and behavioural interventions, such as relaxation, education about the nature of pain and associated cognitions, structured exercise and staff reinforcement for activity.

This is a particularly interesting study because at the end of the treatment intervention there were few differences between the groups. As shown in Figure 10.4 all three groups showed some improvement over time. However, when the patients were followed up about 12 months later, differences between the groups appeared: the two intervention groups had continued to

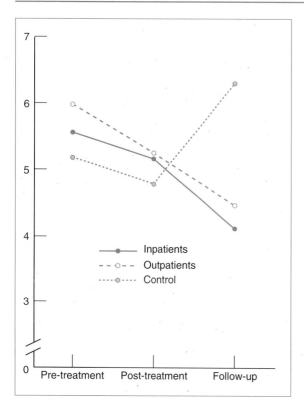

Figure 10.4 Average pain scores using the Visual Analogue Scale at pre-treatment, post-treatment and 12-month follow-up for three groups of patients suffering chronic non-malignant pain and given either routine treatment in hospital (control) or various cognitive–behavioural interventions either as in-patients or as out-patients. (Reproduced from Peters, J. *et al.* (1992) *Pain* **50**: 41–50, with permission.)

improve while the comparison group had worsened. At this point 68 per cent of the in-patients and 61 per cent of the out-patients had met criteria for success, compared to only 21 per cent of the comparison group. Because chronic pain is so prevalent in the general population such programmes as this hold out great hope for the future well-being of chronic pain suffers.

Hypnosis

Hypnosis has only recently gained a measure of acceptance among psychologists, partly because of the difficulty in ascertaining what a hypnotic state might be. Although it can be characterized as a "trance state" - a unique form of consciousness - it is difficult to distinguish hypnotized subjects from those who have been coached in how to behave. Experienced hypnotists cannot always tell the difference. Psychologists interested in hypnosis debate whether it is a unique state or an example of other, more established forms of behaviour such as role playing.

A profitable line of research has investigated susceptibility, defined as the degree to which a person is "able to enter into hypnosis and become involved in its characteristic behaviour".[34] Scales have been developed to test for susceptibility, such as the Stanford Hypnotic Susceptibility Scale.[35] Several short tests are used, such as the willingness of the subject to fall backwards into the hypnotist's arms. Hypnosis can only be used confidently for highly susceptible people. There is evidence that the hypnotized person actually registers the sensation, but there seems to be some barrier to its becoming painful.

The method has been used in a variety of areas, including helping cancer patients and in childbirth. The following case report provides a rather dramatic example:

◆ Hypnosis has also been used in connection with caesarean sections, either planned in advance or in emergencies. A patient who presented an obstetrical emergency illustrates the advantages of having available someone familiar with hypnotic procedures. A woman expecting a baby had been poorly handled on the ward of the hospital. She had been there for hours with an impacted breach before . . . the ward consultant became aware of her. At that time she had a high fever, a systolic blood pressure of over 200, and a heart rate of more than 150 beats per minute. She evidently needed a caesarean operation, but the anesthetist refused to give any general chemoanesthesia, and the operation under local anesthesia was not judged feasible. Hence (the consultant) who was to do the surgery, determined to use hypnosis. Although he had not seen her before and she was completely naive to hypnosis, he hypnotized her during the ten to fifteen minutes in which he was scrubbing and preparing her abdomen. The record obtained by the anesthetist during the course of the operation showed that the vital signs steadily returned to normal despite the progress of surgery. A normal infant was delivered and the mother's recovery was uneventful. The record was later reviewed by a senior obstetrician who described it as remarkable. (Ref. 36, p. 22) ◆

Although hypnosis can certainly be effective, it should be noted that it is more effective for some problems than others. While patients with pain and anxiety respond well, other difficulties such as eating disorders and alcoholism are less successfully treated by hypnosis.[37]

Psychotherapeutic approaches

According to the psychotherapeutic approach, the experience of pain may be a reflection of some underlying conflict or personal difficulty. Thus the aim is to uncover and address this conflict. An extract from a case report illustrates this point of view. The woman involved had a history of cancer:

◆ The present hospitalization was prompted when the woman came into the surgery outpatient clinic complaining of a severe and constant pain in her left side. No apparent cause for this pain could be ascertained by physical examination in the clinic, but a coincident finding was the presence of another enlarged sub-mandibular lymph node. She was admitted for an excision biopsy of this node.

When interviewed, she appeared to be in considerable discomfort and was preoccupied with what she described as a severe and sharp pain in her left side. Signs of depression were immediately noted, including psychomotor retardation, poor eye contact, low-pitched and monotonous voice and expressions of fatigue and despair. Early in the interview it was learned that she was well aware of her diagnosis of reticulum cell sarcoma and the eventual possibility of death as a consequence of that disease.

However, she talked almost exclusively about the pain in her side, which had been the only reason for her seeking help at this time. She stated that the pain had been constant and severe over the last three months and prevented her from being more active around the house and socially. The pain concerned her much more than did the enlarged node in her neck, which she dismissed by stating that the surgeons would simply "cut it out" in the same fashion as they had two years earlier, and there would be no further consequences. The pain in her side was a different story altogether, for it had never occurred before and she was afraid that it represented a new direction of spread or growth of her tumour. Further exploration of this notion revealed concern that this meant death was imminent. The woman confessed that in recent months she had been spending more and more of her time preoccupied with thoughts about her death.

She was encouraged to elaborate some of her thoughts concerning death, and the balance of the interview was focused on this topic. Among her greatest fears was leaving behind her 11-year-old son in the care of his untrustworthy father. She also expressed fear that death would be painful and that in the end her doctors would abandon her. The patient received support from the interviewer for her fears and concerns. She cried spontaneously throughout this part of the discussion.

As the interview ended, all observers noted that the woman's affective state had improved dramatically: she had become more animated, and her eye contact with the interviewer had increased.

One day later, during routine rounds, the woman was seen again. She enthusiastically summoned the interviewer to her bedside and somewhat sheepishly reported that the pain in her side had disappeared immediately following the interview on the previous day and had not returned. It was the first time in three months that she had been without pain in that area. Owing to complications in the subsequent biopsy procedure, she remained in the hospital a total of six weeks, with no recurrence of pain. (Ref. 38, pp. 494–495) ◆

For this patient, simply listening to her concerns and taking them seriously resulted in disappearance of the symptom of pain. Apley,[7] in his work with children with abdominal pains, reported similar findings. Many of the children, once they had been reassured that their abdomens were normal and had been given some attention, had no recurrence of pain. In these cases only minimal psychotherapy was required in order to alleviate the pain.

All of these approaches to pain relief are effective for particular patients. The choice of method will depend on the individual and his or her problems. For a patient who has suffered chronic pain for several months or years, a behavioural or cognitive–behavioural approach could be the most useful for encouraging activity. Many pain clinics now incorporate this method. A psychotherapeutic approach should be considered for patients if no organic cause can be found and they are suffering stress in their lives. For those who are susceptible, hypnosis has found support, but much training is required before it can be used safely. Certainly, the cognitive techniques such as distraction are helpful on an everyday basis. It should be remembered that the efficacy of pharmacological methods, too, varies between patients and many chemical agents have a placebo component, a topic which is considered next.

Placebo effects

Placebo effects are generally defined as those effects of a treatment that are not attributable to the mechanics of the treatment itself, but rather to the circumstances surrounding it. For example, in Figure 10.2 just over 40 per cent of the patients who received a saline solution reported substantial pain relief one hour after its administration, compared to just over 60 per cent who received morphine. When a new drug is tested it is therefore necessary to compare it with a placebo intervention, lest any demonstrated effect is due to non-specific factors. In this sense, placebo effects are something of a nuisance because they make evaluations of treatments more complicated than they otherwise might be.

In another sense, they are a fascinating subject of study in their own right. That a saline solution can affect patients' reports of their pain is very surprising and this phenomenon provides much information about the psychology of medical care. Placebo effects have been shown in dentistry and in surgery. Placebos can be addictive, mimic the effects of active drugs, reverse the effects of potent drugs and have an effect on bodily organs.

Although the results portrayed in Figure 10.2 are not unusual for placebo-controlled studies, they are often misinterpreted, apparently suggesting to some that placebos will be effective for most patients. This is not the case. On average, about 35 per cent of patients obtain relief, but the range is probably from 0 to 100 per cent depending on the treatment in question, the condition, and the situational factors such as the patients' and physicians' belief in the efficacy of treatment. Personality traits (such as suggestibility or IQ) and demographic characteristics (such as age and sex) are not consistently related to whether an individual responds to a placebo. Figure 10.2 can also be taken to suggest that no patients are harmed by placebos, but this too is incorrect. A small proportion can show *reverse* placebo effects, where they report a worsening of symptoms.

That the enthusiasm of the practitioner for the placebo can influence the effectiveness of a placebo has been illustrated in a study on dental patients who were due to have a painkilling injection before a filling.[39] Before the injection, patients were given a placebo pill, but for some of the patients the dentist was very enthusiastic about it, saying, "This is a recently developed pill that I've found to be very effective in reducing tension, anxiety and sensitivity to pain." Other patients received a message in which the dentist expressed some doubt about the pill's effectiveness: "This is a recently developed pill which reduces tension, anxiety and sensitivity in some people. Other people receive no benefit from it at all. I personally have not found it to be very effective." Those patients who were given the enthusiastic message subsequently reported less pain from the injection than those given the more ambivalent message.

In the same study, the manner of the dentist was also varied. For some patients the dentist was very warm and friendly, engaging them in open and reassuring conversation, while for others the dentist was more neutral, being polite but with limited verbal exchanges. This difference in manner also had an effect, with the patients treated by the "warm" dentist reporting less pain from the injection than patients treated by the "neutral" dentist.

How do placebos work?

It has been suggested that the placebo effect is only a myth. It may be the case, for instance, that placebos are given the credit for spontaneous recovery from the illness or that patients only report improvements but actually do not feel any different. It may be that some patients feel obliged to say the treatment has worked when a doctor has taken time to treat them.

These latter explanations do not provide a full explanation, however. When placebos are effective what processes are involved? One theory relies on classical conditioning. In some studies, dogs were given morphine and, as in the case of food and salivation with Pavlov's dogs, some of the animals came to show a response to morphine *before* they were given the injection. The suggestion is that, in humans, the placebo effect works similarly: patients feel better because this is a conditioned response to taking medication.[40,41] The classical conditioning position would predict that as the number of occasions on which placebos are administered increases, the percentage of patients reporting relief would decrease. This is, in fact, what occurs.

A second possibility is based on the notion of expectations and selective attention. In most illnesses the amount of discomfort varies, so a patient will feel better at some times than others. Placebo effects could occur if patients became more aware of the times when they did feel better and paid less attention to the times when they felt unwell. Yet another possibility is that patients may come to interpret their sensations as less unpleasant following the doctor's advice. Gate Theory postulates that the experience of pain is enhanced by anxiety, such that the gate in the dorsal horn is opened by fear. When the doctor says that a pill will make them better – implying that the condition is treatable and not too serious – their anxiety could decrease and the gate close.

Endorphins

There are some clues to the physiological action of placebos. In the case of both placebos and narcotics, there is a tendency to increase the dosage over time. With repeated dosages over long periods both become less effective and there are withdrawal difficulties. These similarities have led to the suggestion that placebos work by releasing endorphins (endogenous morphine-like substances) into the body. This suggestion has been tested through the injection of naloxone, an opiate antagonist that blocks the opiate receptor sites. If the placebo effect is no longer present when naloxone is given, this would provide evidence for a link between placebos and endorphins.

Levine *et al*.[42] studied patients whose impacted wisdom teeth were to be removed. Two hours after surgery, all patients were given a placebo and then, after a further hour, either placebo or naloxone. The first prediction the researchers made concerned the effect of naloxone versus placebo. As expected, those patients who were given naloxone reported greater pain one hour after administration than did those given placebos, indicating that the naloxone enhanced the pain relative to placebos. In addition, the difference in pain reports given by reactors and non-reactors diminished after naloxone administration, providing evidence that placebo effects are naloxone-reversible. Finally, the researchers observed that naloxone had no obvious effect on placebo non-reactors.

Thus, this study suggests that the analgesic effect of placebos is real (i.e. not simply due to response biases) and is based on the action of endorphins. Placebos cannot be used to distinguish functional from organic illnesses. Like morphine, placebos seem to operate on the emotional and evaluative components of pain. This study does not indicate, however, how the message "Take this, it will be good for you" from a trusted physician is translated into the release of endorphins.

Side-effects of placebos

Part of the "magic" of placebos is their apparent ability to induce side-effects. Often, the type of side-effect is related to the type of medication under study, such as nausea with antispasmodic placebos or drowsiness with tranquillizer placebos. This seems very odd indeed and is sometimes used as an indicator of the strength of placebo reactions. However, the emphasis on placebo side-effects may be due to the lack of adequate control groups. Studies reporting side-effects have only a small proportion of their patients presenting complaints. While some of the complaints are dramatic (e.g. visible skin rashes) these are in the minority.

The most likely explanation for the reporting of side-effects to a placebo is a greater awareness of bodily reactions during illness and clinical trials than usual. In a survey of healthy subjects not taking medication, 25 per cent reported an inability to concentrate in the 3 days before the survey, 23 per cent reported excessive sleepiness and 40 per cent fatigue. Had these people been taking medication or placebos, these difficulties might have been attributed to the drugs, and called side-effects.

Suggested reading

Melzack, R. and Wall, P. (1982) *The Challenge of Pain*, Harmondsworth, Middlesex: Penguin, gives a good introduction to pain research. Turk, D. and Melzack, R. (eds) (1992) *Handbook of Pain Assessment*, London: Guilford Press, is an excellent and comprehensive review of pain assessment.

References

1. Beecher, H.K. (1956) Relationship of significance of wound to the pain experienced. *Journal of the American Medical Association* **161**: 1609-1613.
2. Uddenberg, N. (1979) Childbirth pain. In: Oborne, D.J., Gruneberg, M. and Eiser, J. (eds) *Research in Psychology and Medicine*, vol. 1. London: Academic Press.
3. Kosambi, D.D. (1967) Living prehistory in India. *Scientific American* **216**: 105-114.
4. Manne, S., Jacobsen, P. and Redd, W. (1992) Assessment of acute pediatric pain: do self-report, parent ratings, and nurse ratings measure the same phenomena? *Pain* **48**: 45-52.
5. Koopman, C., Eisenthal, S. and Stoeckle, J. (1984) Ethnicity in the reported pain, emotional distress and requests of medical outpatients. *Social Science and Medicine* **18**: 487-490.
6. Craig, K.D. and Prkachin, K. (1978) Social modelling influences on sensory decision theory and psychophysiological indexes of pain. *Journal of Personality and Social Psychology* **36**: 805-815.
7. Apley, J. (1975) *The Child with Abdominal Pains*. London: Basil Blackwell.
8. Walker, L., Garber, J. and Greene, J. (1993) Psychosocial correlates of recurrent childhood pain: a comparison of pediatric patients with recurrent abdominal pain, organic illness and psychiatric disorders. *Journal of Abnormal Psychology* **102**: 248-258.
9. Creed, F. (1981) Life events and appendectomy. *Lancet* **1**: 1381-1385.
10. Craig, T.K.J. and Brown, G.W. (1984) Goal frustration and life events in the aetiology of painful gastrointestinal disorders. *Journal of Psychosomatic Research* **28**: 411-421.
11. Melzack, R. and Wall, P. (1982) *The Challenge of Pain*. Harmondsworth, Middlesex: Penguin Books.
12. Kerns, R. and Jacob, M. (1992) Assessment of the psychosocial context of the experience of chronic pain. In: Turk, D. and Melzack, R. (eds) *Handbook of Pain Assessment*. London: Guilford Press.
13. Rosen, M. (1977) The measurement of pain. In: Harcus, A.W., Smith, R.B. and Whittle, B. (eds) *Pain - New Perspectives in Measurement and Assessment*. Edinburgh: Churchill Livingstone.
14. Melzack, R., Taenzer, P., Feldman, P. and Kinch, R. (1981) Labour is still painful after prepared childbirth training. *Canadian Medical Association Journal* **125**: 357-363.
15. Dubuisson, D. and Melzack, R. (1976) Classification of clinical pain description by multiple group discrimination analysis. *Experimental Neurology* **51**: 480-487.
16. Thompson, K. and Varni, J. (1986) A developmental cognitive–behavioural approach to pediatric pain assessment. *Pain* **25**: 283-296.
17. Philips, H.C. (1989) Thoughts provoked by pain. *Behaviour Research and Therapy* **4**: 469-473.
18. Kleck, R.E., Vaughan, R.C., Cartwright-Smith, J., Vaughan, K.B., Colby, C. and Lanzetta, J. (1976) Effects of being observed on expressive, subjective and physiological responses to painful stimuli. *Journal of Personality and Social Psychology* **34**: 1211-1218.
19. Craig, K.D. and Prkachin, K. (1983) Nonverbal measures of pain. In: Melzack, R. (ed.) *Pain*

Measurement and Assessment. New York: Raven Press.

20. Bond, M. and Pilowski, I. (1966) Subjective assessment of pain and its relationship to the administration of analgesics in patients with advanced cancer. *Journal of Psychosomatic Research* **10**: 203–208.

21. Crook, J., Rideout, E. and Browne, G. (1984) The prevalence of pain complaints in a general population. *Pain* **18**: 299–314.

22. Leventhal, H., Brown, D., Schacham, S. and Engquist, G. (1979) Effects of preparatory information about sensations, threats of pain and attention on cold pressor distress. *Journal of Personality and Social Psychology* **37**: 689–714.

23. Beales, J.C. (1979) The effect of attention and distraction on pain among children attending a hospital casualty department. In: Oborne, D.J., Gruneberg, M.M. and Eiser, J.R. (eds) *Research in Psychology and Medicine*, vol. 1. London: Academic Press.

24. Richardson, R. and Vincent, C. (1986) Acupuncture for the treatment of pain: a review of evaluative research. *Pain* **24**: 15–40.

25. Anon. (1981) How does acupuncture work? *British Medical Journal* **283**: 746–748.

26. Lousberg, R., Schmidt, J. and Goenman, N. (1992) The relationship between spouse solicitousness and pain behaviour: searching for more experimental evidence. *Pain* **51**: 75–79.

27. May, B. (1991) Pain. In: Pitts, M. and Phillips, K. (eds) *The Psychology of Health*. London: Routledge.

28. Bonica, J.J. and Fordyce, W.E. (1974) Operant conditioning for chronic pain. In: Bonica, J.J., Procacci, P. and Pagni, C. (eds) *Recent Advances in Pain*. Springfield, Illinois: C.C. Thomas.

29. Vlaeyen, J., Groenman, N., Thomassen, J., Schuerman, J., van Eek, H., Snijders, A. and van Houtem, J. (1989). A behavioural treatment for sitting and standing intolerance in a patient with chronic low back pain. *Pain* **5**: 233–237.

30. Langer, E., Janis, I. and Wolper, J. (1975) Reduction of psychological stress in surgical patients. *Journal of Experimental Social Psychology* **11**: 155–165.

31. Degood, D. and Shutty, M. (1992). Assessment of pain beliefs, coping and self-efficacy. In: Turk, D. and Melzack, R. (eds) *Handbook of Pain Assessment*. London: Guilford Press.

32. Jensen, M., Turner, J. and Romano, J. (1991) Self-efficacy and outcome expectancies: relationship to chronic pain coping strategies and adjustment. *Pain* **44**: 263–269.

33. Peters, J., Large, R. and Elkind, G. (1992) Follow-up results from a randomised controlled trial evaluating in- and outpatient pain management programmes. *Pain* **50**: 41–50.

34. Engstrom, D.R. (1976) Hypnotic susceptibility, EEG-alpha and self-regulation. In: Schwartz, G.E. and Shapiro, D. (eds) *Consciousness and Self-Regulation*. London: Plenum.

35. Weitzenhofer, A.M. and Hilgard, E.R. (1959) *Stanford Hypnotic Susceptibility Scale*. Palo Alto, California: Consulting Psychologists Press.

36. Hilgard, E.R. (1978) Hypnosis and pain. In: Sternbach, R.A. (ed.) *The Psychology of Pain*. New York: Raven Press.

37. Wadden, T.A. and Anderton, C.H. (1982) The clinical use of hypnosis. *Psychological Bulletin* **91**: 215–243.

38. Kuhn, C.C. and Bradnan, W.A. (1979) Pain as a substitute for the fear of death. *Psychosomatics* **20**: 494–495.

39. Gryll, S.L. and Katahn, H. (1978) Situational factors contributing to the placebo effect. *Psychopharmacologica* **57**: 253–261.

40. Wall, P (1992) The placebo effect: an unpopular topic. *Pain* **51**: 1–3.

41. Richardson, P. (1992) Placebos: their effectiveness and modes of action. In: Broome, A. (ed.) *Health Psychology: Processes and Applications*. London: Chapman and Hall, pp. 34–56.

42. Levine, J.D., Gordon, J.C. and Fields, H.L. (1978) The mechanism of placebo analgesia. *Lancet* **2**: 654–657.

11

The Consultation

CONTENTS

SUMMARY

This chapter reviews three areas of research on communication between doctors and patients. First, the decision to consult a doctor depends not only on the interpretation of symptoms but also on social factors, such as the effects of personal obligations. Second, the development of interviewing skills has been assisted through the development of interviewing models, in which training on response styles, the use of non-verbal behaviour and ways of breaking bad news have been outlined. Third, the treatments recommended for patients are dependent not only on clinical indications but also on social factors such as the background and enthusiasm of the doctor. The patient's perceptions of risk may be different from the professional's.

It is tempting to assume that whenever a person has a symptom – is in ill-health – then he or she will consult a physician. According to this assumption, the physician would see all the people in the practice who are ill. Apparently this is mistaken. If the condition is incapacitating the person may have little choice in the matter, but in most cases there is a series of decisions involved. First of all, there is a problem in defining health. If it is defined as the absence of symptoms, then it appears that most people are unhealthy much of the time. In one survey,[1] the health of over 3000 people living in the community was examined. Only 15 per cent were considered to be free from symptoms, ranging from psychiatric disorders to respiratory problems. Another kind of study has involved asking people to keep a diary of how they felt each day for several days or weeks. Here, again, there is strong evidence that people have symptoms much of the time. In one study conducted over one month, symptoms (such as headaches, backaches and abdominal pains) were recorded about one day in three, lasting an average of 1.6 days.[2] Only about one in every 37 symptoms resulted in a consultation with the physician. There is also evidence that there is much psychiatric illness in the community that does not come to the attention of the general practitioner or psychiatrist.[3]

Even when a doctor is consulted there are many social and psychological factors at work. A physician who concentrates solely on organic difficulties is unlikely to become aware of how health problems are affecting the social and emotional aspects of a patient's life. The doctor may not discover, for example, that one patient is very frightened about any pain which might result from a surgical procedure, or that another patient is unable to comply with a recommendation of bed rest because she cares for an elderly relative.

The decision to consult

Several factors have been identified as being important in the decision to seek medical help for physical or psychiatric complaints. Broadly speaking, these can be grouped into those concerning the interpretation of symptoms and those concerning social and personality variables.

Interpreting symptoms

First, there is the problem of interpretation. As discussed in Chapter 1, signs and symptoms have meaning only in so far as they fit into a larger context. Robinson[4] asked mothers to keep diaries of the signs of illness in their families along with a description of how they reacted to and interpreted them. Clearly, there was a considerable degree of uncertainty about the meaning of these upsets. The mothers would often adopt a "wait and see" strategy, so that a child might feel quite ill for several days or wet the bed on several occasions before a decision to see the doctor would be taken. Steps to consult a professional were taken only once they had decided that the signs were indications of an important illness. Another researcher interviewed myocardial infarction patients about their perceptions at the time of the attack. Often, they first tested alternative explanations for the pains they were feeling, and only after the pains worsened was action taken.[5]

Similarly, psychiatric illness can be difficult to interpret. In one study, the process involved in interpreting psychiatric illness in the family was explored by asking the spouses of patients about their perceptions of symptoms. Initially, unusual behaviour was put down to a physical condition or to a normal response to a crisis. There were attempts to "normalize" the behaviour by finding explanations for it or by looking for similar behaviour in others who were not ill. Only when these strategies did not work satisfactorily on several occasions was the decision taken to seek assistance.[6]

Related to the importance of interpretation are studies concerned with perceived health. Simply because a physician considers a symptom to be serious does not mean that lay members of the public do as well. The discrepancy can be large. In one study, two out of three elderly people who were rated as being in unfavourable health by their physicians gave themselves favourable reports, while one in five who saw themselves as being in poor health had physicians who considered them to be in good condition.[7] Part of this discrepancy might be due to differences in how doctors and their patients view the seriousness of symptoms. When asked about the suitability of self-care for a number of signs, doctors placed more emphasis on self-care for some (e.g. "difficulty in sleeping for about a week"), less for others (e.g. "more than one headache a week for a month") than did patients.[8]

Social factors

Other research has been conducted on the social factors influencing the decision to consult a doctor. The problem may be seen as one of delay: because many patients waited until the disease had been present for several weeks or months, one question could be "Why did they take so long?". Demographic characteristics such as age, sex and social class of the patients are only mildly related to delay. Examination of individuals' particular circumstances, however, is more informative. Through interviewing patients, it has become clear that a visit to the doctor involves costs as well as gains. Although there might be some gain in physiological health, there might also be psychological and social costs. Economics seemed to play a part, not only because of any financial fees but also because of time taken off work. It might be difficult to find someone to look after the children, and so on.[9] Some of these factors are illustrated by the following:

> " I wish I knew what you mean by being sick. Sometimes I felt so bad I could curl up and die, but I had to go on because of the kids who have to be taken care of, and besides, we didn't have the money to spend for the doctor. How could I be sick? Some people can be sick any time with anything, but most of us can't be sick, even when we need to be. (Ref. 10, p. 30)   "

Zola[11] described how he came to view the issue somewhat differently. While interviewing people in an out-patient department of a hospital, he noted that many were attending with difficulties that had bothered them for quite some time. His question became "Why are you coming *now*?", rather than "Why didn't you come before?". He noted that they were attending at that time because their symptoms were beginning to interfere with their normal activities. Zola suggested that people often learn to accommodate themselves to their disabilities and only when this accommodation is upset in some way (which might be the worsening of a condition or equally a new social demand) is action taken. It also seemed that a condition was sometimes used for interpersonal reasons – to relieve the person of unwanted social duties perhaps, as in the following example:

> ◆ Carol Conte was a forty-five-year-old, single book-keeper. For a number of years she had been both the sole support and nurse for her mother. Within the past year, her mother died and shortly thereafter her relatives began insisting that she move in with them, quit her job, work in their variety store, and nurse their mother. With Carol's vacation approaching, they have stepped up their efforts to persuade her to at least try this arrangement. Although she has long had a number of minor aches and pains, her chief complaint was a small cyst on her eyelid (diagnosis: fibroma). She related her fear that it *might* be growing or could lead to something more serious and thus she felt she had better look into it now (the second day of her vacation) "before it was too late". "Too late" for what was revealed only in a somewhat mumbled response to the question of what she expected or would like the doctor to do. From a list of possible outcomes to her examination, she responded, "Maybe a 'hospital'[ization] . . . 'Rest' would be all right . . . " (and then in barely audible tone, in fact turning her head away as if she were speaking to no one at all) "just so they [the family] would stop bothering me." Responding to her physical concern, the examining physician acceded to her request for the removal of the fibroma, referred her for surgery, and thus removed her from the situation for the duration of her vacation. (Ref. 11, p. 683)   ◆

According to this view, social factors act as "triggers" that set in motion the decision to seek aid.

Other researchers have looked at factors associated with family background that affect the decision to consult. The decision as to whether symptoms merit professional assistance is often negotiated within the family. Almost all potential patients seek the advice of relatives about what they should do when they experience symptoms. If the family advises against seeing a doctor, symptoms are usually ignored until they disappear or until they become much worse.[12] Where psychiatric difficulties are involved, friends are more likely than relatives to suggest professional assistance, perhaps because relatives are anxious about the stigma of psychiatric treatment.[13] For physical illnesses in children, the influence of the mother is particularly important. Mechanic[14] showed that mothers tended to treat their children's illness like their own: those mothers who were more likely to take medication or to visit the doctor for themselves, were also more likely to give medication to their children and to take them to see the doctor.

Thus, the relationship between symptom and action is mediated by social and psychological factors. It seems necessary to consider the presentation of symptoms against the total background of the patient's daily life and relationships with others. In this context many writers have made a distinction between disease and "illness behaviour". Disease might be considered a good term for the objective pathology, while the term illness behaviour might be used to describe the processes of evaluation and action connected with the perceptions of symptoms. It may be more useful to consider the decision to consult a physician as a result of difficulties in continuing a lifestyle rather than as a result of the disease itself.

Seen in this way, illness becomes an indication of impaired capacity rather than an indication of disease. If this is the basis upon which a person consults a doctor, it seems likely that some consultations will not be about diseases at all, but rather about interpersonal relationships and emotional difficulties. It would also seem that curing a disease is not the same as curing an illness, so that medical care would involve more than pharmacological or surgical treatments.

Interviewing

There are several reasons why skill in interviewing is important for the practising doctor. As mentioned above, consideration of the patient's social obligations and perceptions of the illness are significant. In so far as these are related to outcome, an understanding of these factors is an important aspect of medical care.

There is a more general reason for competent interviewing, however, having to do with the satisfaction that a patient feels about the consultation. Roughly speaking, satisfaction with care has cognitive and emotional components, although they are often related to each other. Cognitive satisfaction – how satisfied a patient is with their understanding of the diagnosis, treatment and prognosis – appears to be associated with the doctor's verbal behaviour. In general practice consultations, the opportunity to ask questions and to gain information about illness and treatment is predictive of patients' satisfaction. On average, one-third of patients feel they have not received sufficient information about their illness when asked after consultations.[15]

Emotional satisfaction, on the other hand, seems to be related more closely to the doctor's non-verbal behaviour. The ability to show care and concern by tone of voice, body movements and body posture is significant in this respect. Both verbal and non-verbal aspects of interviewing are discussed below.

Problems in interviewing

As discussed in Chapter 1, it seems that physicians often have the expectation that patients have *either* a social/psychological difficulty *or* an organic complaint. Physical illness is often missed in psychiatric patients, while surgeons and general practitioners often do not inquire about personal difficulties associated with physical disease. For example, Maguire[16] found that most of the women who were clearly upset after a mastectomy received little assistance. For only 5 per cent of the women was distress heeded, while in 20 per cent the doctors appreciated their needs but dealt with them by such comments as "Don't worry, there's nothing to be bothered about" or "We'll sort it all out for you". In the remaining cases, there was no evidence that the emotions were noted by the doctors. Consequently, many of the women who were distressed before the consultation were distressed afterwards.

Initially, students encounter many problems when interviewing patients. Beginning the conversation, coping with emotions and keeping an open mind about possible diagnoses are commonly mentioned.[17] This is consistent with research by Maguire and Rutter,[18] who asked students who were close to their final examinations to conduct a 15-minute interview with a psychiatric patient. They were asked to concentrate on the patient's current problems and to write up the history afterwards. In this way Maguire was able first to identify areas where the students required specific assistance in interviewing and then able to develop a model which could help them improve their skills.

An interviewing model
Maguire has shown that students are able to increase the amount of information they acquire by seeing and hearing themselves interview a patient and by following a systematic procedure during the interview. In one typical study,

students were divided into two groups. Those in the experimental group were first videotaped while interviewing a patient. They were then presented with a handout explaining the model outlined below and the course tutor asked the student to consider the problems the consultation presented while referring to the model and to the videotaped interview. Students in the control group also interviewed a patient, but were not given a handout or any other feedback.

When the students in both groups interviewed a second patient a week later, those in the experimental group obtained three times as much relevant and accurate information as those in the control group. Further, the patients of the experimental group rated their student interviewers somewhat more favourably than did patients of the control group, suggesting that the patients benefited as well. There is even some evidence that this type of training has important longer term effects on the students' interviewing styles.[19] In his model, Maguire makes a distinction between content (what information should be collected) and process (how it might be gathered).

Content

Details of the main problems   The interviewer needs to be aware that a patient may have several problems and that these may be physical, social and psychological in nature. After establishing the primary difficulty, the interviewer should ask whether there are any problems the patient would like to mention: in fact, the interviewer should assume they exist. For the problems that there is time to explore, the date of onset, the subsequent development of the problem, precipitating or relieving factors, the help given to date and the availability of support need to be discussed.

Impact of the problem on patient and family   It is likely that physical complaints will have social and psychological consequences. Patients' abilities to do their jobs, to pursue leisure activities and the quality of their relationship with their families are all relevant here.

Patients' view of their problems Since patients' beliefs about their illnesses and treat-

ment are often better predictors of their behaviour than medical views, by obtaining a clear understanding of these beliefs the physician is in a better position to provide effective reassurance and to correct misconceptions. Maguire provides an example of a patient who had been admitted to hospital after a myocardial infarction. Having been led to believe by a staff member that it was of a minor nature, he was unwilling to follow his doctor's advice to restrict his activities.

Predisposition to develop similar problems   The patient's background is significant here, both psychologically and organically. Details of the family of origin, occupation, the patient's early development and childhood, sexual development, interpersonal relationships and previous health may be noted.

Screening questions   Finally, the content of the interview ought to include an exploration of areas not yet covered. If the consultation has been primarily concerned with physical complaints, then it is appropriate to inquire about social and psychological difficulties; if the interview has been biased towards personal problems, then the physical well-being of the patient should be considered.

The interviewing process

Beginning the interview The interviewer should take particular care to greet the patient both verbally, using the correct name and title, and non-verbally (e.g. by shaking hands). The interviewer should also indicate clearly where the patient is to sit and to introduce him or herself if they have not met before.

Discussing the procedure of the interview   As aids to understanding and remembering, a short explanation of the time available and the procedure to be used is helpful. For example, if the interviewer plans to take notes, this should be mentioned and the patient's feelings about it should be elicited. Although note-taking may improve the accuracy of the doctor's memory, it may also inhibit the patient. If the interview is to be conducted in public (e.g. a hospital ward), the patient should be given the opportunity to voice hesitations about talking of personal matters and to move somewhere with more privacy. The theme of this aspect of the consultation is that doctors should make every attempt to put the patient at ease.

Obtaining the relevant information   After the opening of the interview, the patient should be encouraged to outline the important difficulties. Perhaps an open-ended question such as "Can you begin by telling me what problems brought you here today?" could be used. The doctor could encourage the patient to continue by saying "Go on" or "Can you tell me more about that?", rather than by interrupting to ask what seem to be pertinent questions. Beckman and Frankel[20] found that interruptions by the doctor frequently occurred (69 per cent of the consultations in their sample) during patients' initial statements of their concerns.

Most commonly, questions will be used to gain information, but asking several questions at once is not conducive to good communication. Nor are questions that restrict the range of possible answers always appropriate. To ask "Was it because you walked too quickly or ate too much?" forces the patient to choose between two alternatives: perhaps both or neither seems correct. Open questions (e.g. "How do you feel about your mother coming to stay?") allow the patient considerable latitude for reply, while closed questions (e.g. "Will there be enough room?") narrow the possibilities considerably. Frequent use of closed questions will elicit answers to the questions asked, but suffers from the problem that the doctor may not ask the most appropriate questions. This is particularly likely when social and psychological information is being sought.

Listening is another important skill in interviewing. Rather than determining the direction of the interview entirely, it is often important to allow patients to say what they want in their own way. Silence is often needed by patients (and doctors) to consider what has gone on before.

Ending the interview   Students report that ending an interview is often difficult. Two or three minutes should be left at the end to review the information given, to ask if any important information has not been transmitted and to provide the patient with an opportunity to ask questions.

Patient-centred and doctor-centred consultations

A fundamental issue in doctor–patient communication concerns the extent to which the patient or the doctor "controls" the consultation. Traditionally, the doctor has been seen as the person in charge, since he or she has the necessary expertise and experience to decide what is and what is not important. The model outlined above is primarily doctor-centred, in that it concentrates on the tasks a doctor performs in the consultation. However, the patient-centred movement in medicine emphasizes the need for mutuality between doctor and patient, rather than one party deciding what the problem is, how the consultation should be conducted and what action needs to be taken in future.[21] In many respects this change reflects the shift away from paternalism in medicine.

Consider the following two consultations. In both cases the patients had recently suffered a heart attack, so their clinical condition was similar, and they were of similar ages. But the doctors' styles were very different.

The doctors in these two consultations appear to have very different styles of conducting their interviews. The first is giving very clear instructions, but giving the patient little part to play beyond following advice. The second doctor is more concerned with finding out how the patient feels while encouraging him to take some responsibility for his care.

> Case 1   *Doctor:* Okay, put your shirt back on please. Now then, I think it is time that you went back to work. However, I think that you must only go back for a few hours a day and at the least sign of tiredness you must stop. I don't want you smoking any more and you are not under any circumstances to take any form of strong liquor. You will stay on all the tablets for the time being and we will start to reduce the dosage next month. You are not to drive. You're not driving are you?
> *Patient:* No. My wife brought me here today.
> *Doctor:* Good. Let's keep it that way for the time being, shall we?

Case 2 *Doctor:* Well, now, Mr _____ you seem to be making a reasonable recovery. How did you get here today?

Patient: Oh, I came on foot.

Doctor: Mmm. Mmm. How did it feel?

Patient: Out of breath two or three times but I rested.

Doctor: Splendid. Well, that's something you can slowly expect to build up. But whilst you need some exercise you must take it very carefully.

Patient: What about work, doctor?

Doctor: Well, how do you feel about it?

Patient: Well, I think I could manage a few hours a day, you know.

Doctor: Mmm. Mmm. How will you get there?

Patient: My neighbour works in the same office. He could take me.

Doctor: Mmm. Mmm. Well I don't want you in there for too long at first.

Patient: You mean I should stay away?

Doctor: No. I think you must decide when you go back. If you think you can manage now, then it's fine. But two or three hours is enough. (Ref. 22, p. 105)

Bryne and Long[22] argue that the first consultation is very *doctor-centred*, the second more *patient-centred*. By analysing many general practice consultations, Byrne and Long were able to identify several types of responses made by doctors to patients' comments, as shown in Table 11.1. Patient-centred responses tend to follow the patients' expectations and assumptions and use their knowledge and expertise, with a recognition that they are the experts on how they

Table 11.1 Examples of patient-centred and doctor-centred responses

Patient-centred responses	Doctor-centred responses
Open questions	Direct questions
Listening	Closed questions
Reflecting	Reassurance
Clarifying	Giving advice
Indications of understanding and acceptance	

feel. Thus in a patient-centred interview the doctor will tend to use open questions (e.g. "Could you tell me what brought you here today?"), ask for clarification (e.g. "Could you tell me a bit more about what you mean by feeling tense?") and reflect back the words used by the patient (e.g. "You say that you are unhappy with how your son is getting on at school").

Doctor-centred responses follow the doctor's expectations and assumptions, using his or her own knowledge and frame of reference. In a doctor-centred interview the doctor will tend to use closed questions (e.g. "Are you feeling pain here?"), give advice (e.g. "I think that you should go back to work now") and give information and reassurance (e.g. "This lump is benign and not cancerous"). Their model is illustrated in Figure 11.1, which indicates that there is a gradation between these two styles.

This is not to say that one style is necessarily better than the other. For example, a patient who is seriously ill and frightened may need a doctor to take control over the situation, when a doctor-centred style would be appropriate. On other occasions, a patient may wish to be in control

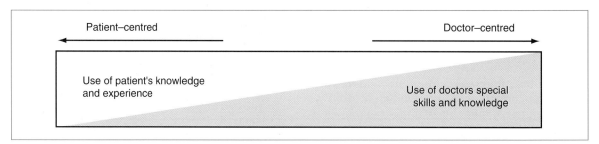

Figure 11.1 A gradation between a patient-centred and a doctor-centred style of consultation (Adapted from Bryne, P. and Long, B. (1976) *Doctors Talking to Patients.* London, HMSO. Crown copyright is reproduced with the permission of the Controller of HMSO.)

and take more responsibility for the conduct of the interview and any decisions which result. The appropriateness of the style may also depend on the stage of the consultation: at the beginning, a patient-centred style might be most helpful, giving an opportunity for the patient to tell his or her story in their own words. At another point, it may be necessary to take control over the interview by asking closed questions.

Non-verbal behaviour

Although verbal behaviour is important in the consultation, the understanding of the relationship between doctor and patient requires consideration of non-verbal behaviour as well, since the gestures and bodily movements that surround a verbal statement modify its meaning. For instance, the comment "Come in, Mr Smith" can give very different impressions depending on the speaker's non-verbal behaviour. If the speaker looks at the visitor, rises in greeting and perhaps shakes hands, friendliness is indicated, but if the speaker continues to look down at the desk and issues the invitation in a routine manner, indifference is the likely impression.

Non-verbal aspects of conversation are mainly responsible for the emotional quality of the relationship between two people whereas verbal communication is more relevant to their shared cognitive tasks and problems. For example, non-verbal signals have a greater impact than verbal ones on assertiveness and friendship. The aim of this section of the chapter is to explore the importance of non-verbal behaviour in doctor–patient communication.

Broadly speaking, researchers in this area have taken one of two positions. One group of workers has maintained that every expression or bodily movement is part of a larger context that will influence its meaning to a large extent. For example, eye gaze can have two distinct and incompatible meanings, depending on the circumstances. When two people know each other well and the circumstances are friendly, long periods of looking at each other suggests intimacy, but when issues of status are at hand, gaze may indicate aggression. Similarly, touching may indicate caring or dominance.

A second group of researchers has suggested that many expressions bear a close relationship to emotional state. They are concerned with the relationship between behaviour and emotional feelings – that looking downwards is a sign of embarrassment, for example. This tradition is more closely related to evolutionary approaches to understanding behaviour. Paul Ekman[23] is an important researcher in this field, taking as his starting point Darwin's observations about the cross-cultural nature of many facial expressions. Ekman presented photographs of models portraying various expressions to people from very different cultures. There was considerable agreement in identifying the nature of emotions shown (happiness, surprise, anger and so forth).

It seems that both approaches have much to offer, providing insights into this topic. In the outline of research given in this section, both approaches are used and their implications for doctor–patient communication considered.

Vision

Eye gaze is not necessary for person-to-person interaction (talking over the telephone is possible, for instance), but it does play an important role. Speakers look at their conversational partners from time to time, apparently to gain information as to whether they are being understood. Observation of conversations indicates that it is during these times that listeners provide feedback, nodding their heads and murmuring agreement. When listening, a person will spend most of the time looking at the speaker, showing attention to what is being said. Listeners who do not look and who do not nod their heads are often judged to be unfriendly or uninterested. Whether speaking or listening, the amount of gaze a person gives appears to affect others' perceptions of friendliness and warmth.

We often make judgements about the relationship between two people by the amount of time they spend looking at each other. One way to explore the importance of different non-verbal cues is by experimenting with various combinations and testing for general principles. For example, the amount of time two people look at each other and the physical distance between them appear to be inversely related. Argyle and Ingram[24] suggest that eye gaze and distance can substitute for each other as signs of intimacy, so that in order to keep a constant level of intimacy people will look at each other less often and for shorter periods of time as they come closer together. An example of a similar situation to this experiment can be found in crowded buses – everyone is standing close together and studiously looking out of the window or at the advertisements.

Patients who are not looked at by their doctors may well feel that the physician is not especially warm or caring. Several examples of the practical importance of these considerations are given by Byrne and Heath.[25] They videotaped consultations and related the physicians' behaviour to the patients' reactions. In several cases, patients hesitated or fell silent when their doctors began to read or write on the medical records. In the following example, the patient stopped talking about her problem at item 3, just when the doctor began writing. Only at item 4, when the doctor looked up, did the patient begin again:

> **1** *Patient:* No, well, even the training centres for the unemployment . . . unemployed . . . they don't like them after a certain age to return there 'cos they say it's . . . they're too old . . . you see.
> **2** *Doctor:* I see.
> **3** *Patient:* So . . . (3.5 seconds)
> **4** *Patient:* So I don't think there's . . . (Ref. 25, p. 30)
> It seemed that the shift of eye gaze and attention away from the patient and towards the records effectively suspended the consultation.

Posture and gestures

Posture is also important for conversation. A slight forward lean has been shown to be associated with perceptions of warmth. Although closed arm positions appear to indicate coldness, rejection and inaccessibility, moderately open arm positions convey warmth and acceptance. Movement is often used to emphasize a point or to demonstrate an idea. The representation of size with the hands is common: people often hold their hands and arms far apart when describing a large object, close together when describing something small. Changes in posture can convey

a wealth of information. They often accompany a change in topic and can be used to signal the end of a conversation. People may serve notice that they want to say something important by changing position or becoming restless.

It is important that physicians recognize the significance of movements not only in their patients but also in themselves. Doctors who find themselves changing position constantly and keeping their arms closed around their bodies might reflect on their feelings towards their patients. Counsellors who often smile and who show interest by nodding their heads frequently are rated as being more facilitative than counsellors who show little emotional involvement.[26]

Proximity

One way of describing the distance between people is in terms of "personal space" – a kind of bubble of territory that surrounds people. One method to discover the size of this space is simply to observe conversationalists and measure the distance between them. When standing or talking casually, interactants usually keep about 60–75 cm apart. A way of testing the validity of this observation is simply to walk closer to someone and measure the distance at which he or she begins to move backwards. The point at which this occurs is the edge of the bubble. It seems, from experiments of this type, that the bubble is not round: people will tolerate more proximity at their sides than at the front or back.

The boundaries of personal space vary according to several situational factors. Intimacy of topic is one variable, as is the relationship between the participants (e.g. friends or strangers) and cultural background (e.g. Mediterranean peoples generally stand closer together than Anglo-Saxons). Hall[27] categorized proximity into four zones: intimate (0–45 cm), personal (45–120 cm), social (1.2–4 m) and public (greater than 4 m). The topic of conversation and the relationship between the participants using these different zones varies. For example, two people standing or sitting 1.2–4 m apart are more likely to be speaking socially than personally or intimately. We often first recognize that two people are developing a close relationship with each other when they start sitting or walking more closely together.

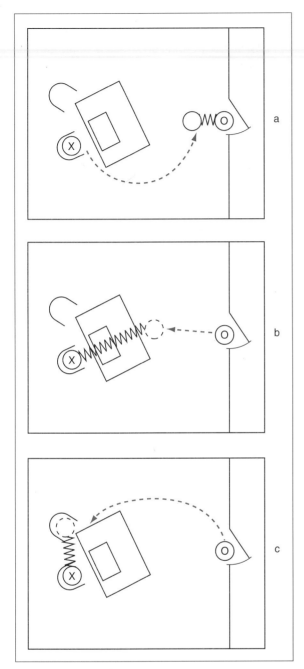

Figure 11.2 Three examples of the way one person could enter another's office. In (a), person O steps into the office while person X rises and greets him: O was considered to have higher status than X. In (b), O moves towards X, who remains seated: O was seen as being of lower status than X. (c) One situation in which both were considered to be of equal status: O moves towards X and sits beside him without hesitation. (Reproduced from Burns, T. (1964) *Discovery* **25**: 30–37.)

Status is also related to proximity. Those with high status have more territory than those with low status. A director of a company will not only have a large office but also a large desk that serves to maintain a large personal space. As illustrated in Figure 11.2, the way in which a person enters another's office is a good example of how non-verbal behaviour can indicate relative status.[28] If you are ever asked to meet the Dean of your Medical School, it is better to follow example (b) than (c)!

To some extent, patients entering a doctor's office are entering territory that "belongs" to the physician. The way in which they act may provide a good indication of how comfortable or uncomfortable they feel in a doctor's presence. Conversely, the way patients are greeted may give them an indication of the doctor's concern with status. If the doctor stays seated and waits for patients to come to the desk, they may consider the doctor to be asserting higher status. Ley and Spelman[29] and Robinson[30] suggest that patients often feel diffident about asking questions or feel unable to contribute to the interview. Perhaps any feature of the consultation that emphasizes a difference in status may not be conducive to good communication.

Associated with proximity are studies on touching. In one study, observations of couples seated in restaurants illustrated how the extent of touching is affected by cultural background. There were 110 contacts per hour in France, 2 in the United States, and none in England. The nature of the relationship between two people is also relevant. Jourard[31] asked students to indicate who touched them (e.g. mother, father, same-sexed friend) and how frequently they were touched on various parts of their bodies. As would be expected, only the hands were touched by everyone and the trunk of the body and the genitals were touched infrequently.

The relevance of this study to doctor–patient communication is that touching and intimacy seem to be closely related to each other, such that if touch occurs the relationship is interpreted as a close one. Johnson[32] reported that nurses often find their patients begin disclosing very personal information during intimate forms of touching. Conversely, patients may feel violated when being physically examined by a doctor who has not taken time to establish some rapport.

Breaking bad news

Perhaps the most important psychological aspect of the consultation is the physician's sensitivity to the behaviour and feelings of the patient. It is not possible to specify the "best" way to communicate with all patients. Perhaps because people under the care of doctors are given the same label – patients – there is a tendency to consider the people in this heterogeneous group as being more similar to each other than they are.

Psychology has been able to provide some guidelines – for example, it is important not to assume that once information has been given to a patient it has been understood or that further information is unnecessary – but studies in this area indicate that all patients should be treated as individuals. What might be appropriate for one person may be hurtful or shocking for another, so that it is important to be sensitive to patients' non-verbal behaviour, such as hesitations, restlessness and signs of embarrassment. In many of the studies on preparing patients for hospitalization and surgery mentioned elsewhere in the book, providing information about procedures and sensations they are likely to experience has been useful for most patients, but not all.

That individuals have different needs makes breaking bad news to patients or their families very problematic, particularly perhaps at the end of a long and busy day. While junior staff might not have the formal responsibility of telling patients about, for instance, a child's handicap or a poor prognosis, they often have more contact with patients than senior staff. Students report that this is one of the more stressful aspects of practice.

An example of a difficult communication is telling parents that their child is handicapped. Parents of children with Down's syndrome have complained that they were not told together (one spouse being left to inform the other), that they were not told soon enough, that they were told in front of a large group of people rather than in private, and that they were not given enough information.[33] Svarstad and Lipton[34] reported a significant relationship between parental acceptance of mental handicap in their child and the nature of professional communication to them about the condition. Parents who received specific, clear and frank communication were more likely to accept the diagnosis than those who received vague and hurried information. Coming to terms with the disability was not related to any measured characteristics of the child (age, sex and IQ), the parents (social class) or the professional who informed them (age, sex and level of experience).

These findings do not, however, indicate that all parents should be informed in the same way. While 60–80 per cent of parents would have liked to have been told together, there remains the 20–40 per cent who would not have wished this. While some were glad that they had been told about the mental handicap straight away, others report that they would "prefer to wait until the diagnosis is confirmed" or were "glad they waited a week – we might have rejected him".[35]

Memory

People in a shocked state often retain little of what is said to them. This could apply equally to informing someone of a terminal prognosis as to telling parents that their child is handicapped. This implies that it is important for doctors to make themselves available on subsequent occasions and to be prepared to repeat information that has already been given.

In order to assess the importance of repeating information, patients with cancer were given a tape recording of their "bad news" consultation with their surgeon to take home with them. Although the content of the consultation was often very distressing, both the patients and their families were deeply appreciative of the efforts to inform them clearly, and the tape provided a way not only of recalling what occurred but also a way of informing other relatives, as indicated by the following:

    66 We both appreciated the frank and honest way the doctor spoke to us about cancer. Listening to the tape again gave us great confidence in him. It stopped me feeling so anxious about what was to come.[36]   99

BOX 11.1

Breaking bad news

Rob Buckman,[39] an oncologist, has developed a model which is helpful to those who have to break bad news to patients and their families. He defines bad news as information "that drastically and negatively alters the patient's view of his or her future". This means that the impact of the news on the patient or relative depends on the size of the gap between expectations (including ambitions and plans for the future) and the medical reality of the situation. This definition therefore stresses the importance of knowing how much a patient knows and expects of his or her condition.

Buckman believes that there are, essentially, six basic steps:

1 *Get the physical context right*. The conversation should be in person and not over the phone, and should take place in a private room. The physical context includes helping the person to be comfortable and organizing who should be present.

2 *Find out how much the patient knows*. What do they know about the impact their illness will have in the future? This involves determining present knowledge, understanding of the medical situation, emotional state, and the verbal and emotional content of the patient's statements.

3 *Find out how much the person wants to know*. An open question, such as "How much would you like me to tell you about the diagnosis?" is one possibility. It depends on your personal style. It is also important to leave the door open for future questions if the person does not wish to discuss the information now.

4 Only when the first three preparatory steps are complete is it time to *impart information*. It can be useful to have an agenda – diagnosis, treatment plan, prognosis, support. It is important to share the information by aligning and educating. Aligning means adjusting the information to the baseline of the patient's knowledge. Education means bringing the patient's perception of the situation closer to the medical facts. Avoid medical jargon, check the reception of the facts and clarify, repeat important facts, listen to the patient's anxieties and concerns.

5 *Assess the patient's reactions and respond to them*. Aim to respond in an individualized way. Possible reactions are denial, shock, fear and anxiety, anger and blame. Identify these reactions and try to understand their cause.

6 *Organize a plan for the future and follow through*. Offer support and make a contract for the future – however simple.

Sensitivity

There has been considerable emphasis on the concept of "accurate empathy", particularly in the literature on psychotherapy. Empathy requires an ability not only to understand feelings but to *express* this understanding as well. The ability of physicians to understand the emotions of their patients and the ability to communicate this understanding is associated with patient satisfaction.[37] Some studies have shown that sensitivity can be improved through teaching programmes. These often include an opportunity for trainees to role-play a consultation and then the patients (who are sometimes actors and actresses, and sometimes patients living nearby) provide information on how they felt about the interview.[38]

Hiding bad news

Another aspect of this difficult area is a recognition that the physician's own behaviour will be studied and interpreted by patients, particularly when they are unsure about diagnosis and treatment. To take Down's Syndrome as an example again, Cunningham[33] describes how it was the changes in hospital routine and reactions of the staff that had made some parents concerned about their children:

> I knew something was wrong as soon as he was . . . born. They all looked at each other and went very quiet. Some other people then came in . . . but when I asked was he all right, they said he was fine and not to worry . . . but I knew they knew all the time, so why didn't they say something instead of keeping me wondering and worrying all that time?

and

> I guessed she wasn't all right. She was always the last baby brought up from the nursery after feeding and people – doctors, students and nurses and all that – kept

popping in to see us but never seemed to want anything. (Ref. 33, p. 314)

It can be tempting to attempt to deceive or at least to mislead a patient when the consequences of telling the truth may be negative. You might be anxious about causing hurt, the patient may become angry or distressed, or it might just be easier to leave the responsibility to someone else. There is very little research on this area of medical care but, as the quotations given above show, patients are often very sensitive to unusual changes in the behaviour of doctors and nurses. Although non-disclosure of information is not the same as deception, they can both have negative effects on patients' well-being and staff morale. The emotional costs of collusion in deception can be high and the need for teamwork in

BOX 11.2

Ethical rules in doctor-patient communication

There are a number of obligations involved in doctor–patient communication. These include:

- *Veracity* This concerns rules about telling the truth. Lying is wrong, but is not the same as non-disclosure of information. A doctor may not disclose all the relevant information to a patient at one time, preferring instead to "titrate" the information in a sensitive and appropriate way. For example, it might be more appropriate to communicate a terminal prognosis over the course of a few days, rather than all at once.
- *Privacy* This is respect for limited access to the thoughts, feelings and physical state of another person. Patients may grant access to themselves when they consult a doctor, but not unlimited access, and they have the right to refuse to divulge information or to be physically examined. Recently, there has been discussion about whether patients should be required to be tested for HIV before surgery, a question of privacy.
- *Confidentiality* A patient may grant

access to him or herself, but may not relinquish control of the information obtained. There ought to be no disclosure of information without the individual's permission. This applies to both communication and medical records. Confidentiality can be violated when there is deliberate disclosure or when there is negligence (e.g. leaving notes in a public place). Patients may not realize the extent to which information is shared between various doctors, hospital administrators and students,[41] and tend to believe that the rule of confidentiality is more closely observed than it seems to be.[42]

- *Fidelity* This rule concern promise-keeping, especially the implicit promises made by a doctor to promote the patient's welfare and be careful about information. Fidelity can be problematic in some situations, such as in clinical research or during immunization programmes. Although the clinical role is primarily concerned with a patient's welfare, a research project or immunization of the population may be for society's benefit, not the patient's.

maintaining deception increases the risk of discovery. For all these reasons, the use of deception in health care is a high risk strategy.[40]

There are also ethical issues involved. When dealing with patients, medical staff have a number of explicit and implicit obligations. As described in Box 11.2, these include veracity, respect for privacy, confidentiality and promise keeping.

Deciding on treatment

The research into the personal and psychological factors that influence treatment decisions has explored issues concerning prescribing and surgical treatment, showing that the views of the individual physician, prevailing medical norms and patients' wishes are all relevant.

Prescribing

The most important decision is whether to provide medical treatment at all. Perhaps 3 in 10 patients who consult a general practitioner require only reassurance and support.[43] This has led Bain[44] not to intervene for about 20 per cent of the patients who consult him and there is some evidence to suggest that more stringent prescribing would not work to the detriment of patients. Marsh, a general practitioner, reports that he avoids prescribing when social, psychological or interpersonal needs seem more relevant than pharmacological ones. He has also attempted to reduce the number of drugs he uses, claiming that by using a limited range of medications he understands their effects well and can monitor their side-effects. When asked, only 1 per cent of his patients felt that they were not given a prescription often enough.[45]

There is a wide variation amongst doctors in their tendency to intervene, some giving up to six times as many prescriptions than others. Part of this variation might be due to patient selection: in group practices patients can choose one doctor when they have a complaint which requires medication and another doctor when they prefer a sympathetic ear. However, it seems unlikely that all the variation could be due to this kind of patient selection and several other factors have been found to be associated with prescribing patterns. The doctor's training, use of advice from colleagues and the advertising of pharmaceutical companies all seem important.[46]

The quality of prescribing

Besides the number of prescriptions written, the quality of prescribing is also important. In one study, an indication of physicians' dissatisfaction with their job was related to incautious prescribing. A group of doctors were asked to indicate their degree of agreement or disagreement with a number of statements, such as: "Assuming that pay and conditions were similar, I would just as soon do non-medical work" and "My work still interests me as much as it ever did". Those doctors who disagreed with items like the first one and who agreed with items like the second were said to have high job satisfaction. Prescribing records were then reviewed, particularly those prescriptions for drugs which current pharmacological research has suggested were contraindicated in some way. The results showed that the more satisfied doctors were less likely to prescribe these medications than the less satisfied ones. They were also less likely to sign prescriptions without first seeing the patient and so were perhaps in a better position to observe signs that could lead to adverse reactions.[47]

In another similar project, physicians' attitudes towards emotional disturbance in their patients was found to be related to prescribing patterns. Those who agreed with such statements as: "The distress shown by many neurotic patients is due more to a lack of control than real suffering"; and "Until the advent of more effective methods of treatment there is little to be done for psychiatric patients", were more likely to issue repeat prescriptions for tranquillizers and to ask ancillary workers to fill out the forms. Agreement with such statements was also related to low job satisfaction and low general morale.[48]

The enthusiasm of the physician for a particular drug may actually alter its effectiveness. Haefner et al.[49] first divided their sample of physicians into two groups: those whose attitudes were favourable towards the use of medication and those whose attitudes were less positive. Then 111 newly admitted patients (diagnosed as schizophrenic) were randomly assigned to the physicians. For the first 4 weeks of the patients' stay, all doctors were asked to give the same dosage of medication. Measures of patient improvement were based on interviews (where the assessors did not know which doctor the patient had seen) and on observation of behaviour on the wards. Patients who were under the care of doctors with more favourable attitudes towards chemotherapy showed greater improvement than did patients under doctors with less favourable attitudes, despite the fact that they were given the same dosages of the same medication. Such studies support the suggestion that the doctor is one of the most potent drugs available to his or her patients.

Personal characteristics of the physician are also relevant. One study[50] examined the effects of the sensitivity of junior doctors on patients with chronic asthma. The doctors' supervisors rated their sensitivity according to the following instructions:

◆ Please rate each physician according to the degree to which each treated his patients as real, whole persons with feelings rather than a representative case of pulmonary pathology. ◆

In making their ratings, the supervisors felt that concerns about the general welfare of the patient and willingness to respond to the patients' demands were two important features of a sensitive physician. The researchers then took several measures of how the doctors cared for their patients, particularly their prescribing patterns. Those doctors who were rated high in sensitivity were less likely to give medications which had adverse side-effects and were more likely to treat different kinds of patients in different ways, adjusting their prescribing practice to suit each patient. There was also evidence that they took the patients' general welfare into account in their prescribing, giving aid to other difficulties more frequently.

It seems, then, that prescribing patterns are not altogether rational and scientific or based solely on the appropriateness of a particular drug. Some doctors prescribe drugs much more frequently than others, with those who are pessimistic about the treatment of psychiatric patients being more likely to use tranquillizing drugs.

Doctors who have favourable attitudes towards medication seem to achieve better results when using drugs, whereas incautious prescribing is related to low job satisfaction.

Surgery

Similar points can be made about surgical procedures. Like prescribing, there is evidence that the decision to operate depends on the physician's expectations and the resources available. The classic study on surgical procedures was conducted in the 1930s. At that time, most children had their tonsils removed, a procedure that is currently practised much less frequently. At first, 1000 children, 11 years of age, were examined. Some 61 per cent of these had had their tonsils removed previously. The remaining 39 per cent were then examined by a group of physicians who selected 45 per cent of these for tonsillectomy and passed the rest as fit. Those said to be healthy by this group of doctors were then re-examined by a second group of physicians, who recommended that 46 per cent of these be given a tonsillectomy. When the remaining 116 children were seen again by a third group of doctors, 51 more were advised to have the operation. After three examinations, only 65 children remained. These were not examined further because the supply of doctors ran out. There seemed to be no correlation between the recommendation of one physician and that of another regarding the advisability of the operation, so that the probability of a child being given a tonsillectomy depended principally on the physician rather than on the child's health.[51]

Even today there is a wide variation in the use of surgical interventions. Here again, it is unlikely that this is due only to medical factors. Part of the variation seems to be related to the supply of surgeons: it has been estimated that a 10 per cent increase in the surgeon:population ratio results in about a 3 per cent increase in the per capita utilization of their services. An increase in the number of surgeons living in an area does not appear to be the result of increased demand; rather, demand seems to follow supply to some extent. In one study, the surgical rates in Ontario, Canada, were examined. Considerable variation in the proportion of patients who underwent operations was found for different areas of the province: 7-fold differences for colectomies, 5-fold for appendectomies. The factors which could explain most of the variation in these rates were the availability of hospital beds and the number of physicians living in the area. The more resources available, the larger the number of operations that were performed.[52]

Even within one hospital there is variation in the number of operations performed, with some surgeons taking a more "radical" approach than others. Howie[53] studied five surgical units that worked in strict rotation on emergency admissions. Three of the units took a cautious or conservative approach to appendectomies, preferring not to operate if the patient seemed to have a reasonable chance of recovery. The surgeons in the other units were more radical, believing that it would be proper to operate in most instances and only refraining if there were good reason not to intervene. Over a period of 9 months, the radical surgeons removed an average of 72 acutely inflamed appendices per unit, while the conservative surgeons removed only 46 per unit.

Thus, it seems that the decision on how to treat a patient is not determined solely by the condition. Such variation in treatment rates have been found with several other types of intervention, including use of endoscopy services and admissions to neonatal care units. In East Anglia, England, some units admitted 30 per cent of newborn babies, others only 6 per cent. However, such differences did not correlate with clinical need (such as the percentage of low birthweight children). Again, this variation could be explained by the size of the hospital and the number of cots available. Further, physicians who felt sympathetic about the problem of separating the mother and her infant were less likely to admit neonates to units. Each physician has his or her own personal experience and beliefs that will influence treatment decisions.[54]

The patient's point of view

There is relatively little research on how patients view treatment decisions. Perhaps this is because the responsibility has, traditionally, been the doctor's alone. However, there is much more rec-ognition being given to the rights of patients in recent years. One important area is how patients perceive the risks involved in treatment.

An example of how doctors and patients can use different criteria for deciding between courses of treatment is provided by some work in oncology. As a measure of clinical effectiveness, a 5-year survival rate is generally used: using this criterion, surgical procedures are preferable to radiotherapy. The operation provides a better chance of prolonged life at the risk of an early death, whereas radiotherapy provides a smaller chance of prolonged survival but with little risk of an early death. However, this criterion may not be the most suitable from the patient's point of view. McNeil[55] found that for elderly patients at least, the longer term gain offered by surgery was not as important as its short-term threat. Many patients preferred radiotherapy. Here, the 5–year survival rate criterion was not the optimum one from the patients' standpoint.

Perceptions of risk

The determination of risk is important, since patients may use this information in order to make choices about treatment. However, assessment of risk is a complex area and there is a substantial literature on how people make choices under conditions of uncertainty. Perhaps part of the difficulty is that different people attach different meanings to such terms as "usually", "rarely" or "frequently". For example, Sutherland et al.[56] first reviewed 15 consent forms at the cancer centre where they worked. They selected words or phrases that described the probabilities of various risks or benefits, such as "may occur", "occasionally", "rarely" and "possible". Then interviewers asked patients who were receiving treatment for cancer to indicate their understanding of the terms on scales ranging from 0 to 100. Patients often disagreed amongst themselves about the meanings of these words. For example, the mean value for the word "frequently" was 67.8, but the standard deviation was 20.5; for "unlikely" it was 29.4 (SD = 33.0); and for "rare" 24.6 (SD = 30.5). Patient characteristics (age, sex and level of education) were not related to estimates.

Even if there is agreement between doctor and patient about the understanding of terms, the *meaning* of risk might be very different for a patient than the professional. A good example of this is provided by some research on parental choices about whether to have children after counselling for genetic diseases. Information given by genetic counsellors is often not used in the expected way. Instead of basing decisions on objective probabilities, prospective parents see the situation differently. Tymstra[57] quotes a woman who had a small chance of having an affected baby, but for her the probabilities were different: "There is a 2% chance that our child will be affected, but I always say: it might happen and it might not, so to me that means 50–50".

Patients may take many other factors into account when making a decision. Lippman-Hand and Fraser[58] found similar results. Instead of basing their decision to have children or not on the probabilities, they calculated whether they could or could not cope with the burden of having an affected child. If they felt they could cope, they would go ahead and attempt to become pregnant. Effectively, they made the decision on the basis of whether their resources were sufficient to cope with a negative outcome, not the objective probabilities. Perceptions of risk and benefit are also affected by the context. As shown in Box 11.3, the decision made can be heavily influenced by the context in which the information is given.[59]

Not only might a patient have preferences because of possible risks, but he or she might also be involved in the negotiation about the choice of treatment because of its effects on psychological well-being or social functioning. Attempts to define the efficacy of treatment come up against the difficulty of knowing what a "cure" might be. As in the case of psychiatric illness (Chapter 4), it is not always possible to say that a patient has completely recovered from a physical illness. No one measure is adequate to give a complete picture of recovery. A patient may recover from a myocardial infarction from a physiological point of view, but never return to work. Renal dialysis may prolong a life but create feelings of dependency. The word "cure" is certainly a relative term when it is applied to cancer, where there may be much suffering due to the treatment.[60]

BOX 11.3

Perceptions of risk

One of the better known studies on context was conducted on choices for receiving radiotherapy or surgery for cancer. Patients, doctors and students were first given a brief description of two treatments for lung cancer – radiotherapy and surgery. They were then given some statistics about the chances of living or dying as a result of these treatments. For *survival*, the descriptions were:

◆ Of 100 people having surgery, 90 will live through the surgery, 68 will be alive at the end of the first year, and 34 will be alive at the end of 5 years.

   Of 100 people having radiation therapy, all live through the treatment, 77 will be alive at the end of the first year, and 22 will be alive at the end of 5 years.   ◆

Which would you choose? In the sample studied, 18 per cent chose radiation therapy. However, your decision might change if you were given the chances of *dying*, as were another sample:

◆ Of 100 people having surgery, 10 will die during treatment, 32 will have died by one year, and 66 will have died by 5 years.

   Of 100 people having radiation therapy, none will die during treatment, 23 will die by 1 year, and 78 will die by 5 years.   ◆

Although the information was technically the same, the way it was framed made a significant difference to choices. Instead of 18 per cent favouring radiotherapy in the survival frame, 44 per cent chose radiotherapy in the mortality frame. This difference was no smaller for experienced physicians or for statistically sophisticated business students than for clinical patients.

In other words, the measures used to assess outcome may give results that are inconsistent with each other. The weighting given to one kind of measure (e.g. organic) over another kind (e.g. psychological) is largely a value judgement, rather than a scientific one. There is the need to choose treatments and assess their outcomes on the basis of several criteria, including the beliefs and attitudes of patients themselves.

Suggested reading

For a more comprehensive review of the doctor–patient relationship, see Pendleton, D. and Hasler, J. (eds) (1983) *Doctor–Patient Communication*, London: Academic Press. Winefield, H. (1992) Doctor–patient communication: an interpersonal helping process, in *International Review of Health Psychology*, vol. 1, Chichester: Wiley, pp. 167–187, provides a useful summary of research into doctor–patient communication. For a consideration of how patients, families and physicians cope with medical uncertainty, see Bursztajn, H., Feinbloom, R., Hamm, R. and Brodsky, A. (1990) *Medical Choices Medical Chances*, London: Routledge.

References

1. Epsom, J.D. (1978) The mobile health clinic: a report on a first year's work. In: Tuckett, D. and Kaufert, J. (eds) *Basic Readings in Medical Sociology*. London: Tavistock.
2. Banks, M.H., Beresford, S., Morrell, D., Walker, J. and Watkins, C. (1975) Factors influencing the demand for primary medical care in women aged 20–24 years. *International Journal of Epidemiology* 4: 189–195.
3. Goldberg, D. and Huxley, P. (1980) *Mental Illness in the Community*. London: Tavistock.
4. Robinson, D. (1971) *The Process of Becoming Ill*. London: Routledge and Kegan Paul.
5. Cowie, B. (1976) The cardiac patient's perception of his heart attack. *Social Science and Medicine* 10: 87–96.
6. Radye-Yarrow, M., Schwartz, C., Murphy, H. and Deasy, L. (1955) The psychological meaning of mental illness in the family. *Journal of Social Issues* 2: 12–24.
7. Suchman, E. and Phillips, B. (1958) An analysis of the validity of health questionnaires. *Social Forces* 36: 223–232.
8. Cartwright, A. (1979) Minor illness in the surgery: a response to a trivial, ill-defined or inappropriate service? In: *Management of Minor Illnesses*. London: King Edward's Hospital Fund.
9. Adam, S.A., Horner, J. and Vessey, M. (1980) Delay in treatment for breast cancer. *Community Medicine* 2: 195–201.
10. Koos, E.L. (1954) *The Health of Regionville*. New York: Columbia University Press. Copyright, by permission.
11. Zola, I.K. (1973) Pathways to the doctor – from person to patient. *Social Science and Medicine* 7: 677–689.
12. Sanders, G.S. (1982) Social comparisons and perceptions of health and illness. In: Sanders, G.S. and Suls, J. (eds) *Social Psychology of Health and Illness*. London: Lawrence Erlbaum.
13. Horwitz, A. (1978) Family, kin and friendship networks in psychiatric help-seeking. *Social Science and Medicine* 12A: 297–304.
14. Mechanic, D. (1964) Influence of mothers on their children's health attitudes and behaviour. *Pediatrics* 33: 445–453.
15. Ley, P. and Morris, L.A. (1984) Psychological aspects of written information for patients. In: Rachman, S. (ed.) *Contributions to Medical Psychology*, vol. 3. Oxford: Pergamon.
16. Maguire, G.P. (1976) The psychological and social sequelae of mastectomy. In: Howells, J. (ed.) *Modern Perspectives in Psychiatric Aspects of Surgery*. New York: Brunner/Mazel.
17. Batenburg, V. and Gerritsma, J. (1983) Medical interviewing: initial student problems. *Medical Education* 17: 235–239.
18. Maguire, P. and Rutter, D. (1976) Training medical students to communicate. In: Bennett, A.E. (ed.) *Communication between Doctors and Patients*. Oxford: Oxford University Press.
19. Maguire, P., Fairbairn, S. and Fletcher, C. (1986) Consultation skills of young doctors: 1 Benefits of feedback training in interviewing as students persist. *British Medical Journal* 292: 1573–1576.
20. Beckman, H. and Frankel, R. (1984) The effect of physician behaviour on the collection of data. *Annals of Internal Medicine* 101: 692–696.
21. Winefield, H. (1992) Doctor-patient communication: an interpersonal helping process. *International Review of Health Psychology*, vol. 1. Chichester: Wiley, pp. 167–187.
22. Bryne, P. and Long, B. (1976) *Doctors Talking to Patients*. London: HMSO.
23. Ekman, P. (1973) *Darwin and Facial Expression*. London: Academic Press.

24. Argyle, M. and Ingram, R. (1972) Gaze, mutual gaze and proximity. *Semiotica* **6**: 32-49.

25. Byrne, P.S. and Heath, C. (1980) Practitioners' use of non-verbal behaviour in real consultations. *Journal of the Royal College of General Practitioners* **30**: 327-331.

26. Hall, J., Harrigan, J. and Rosenthal, R. (1995) Non-verbal behaviour in clinician–patient interaction. *Applied and Preventive Psychology* **4**: 21-37.

27. Hall, E.T. (1969) *The Hidden Dimension*. London: Bodley Head.

28. Burns, T. (1964) Non-verbal communication. *Discovery* **25**: 30-37.

29. Ley, P. and Spelman, S. (1967) *Communicating with the Patient*. London: Staples Press.

30. Robinson, E. (1992) Patients' contributions to the consultations. In: Broome, A. (ed.) *Health Psychology*. London: Chapman and Hall, pp. 131-150.

31. Jourard, S.M. (1966) An exploratory study of body accessibility. *British Journal of Social and Clinical Psychology* **5**: 221-231.

32. Johnson, B.S. (1965) The meaning of touch in nursing. *Nursing Outlook* **13**: 59-60.

33. Cunningham, C. (1979) Parent counselling. In: Craft, M. (ed.) *Tregold's Mental Retardation*, 12th edn. London: Baillière Tindall.

34. Svarstad, B.L. and Lipton, H. (1977) Informing parents about mental retardation. *Social Science and Medicine* **11**: 645-651.

35. Armstrong, G., Jones, G., Race, D. and Ruddock, J. (1980) *Mentally Handicapped Under Five*. University of Sheffield: Evaluation Research Group Report 8.

36. Hogbin, B. and Fallowfield, L. (1989) Getting it taped: the "bad news" consultation in a general surgical outpatients department. *British Journal of Hospital Medicine* **41**: 330-333.

37. DiMatteo, M.R. and Taranta, A. (1979) Non-verbal communication and physician–patient rapport. *Professional Psychology* **17**: 540-547.

38. Kent, G., Clarke, P. and Dalrymple-Smith, D. (1981) The patient is the expert. *Medical Education* **15**: 38-42.

39. Buckman, R.(1992) *How to Break Bad News. A Guide for Health Care Professionals*. London: Papermac.

40. Teasdale, K. and Kent, G. (1995) The use of deception in nursing. *Journal of Medical Ethics* **21**: 77-81.

41. Siegler, M. (1982) Confidentiality in medicine - a decrepit concept. *The New England Journal of Medicine* **24**: 1518-1521.

42. Weiss, B. (1982) Confidentiality expectations of patients, physicians and medical students. *Journal of the American Medical Association* **247**: 2695-2697.

43. Thomas, K.B. (1974) Temporarily dependent patients in general practice. *British Medical Journal* **1**: 625-626.

44. Bain, D.J.G. (1983) Diagnostic behaviour and prescribing. *British Medical Journal* **287**: 1269-1270.

45. Marsh, G.N. (1981) Stringent prescribing in general practice. *British Medical Journal* **283**: 1159-1160.

46. Hemminki, E. (1975) Review of literature on factors affecting drug prescribing. *Social Science and Medicine* **9**: 111-115.

47. Melville, A. (1980) Job satisfaction in general practice: implications for prescribing. *Social Science and Medicine* **14A**: 495-499.

48. Melville, A. (1980) Reducing whose anxiety? In: Mapes, R. (ed.) *Prescribing Practice and Drug Use*. London: Croom Helm.

49. Haefner, D.P., Sacks, J. and Mason, A. (1960) Physicians' attitudes towards chemotherapy as a factor in psychiatric patients' responses to medication. *Journal of Nervous and Mental Diseases* **131**: 64-69.

50. Staudemayer, H. and Lefkowitz, M.S. (1981) Physician–patient psychosocial characteristics influencing medical decision-making. *Social Science and Medicine* **15E**: 77-81.

51. Bakin, H. (1945) Pseudocia pediatrica. *New England Journal of Medicine* **232**: 691-697.

52. Stockwell, H. and Vayda, E. (1979) Variations in surgery in Ontario. *Medical Care* **17**: 390-396.

53. Howie, J.G.R. (1964) Too few appendectomies? *Lancet* **1**: 1240-1242.

54. Campbell, D.M. (1984) Why do physicians in neonatal care units differ in their admission thresholds? *Social Science and Medicine* **18**: 365-374.

55. McNeil, B. (1978) Fallacy of the five-year survival in lung cancer. *New England Journal of Medicine* **299**: 1397-1404.

56. Sutherland, H., Lockwood, G., Tritchler, D., Sem, F., Brooks, L. and Till, J. (1991) Communicating probabilistic information to cancer patients: is there noise on the line? *Social Science and Medicine* **32**: 725-731.

57. Tymstra, T. (1989) The imperative character of medical technology and the meaning of "anticipated decision regret". *International Journal of Technology Assessment in Health Care* **5**: 207-213.

58. Lippman-Hand, A. and Fraser, F. (1979) Genetic

counselling: Parents' responses to uncertainty. *Birth Defects: Original Article Series* **15** (5C): 325–339.

59. McNeil, B., Pauker, S. and Tversky, A. (1988) On the framing of medical decisions. In: Bell, D., Raiffa, H. and Tversky, A. (eds) *Decision making. Descriptive, normative and prescriptive interactions*. Cambridge: Cambridge University Press.

60. Rosser, J.E. and Maguire, G.P. (1982) Dilemmas in general practice: the care of the cancer patient. *Social Science and Medicine* **16**: 315–322.

12
Compliance

SUMMARY

This chapter concerns compliance – the extent to which patients do or do not follow their doctors' advice and the factors which affect this aspect of doctor–patient communication. Factors include family support, the patient's own views about the illness, and difficulties in remembering and understanding advice.

Medical care can result in negative as well as positive consequences for patients, including the side-effects of drugs and adverse reactions to hospitalization. One of the more significant recent developments in medicine involves screening for genetic diseases, which raises a number of ethical and emotional issues.

Non-compliance is said to occur if a patient makes an error in dosage or timing or takes other medications that interact dangerously. Davis[1] reported that most of the physicians in his sample believed that when they prescribed a drug, most or all of their patients complied promptly and accurately. However, empirical investigations of adherence suggest that this expectation is an unrealistic overestimation. Further, doctors do not seem able to distinguish between patients who comply and those who do not.[2]

Studies on this issue have given various indications of the degree of non-compliance, ranging from about 4 to 92 per cent, with a median of about 45 per cent. The wide range of reported findings may be due to various factors such as design and measurement. Some researchers have taken 90 per cent compliance as satisfactory while others have insisted on 100 per cent. If patients are simply asked about their adherence, the rate can appear reassuring but if objective tests are taken (e.g. urine or stool analysis) the rate of adherence is often much lower. Thus simply asking a patient if he or she has followed advice does not seem to be a valid way of measuring compliance.[3]

One study which demonstrates low compliance was conducted with parents of children who were on a 10-day course of penicillin prescribed for streptococcal infection. Although most of the parents correctly identified the child's diagnosis, knew the name of the medication and how to obtain it, few of them ensured the completion of the programme. Although the medication was free, their physicians were aware of the study and the families were given advance notification that they would be visited, by the third day 59 per cent of the children were not receiving penicillin and by the sixth day only 29 per cent were continuing treatment. The first section of the chapter includes suggestions about how adherence to doctors' advice can be improved.

The emphasis placed here on compliance is not intended to suggest that it is necessarily important that patients always follow advice. It has been noted that there is often an implicit assumption that patients should obey their doctors' instructions and failure to do so indicates some kind of deficiency within the patient. The terms used by some researchers – obedience, refusal, failure to co-operate, indeed the words "patient" and "compliance" themselves – suggest that some blame lies with a person who does not follow advice. Such a view can be justified only if the doctor–patient relationship is seen as an authoritarian one, with the physician being the expert who knows what is best.

This paternalistic view has been strongly challenged in recent years, with many preferring to consider the relationship as one in which both parties *negotiate* a course of action. Seen in this way, it may not be appropriate for patients always to adhere to their doctor's advice. Indeed, it has been argued that this is unimportant for many conditions.[4] As considered here, compliance is used as an example of how doctor–patient communication can succeed or fail, depending on the care physicians take in understanding patients' needs and circumstances. Compliance is more appropriately seen as a dependent measure of communicative success, rather than an end in itself.

In another respect, compliance can be detrimental to health. This chapter also gives a brief outline of some of the research on iatrogenic illnesses – difficulties that result from medical care. In part, such conditions are a result of a medical system that includes large hospitals, where the risk of infection is high, and a reliance on drugs that may have unexpected side-effects. Because of such risks, people may come to believe that the disadvantages of medical care outweigh the advantages.

Factors affecting compliance

Several suggestions have been put forward to account for the low rates of compliance mentioned above. One aim of research in this area has been to identify factors which are associated with reduced compliance. A secondary aim has been to take steps to minimize their influence. Although Davis[1] reported that two-thirds of the doctors in his sample attributed non-compliance to patients' uncooperative personalities, few associations between compliance and this aspect of personality have been found.

There is evidence that examining factors which affect compliance can have positive results. Inui *et al.*[5] randomly assigned hospital doctors responsible for hypertensive patients to one of two groups. One group received a 1–2-hour tutorial on compliance while the other group served as a comparison. The experimental group was encouraged to be sceptical about compliance and many of the factors which will be outlined below were discussed. For the patients of the doctors in the tutored group, there was a 40 per cent increase in the number taking most of their pills, and at the end of the study hypertension was considered to be adequately controlled in 67 per cent of the patients of the tutored group but in only in 36 per cent of the patients of the untutored group. The patients of the tutored doctors were also found to be more knowledgeable about their drug regime and dietary requirements and had more accurate views of the seriousness of the disease, the efficacy of the drugs, and the consequences of not taking them. These results indicate that, with greater awareness on the part of physicians, non-compliance can be reduced. Aspects of the problem have been investigated as described below.

Family circumstances

An individual's unique circumstances, such as the level of family support, influence the decision to comply or not comply with medical advice. For example, mothers who report that they have difficulty in caring for their children tend to be non-compliant and the example set by others in the family is also significant. Osterweis *et al.*[6] looked at the strength of the association between use of medication in individuals and their families. They found that use by other family members was a good predictor, a better one than severity of the illness.

The actual presence of family members living with the patient seems to be related to compliance in adults as well. In one study patients living with a spouse or relatives were found to be twice as likely to take their medication as those living in isolation. There is also evidence that the degree of medical supervision is relevant. Hare and Wilcox[7] reported that non-compliance was found in only 19 per cent of in-patients, 37 per cent of day patients and 49 per cent of out-patients. Results such as these have led to the suggestion that teaching self-medication while in hospital may increase out-patient compliance.

It should also be pointed out that compliance with medical advice is often considered in broader terms than simply pill-taking. Francis *et al.*[8] asked mothers why they missed appointments made for their children. Some of the most frequent replies were lack of transport and the presence of other family problems. It seems that the decision to make and keep appointments is not as closely related to the severity of the illness as to its relative urgency. Gabrielson *et al.*[9] examined factors that affected parents' decisions to make an appointment with a doctor when a school nurse indicated one was needed. Over 90 per cent of the parents who saw the condition as more urgent than other family problems complied, whereas 50 per cent of the parents who felt it was not as urgent disregarded the advice. Compliance appears to be related to the costs and benefits to the individual and these will be affected by his or her unique circumstances.

The treatment regime

The treatment regime influences the degree of compliance in several ways. One reason for non-compliance is disruption to normal routines. The complexity of the regime is important, in that as the number of drugs or their frequency is increased, the likelihood of compliance is decreased. Hulka *et al.*[10] who examined the compliance rates of patients with diabetes or congestive heart failure, found fewer than 15 per cent errors when only one drug was prescribed, 25 per cent when there were two or three, and 35 per cent errors when more than five drugs were used to control these conditions. Similarly, the frequency with which pills should be taken is associated with compliance. One report indicated a doubling in the number of patients not complying when the frequency was increased from one to four tablets per day.

Side-effects

Another way in which a treatment regime may affect compliance concerns unpleasant side-effects. Adherence could be expected to decrease if the treatment feels more painful than the illness. However, the relative contribution of this aspect of treatment may be smaller than imagined: only 17 per cent of patients treated for hypertension mentioned this as a reason for stopping treatment. Possibly the degree to which side-effects lower compliance is related to whether patients have been led to expect them. The type of side-effect is also important. Patients report that they are more likely to stop taking medications if the drug alters cognitive abilities – e.g. ability to concentrate and sense of balance – than if it affects physical well-being – such as nausea or aches.

Nor would side-effects necessarily have to be actually experienced. Elling *et al.*[11] reported that one reason why mothers gave inadequate dosages of penicillin to their children with rheumatic fever was their concern over the long-term effects of such a medication. One mother gave her child only some of the medication because she believed strong drugs should be given sparingly.

Patients' beliefs

This last point is related to another factor: patients' beliefs about the efficacy of a particular treatment. On the one hand, there is the question of diagnosis. A patient could not be expected to follow a physician's advice if he or she did not believe that the doctor had the condition correctly identified. Becker *et al.*[12] measured both the degree to which mothers agreed with the physician's diagnosis and their opinions of how certain the doctor was of the diagnosis for their children. They combined these measures to give a "degree of certainty" score and found that this measure was predictive of compliance. The higher the certainty score the more closely were the doctor's recommendations followed.

Even if both doctor and patient agree on the diagnosis, however, there is agreement about the treatment to be considered. This, too, must make sense to the patient. It may be necessary for the patient's beliefs about the causes of the illness to be similar to the doctor's. For example, many people believe that the "cause" of ulcers is emotional (e.g. anger), while few see the stomach's acidity as relevant. If a patient believes that emotions alone are responsible, then the necessity for acid neutralization would not be apparent and the point of small meals and drugs less sensible.

In attempting to reduce the incidence of cervical cancer, screening clinics have been operating for several years. Yet only some women attend these clinics. Compared with non-attenders, women who followed the advice for screening were more likely to believe that (1) the test could detect the cancer, (2) the test could detect the cancer before the women themselves could notice it, and (3) that early detection leads to a more favourable prognosis.[13] The non-attenders apparently saw little reason to come since they did not believe in the efficacy of the screening. Similarly, Gabrielson et al.[9] found a relationship between parents' faith in the effectiveness of professional care and their decision to take up the school nurse's advice to seek further help. Thus, the patient's beliefs about the illness and treatment are of clear relevance to compliance.

A different kind of issue concerns the loss of control over one's routines. People with diabetes, for example, may be required to adhere to a strict diet or take insulin at specified times. Many studies have shown that adolescents in particular can come to resent such restrictions, partly because they set them apart from their friends. As a result many diabetics test the limits of their diets or treatments in order to gain some control over the regime. Although such testing can have negative consequences, it is possible to use this need for control in positive ways, as in giving patients choices about the treatment to be used. For example Bradley et al.[14] offered diabetic patients the choice of an insulin pump, intensified conventional treatment or continuation with the current regime of injections.

Nature of the illness

The severity of the illness could be expected to affect the degree of compliance. However, it is not the objective severity but the patient's *perception* of severity that is significant. There is little relationship between doctors' views of seriousness of condition and compliance, but the way in which a patient views the illness does have some predictive value. In the research mentioned above by Gabrielson et al.,[9] parental belief that their child's condition was sufficiently serious to affect their school work was associated with seeking help.

Related to perceived seriousness is perceived susceptibility. Continued use of penicillin prophylaxis in patients with a history of rheumatic fever was related to their subjective estimate of the likelihood of having another attack as well as their view of the seriousness of the attack.[15] Similarly, mothers who felt that their children contracted illness easily and often and who perceived illness as a serious threat to children in general, were more likely to give medication and to keep follow-up appointments than mothers who did not hold these views.

Other indications that perceived seriousness is important for compliance come from work concerning patients' decisions to end treatment. If how the person feels is a significant factor, then it would be expected that as symptoms are reduced, compliance would decrease. This expectation is supported by several studies. For example, Caldwell et al.[16] asked patients why they had discontinued therapy: the most frequent reason, mentioned by 39 per cent, was that they now felt well. Again, compliance seems to be related to the sick role: if someone no longer feels ill, then some of the expectations surrounding the sick role – which include co-operation with the doctor – may no longer apply.

A third feature of illness is its duration. A good example of an illness that requires long-term control is diabetes. Charrey[17] examined the adherence rates in people with diabetes who had been diagnosed either 1–5 years or more than 20 years before the study. Although non-compliance was 30 per cent in the newly diagnosed group, longer term patients showed an 80 per cent non-compliance rate. Other studies have indicated that as illness passes the acute stage patients seem less likely to adhere to the treatment regime.

Understanding

Even if patients felt able to cope with situational factors, had confidence in their treatment and believed that non-compliance could have serious consequences, they would nevertheless be unable to adhere to their physician's recommendations if they did not understand them.

The extent of misunderstanding can be surprising. For example, Boyd et al.[18] found that about 60 per cent of patients misunderstood their doctors' verbal directions about the method for taking medication. This is not an unusual result. The lack of understanding may be due to factors such as doctors' belief that patients are not concerned with understanding their treatment (and therefore do not take care to explain it) or because patients do not ask questions when they are unclear about recommendations.

Doctors may also overestimate the knowledge that patients possess. Boyle[19] found a high proportion of people had incorrect beliefs about the location of their internal organs: 80 per cent wrongly located their stomachs and 58 per cent their hearts. Another possibility is that material given to patients is too difficult for many to understand. There are ways of estimating the percentage of the population who could be expected to understand a given piece of writing. In one study these techniques were applied to leaflets explaining X-rays: for some of these leaflets, only 40 per cent of the target population could be expected to understand them.[20] Some suggestions for improving the way in which leaflets are written are outlined later in the chapter.

Studies concerning the interpretation of labels on medicine bottles indicate that here, too, lack of understanding is prevalent. Often, this is due to ambiguity in the instructions. In one project, the researchers asked people to specify when they would take the medication given the instructions on the bottles. Some of the results from this study are shown in Table 12.1. Taking thioridazine first, only 13.4 per cent interpreted the instructions correctly – three dosages spread throughout the 24 hours. Apparently, many considered the day to mean only the waking day, some 18 hours. In the case of penicillin G, 89.5 per cent would take the drug after meals, whereas it ought to be taken on an empty stomach. Conversely, nitrofurantoin should be taken on a full stomach, but 53.7 per cent said they would take it before eating. These results can be compared with interpretations when the instructions are more specific and less ambiguous, as shown in Table 12.2. Here a much smaller proportion made mistakes.[21]

Remembering

Yet another factor to be considered is memory. Patients would need to remember the recommendations if they are to take medication

Table 12.1 Interpretations given to some labels on medicine bottles (Reproduced from Mazzulo, J.M., Lasagna, L. and Griner, P.F. (1974) *Journal of the American Medical Association* **227**: 929–931, with permission of American Medical Association.)

Medication and instructions	Interpretation	% Subjects giving interpretation
1 Thioridazine '3 times a day'	With meals	80.5
	Every 8 hours	13.4
	10 a.m., 2 p.m., 6 p.m.	4.4
2 Penicillin G '3 times a day and at bedtime'	After meals and at bedtime	89.5
	10 a.m., 2 p.m., 6 p.m., 10 p.m.	4.5
	Other	5.0
3 Nitrofurantoin 'with meals'	Before	53.7
	With	32.8
	After	13.4

Table 12.2 Percentages of subjects who gave correct and incorrect interpretations to instructions on medicine bottles when the instructions were made less ambiguous (Reproduced from Mazzulo, J.M., Lasagna, L. and Griner, P.F. (1974) *Journal of the American Medical Association* **227**: 929–931, with permission of American Medical Association.)

Medication and instructions	Interpretation	Percentage
1 Penicillin G '30 minutes before meals and at bedtime'	Correct	91.0
	Incorrect	9.0
2 Nitrofurantoin 'to be taken immediately after meals, 4 times a day'	Correct	85.1
	Incorrect	14.9

without error. Svarstad[22] reported that more than 50 per cent of the patients he interviewed made at least one error in describing their doctors' recommendations one week after the consultation. As expected, those patients who remembered more accurately adhered more completely. Other evidence indicates that many of the doctor's statements are forgotten much more quickly than within one week. Different studies have found that patients had forgotten about 40 per cent within 80 minutes, 50 per cent within 5 minutes and over 50 per cent immediately after the consultation. It also seems that the number of statements forgotten increases with the number given, such that a patient could be expected to remember three out of four statements, but only four out of eight. Perhaps the high rate of forgetting found in these studies is due to a tendency to give too many directions at one time.

Improving recall

Some solutions to the difficulties that memory poses to doctor–patient communication have been suggested. One possibility is to reduce the number of instructions to a minimum, reserving advice for only the most important aspects. Another suggestion comes from experimental work on the psychology of memory – the "primacy effect". People remember the first item they hear better than subsequent items. That is, they recall best what they hear first. Ley[23] reported that when advice in a consultation was given first, as compared to when it was usually given, recall increased from 44 to 75 per cent. In the same study, he also asked physicians to stress the significance of advice that they considered crucial: in this condition recall increased from 44 to 64 per cent. A third possibility concerns the specificity with which advice is given. Bradshaw et al.[24] provide evidence that recall of instructions about dieting increases if the advice is specific (i.e. "You must lose 7lb in weight") rather than general (e.g. "You must lose weight"). Patients who were given specific instructions recalled 49 per cent of the advice, whereas patients given general recommendations remembered only 19 per cent. It was shown above that precise instructions are understood more readily than vague ones: it also appears that precise advice can be recalled more readily.

There are other ways to assist memory. One approach is to give patients a tape recording of the consultation which, as shown in Chapter 11, can be a very powerful aid for patients when transmitting bad news, but it can also be used more routinely, as was illustrated by a study in one hospital where patients were given a tape recording of their final interview before discharge. At this time the history was reviewed, a final physical examination was given, the

---

BOX 12.1

Writing leaflets

Many hospitals now provide short leaflets for patients which give information about general hospital procedures as well as some details about their care. However, many patients have difficulty in understanding these leaflets, partly because the educational attainments of the readers will often be less than that of the writers. Reading ease can be calculated through the following formula:

Reading ease $= 206.835 - 0.84wl - 1.05sl$

where wl = the number of syllables per 100 words (a measure of word length) and sl = number of words per sentence. A score below 60 is considered fairly difficult, below 50 difficult. For material designed for children, the score should be much higher, perhaps over 90 plus.[28]

Several stylistic factors need to be taken into account.[29] These include:

1 Using active rather than passive verbs
2 Using concrete rather than abstract words
3 Stating ideas explicitly rather than implicitly
4 Using numbering when presenting facts
5 Using the same words consistently when referring to a disease or treatment

In addition, the typeface is important. Poulton et al.[30] give some guidelines:

1 Type should be at least 10 point
2 Printing in capital letters reduces speed of comprehension
3 Printing in italics reduces speed of reading
4 Headings will stand out better if a different typeface is used
5 Unjustified lines are easier to read.

laboratory findings were outlined and the treatment discussed. When asked about the usefulness of the tape recording later, the patients reported that they had listened to it $3\frac{1}{2}$ times on average, indicating that most were unable to assimilate all the information on first or even second hearing.[25]

Many doctors now use written information.[26] In one study, patients leaving hospital were given detailed information concerning their diagnosis, the name, dosage and purpose of the drugs prescribed, and some general advice on diet. All were given this material verbally but, in addition, about half were also provided with the information in written form, which they could take away with them. When they returned for follow-up, both groups were asked about their recollections of the information: significantly more material was remembered by those patients who had been given both verbal and written material.[27] Box 12.1 gives some advice on writing material for patients.

The doctor–patient relationship

The quality of this relationship (often measured by patients' satisfaction with their care) is also relevant to compliance. Ben-Sira[31] points out that patients can have little knowledge of the principles of diagnosis and treatment, being unable to judge the technical competence of their doctor accurately. Also, since medical treatment usually does not give immediate relief from physical disturbance, the quality of the relationship is the main source of information available to the patient about the doctor's skill. Ben-Sira found that patients' satisfaction was closely related to their doctors' show of concern and interest. Satisfaction was highest when the doctor related to the patient as a person and not as a "case". Patients were more likely to turn elsewhere when they felt dissatisfied with the personal aspects of their care than with the technical aspects. In other words, the way the doctor cared for the patients seemed more important to them than the treatments given.

This raises an interesting question about physician style. Should doctors be informal and friendly, or should they be distant and authoritarian? Szasz and Hollander[32] distinguish three approaches. The first is where the doctor is active and the patient passive. This approach is very "doctor-centred", with the physician being completely in charge, deciding on treatment without taking the patients' wishes and views into account. Such a relationship would be appropriate to emergency settings, where the treatment takes place with little psychological involvement from the patient. The second approach is termed guidance–co-operation where, like a teacher guiding a student, the doctor would tailor treatment to the individual but nevertheless knows "what is best". In such a relationship the power resides with the doctor who can ask many questions while the patient simply replies. In the third approach, mutual participation, the consultation becomes a negotiation where both participants are aware of each other's individuality. The doctor has knowledge and skills that the patient does not possess, but these are put at the patient's disposal. The patient has the right to accept or refuse them.

Most studies have found that the authoritarian approach is not conducive to compliance and satisfaction. It is likely that the "correct" approach depends on the individual patient (some may prefer and expect the guidance–co-operation approach, for example) and the condition (for long-term compliance, as for diabetes mellitus and chronic heart disease, mutual participation seems best). Problems may arise when the doctor is working under one approach (perhaps being authoritarian) while the patient would prefer another approach (perhaps more mutual negotiation).

In any case, intimacy seems important. Patients who did not keep appointments in one study tended to be those who felt they could not talk easily and intimately with their doctor.[33] Similarly, patients who described their physicians as "personal" adhered to instructions better than those who described them as "business-like".[34] Some continuity of care may be significant: seeing the same doctor on subsequent visits increases the probability of compliance and appointment-keeping.[35]

Satisfaction with care
Some of these aspects of doctor–patient communication are often out of an individual doctor's

control or awareness, but many of the factors discussed above (taking care that patients are able to remember recommendations, using time to understand the patient's beliefs about his or her illness, and taking the patient's unique circumstances into account when giving advice) can all be expected to improve the quality of the relationship. Other research has shown that ensuring adequate understanding of information given to patients in hospital increases their satisfaction with care. Certainly, inability to find out what they want to know about their condition, their treatment and the hospital routine have been found to be among the most frequently expressed complaints by hospitalized patients.[35]

One difficulty with some of these studies is that the researchers simply asked patients about their understanding, compliance and satisfaction. The relationships discovered between these variables could therefore simply be due to patient characteristics: i.e. that the same people who report they were satisfied would also report that they understood and would adhere to their physician's advice. Other patients may report that they are unhappy with their care regardless of the behaviour of the physician. An alternative method could be to measure what a patient knows about the treatment and compare this with what the doctor said the patient was told. If these two measures correspond, the communication could be said to be successful. This procedure, used with patients with diabetes mellitus, has indicated that there is an association between these two measures: patients who receive the message which the doctor intends to give tend to be satisfied with their care.[36]

An alternative research approach would be to observe examples of doctor–patient communication, take measures of behaviour which could be important, and then see if these measures relate to feelings of satisfaction and evidence of compliance. Using this method, failure to follow advice has been related to certain kinds of doctors' behaviour: these include collecting information but ignoring patients' requests for feedback, and concentrating on their patients' medical situation but ignoring their psychological and social circumstances.[37]

BOX 12.2

A summary of the findings related to patient compliance and successful doctor–patient communication

- *Family circumstances* The support given by the patient's family and the difficulties the family faces are relevant. Complying with a physician's advice involves costs as well as benefits.
- *Treatment regime* The frequency and number of drugs prescribed have an effect, as do the patient's views of the side-effects and efficacy of treatment.
- *Nature of the illness* The patient's perception of the severity of the illness and of the consequences of non-compliance (rather than medical views) are significant. Compliance decreases with length of illness and with improvement in health.
- *Understanding* Patients cannot adhere to a doctor's recommendations if they do not understand them. The difficulty and ambiguity of material given to patients is often underestimated.
- *Remembering* Many patients do not comply simply because they cannot remember the doctor's instructions. Some solutions to this problem include giving important instructions first, reducing the number of instructions to a minimum and making recommendations specific.
- *The doctor–patient relationship* The quality of the relationship is associated with compliance, in that patients who are satisfied with the interpersonal aspects of their care are more likely to follow advice.

Some important work has been conducted on communications between paediatricians and mothers who had brought their children to emergency casualty clinics. Medical interviews were tape recorded, the patients' charts reviewed and follow-up interviews were conducted. In this research, mothers' satisfaction with their care was related to the friendliness of the doctors and their show of understanding and concern for the children. The use of medical jargon was inversely related to satisfaction. In another study using the same research methods, a significant positive correlation was found between doctors' warmth and patients' compliance.[38]

Interestingly, there was little association between the duration of the consultation and mothers' satisfaction or mothers' knowledge of the diagnosis,[39] a result also found in studies of general practice. Patients report that they are satisfied with the length of the consultation if they are given the opportunity to say what they want to say. These findings indicate that the way in which the time is used is more important than the actual length of the consultation. The type of verbal behaviour that made the largest single contribution to patient satisfaction was the giving of objective information about the illness and treatment. Many of the verbal and non-verbal aspects of interviewing discussed in the previous chapter are important for the quality of the doctor–patient relationship. Box 12.2 presents a summary of the variables found to be important for compliance and satisfaction with care.

Iatrogenic illness

Behind the research on compliance lies the assumption that it is always in patients' best interests to follow their physicians' advice. Not all writers agree with this. Some have contended that the way medicine is organized in Western societies sometimes works to the detriment of patients. A leading proponent of this position is Illich,[40] who discusses iatrogenic illness (*iatros*, Greek for physician; *genesis*, meaning origin).

Clinical iatrogenic illness refers to the ways in which physicians, hospitals and medical technology more generally can be pathogens or "sickening agents". The prescription of thalidomide to help women during pregnancy is an instance that is often cited in this respect, but there are other more recent examples. In one project, all the patients who entered a hospital over a one-year period were studied. One in 12 had some major adverse reaction to their care, particularly to the drugs they were given. About one-quarter of the deaths in the hospital during that time were considered to be due to adverse drug reaction.[41]

Hospitalization

In fact, hospitals can be particularly dangerous places. Earlier in the book, several studies have been described which illustrate that entering hospital can be stressful and distressing. Such studies have included the need to cope with unfamiliar surroundings and the disturbing experience of viewing other patients' deaths (Chapter 9). There can also be problems with infections. In a survey of British hospitals, 19 per cent of the patients were diagnosed as having an infection – about half of these were acquired while in hospital.[42] Even in many cases of severe and acute illness, hospital care may not be necessary. Some studies of the effectiveness of coronary units have suggested that their popularity is not commensurate with their clinical effectiveness. Mather[43] randomly assigned coronary patients to home care with the support of family doctors or to intensive care in hospitals: they found no difference in mortality.

Another area of medical care which has received criticism concerns childbirth. Some advocates argue that women who are giving birth are not "patients" but women performing a natural act. They cite evidence that women who have babies at home run a lesser risk for themselves or their children than those who enter hospital,[44] a result which does not seem to be due to more "at-risk" women being hospitalized.[45] However, the evidence is not unequivocal in this respect. A recent randomized trial with women who had low-risk pregnancies showed that transfers from a midwifery unit to the labour ward were required in about half the deliveries, and that it was difficult to determine before labour whether difficulties would arise.[46]

It may be that part of the problem is the way women are confined to bed soon after they arrive at hospital. Flinn et al.[47] asked mothers-to-be if they would be willing to walk about during the first stage of labour (when the cervix is dilating) rather than be kept in bed. Of those women who expressed an interest, half were nursed in bed with traditional procedures. The other half were allowed to walk about, visiting the television room to be with friends and relatives or making a drink in the kitchen. All women were nursed in bed during the second and third stages of labour. When the birth records of these two groups of women were compared, the ambulant mothers had shorter first stages (on average 2 hours shorter), were more likely to have a normal delivery, and required less analgesia. Their foetal heart rate pattern was also more satisfactory during the birth. The researchers took Apgar scores of the infants, which gave an indication of their general health and responsiveness at birth: the scores of the ambulant group were significantly better. Results such as these argue against routine medical interference at birth.

The value of episiotomy during birth has also been questioned: cutting the perineum causes much discomfort for months afterwards, and there is little empirical justification for its routine use.[48] Additionally, there is disagreement about the currently routine practice of delaying discharge of low-birthweight babies until they have reached some criterion weight. Such enforced separations may have negative consequences for the parents' relationship with the baby and are certainly distressing for the parents.[49] When the policy at one maternity hospital was changed so that the timing of discharge was determined not so much by weight as by feeding patterns and satisfactory conditions at home, no increase in complications was found.[50]

Genetic screening

One area where there have been considerable advances in knowledge in recent years is in the identification of genetic links for certain diseases. People have become aware that certain diseases can run in families. For some, such as coronary heart disease and breast cancer, only vulnerability can be ascertained, while for others, such as Huntington's, it is now possible to carry out a test in order to determine whether a person will develop the disease in the future.

This information has a number of possible benefits. In the case of coronary heart disease, for example, people can take steps such as increasing their level of exercise or altering their diet to reduce their susceptibility. In the case of Huntington's, prospective parents can make more informed choices about reproduction.

However, this information has costs as well.

Giving news of possible heart disease can increase anxiety. Some patients report that they often suffer from such intrusive thoughts as "I find myself thinking about it at odd moments" and "any reminder brings back emotions about it" or avoidance reactions such as "I avoid letting myself get emotional about it when I think of it". For some people such concerns may last for several months or years.[51]

Boutte[52] explored the meanings of being at risk for Machado–Joseph disease amongst adults whose parents or siblings had been affected. Machado–Joseph disease is similar to Huntington's disease in both hereditary pattern (an autosomal dominant disorder meaning that a child of an affected patient has a 50 per cent chance of developing the disease) and in symptoms of spinocerebellar degeneration (including muscular weakness, a staggering gait and uncoordinated body movements) which generally begin to appear between 20 and 40 years of age. Death usually occurs after 10–15 years of steady deterioration, often as a result of a respiratory infection.

One of Boutte's main findings was that, in common with other genetically determined diseases, those at risk were forever vigilant for symptoms of the disease, often mistaking occasional stumblings and other normal incidents as early manifestations of progression of the disease. Such vigilance could dominate their lives and their plans for the future, as indicated by the following quotations from interviews:

66 My friends say they don't watch me for symptoms. I do. Every time I trip over a telephone cord I get worried. My husband says just to relax, but he never saw my father. He doesn't know what this disease does to you. (p. 842) 99

66 When my daughter wanted to get married I told her boyfriend point blank and matter of fact that my mother had died of it and that I had two sisters with it. I said that we didn't know if I was going to get it or not . . . If I did then there was a 50 per cent chance that my daughter would get it and the possibility of any children they might have of getting it . . . Only one of my kids got married without telling. One son got

married without telling his wife and they are now divorced. (p. 842) "

On the face of it, the development of tests to ascertain whether or not the person carries the relevant gene could reduce emotional distress. As we saw in Chapter 1, people strive to reduce uncertainty in their lives. Information from genetic assessments could be used to inform the choices people make about their lives by increasing certainty about the future. The difficulty is that these tests are themselves not 100 per cent certain: there will always be a proportion of false positives (some people who appear to have the gene will in fact not be affected) and false negatives (the genetic marker will be missed). In screening for children with Down's syndrome, for example, about 40 per cent of affected foetuses will not be detected. It seems possible that parents who had been given a false negative result might have increased difficulties in adjusting to the birth of a child with Down's than if the test had never been offered. Conversely, some parents are given a false positive, which could result in the termination of an unaffected child.

There is the concern that screening can increase anxiety and distress, at least until a result is known. For example, Robinson *et al.*[53] interviewed women whose blood samples indicated raised amniotic fluid alpha foeto-protein (AFP) levels, which is an indication for open neural tube defects found in anencephaly and spina bifida. They found that the women's levels of anxiety were extremely high and only returned to normal levels after they had received a normal result. It some instances, anxiety can remain high even when the test indicates no abnormality. Because of such distress, it can be argued that clinicians have an obligation to take any steps which could reduce anxiety.[54]

Ethical issues

Several ethical problems associated with genetic testing have already been mentioned, particularly the emotional distress and unnecessary interventions due to false negatives and false positives. There are two additional concerns which deserve notice. First, the implications of gathering this information when no intervention is possible can be severe. Little is known about the longer term

effects on those who initially seem able to cope with bad news about Huntington's but who may become increasingly distressed as the time of onset draws nearer.[55] The rate of suicide amongst people affected by Huntington's disease is much higher than for the general population, although it is unclear whether this is due to an awareness of unavoidable deterioration or to progression of the disease.[56]

Foetal screening is particularly problematic because of its association with eugenics. Part of the justification for pre-natal screening is that the pregnancy could be terminated if the parents so wished. Such a course of action might be justified on the basis of cost to society, of distress to the parents and of the child's own future. However, the quality of life of people affected by genetically based diseases can be as good as for unimpaired people. Many Down's children live long and fulfilling lives. Ethical questions about screening for Down's include whether screening is designed for the well-being of the family or whether its purpose is more economic (a termination is much cheaper than the possibility of life-long care), and whether a decision to terminate is made on the basis of inaccurate beliefs about the severity of conditions (many Down's children are very competent and do not conform to the stereotype of severe incapacity). For all these reasons, genetic screening raises a number of ethical and emotional issues.

Suggested reading

More detail about research on compliance can be found in DiMatteo, M.R. and DiNicola, D.D. (1982) *Achieving Patient Compliance*, Oxford: Pergamon, while Marteau, T. (1993) Health-related screening: Psychological predictors of uptake and impact. *International Review of Health Psychology*, vol. 2, Chichester: Wiley, pp. 149–174, discusses various aspects of screening.

References

1. Davis, M.S. (1966) Variations in patients' compliance with doctors' orders. *Journal of Medical Education* **41**: 1037–1048.
2. Kasl, S.V. (1975) Issues in patient adherence to health care regimes. *Journal of Human Stress* **1**: 5–18.

3. Norell, S.E. (1981) Accuracy of patient interviews and estimates by clinical staff in determining medication compliance. *Social Science and Medicine* **15E**: 57-61.

4. Leading article (1979) Non-compliance: does it really matter? *British Medical Journal* **2**: 1168.

5. Inui, J.F., Yourtee, E. and Williamson, J. (1976) Improved outcomes in hypertension after physician tutorials. *Annals of Internal Medicine* **84**: 646-651.

6. Osterweis, M., Bush, P. and Zuckerman, A. (1979) Family context as a predictor of individual medicine use. *Social Science and Medicine* **13A**: 287-291.

7. Hare, E.H. and Wilcox, D. (1967) Do psychiatric inpatients take their pills? *British Journal of Psychiatry* **113**: 1435-1439.

8. Francis, V., Korsch, B. and Norris, R. (1969) Gaps in doctor–patient communication. *New England Medical Journal* **280**: 535-540.

9. Gabrielson, I.W., Levin, L. and Ellison, M. (1967) Factors affecting school health follow-up. *American Journal of Public Health* **57**: 48-59.

10. Hulka, B.S., Cassel, J., Kupper, L. and Burdette, J. (1976) Communication, compliance and concordance between physicians and patients with prescribed medications. *American Journal of Public Health* **66**: 847-853.

11. Elling, R., Whittemore, R. and Green, M. (1960) Patient participation in a pediatric program. *Journal of Health and Human Behaviour* **1**: 183-191.

12. Becker, M.H., Drachman, R. and Kirscht, K. (1972) Predicting mothers' compliance with pediatric medical regimes. *Journal of Pediatrics* **81**: 843-854.

13. Kegeles, S.S. (1969) A field experiment attempt to change beliefs and behaviour of women in an urban ghetto. *Journal of Health and Social Behaviour* **10**: 115.

14. Bradley, C., Gamsu, D. and Moses, J. (1987) The use of diabetes-specific perceived control and health beliefs to predict treatment choice and efficacy in a feasibility study of continuous subcutaneous insulin transfusion pumps. *Psychology and Health* **1**: 133-146.

15. Heinzelmann, F. (1962) Factors in prophylaxis behaviour in treating rheumatic fever. *Journal of Health and Human Behaviour* **3**: 73.

16. Caldwell, J.R., Cobb, S., Dowling, M. and deJongh, D. (1970) The dropout problem in hypertension therapy. *Journal of Chronic Diseases* **22**: 579-592.

17. Charrey, E. (1972) Patient-doctor communication: implications for the clinician. *Pediatric Clinics of North America* **19**: 263-279.

18. Boyd, J.R., Covington, T., Stanaszek, W. and Coussons, R. (1974) Drug defaulting. *American Journal of Hospital Pharmacy* **31**: 485-491.

19. Boyle, C.M. (1970) Differences between patients' and doctors' interpretation of some common medical terms. *British Medical Journal* **2**: 286-289.

20. Ley, P. (1973) The measurement of comprehensibility. *Journal of the Institute of Health Education* **11**: 17-20.

21. Mazzulo, J.M., Lasagna, L. and Griner, P. (1974) Variation in interpretation of prescription instructions. *Journal of the American Medical Association* **227**: 929-931.

22. Svarstad, B. (1976) Physician-patient communication and patient conformity with medical advice. In: Mechanic, D. (ed.) *The Growth of Bureaucratic Medicine*. New York: Wiley.

23. Ley, P. (1976) Towards better doctor–patient communications. In: Bennett, A.E. (ed.) *Communication between Doctors and Patients*. Oxford: Oxford University Press.

24. Bradshaw, P.W., Ley, P., Kincey, J. and Bradshaw, J. (1975) Recall of medical advice. *British Journal of Social and Clinical Psychology* **14**: 55-62.

25. Butt, H.R. (1977) A method for better physician-patient communication. *Annals of Internal Medicine* **86**: 478-480.

26. Ley, P. and Morris, L. (1984) Psychological aspects of written information for patients. In: Rachman, S. (ed.) *Contributions to Medical Psychology*, vol. 3. Oxford: Pergamon.

27. Ellis, D.A., Hopkin, J., Leitch, A. and Crofton, J. (1979) Doctors' orders: controlled trial of supplementary written information for patients. *British Medical Journal* **1**: 456.

28. Flesch, R. (1951) *How to Test Readability*. New York: Harper and Row.

29. Kanouse, D. and Hayes-Roth, B. (1980) Cognitive considerations in the design of product warnings. In: Morris, L., Mazzio, M. and Barofsky, I. (eds) *Banbury Report 6: Product labeling and health risks*. Cold Spring Harbor Laboratories.

30. Poulton, E., Warren, T. and Bond, J. (1970) Ergonomics in journal design. *Applied Ergonomics* **13**: 207-209.

31. Ben-Sira, Z. (1976) The function of the professional's affective behaviour in client satisfaction. *Journal of Health and Social Behaviour* **17**: 3-11.

32. Szasz, T.S. and Hollander, M. (1956) A contribution

to the philosophy of medicine – the basic models of the doctor-patient relationship. *Archives of Internal Medicine* **97**: 585-592.

33. Alpert, J.J. (1964) Broken appointments. *Pediatrics* **34**: 127-132.

34. Geersten, H.R., Gray, R. and Ward, J. (1973) Patient non-compliance within the context of seeking medical care for arthritis. *Journal of Chronic Diseases* **26**: 689-698.

35. Cartwright, A. (1964) *Human Relations and Hospital Care*. London: Routledge and Kegan Paul.

36. Romm, F.J. and Hulka, B. (1979) Care process and patient outcome in diabetes. *Medical Care* **17**: 748-757.

37. Davis, M.S. (1968) Variations in patients' compliance with doctors' advice. *American Journal of Public Health* **58**: 274-288.

38. Freemon, B., Negrete, V., Davis, M. and Korsch, B. (1971) Gaps in doctor-patient communication. *Pediatric Research* **5**: 298-311.

39. Korsch, B.M. and Negrete, V. (1972) Doctor-patient communication. *Scientific American* **227**: 66-74.

40. Illich, I. (1977) *Limits to Medicine*. Harmondsworth, Middlesex: Pelican.

41. Ogilvie, R.I. and Ruedy, J. (1967) Adverse drug reactions during hospitalisation. *Canadian Medical Association Journal* **97**: 1450-1457.

42. Meers, P.D. (1981) Infection in hospitals. *British Medical Journal* **1**: 1246.

43. Mather, H.G. (1971) Acute myocardial infarction: home and hospital treatment. *British Medical Journal* **3**: 334-338.

44. Barry, C.N. (1980) Home versus hospital confinement. *Journal of the Royal College of General Practitioners* **30**: 102-107.

45. Tew, M. (1979) The safest place of birth. *Lancet* **1**: 1388-1390.

46. Hundley, V., Cruickshank, F., Lang, G., Glazener, C., Milne, J., Turner, M., Blyth, D., Mollinson, J. and Donaldson, C. (1994) Midwife managed delivery unit: a randomised controlled comparison with consultant led care. *British Medical Journal* **309**: 1400-1404.

47. Flinn, A.M. Kelly, J., Hollins, G. and Lynch, P. (1978) Ambulation in labour. *British Medical Journal* **2**: 591-593.

48. Harrison, R.F., Brennan, M., North, P., Reed, J. and Wickham, E. (1984) Is routine episiotomy necessary? *British Medical Journal* **288**: 1971-1975.

49. Jacques, N., Amick, J. and Richards, M. (1983) Parents and support they need. In: Davis, J.A., Richards, M. and Robertson, N. (eds) *Parent-Baby Attachment in Premature Infants*. London: Croom Helm.

50. Derbyshire, F., Davies, D. and Bacco, A. (1982) Discharge of preterm babies from neonatal units. *British Medical Journal* **284**: 233-234.

51. Horowitz, M., Hulley, S., Alvarez, W., Billings, J., Benfari, R., Blair, S., Borhani, N. and Simon, N. (1980). News of risk for early heart disease as a stressful event. *Psychosomatic Medicine* **42**: 37-46.

52. Boutte, M. (1990) Waiting for the family legacy: the experience of being at risk for Machado-Joseph disease. *Social Science and Medicine* **30**: 839-847.

53. Robinson, J., Hinnard, B. and Laurence, K. (1984) Anxiety during a crisis: emotional effects of screening for neural tube defects. *Journal of Psychosomatic Research* **28**: 163-169.

54. Marteau, T. (1990). Reducing the psychological costs. *British Medical Journal* **301**: 26-28.

55. Craufurd, D., Dodge, A., Kerzin-Storrar, L. and Harris, R. (1989) Uptake of presymptomatic predictive testing for Huntington's disease. *Lancet* 603-605.

56. Terrnoire, G. (1992) Huntington's disease and the ethics of genetic prediction. *Journal of Medical Ethics* **18**: 79-85.

Appendix: Studying Skills

You already have a wide range of effective studying skills. Otherwise, you would not have made it to medical school. It is important to remember these accomplishments when you are anxious about your work. It is also important to remember that staff want you to pass and to do well. Work of a high quality not only reflects well on them as teachers but also means that they do not need to set further examinations.

Higher education does place particular demands on students. There can be more uncertainty about requirements resulting from less direction and less contact with staff. You have to manage your own time and make choices about what you study. Medical courses involve a combination of factual material and understandings of processes, relationships and effects as required in writing essays. It is not possible to remember facts without an overall understanding of why particular facts are important and relevant, and understanding needs to be informed by facts. The purpose of this appendix is to provide some help in achieving a balance between these two aspects of your education.

Studying facts

Several suggestions about effective study have already been mentioned in the text. In Chapter 2, on memory, the notion that factual information can be assimilated more readily if it is integrated with meaning was stressed. Having an overall view of a physiological process, for example, can assist in remembering the various pathways. Chapter 2 also introduced the notion of spacing reviews and skimming over the material to be learned before settling down to read it thoroughly, for example by reading the main headings of a chapter. In Chapter 3, some studies which examined ways of helping students were discussed. These studies indicated that those who reward themselves for studying (e.g. by promising themselves they will engage in some pleasurable activity after accomplishing a certain amount of work), who gradually build up the amount of studying time, and who give themselves positive rather than negative self-statements (e.g. "I am a capable student who needs to organize my work" rather than "There is so much work to do I will never get through it") tend to do better at examinations.

One method used to encourage good studying skills is the SQ3R method:[1] Survey, Question, Read, Recite, Review.

The SQ3R method for learning

- *Survey* The first step is to read the main headings of a chapter in order to prepare yourself for the information to be learned. This initial step should not take more than a minute. In this book, the major headings are given at the beginning of each chapter.
- *Question* Turn the heading into a question before you read the section of the chapter. For example, the heading to this appendix, Studying Skills, could be turned into the question: "How can research in psychology help me to study more effectively?"
- *Read* Now read to answer the question. Particular words or phrases which contribute to the answer can be jotted down, as briefly as possible.
- *Recite* Now look away from the book and try to recite your answer to the question. If possible, use your own words and give an example. If you can't answer the question, read the material over again quickly.

The last three steps (turning the heading into a question; reading to answer the question while making brief notes; reciting the answer) can be repeated for each section of the chapter.

- *Review* Finally, when all the information has been learned in this way, look over your notes once more to gain an overall view of the material. Check your memory by reciting the major points again.

There are a number of other suggestions which can be used to increase efficiency. Time management was outlined in Chapter 9 in connection with reducing stress at work. The essentials of time management which also apply to studying are:

1 To get organized, which allows you to concentrate on one task at a time
2 To maintain an overview of your work, which allows you to set priorities

3 To manage interruptions, so that you can work without distractions
4 To pace yourself, being realistic about what you can achieve
5 To set some personal objectives, by setting personal deadlines for your work's progress.

Two cautions. First, never purchase several books on the same area. Some students find that they begin to panic when they buy or are given, say, three anatomy textbooks. One is enough. Second, do not use alcohol to try to control your anxiety. If you are getting panicky, ask for help with your work from staff. Although alcohol may induce a relaxed feeling in the very short term, physiologically it can increase feelings of anxiety the next day.

Essay writing

Writing essays requires skills somewhat different from those used for studying factual information. Here the emphasis is firmly on understanding the material, so that it is important to ask questions of yourself and the material you read.

For example, you may want to write an essay on anorexia nervosa. The traditional questions of "Who", "When", "Where", "What", and "Why" are all useful. Providing a discussion of who is affected, when or at what age, and from which social backgrounds are all topics to consider. The what and why questions are more difficult, because answers to these questions require more than factual or empirical responses. They also require thought and criticism of the facts. The question "What is anorexia nervosa?" can be answered in several ways, because it is open to several definitions, such a weight loss, particular kinds of behaviour, or physiological changes. It is not clear which definition is the most appropriate. The question "Why does it occur?" is similarly difficult, since there are many and varied theories about the aetiology and maintenance of anorexia.

Asking yourself such questions provides a guide to your reading. You may realize that after having read some books and articles you have covered most questions, but not some others. This gap can then guide further reading. The questions you ask can also guide your writing. When you come to write the essay, it is very useful to sketch out a plan – perhaps along the lines of the questions you have asked yourself – before you begin to write. Many academics begin their organization by physically placing copies of articles and books in separate piles which represent different aspects of the paper they are going to work on. Then it is possible to write each section as a manageable task, rather than trying to complete the whole essay in one sitting.

Finally, it is important to ask questions of your tutor. Be clear about what he or she is looking for in a quality essay. You have the right to know the criteria which will be used in marking. Ask to see examples of successful work completed by previous students and ascertain the important characteristics of their essays.

Suggested reading

Barnes, R. (1992) *Successful Study for Degrees*, 3rd edn, London: Routledge, provides a more detailed review than given here.

References

1. Robinson, F. (1946) *Effective Study*. New York: Harper and Row.

Index

Entries in **bold** are main discussions; entries in *italics* indicate reference to illustrations and tables